ThinkPad®

A Different Shade of Blue

Deborah A. Dell
J. Gerry Purdy, Ph.D.

SAMS

A Division of Macmillan Computer Publishing
201 West 103rd Street, Indianapolis, Indiana 46290

ThinkPad®
A Different Shade of Blue

Copyright © 2000 by Sams Publishing

International Standard Book Number: 0-672-31756-7

Library of Congress Catalog Card Number: 99-63812

Printed in the United States of America

First Printing: September 1999

02   01   00   99   4   3   2   1

Trademarks

Warning and Disclaimer

Associate Publisher
Bradley L. Jones

Acquisitions Editor
Chris Webb

Development Editor
Thomas Cirtin

Managing Editor
Lisa Wilson

Project Editor
Heather Talbot

Copy Editor
Kate Talbot

Indexer
Johnna VanHoose

Proofreader
Jill Mazurczyk

Production Control Team
Dan Harris
Heather Moseman

Team Coordinator
Meggo Barthlow

Interior Designer
Gary Adair

Cover Designer
Nathan Clements

Copy Writer
Eric Borgert

Layout Technicians
Darin Crone
Jeannette McKay
Louis Porter, Jr.

Contents

Foreword

The Seven Qualities of Enduring Brands

by Thomas J. Kosnik

It brings me great pleasure to write the foreword to a book about a product family—and a company—that has changed my life: the IBM ThinkPad family of notebook computers. I don't often add my "seal of approval" to books that other people write. I turn most requests down because, although I buy more than one hundred business books a year, I'm picky about the books I recommend. In fact, I think of myself as the people's critic of the business books category, similar to the role that Roger Ebert and (the late) Gene Siskel have played for the movie industry since 1982. *Kosnik's Short List of Best Books*—which is available at http://ieem.stanford. edu/faculty/kosnik.html—has become a useful reference for the students, alumni, business executives, and entrepreneurs in my network who read only a few books a year. Only one in twenty books that I read makes the list.

The book that Gerry Purdy and Debi Dell have written about the IBM ThinkPad brand is on my "Highly Recommended" list. It is for anyone who faces the challenges of building a mobile team, a global business, and an enduring brand. It is also a great book if you think of yourself as a "road warrior"—if your daily work requires that you spend considerable time in cars, taxicabs, airplanes, airports, hotel rooms, or other people's offices. Why should road warriors read this book? Because it describes the inside story about the people, technologies, and competitive dynamics that have shaped the world in which you work and the portable computing products that you use. If you own an IBM ThinkPad, you can learn the inside story about how the brand you trust came to be. If you swear by a competing mobile computer from Dell, Compaq, Toshiba, HP, Apple, and so on, then Sun

Tsu's timeless advice to know your enemy applies. You should *not* read this book if you hate computers and believe that they are ruining our lives. The IBM ThinkPad story was written by road warriors for other road warriors. If you enjoy reading it half as much as I did, you, too, will give it a "thumbs up."

As you read this book, think back through the years and retrace your own path as a road warrior. Try to remember what work you were doing, the mobile computing and communications tools you were using, and the products and companies that you learned to love and hate in your own career on the road. Taking time to remember your own story will give you a personal context that makes the story that Gerry and Debi have created about the ThinkPad more relevant, more useful, and more enjoyable for you.

My own ThinkPad journey started in the spring of 1996, when I began two years of cross-country commuting. I had one requirement for my mobile machine: It had to be the lightest possible computer that provided the functionality of a desktop. Because of its light weight, the IBM ThinkPad 560 was my choice in the IBM-compatible world. The ThinkPad 560 won the Mobility Award from Mobile Insights for two successive years because it combined light weight with full functionality, bundled in a sleek, black package. By today's standards, its Pentium 166 processor, 16 megabytes (MB) of memory, and 2 gigabytes (GB) of storage are slightly archaic when compared to the ThinkPad 600, with its Pentium II 300MHz processor, 96MB of memory, and 6GB of storage. The ThinkPad 560's elegant design still looks great next to the IBM ThinkPad 600 that is now my primary mobile machine.

Over those two years, the ThinkPad 560 became the machine that kept my e-mail and my Internet browser, with all of its bookmarks. It emerged as my mission-critical mobile machine. Like the American Express card in my wallet, I never left home without it. Over time, in side-by-side comparisons on many a late night at work, the ThinkPad's brighter, crisper screen stood out when I compared it with my Mac PowerBook and the two Macintosh desktop systems I was using. Not only was the ThinkPad much easier on my back than the PowerBook, it was easier on my eyes than any computer I had ever owned. Those two benefits turned me from a satisfied, sophisticated customer who liked many mobile brands to a die-hard loyalist for the IBM ThinkPad.

When my bi-coastal commute ended, I returned to Stanford full time. I began planning for a new course that would link Stanford with two locales known for innovative use of computing and communications technology: Sweden and Singapore. In 1998, my ThinkPad 560 traveled with me from the Stanford School of Engineering to the Royal Institute of Technology (KTH) in Sweden and the National University of Singapore as we launched the first generation of a course called *Global Project Coordination (GPC)*.

In GPC, students and faculty on three continents work on real projects for real companies, with real funding. These are students who want to learn more about how to use cutting-edge mobile and Internet technologies to coordinate the work of global teams. I am now part of a six-person faculty team from these three universities; we design and deliver courses to students in Sweden, Silicon Valley, and Singapore *simultaneously*. On any Wednesday night, drop by Stanford at 11 p.m. and go to the GPC class with a group of Stanford night owls, Swedish early birds (it's 8 a.m., Thursday, in Sweden), and Singaporeans just after teatime (it's 3 p.m. in Singapore). We have lively three-way, interactive class discussions that literally span the globe.

These global mobile students are building skills to be future business leaders through hands-on distance learning. Mobile computing—combined with low-cost, three-way interactive video teleconferencing over the Internet—has made possible in 1999 what was technologically not feasible and economically not affordable in the past. I know that the IBM ThinkPad family will be part of this effort, as IBM continues the great innovation, service, value, and cool industrial design that the brand has come to represent. These qualities have resulted in the IBM ThinkPad becoming one of the most successful brands in portable computing. These qualities are included in the Seven Qualities of Enduring Brands, which I have developed and documented.

I developed the Seven Qualities of Enduring Brands from research and consultations with numerous global high-tech entrepreneurs. I wanted to provide the basics to assist young people starting their own companies. I also wanted to help engineers learn what it takes to develop a successful business beyond the technology. Thus, I teach a course titled *Global Entrepreneurial Marketing* at Stanford School of Engineering. I complement this academic endeavor with an active consulting practice in the real world. As a consultant, I help emerging companies with the difficult issues of building successful enterprises. In both my classes and my consulting engagements, I offer the Seven Qualities of Enduring Brands. These qualities are defined as follows:

- A growing market
- Innovative technologies
- World-class products
- Profound leadership
- A trustworthy brand
- A balanced business
- A global learning network

I wish that I could just hand this list to my students and consulting clients, but it's not as easy as it sounds. In fact, *it is how leaders working in teams at all levels of an organization achieve these seven qualities that makes the difference.*

The IBM ThinkPad achieved excellence in every one of these seven qualities, through several generations of leaders and support teams. Moreover, it launched a successful global business at a time when ThinkPad's parent company, IBM, was going through one of the most difficult and wrenching transformations undertaken by any global company in history. The tenacity, resourcefulness, and entrepreneurial spirit of the many people who contributed to the ThinkPad story is a lesson for any of us who think it is not possible to be an entrepreneur when buried in the bowels of a large, established company—especially one that must downsize and restructure to survive.

A Growing Market

The market for portable computers is growing rapidly, and the IBM ThinkPad has "crossed the chasm," as my colleague Geoffrey Moore would say.[1] IBM sputtered with many false starts in portable computing before the ThinkPad came on the scene in late 1992. But, the portable computing market in general and the IBM ThinkPad in particular are now part of portables being purchased and used everywhere. Every indicator—unit sales, revenue, and market share—shows a growing opportunity. ThinkPads are no longer relegated to the business environment. My students are now buying ThinkPad iSeries, and many faculty colleagues want ThinkPads. It is the premier brand in the growing market of portables.

Innovative Technologies

To have a successful brand, one or more innovative technologies are integral to the product offering. In the case of the ThinkPad, it was a combination of innovations. Back in 1992, IBM was the only portable manufacturer in the world to deliver a 10.4-inch color display. It was the only company with a little red eraser pointing device in the keyboard. The industrial design was jet black and futuristic in style. From the onset, the team continued its innovation with larger, clearer, brighter displays, thin and light designs, modularity, and ease-of-use functionality. To describe ThinkPad, *innovation* is a word that is usually at the top or near the top of everyone's list.

---

1. Geoffrey Moore, *Crossing the Chasm* (1991) and *Inside the Tornado* (1995).

World-Class Products

Every marketing book talks about the importance of product excellence. IBM did not just build a little better portable. It built a world-class, multi-generation family of portable computers that are easier to use. The thin and light design is easier on our backs and shoulders. The product family has consistently delivered one of the best keyboards, which is easier on the fingers, reduces keystroke errors, and makes writing more fun and less of a chore. The screens make the ThinkPad easier on the eyes than those of IBM's competitors. Lessening eyestrain provides intangible benefits to us as individual users as we get a little older and don't want to risk damaging our eyes for our careers. It also has potential business benefits to employers of knowledge workers by reducing the number of workdays lost because of visits to the eye doctor or sick days taken for job-related stress. Scientific studies have not yet been conducted that verify the benefits I am suggesting might be true. However, in my own unscientific research, using me as a guinea pig, I know that my eyes hurt less and I am less stressed out when I am writing on my ThinkPad than when I use my other computers.

I'm not a lone voice in the wilderness in praising the ThinkPad product line. Numerous industry watchers believe that no one else has matched IBM's ergonomics and human-computer *interface* (how a person interacts with the portable). ThinkPads have consistently been among the best portable products on the market from 1992 to the present. IBM focused on building world-class products generation after generation, which, in turn, contributed to a successful brand.

Profound Leadership

Most high technology companies that create successful brands and businesses have a deep bench of leadership talent. They *do not* rely on one great individual to show the way. Rather, they create an environment in which people at every level, in every function, step up to lead when it is their turn. Like runners in a relay race, each leader runs at maximum effort when it is his or her turn and smoothly hands off the baton to the next runner so that the team overall can win. These leaders also cheer on the other team members during their leg of the race. They don't motivate their teammates in the same way, but their teammates know that each leader is motivated. The teammates become more fired up because they all are on the same team.

In the case of IBM's ThinkPad, the depth, breadth, and diversity of leadership talent across multiple generations of the product line are remarkable. The first leader of product development, Hajime Watabi, was technologically adept and laid the groundwork for the generations of product innovation that followed. The first general manager, Bruce Claflin, exuded charisma, established a vision for the market and the business, and made some very tough decisions to focus attention and accountability for results. Following such technological and marketing leadership, Joe Formichelli demonstrated manufacturing skills to correct the notorious supply problems surrounding ThinkPad. Customers were able to get ThinkPads when they wanted them, not a year later. Finally, Steve Ward brought operational excellence to the organization, positioning it for the stewardship continued by Adalio Sanchez. Each leader demonstrated a proficiency necessary to build ThinkPad into a successful business at IBM. Each leader also surrounded himself with an extraordinarily talented team, set the bar high, and gave people in the organization an opportunity to make a difference.

A Trustworthy Brand

Building a brand is difficult. Investments in advertising and other forms of marketing communications will not build a brand unless customers trust the brand, based on their experiences with product usage, customer service, and technical support. Can you think of a brand that you love to hate because of bad quality, lousy customer service, and so on? What happens when you see advertising for that brand? If you are like most people, you turn to someone sitting next to you and say something like, "That advertisement is a bunch of B.S. I tried that product and hated it. Let me tell you why." Advertising a defective brand will actually stimulate negative word of mouth, which can *reduce* sales because disgruntled customers respond to the ad by brand bashing.

Great products are necessary, but not sufficient, to build a brand. Plenty of brands grow slowly because happy customers have no incentive, and might even have disincentives, to spread the good word to other potential customers. Great brand builders use marketing to *accelerate the velocity of positive word of mouth from die-hard customers to other potential customers.*

Trustworthy brands are also built through the continuous, two-way communication between the people in the company creating the products and the people who use them. Very few organizations have mastered the new marketing skill of initiating and guiding customer-company dialogues. Early on, the IBM ThinkPad group implemented a process for customer dialogue by creating councils of leading thinkers in the mobile computing industry. By sustaining a dialogue with these most visionary customers year after year, IBM was able to keep a finger on the rapidly changing rules of the portable computing marketplace. Trust increased across this customer network, evolving into a kind of early warning system that could signal changes in the marketplace that might impact the ThinkPad brand.

The IBM ThinkPad team did the three things that are needed to build a trustworthy brand. First, they used great industrial design to build quality products with innovative technology. Second, they accelerated positive word of mouth through their creative marketing tactics. Third, through ongoing dialogs with leading-edge customers, they improved their ability to anticipate latent customer needs and create products that delighted customers through a series of pleasant surprises. As a result, IBM created a position in the minds of the user (and the prospective customer) that ThinkPad was a brand people can trust, admire, and enjoy.

A Balanced Business

What good is innovation or a world-class product if it does not translate into a sustainable, profitable business? The team worked hard to run ThinkPad as a successful business, even during IBM's most challenging times. What does it mean to be a great business? Is it just being number one in market share? What if market share leadership was achieved by selling the most products at a loss? Is it selling products at a profit? What if that meant becoming viewed as a luxury product that most customers could not afford?

Professor Robert Kaplan at Harvard Business School asserts that a business can be successful in the long term only if it manages itself using a *balanced scorecard*.[2] The firm should monitor measures of financial performance (such as growth and profitability), customer performance (such as share of market and customer loyalty), internal processes (such as cycle time and quality), and organizational learning and innovation (such as employee retention and percent of revenues from new products). IBM has built a portable business that, by all estimates, is in excess of five billion dollars a year—and is a very profitable unit within IBM. As you read the chapters that follow, see whether you can identify the areas of the balanced scorecard where IBM has performed well and the areas where it could improve.

2. Robert Kaplan, *The Balanced Scorecard* (Boston: Harvard Business School Press).

A Global Learning Network

No one individual or team was responsible for the ThinkPad's success. With each generation of the product family, groups of designers, planners, and engineers melded into cohesive teams to develop award-winning products. A network of industry influencers molded each team's approach to the market. An evolving network of channel partners delivered ThinkPads to successive generations of customers. Legions of sales representatives touted the ThinkPad benefits while they assisted clients with integrating them into their organizations. As IBM employees moved on to other organizations or left IBM to build other companies, they kept in touch with the teammates they left behind. The importance of the ThinkPad network—a web of trustworthy relationships that has spanned product generations and company and country boundaries—is exemplified throughout the story and deserves additional comment. I have had the opportunity to compare the operation of high-tech business networks in greater Boston and the Silicon Valley firsthand, from 1980 to the present. Professor Annalee Saxenian has written a great book on that subject, titled *Regional Advantage*.[3] She compares the Silicon Valley to the Boston area as a hotbed of high-tech innovation and analyzes why the Bay Area has been so much more successful as an economic region than Boston. One of the major differences that Saxenian attributes to the success of Silicon Valley is its vibrant network of relationships among engineers, entrepreneurs, venture capitalists, and global companies willing to invest in startups. Employees left established companies to join startups, partnered with their former employers, and sometimes came back if their new business went out of business. The Boston area did not have a similar network. Companies operated more as separate entities, and when employees left, they did not phone home to their former employers.

3. Annalee Saxenian, *Regional Advantage: Culture and Competition in Silicon Valley and Route 128* (Cambridge: Harvard University Press, 1994).

I believe that the IBM ThinkPad story is a great example of a variation of the Silicon Valley success story: *a global, mobile network collaborating to build a multi-billion dollar business and an enduring brand*. Although this phenomenon is not well understood, I believe that the IBM ThinkPad brand is a living example of what some futurists have described as the *virtual corporation*.[4]

As fewer companies offer lifetime employment, and fewer employees put all their eggs in the basket of one company for entire careers, more businesses are thinking of themselves as networks. If we create a dynamic family tree of the IBM ThinkPad network, everyone inside and outside IBM who has contributed to the brand's success would be represented. Our potential for continued learning and innovation is much greater than if we focus narrowly on just the IBM employees on the ThinkPad team in any given year.

Want to learn more? The remainder of this book ties all seven of these elements together using a narrative style that most readers will find pleasing. You get a rare chance to read the inside scoop on how one company followed the Seven Qualities of Enduring Brands and created one of the most successful global entrepreneurial ventures in high-tech history. Enjoy your journey!

Thomas J. Kosnik
Consulting Professor
Stanford School of Engineering
Kosnik@stanford.edu

---

4. William H. Davidow and Michael S. Malone, *The Virtual Corporation* (New York: Harper Business, 1992).

Preface

Many books have been written on high tech failures. Books such as *Start Up: A Silicon Valley Adventure*, by Jerry Kaplan, which explains how more than one hundred million dollars was poured down the drain chasing what was supposed to be the sequel to personal computing: pen computing. Books such as *Apple: The Inside Story of Intrigue, Egomania, and Business Blunders*, by James Carlton, which appropriately blasts Apple Computer and its management for blowing opportunity after opportunity in its campaign to become a leader in personal computing. These books are interesting to read. They elicit responses such as "I don't believe this," "Ugh," "Yikes!" and "Oh, no."

It is hard to write a book about a high tech success. Why? Oftentimes, it is not nearly as interesting as a disaster. "They succeeded, so what is there to discuss?" We have been taught to learn from our mistakes, but we can learn equally well from our successes. The headlines blast away at the failures but seldom celebrate the successes. It is also harder to dig up factual information, especially when the story deals with IBM. A former IBM executive, Bill Lowe said that getting information from IBM used to be harder than getting information from behind the Iron Curtain. But, all of that is changing, as you will see from the interviews and stories within this book. And, finally, it is hardest to put the pieces of a story together so that people will want to tell someone else, "You've *got* to read this book."

We spent years working with IBM on the creation of the IBM ThinkPad. I am a leading analyst in mobile computing and a consultant to IBM; Debi is now developing IBM's mobile services business and was a member of the initial ThinkPad marketing team. During the past three years, we kept saying to each other, "We really should write a book on how IBM created the ThinkPad and then developed a successful business in mobile computing."

The story is fascinating and every bit as enjoyable as any high-tech failure treatise. Business lessons can be gleaned from this story as well—for one, how it is possible to create a successful line of portable computer products and a recognizable brand in a relatively short time.

We set our goal to write a book that is fun to read. Each chapter is a story unto itself. The main characters tell the ThinkPad story in their own words. Events sometimes seem almost magical. The tone is "up close and personal." Some people said unrefined things along the way, but these reflect the personalities involved and the mood of the moment. People did not always get along, but they were always focused on the same goal: to build a very successful line of portable computers, the ThinkPad brand, and a profitable and successful business within IBM. And they did.

We began discussions about the book at the Mobile Insights '96 conference at the Arizona Biltmore in Phoenix. IBM had just won the Mobility Award for best notebook, selected by twenty-five editors and analysts. Debi approached me with the idea because she had saved quite a bit of information on the early ThinkPad years.

Little did we know that it would take more than eighteen months to get the necessary approvals to begin the project. We signed a partnership agreement contingent on IBM's approval. We developed an outline and submitted it to the ThinkPad management team. However, a key executive did not feel that it was the right time for such a book. According to the terms of Debi's employment agreement, she could not work on the book without his approval. We were told that the effort was not authorized and our relationship with IBM (me as a consultant and Debi as an employee) could be negatively affected. We thought about the situation and determined that it was better to wait until the political climate improved.

Luckily for us, nothing ever stays the same at IBM. Some of the ThinkPad executives who felt that it was premature to have a book written about ThinkPad left the business. Others, who had their own personal agendas, changed jobs within IBM. Finally, in the fall of 1997, the IBM ThinkPad management team agreed to allow Debi to pursue the creation of this book. The only requirement: They wanted to review the book to ensure the accuracy of any references to IBM. That seemed fair to us.

This tale needed to be told for a variety of reasons. First and foremost, the participants relate interesting stories about their feelings and experiences regarding the brand, the process, and their fellow team members. Second, the lessons they learned might help others to create world-class high technology brands. Third, IBM deserves to have a book written about one of the more positive things that has happened in the past decade. This story represents an effort of which IBM should be proud. Although they did not write the actual book, the story is IBM's. The ThinkPad management team had the vision and commitment necessary to make ThinkPad happen.

But, this story is not just about IBM's journey to create the most recognizable brand in portable computing history. It is also a roadmap for any individual or company that wants to build a team, develop a product or service, and create a brand recognized within its market. The Authors' Insights summarize the lessons learned in each chapter and provide the reader with food for thought—these lessons can be applied to almost any industry.

One last comment, on an aspect of writing this book that reflects today's business climate. I live in the San Francisco Bay area; Debi resides in Delray Beach, Florida. I run my own business; Debi is managing the mobile services business within IBM. Whereas I use Microsoft Word, Debi uses Lotus Word Pro, the

IBM standard (Microsoft Word was used because most publishers prefer it). We both use an IBM ThinkPad as our system of choice. This endeavor, accomplished in a short time, clearly illustrates the advantages of a mobile environment where you can work and communicate any time, any place.

February 1999

J. Gerry Purdy, Ph.D.
President and CEO
Mobile Insights, Inc.

gerry.purdy@mobileinsights.com
650-937-0938

Deborah (Debi) Dell
IBM National Principal
Mobile and Wireless
Services

dell@us.ibm.com
561-496-4603

Acknowledgments

The authors acknowledge the help and assistance of James Levine, our agent, critic, coach, ThinkPad fan, and, most of all, good negotiator in helping to get this story molded into a shape that would result in a marketable book. We wish to thank Bruce Stephens of International Data Corporation (IDC) for providing statistical data that appears throughout the book. We appreciate Brodeur & Partners for providing copies of all IBM portable computing press releases so that we could check facts. We recognize the research and copyediting provided by Theresa Nozick and the graphical support of Tracey Gilbert. This book would not have been possible without the encouragement and support of Chris Webb, our advocate within Macmillan Publishing USA and his excellent team.

Gerry acknowledges the patience of his family—notably, his wife, Melanie, who put up with evenings and weekends spent working on this book—and the support of his five children—Jill and her spouse, Paul Sarkozi; Kristi and her spouse, Randy Riggs; Jennifer; Bryan; and Jason. Gerry also wants to acknowledge the friendship and mentoring support of Professor Tom Kosnik of Stanford University. Acknowledgment is made to the entire Mobile Insights team, who tolerated their boss working on a book at the same time they were working hard to develop a small, but growing company in mobile computing professional services. Finally, Gerry wishes to acknowledge the friendship, support, and professional affiliation with all members of the IBM Industry Advisory Council.

Debi is grateful to her husband, Fred Adolphson, and her family for their patience during IBM's massive changes, her latest master's program, and the writing of this book. She is indebted to Dr. David Bradley, IBM Senior Technical Staff Member, Dr. Gina Dell, and Peter Golden for their edits and critiques of this effort;

their comments were invaluable. She recognizes the original ThinkPad team members, who were so generous with their time and insights: Jim Cannavino, Bruce Claflin, Joe Formichelli, Scott Bower, Maurice Fletcher, Sue King, and Rick Thoman. Debi sends special appreciation to Dolly Salvucci and Jean DiLeo for the photos they provided, Chris Farrell for his paper on the Butterfly development project, and Bob Sztybel for his detailed descriptions of the press and media programs. The story would not have been complete without Tom Hardy's extensive comments, written inputs, and edits on the industrial design, an integral aspect of the ThinkPad's success. She wishes to thank those lifelong Notre Dame and IBM friends who provided ongoing encouragement and suggestions during this project and who remain phantoms of wonderful memories and feelings. Finally, she is indebted to Mrs. Irene Dougherty, Mr. Roger Schram, Dr. William Heisler, Father Matthew Miceli, C.S.C., Sister Anne Richard, and Dr. Arum Sharma—some of the teachers throughout her life who taught her to love reading, writing, and the management of technology.

In addition to the special acknowledgments, the authors thank the following individuals, who contributed their time and memories in the writing of this book: Sam Albert, Tim Bajarin, Chris Barr, Jim Bartlett, Kevin Clark, Sam Dusi, Rob Enderle, Leslie Fiering, Jim Forbes, Randy Guisto, Tom Grimes, Heinz Hegmann, Koichi Higuchi, David Hill, Toshiyuki Ikeda, Bob Kanode, John Karidis, Per Larsen, Pete Leichliter, Bill Lowe, John Madigan, Mark McNeilly, Nobuo Mii, Adam Myerson, Jerry Michalski, David Nichols, Joseph Rickert, Janice Roberts, Adalio Sanchez, Dr. Ted Selker, Chris Shipley, Ron Sperano, Ken Stoffregen, Bruce Stephen, Leo Suarez, Bill Tsang, Peter Tulupman, Kathy Vieth, Steve Ward, Hajime Watabe, Dr. Frank Wilbur, Steve Wildstrom, Mike Wiley, and Jan Winston.

Kudos to the members of the original ThinkPad team and the friends who started it all, including Patty McHugh, Mark Hofert,

John Madigan, Dick Greene, Chuck Pecnik, Lew Brown, Gary Buer, Lou Yovin, Paul Turner, Gene Yaffe, Howard Dulany, Jim Geis, Lucy Hanks, Joyce Sykes, Sam Lucente, John Wiseman, Bob Sachsenmeier, and Dick Powell. Finally, a heartfelt thanks to everyone who touched the ThinkPad product line as part of industrial design, finance, competitive analysis, planning, engineering, programming, manufacturing, marketing, or sales who may not have been named here. Without them, this story would not have been possible.

About the Authors

Deborah A. Dell

Deborah (Debi) Dell is currently the national principal–Mobile and Wireless Solutions for IBM Global Services. With her small team of senior professionals, the practice develops and enables IBM's participation in the mobile and wireless market. Working with airtime, hardware, and software providers, her organization develops service and support offerings for the U.S. market. The group also provides consulting and sales support for client and industry sales teams. Her team operates remotely with employees based in Dallas, Atlanta, Raleigh, Denver, and Peoria. Interviewed in such publications as Andy Seybold's *Outlook*, *Computer Reseller News*, *Washington Technology*, and *Wireless Week*, she is a frequent speaker on the topics of brand management and telecommuting.

Debi's love of mobility stems from her previous assignment as product manager for Mobile Computing Strategy and Development. She was responsible for the worldwide development and implementation of the ThinkPad out-of-box experience, as well as its business strategy, from 1993 through 1995. In addition, She enjoyed managing the ThinkPad Industry Advisory Council during its formative years. She also worked on the development of IBM's pen systems and their associated marketing programs. Debi held numerous management and staff positions in the Personal Computer Company since its 1981 inception. She worked on products such as the PC AT, the PS/2 Model 30, and the PS/2 Models 90 and 95. She was mentored in her early career by several individuals who helped her learn the personal computer business—especially George Andersen, Dennis Andrews, Dr. David J. Bradley, Dick Cook, Howie Davidson, Mike Hyland, Sue King, Cynthia McFall, Tom O'Donnell, Tom Pitts, Paul Schlick, Connie Scott, and Pres Stratton III.

She holds a bachelor's degree in business administration from the University of Notre Dame, graduating in the first class of undergraduate women. Inspired by her father, attending Notre Dame was a lifetime objective from the age of five. In addition to the ThinkPad and PC years, it provided her with one of life's truly great experiences. And, yes, she knew Rudy.

Debi completed a master's degree in business administration from the University of Loyola, Chicago, while working for Commonwealth Edison Company as a technical sales representative. She graduated with a Master of Science degree in the management of technology from the University of Miami in 1995. Work for this master's program—with her teammates John Bilanych, Steve DelGrosso, and Nora Mosher—resulted in several ThinkPad papers and inspired the dream of writing this book.

Raised in southern Florida, her parents encouraged her to pursue her career in the big city—Chicago. She met her husband, Fred Adolphson, at Commonwealth Edison and married in 1978. After the Blizzard of 1979, they decided to return to Florida, where she now works from her Delray Beach home. In recent years, she has experienced the joys and tribulations associated with working from home—but that's another story!

J. Gerry Purdy, Ph.D.

Dr. Purdy is president and CEO of Mobile Insights, Inc., a professional services firm located in Mt. View, California. Dr. Purdy is also editor-in-chief of *Mobile Letter*, a publication of Mobile Insights and MobileTrax Online, a Web-based continuous information service. Dr. Purdy has focused on mobile markets and products since 1986 and has become recognized as an industry authority in the mobile computing industry. He is often quoted in publications such as *The Wall Street Journal, Business Week, PC Week, The San Jose Mercury News, InfoWorld*, and *The New York Times*. He has appeared on CBS Radio Business Report and Voice of America.

Dr. Purdy also conducts a number of consulting engagements for major firms in the mobile computing and communications market. Recent engagement clients include 3Com, Apple, AT&T Wireless, Compaq, Dell, Fujitsu, Hayes, HP, IBM, Intel, Microsoft, NEC, Motorola, TI, and Xircom.

Before founding Mobile Insights, Dr. Purdy was vice president and chief analyst for Mobile Computing at Dataquest. Previously, he held marketing positions with Connecting Point (now Intelligent Electronics), Compaq, Fujitsu (Poqet division), and Phoenix Technologies. Dr. Purdy has had significant experience producing major mobile computing conferences. He produces Mobile Insights conferences for leaders in mobile computing and communications and the Go Mobile conference for leading IT decision makers.

Dr. Purdy is a member of the IBM Mobile Computing Industry Advisory Council, the AT&T Wireless Analyst Council, the NEC Analyst Exchange, and the Dell Industry Advisory Council.

Dr. Purdy earned his B.S. degree in engineering physics from the University of Tennessee (1965), an M.S. degree in computer science from U.C.L.A. (1968), and a Ph.D. in computer science and exercise physiology from Stanford University (1972). He also completed a Market Strategy for High Technology course at Stanford University (1987).

THE 1980s:
A DECADE OF LEARNING

The 5th Wave By Rich Tennant

"A PORTABLE COMPUTER? YOU'D BETTER TALK TO OLD BOB OVER THERE. HE'S OWNED A PORTABLE LONGER THAN ANY ONE HERE."

The Defining Moment

Some memories are realities, and are better than anything that can ever happen to one again.

—Willa Cather

It was always a challenge to summon the motivation and dedication to work late at night but, in early 1990, it was even more so. Building 31, once at the center of IBM Boca Raton's development efforts, was nearly empty. Unlike the early days of the IBM PC, employees were finding it difficult to stay late, much less stay focused. Because many of their friends had been affected by the various personnel actions that had occurred in Boca Raton, Florida, employees constantly wondered whether they would be next. Since 1988, when manufacturing had moved from Boca to Raleigh, North Carolina, the PC Company had taken headcount reductions every year. Downsizing had become a way of life, not only in IBM but also across the industry.

Walking down the hallway from the coffee machine, I could not believe how desolate the offices looked. Some of the desolation was attributable to the hour—after all, it was after 10 p.m.—but some of the forsaken atmosphere was because the offices were taking on the appearance of temporary spaces.

Employees had fewer and fewer personal items decorating their offices because no one was sure when the next personnel cut was going to occur. Also, fewer and fewer people could be found in those offices late at night. After all, what was the purpose? No one felt that he or she could make a difference in the troubles facing IBM in those days.

Deep in thought, I found myself startled by my own shadow reflected on the concrete walls. When I heard footsteps behind me, nervousness caused me to spill hot coffee on my hand. Turning quickly, I was relieved to see one of my employees, Denny Wainright, approaching.

I was lucky to have two employees in my market planning department who consistently put their jobs first. Roseann Conforti often had to be counseled that I did not expect her to work through the night and that she really should not be the last one in the office. Conforti usually counted on fellow team member Denny Wainright to walk her out, no matter how late she stayed.

Wainright seldom left before he was sure that everyone (especially the women) had gone home. He was always the one to check the department offices to make certain that the area was secure. IBM had a clean desk policy that required confidential materials and desks to be locked at night. Failure to do so resulted in security violations that were reported to the executive management team. Wainright wanted to be sure that our department did not fail any of the periodic security audits, so he took it on himself to check the team offices nightly. Both he and Conforti were always doing things to ensure the reputation of the department.

These thoughts entered my mind as I saw Wainright approach. Wainright reflected his thirty-year tenure with IBM in his manner of dress. He continued to wear a white shirt and a tie, even after casual dress was accepted. His actions were always grounded in IBM's three basic beliefs, with an emphasis on customer service.

If something did not support these beliefs or contribute to IBM, Wainright would not become involved. He had a reputation for excellence in customer service and product planning. This background resulted in a broad knowledge of the IBM Personal Computer family of products and the associated service requirements. Because of this expertise, I assigned him to product naming and model numbering. These two dimensions of a product were closely tied to how service issues were reported and addressed in the field. Although I personally felt that *naming* was a four-letter word and hated the political battles that usually accompanied their recommendations, Wainright handled it in his stride. Product naming was the reason he was working late on this particular night.

After wiping up the spilled coffee, I caught my breath. I asked Wainright how the "name game" was going. We had been struggling to name a soon-to-be-announced, pen-based portable computer. Quite different from anything IBM had ever done, the development team wanted something that reflected the personality, the purpose of the system. Wainright had been trying to come up with a name that reflected this new system's capabilities while meeting the many IBM naming guidelines.

For the first time in weeks, Wainright actually smiled. He responded, "You know, Debi, I think I've been carrying around the answer in my shirt pocket for the past thirty years. Look at this." He pulled a little paper tablet from his shirt pocket; it was black with the word *THINK* embossed in gold on the cover. Having worked at IBM during the years when sales and service personnel carried this type of notepad in their shirt pockets, Wainright always kept a supply of these paper tablets in his office.

Wainright continued, "Deb, I think we have something that the development team and Corporate Naming will be proud of. They may even get excited about it. I can't really say how we got to the actual name—exactly what meeting or what day we all came to the same conclusion—but I am sure that this is the right one to carry forward. I think you will agree that this is worth fighting for. It won't be easy getting the IBM PC Company to move away from its current numbering scheme, but I know it's worth the effort.

"This new tablet computer needs to be called *Think-pad*—you know, the computer pad that lets you do some serious thinking while using it in a way that is comfortable for you. It's friendly. It's descriptive. Even better, it ties to IBM's heritage. God knows, we need something like that right now."

We could not know the profound effect this name would have within IBM and across the industry. By capturing the essence of the pen machine, *ThinkPad* would be a departure for IBM in its naming of personal computers. It was also the departure point for the mobile computing team's journey to create the most recognizable brand in portable computing history.

CHAPTER 1

The IBM PC: Teaching the Elephant to Dance

A horse never runs so fast as when he has other horses to catch up and outpace.

—Ovid

The IBM Personal Computer (PC) was originally developed and manufactured in Boca Raton, Florida. IBM Boca Raton was a palatial facility located just off I-95's Yamato Road exit on IBM Drive (some visitors believed that IBM, with its development lab in Yamato, Japan, named the exit for the PC facility, but it was just a coincidence). Around a small pond, IBM built two large semicircular office buildings distinctively designed by architect Marcel Breuer. With its manufacturing facility on the south and an extensive recreation site on the western side of the property, the Boca Raton site was, in essence, a small city.

Visiting this property was an impressive experience. You drove up a tree-lined drive, stopped at the guard gate, identified yourself, and got a pass. Security did not stop there, however. You were never allowed to traverse the property on your own. An IBM employee always accompanied you—even to the restroom! It felt more like an encounter with the CIA than with a computer manufacturer.

IBM Boca Raton, Home to the IBM PC.

Contrary to popular belief, the IBM PC was not the result of divine intervention; three threads entwined to create this technology icon.[1] These threads were the development, marketing, and research efforts already directed toward a new market space known as desktop computing. The first thread, development, was the IBM 5100 desktop computer.

Developed in Rochester, Minnesota, the 5100 design was conceived from the technologies surrounding the emerging concept of small computers. At the time that the San Francisco Bay area was in the early stage of becoming known as *Silicon Valley*, with research work at Stanford University, Xerox PARC, and start-up Intel, IBM sent its industrial engineers to visit its Palo Alto research facility and come back with creative designs. These designs influenced the 5100 (which shipped in 1975), as well as its follow-on products, such as the 5110 and the Datamaster. The Datamaster development later migrated to Boca Raton and was the first use of an Intel processor in an IBM product.

The second thread, marketing, was an experiment in which retail stores could sell IBM's general business products. A predecessor to IBM's placement of the IBM PC in Sears business centers, this effort introduced the concept of retail sales to IBM. Based out of Atlanta, key marketing personnel were educated on an area of sales and marketing unfamiliar to those traditionally successful "blue suiters." No longer would marketing only be to large corporate customers.

The final thread, a 1976 research effort, combined a small computer and a video disk into a home/education/business product. Eventually, a company called *Discovision* picked up the video disk work, which did not figure into the initial PC effort. The remaining small computer project moved to Boca Raton and greatly influenced the initial application development surrounding a home computer effort code-named *Aquarius*.

---

1. Cliff Cullum, "History: IBM Personal Computer," IBM internal paper (1988).

According to Tom Hardy, the industrial engineer on Aquarius, "A small engineering group, under an executive by the name of Bill Lowe, started to develop a computer concept that utilized bubble memory cartridge technology. Working on the industrial design for Aquarius, I refined one of my earlier 1977 small laptop-size computer forms as the starting point. Engineering did an incredible job packaging the components and keyboard into a small space and making it work. The resulting working prototype was more than fifty percent smaller than the Apple II announced in 1977.

"We were all very excited about Aquarius as a way for IBM to leapfrog the competition and take both a technology and design leadership role. No other company had anything close to this product idea. However, the project was not developed beyond the prototype stage. Maybe the bubble technology was considered too new and risky. Whatever the reason for its demise, the team was disappointed that it did not proceed further. But, it allowed us [industrial engineering] to be creative and try something new. This experience proved valuable in later personal computer efforts."

By 1979, IBM's corporate strategy group had evaluated the Apple computer phenomenon and urged the Management Committee (MC) to act. The strategy group asserted that many IBM technical employees were writing software programs for Apple computers at home.[2] During this same period, Lowe assigned another small group in Boca Raton to put together another home computer project based on the Atari 800 home computer. Hardy, as the project's industrial engineer, recalled visiting Atari in California and learning how the model 800 components were packaged. Although Atari invited IBM to visit, Hardy was not introduced as an IBM representative. This action was to prevent leaks to the market of any potential implications of a relationship between Atari and IBM.

2. James Choposky and Ted Leonis, *Blue Magic, The People, Power and Politics Behind the IBM Personal Computer* (New York: Facts on File Publications, 1988), 9.

Based on an Atari computer board packaged in an IBM box with an IBM keyboard, Bill Lowe and George Beitzel presented this concept to the Management Committee. The initial proposal was poorly received and strongly criticized for its lack of IBM content. However, part of this presentation intrigued the MC; it outlined the growth in the desktop computer phenomenon and the viability of IBM's participation in this new industry. Lowe concluded this presentation saying that "The only way we can get into the personal computer business is to go out and buy part of a computer company or buy both the central processing unit (CPU) and software from people like Apple or Atari—because we can't do this within the culture of IBM."[3]

Lowe and Beitzel promised the MC that they would return within two weeks with an IBM proposal to address this emerging industry. A task force of thirteen convened in Boca and consisted of employees from the Datamaster and Aquarius product development teams, as well as the Atlanta marketing organization. The Datamaster team brought forward a concept for its next machine based on the Intel 8088 processor. Combining this framework with the team's knowledge of systems, applications, and retailing, the task force put together the proposal for what eventually became the IBM Personal Computer.

The team received the MC's approval for the project. The product forecast was a major contributing factor to the MC's approval. Familiar with the volumes associated with mainframes, the executive committee was intrigued by the five-year forecast showing U.S. volumes of 241,683 units. Of course, the IBM PC well exceeded this projection, and the story of the forecast is now an integral part of the myth and lore associated with its success. Much speculation goes into the reasons behind such knowledgeable individuals so underestimating this new product's market potential. Throughout its history, understanding emerging

3. F.G. "Buck" Rodgers and Robert L. Shook, *The IBM Way* (New York: Harper & Row Publishers, 1986), 209–210.

markets and projecting their viability has always proved a challenge for the IBM team.

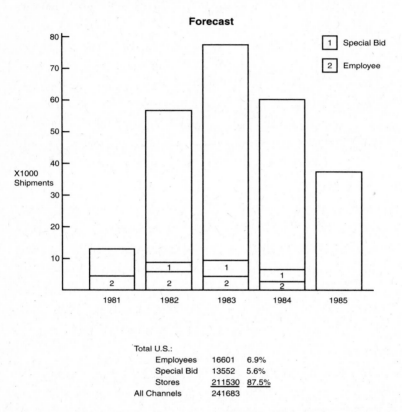

The original IBM PC forecast showed a five-year volume, which was achieved in the first year of operation.

With this approval came funding and the use of IBM's time-honored practice of code names. Jan Winston, who later had a role in IBM's portable efforts, was a nascent member of the task force. Winston later provided a connection from the original entrepreneurial PC endeavor to the burgeoning portable effort. From his position as the original PC director of planning, he became the director of planning–Boca Raton in 1991 with responsibility for overall product strategy. His strategy decisions laid the groundwork for the use of several technologies in the early ThinkPads.

On the topic of code names, Winston offered this reflection: "The first code name for this effort was the *Manhattan Project*, but for obvious reasons, the name was changed. Bill Lowe, the Boca Raton laboratory director and head of the task force, established Project Chess to be responsible for the product code-named *Acorn*. Lowe continued in his role of advisor to the Project Chess team, but his other responsibilities as lab director and his eventual move to run the Rochester lab dictated that he put a strong development manager in place. The eventual outcome was Don Estridge, a dark horse candidate for the position.

"Don [Philip D.] Estridge was a recognized 'wild duck' in the Boca laboratory. He gained fame when State Farm decided to purchase thousands of IBM's Series/1 minicomputers and required a software expert to alter the systems to fit State Farm's needs. This success overshadowed a previous assignment where he had run into some difficulties. In fact, in IBM vernacular, Estridge had been in the penalty box and certainly wasn't the obvious choice for this project."

Despite some questions about Estridge's ability to manage this project, Lowe's decision prevailed, and on September 4, 1980, he announced Estridge as the manager of entry-level small systems. Estridge was asked to lead and staff Project Chess. He was guaranteed direct communications to IBM's MC and the resources necessary to make this product happen.

Because this product was a definite departure for IBM, staffing presented an initial resource challenge. Many candidates were concerned that such career moves were very high risk and could negatively affect their careers. The end result of the recruiting process, however, was a team of people who really wanted to be part of the challenge. Project Chess members went forward with a strong "We are going to do it our way, not the IBM way" attitude that started at the top with the "Father of the IBM PC," Don Estridge. According to Buck Rodgers' book *The IBM Way*, "They [the original team] were high achievers. But more than that, they were true entrepreneurs, who didn't hesitate to put their careers on the line when a challenging opportunity was presented."[4]

These individuals peppered the PC history with a variety of engaging stories. One of the favorites, without fail, refers to a group called the *Dirty Dozen*. These stories resulted in many more than twelve people being counted as part of the Dirty Dozen.

Winston clarified the confusion: "Three key groups have been associated with the *Dirty Dozen* reference. The original task force and Estridge's 'inner circle' have both been considered the Dirty Dozen. But, the real Dirty Dozen was a group of twelve engineers who were brought into the project by Bill Sydnes, the first engineering manager in IBM's personal computer history. These engineers had a far-reaching effect on IBM's Personal Computer history and included a junior engineer named Patty McHugh. McHugh was to be the ThinkPad's planning manager through its formative years. She brought the 1980s entrepreneurial spirit to the portable team that significantly changed IBM's history in the 1990s."

Other individuals from this first personal computer team also migrated into key product development efforts throughout Boca's development history. Leo Suarez was such a person; he also later had a significant role in the ThinkPad story.

Suarez recalled those early personal computing days: "I always considered myself part of the original PC group, although not really a formal member. I was assigned to work with the group, but I was not part of the original twelve. I was probably part of the original thirty or forty. So, although I wasn't one of the 'twelve disciples,' I've been in the PC business with IBM since its inception. I worked on the original PC, as well as its follow-ons. Following these early

4. Ibid.

engineering assignments, I went to work as a technical assistant to the manufacturing plant manager. He knew that engineering skills were critical to building factories that could make millions of machines. I didn't know at the time that these experiences would pay off in the area of mobile computing."

On August 12, 1981, IBM announced its first personal computer and, in essence, jump-started the personal computer market with the IBM PC, the product originally code-named *Acorn*. The IBM press release read:

> IBM Corporation today announced its smallest, lowest priced computer system—the IBM Personal Computer. Designed for business, school and home, the easy to use system sells for as little as $1,565. It offers many advanced features and, with optional software, may use hundreds of popular application programs.

IBM's first recognized brand in personal computing history.

Philip "Don" Estridge, called the Father of the IBM PC by the press.

IBM had learned some lessons from its brief foray into retail with its general business products. The press release led with a price deemed acceptable to the home user instead of the business decision-maker. For the record, the typical expanded system for business—with color graphics, two diskette drives, a printer, and a price of $4,500—would have killed market interest before it had a chance to germinate. Interestingly, the 1981 price range of $4,500–5,000 remained the market threshold for leading-edge performance personal computers for the industry's first decade.

IBM's initial entry into the personal computer market was successful because of, in part, the efforts of its own marketing team. Headed by H. L. "Sparky" Sparks, this team was innovative in its approach to marketing collateral, advertising campaigns, and sales incentive programs. It was this team, working with IBM Corporate Communications, that brought forward the Charlie Chaplin ad campaign of a "personal computer for every man." An award-winning campaign, it quickly solidified IBM's participation in this dramatically growing technology segment. It introduced the concept that computers are not just for corporations but also for individuals who want to increase their personal productivity.

This productivity was made possible with the IBM PC, which, interestingly enough, was made with a number of common industry parts. Most of this first machine contained minimal technology proprietary to IBM, according to Dr. David J. Bradley, one of the key members of the original IBM PC team.

For example, the Microsoft contract for the development of the MS DOS operating system required IBM to develop two major pieces of system software: (1) the "boot" sequence that would start up the computer, check system status, and then load the operating system and (2) a basic input output system (BIOS) to provide all drivers to control the hardware as directed by "system-level calls" from the operating system during operation. The industry used the term *BIOS* for both the boot and driver system–level software. Microsoft wanted to keep the operating system independent of any underlying hardware. This system-level software was needed to tie the higher level operating system to a specific central processor unit (CPU) and to support the core logic that controlled the keyboard, display, and ports.

IBM copyrighted the BIOS code, preventing other companies from using it. So, although the BIOS code was published in the *Technical Reference Manual*, no one else could use it without getting a proper license from IBM. At that time, IBM's practice was to retain all rights to copyrighted material, a practice developed with the S/360 Operating System. Consequently, the IBM BIOS became proprietary.

With these restrictions on the BIOS code, it became one of the most difficult challenges to those companies that wanted to develop a computer compatible with IBM. Their choices were to license the BIOS from IBM, write a clean BIOS from scratch, or license it from a third party that created its own clean BIOS code. IBM's approach to this core element of the personal computer dramatically affected the course of the personal computer industry.

The Authors' Insights

Three threads entwined to create the success of the IBM PC: innovative development, profound marketing, and technologically advanced research. These three divergent plans were brought together from totally separate organizations and woven into a cohesive, market-winning strategy. This strategy convinced IBM's executive management to invest in personal computers. Little did they know that this decision would change the course of not only the industry, but also IBM.

Few industry analysts had believed that IBM could or would address the personal computer market. As the IBM PC garnered sales and market share, consultants and analysts alike realized that the IBM Corporation was changing. In fact, it was remarked in the press that IBM trying to deliver the IBM PC was like trying to teach an elephant to dance. Few realized that IBM was not only learning to dance but also to lead.

CHAPTER 2

Compaq: Pie House Luggables

*...Compaq produced a portable that not only secured its future but
showed legions of other companies how to compete with IBM.[1]*

—Paul Carroll

The computer industry refused to sit back and allow IBM not only
to lead but also to own the personal computer market. The industry was also unwilling to accept that IBM was the only company
with innovative personal computing ideas—nor did it believe that
only one brand was going to dominate this market. Thus, to
understand how IBM created the world's most respected brand in
personal computing, ThinkPad, you have to understand how
portable computing was created in relation to the personal computer. For this historical perspective, the story of how three young
Texas Instruments (TI) engineers left to form a new company in
the emerging world of personal computing has been told numerous times. However, this story adds interesting insight into IBM's
eventual participation in the portable market.

1. Paul Carroll, *Big Blues: The Unmaking of IBM* (New York: Crown
Publishers, 1993), 71.

A typical hot Houston afternoon in 1982, skies were overcast, muggy with threatening thunderstorms. The three young TI engineers met at the Pie House restaurant on FM-1960, one of the main drags in north Houston. *FM* stands for *farm to market*, but because of the expansive growth that occurred after air conditioning became viable in the 1950s, these farms were often sold to land developers. Although silicon chips were now replacing cow chips, the street names remained. Directions stated, "You just go down a ways to FM-1960 and then hang a right on FM-149."

Rod Canion, Bill Murto, and James Harris had a dream. They had presented a creative idea in the form of a business plan to Ben Rosen of Sevin-Rosen, a major venture capital firm in New York and Dallas. The three engineers had decided that it was time to move on from designing portable terminals for TI. IBM's 1981 announcement of the IBM Personal Computer had legitimized a new industry. The IBM PC contained slots to allow for expansion of the computer's capabilities through the addition of function-specific boards. The engineers had told Sevin-Rosen that there was "big business" in developing expansion boards for these new personal computers—and they had great ideas for expansion boards.

Ben Rosen and L.J. Sevin reviewed their plan and expressed interest in helping these experienced engineers, with a proven track record, to form a new company. However, Sevin did not think that the expansion board business would be big enough to warrant their investment. Rosen told them that they would be funded if they came up with a company that did more than just build expansion boards for the PC. "Get creative," he told Canion.

So, Canion, Murto, and Harris were sitting at the Pie House that eventful day while Canion reported the feedback from the meeting. The three discussed the need for something really innovative, not just expansion boards for the IBM PC. They also knew that, given the size of IBM's financial coffers, they did not want to do a machine that competed head-on with the IBM PC. They wanted to get one step ahead of IBM and yet stay out of IBM's way and not go into direct competition.

The conversation continued for quite a while. Then, Canion turned over his place mat, damp with Coke stains, and took out his pen. He began drawing some conceptual diagrams. The group discussed the positives and negatives of the IBM PC and ways to address its deficiencies. All felt that the IBM PC was clunky and that inside the box was a lot of wasted space. Also, when the computer system was coupled with the required external monitor, the entire package was big and bulky. Harris, the consummate engineer, felt that a better system could be designed in less than half the space and at half the weight of the IBM PC.

Suddenly, the team started talking about the possibility of building a personal computer in half the space, integrating a monitor, and putting a handle on it. Harris believed that, by using available nine-inch monochrome monitors, the whole package would weigh less than thirty-five pounds. The system would be light enough for someone to carry around. The three had just turned the discussion focus from the *personal* computer to a *portable* computer.

They were on a roll. Of course, this system would not be truly portable because it would require an AC outlet in order to run. It would, however, be portable enough that people could take it home from the office or to a client site for extended periods of time. They were beaming now. They had taken Ben Rosen's recommendations and turned their idea of an expansion board into an innovative personal computer—but they did not stop there.

Canion looked up and asked, "What do we call this new company?" Harris considered the design on the place mat and said, "Well, it's a very compact design. Can we do something like *Compact Computer Corporation*?" Murto joined in, "I doubt we could ever get a registered trademark for such a common name." Canion felt that he had the answer, "Let's use a variant of com-pact—something we can get trademarked." Murto concluded, "How about if we used a different form of the word, something like *Compaq*—you know, with a *q* instead of *ct*?" The three stared at each other. Canion concluded, "Let's get back to Sevin and Rosen as soon as possible. I'm ready to get going on this."

Canion called Ben Rosen the next morning and related the events of the preceding day. Rosen responded enthusiastically to both the product concept and the name. So it was that Compaq Computer Corporation and the portable computer industry were founded.

Their initial offices were located on Perry Road in Houston. Eventually, they expanded into more office space in the Chasewood Bank Building in an area surrounded by luxurious housing developments with names such as Champion Forest and Memorial Northwest. In addition to Canion, Murto, and Harris, Ben Rosen became an integral part of Compaq. Rosen joined the company's board and provided ongoing financial perspective to their formative endeavors.

With funding approved and a technical plan in place, Compaq introduced its first portable at Fall Comdex 1982. Its small booth was crowded from the opening bell. Everyone wanted to see this innovative new personal computer that included integrated text and graphics and a nine-inch green monitor—all in a single box. By today's standards, it was a thirty-three-pound albatross, but it was quite something back in 1982!

Imagine what it was like to create a portable computer that was so heavy it could not really be called a *portable*. Rather, it was called a *luggable* because it weighed close to thirty pounds and looked more like a sewing machine. People made jokes about how carry-ing the luggable lengthened your arms a few inches. Yet, despite some early development challenges, it was innovative and pro-vided users with the ability to take their computers with them.

Compaq Portable	
Processor	8086
Memory	64KB
Disk	Two 5 1/4" Floppies
Display	9" Monochrome
Weight	33 pounds

Compaq Portable product specifications.

One of Compaq's initial challenges was how to get the system to start. Although IBM's entire system was based on an open archi-tecture, IBM had maintained one very important proprietary piece: the start-up software, or binary input/output software (BIOS). Because the BIOS was developed and owned by IBM's engineers, without a license from IBM, Compaq would never be able to enter the market. Jim Harris's software team decided to develop a compatible but independent BIOS as important as the integrated text and graphics capabilities. This entrepreneurial team made the pieces fit together just as it was first sketched in the Pie House back in early 1982.

As orders rolled in for this innovative portable computer, man-ufacturing became another important challenge. Distribution pre-sented an additional hurdle. When the IBM PC dealers saw the new Compaq portable, they asked, "How do we become author-ized dealers?" The Compaq executives took these requests back to Houston to discuss how to handle the burgeoning interest. Murto told Canion, "You know, we really have to figure out how to man-age all these dealers who want to carry the Compaq portable.

I think we should get some people in here who have the experience. Someone recently introduced me to a guy at IBM named Sparky Sparks. I talked to him on the phone, and, to my surprise, he expressed interest in talking to us."

Sparks not only interviewed but also landed, according to the industry press, a significant signing bonus to leave IBM and come to Houston. He put together a team that would take Compaq into the big leagues. He brought in a host of employees from IBM Boca Raton to set up Compaq's Authorized Dealer program. Compaq's first full year of operation in 1983 resulted in sales of $103 million, the most successful first year in the computer industry's brief history.

Times were good at Compaq Computer Corporation. Success was due in part to the company's ability to quickly follow the successful introduction of the Compaq Portable with the Compaq Plus. In October 1983, the Compaq Plus greatly expanded the usability of the PC with the addition of a ten-megabyte (MB) hard disk, similar to what IBM had done on its IBM XT desktop systems. A dual-display mode also allowed users to switch from high-resolution text to color graphics.

The expanding business and technology advances required lots of new engineers. Compaq looked to the storehouse of engineering talent around the corner at Texas Instruments. There was an added advantage to this close geographical recruiting practice: The three founders knew just about everyone there. When they had a specific staffing need, they called someone at TI who they thought could do the job. They offered the person a nice stock option and got him or her to work for Compaq—no relocation costs, minimal delays.

Texas Instruments eventually took legal action to prevent Compaq from such overt recruiting. However, the floodgates were now wide open because not only TI but also the entire high tech industry recognized that Compaq was really going places. With

Compaq on a financial and technological leadership roll, the engineers applied on their own to transfer from TI to Compaq. This influx of new talent resulted in Compaq's engineering team being technically proficient, yet steeped in TI culture.

At the same time, another very different culture was developing at Compaq. Sparky Sparks, the IBM industry veteran who created the sales and marketing operation for IBM's PC operations, hired Max Toy from IBM as Compaq's vice president of sales. He, in turn, brought in other IBM veterans such as Bob Bauer, Mac McLaughlin, Jim "Bart" Bartelemeo, and Ross Cooley. These savvy marketing veterans saw the opportunity to work for a successful computer start-up that would likely go public and provide an increase in personal financial wealth far beyond what they would ever get working at IBM.

The IBM marketing and sales team set up a contrasting culture with the TI engineers. Gerry Purdy, at Compaq from 1986 until the end of 1987, attended numerous meetings where the contrasting cultures were evident. In one meeting, Max Toy told Bill Murto, "Look Bill, that's just not the way we did it at IBM," to which Murto replied, "That may be true, Max, but we found at TI that it simply was better to do it another way."

When these meetings were over, the IBM alumni would gather in small groups and say things such as, "When are these engineers ever going to learn that we're trying to run a business here?" The TI veterans would say things such as, "Damn it, if we don't watch out, we're going to turn into another bureaucratic operation like IBM and lose our reputation for building better personal computers." Some meetings were like a tennis match, with exchanges going back and forth from one side of the table to the other.

Eventually, the separate TI and IBM cultures merged into a "can do" culture at Compaq. As market success grew, so did the pride of employees and management alike. Talk centered on being number one. Employees within the company began to believe that they were part of something special, something that was challenging the legacy of Big Blue. They were excited about the success and committed to the vision of becoming number one in the PC market. Everyone was enjoying career and personal financial success.

By combining the best of the old with the new attitude, Compaq had gone up against the biggest and best in the world and succeeded. Despite the initial internal counter-productive culture struggle, Compaq's external aura was glowing. Compaq was perceived as a company with a "can do" attitude. Positive self-esteem was everywhere and, with recognized industry success, pride was a driving force behind coming to work each day. Individuals forgot that they came from TI or IBM; they were now a vital part of Compaq Computer Corporation.

At year end, the company gathered everyone in the factory (and, in later years, at larger facilities such as a major church and public facilities) and held a celebration. Rod Canion related how the success was due to the hard work of the entire staff. A music video was played, put together to add to the emotional excitement. One of the favorites was Irene Cara's "Flashdance...What a Feeling" tied to scenes of employees smiling and giving "thumbs up." Such meetings solidified the feeling of belonging to the team, of contributing to the overall company success.

Although this positive attitude was rampant throughout the company, the senior management exercised caution. The former IBM marketing team fully expected IBM to respond to Compaq's success in this market space now called *portable computers*, a concern they shared with Canion and Murto. Ross Cooley told Gerry Purdy a number of times, "Surely IBM will take notice of what we're doing and develop a portable computer that will give us a run for our money."

Surprisingly, IBM's initial response to Compaq was slow. IBM was focusing on satisfying demand for its desktop machines while growing its own infrastructure. Although trying to prevent the clone market from enveloping them, it was not actively pursuing new markets like portable computers. However, a substantial change was in the wind.

Compaq announced the Deskpro personal computer for the office, just two years into its history. Compaq's decision to do a desktop system was not based on a desire to compete directly against IBM; rather, it was a response to the wide range of incompatible systems manufactured by the other "clone" companies.

In 1986, analyst Portia Isaacson of Future Computing brought the compatibility issue to the forefront. Running around Comdex (the premier computer trade show) with a copy of Microsoft Flight Simulator, she would install the software on a clone maker's PC and announce to the press, in real time, whether the manufacturer's system was truly compatible. Imagine! *Compatibility* simply meant that you could run any popular application on any IBM-compatible machine!

Compaq, with its solid software engineering resources, quickly entered the already crowded desktop field and immediately offered users a higher level of compatibility. Compaq even developed a tag line of "It simply works better," which quickly caught on with users. The press declared that Compaq provided performance as good as or better than IBM and that it assured compatibility.

IBM would finally wake up and take notice of Compaq. The little upstart Houston company was becoming more than a niche player. In retaliation for Compaq's threat to IBM's desktop dominance, it was time for IBM to "get serious" about portable computing.

The Authors' Insights

Compaq's founders capitalized on their technological strengths while taking advantage of their competitors' weaknesses. They kept their fingers on the pulse of the market and delivered affordable products that customers wanted—a well-tested formula of success.

Success is a wonderful elixir. The company's prosperity attracted top talent from around the world. Compaq executives knew not only where to get the best people with the experience necessary to fill the company's skill gaps, but also how to give these individuals incentive to join the fledgling company. Somehow, the varying company cultures blended together to challenge IBM in the personal computer market. With strong leadership, this talent fueled Compaq's success through the 1980s and built the cultural foundation of a formidable competitor.

Compaq's success exemplified several of Professor Kosnik's qualities of highly enduring brands (see the Foreword). Compaq participated in the fast-growing personal computer market and possessed the innovative engineering skills to do so. Compaq grew its own style of leadership, beginning with the personnel grafts from both TI and IBM. As the first in the emerging market of portable computers, Compaq created a unified brand that stood for both the company and its product line. Its name was a play on the fact that its leading product was a *compact* personal computer you carried from place to place. Years later, when Compaq's corporate brand stood for "excellence in computing," the company developed sub-brands for its portable computers: Presario for its consumer portables and Armada for its commercial portables. Compaq was cautious in its brand evolution, an evolution that proved effective.

CHAPTER 3

The IBM PC Company: From a Small Acorn

Clearly, our accomplishments are the result not of products, but of people...who sensed the urgency...and who knew that the life-support system relied totally on IBM's basic beliefs at every turn in the road.

—P. Don Estridge, August 1981

The success of the IBM Personal Computer fueled not only market growth but also competition such as the emergence of Compaq on the personal computer scene. It also caused dramatic staffing challenges for the Boca Raton team. During the early 1980s, IBM's personnel practices still touted founder T.J. Watson's three basic beliefs: respect for the individual, pursuit of excellence in all things, and best customer service.

The IBM PC management juggled these beliefs while trying to move their fledgling business forward. They had to staff with IBM employees—at the time, there were few external (that is, professional) hires—many of whom did not understand the requirements of this new market. Management had to find office space to accommodate employees whose number compounded daily. They had to find ways to recognize the long hours and the toll on family life with a compensation plan grounded in the practices of the 1960s. Despite the executives' efforts, the burgeoning Boca site was a hothouse for affairs, alcoholism, drug problems, and the occasional suicide. Many marriages failed because employees spent too many hours at the plant or on the road. These times wrought intense personal problems, in addition to the product and business challenges.

Despite these challenges, staffing continued, growing from the initial Dirty Dozen to 135 employees at the time of product announcement. By January 1982, when Estridge was named division director of the entry systems business unit, the organization had swelled to 330. It then grew tenfold in the next twelve months to 3,300 in January 1983. The most dramatic expansion occurred in 1983, driving the January 1984 head count to almost 7,000 in Boca Raton and 10,000 employees worldwide.

The tremendous growth required employees not only to put careers on the line but also to accept changes in established standards. Arrangements such as office space, furniture, and secretarial support were affected. Debi Dell, then operations manager for the PC business unit, described several instances when executives had difficulty adapting to such a fluid environment: "I remember meeting with the director of marketing about his office. He had joined the PC effort after Sparky Sparks had left to join Compaq. Coming to Boca Raton from New York, he was not familiar with the site dynamics and expected to have an executive office similar to the one he had just left.

"On his arrival, he actually measured his office and found that it was six inches shorter than the published office standard. He called me into his office to tell me to move one of the walls to achieve the standard. At a time when we were doubling and tripling engineers and programmers in offices to accommodate the immense staffing, I had to bite my tongue. I really wanted to tell him what to do with his six inches.

"After I politely told him that I was not going to move the wall and that I had better things on which to spend my limited facilities funds, he reported me to Estridge. Estridge supported my decision and issued a memo that eliminated any requirement to meet the existing IBM office guidelines.

"Estridge was not one for the trappings that accompany position. In March 1982, Estridge became the division vice president and general manager of the entry systems business unit. With this promotion, he was entitled to a suite of offices, which he declined. Despite his pleas, I was asked to put a plan in place to make this happen, working with Paul Rand. The original designer of the IBM eight-bar logo, Rand had recently completed the PC customer briefing center, and its innovative design had captured the interest of IBM's corporate facilities management. Meeting Rand and having design discussions with one of the world's premier designers was a definite career highlight.

"As part of the office design, we decided to use a modern teak oval table as the desk. This decision started a trend—all the PC business unit executives wanted the same table. I remember meeting once with the product manager for the PC advanced systems group. He had just brought onboard a new planning manager who had been given a rickety old rental desk because of the furniture constraints resulting from such exponential headcount growth. This planning manager got down on his knees and begged me to find him an oval table. It's still hard to believe that the people involved with a phenomenon the magnitude of the PC effort were so concerned about such trappings."

Estridge headed the PC effort through 1985. During his tenure, he made every attempt to help his managers address the growth challenges by personally staying in touch with his ever-expanding organization. According to Jan Winston, one of Estridge's key executives, "Estridge had been humbled during his time in the IBM penalty box. It made him a better manager. It put him in touch with the feelings of his team. I don't think he ever lost sight of the importance of each and every individual who was a part of the fledgling PC business unit. Many a night, he walked the halls talking to anyone who was working late, feeling the pulse of the organization. He never forgot to host team celebrations with each product announcement that followed the IBM Personal Computer."

P. Don Estridge.

Dell specifically remembered a celebration held at Broward Community College. The auditorium was filled to the brim when Estridge asked the audience to stand. He then proceeded to ask people to sit down when they were identified with a specific product effort. He called out the Circus team (the code name for the product that eventually became the IBM PC AT), the Peanut team (the code name for the IBM PCjr), and so on. He eventually asked for the original Dirty Dozen to remain standing. A glance around the room showed at least thirty individuals who considered themselves part of the original IBM PC team—and that alumni group has only grown in number with each passing year! Estridge's closing remark to this assemblage was "From a small acorn, we have grown."

Celebrations were not the only reflection of Estridge's concern and respect for the individual. This attitude was also evident in a memo he issued on May 2, 1984. The memorandum, addressed to the management team, referenced the subject of telephone answering machines. He told his team:

> Effective immediately, I want all telephone answering machines removed. I do not want any answering devices rented, purchased or brought onto ESD [Entry System Division] premises.
>
> IBM's deep-seated belief in respect for the individual cannot be carried out by an answering machine. We are all responsible for answering our own phones, and when that is not possible, our phones should be answered promptly by the appropriate individual.

In addition to answering machines, the PC team was also discouraged in the use of the VM/PROFS system for internal communications. Estridge's management style encouraged face-to-face communication as the best way to share ideas and build teamwork. Of course, such communications often led to lengthy meetings and a significant amount of travel. However, these directives were part of Estridge's management style and his pursuit of "Respect for the Individual."

Adalio Sanchez, another participant in these early days, remembered the management styles in Boca Raton at the time. Sanchez was born in Cuba in 1959 but came to the United States when he was two years old. His family lived for a year in South Florida and then moved to the Washington, D.C., area. In 1970, he moved back to South Florida, where he went to high school. He then attended the University of Miami, graduating in 1981 with a bachelor's degree in electrical engineering. He recalled, "After college, I got an offer to work for IBM. Instead, I decided to work for Eastern Airlines as an avionics engineer. I thought it was more fun to play pilot. However, I crashed a lot in the flight simulators. After playing for about a year and a half and seeing the airline industry go down the tubes under deregulation, I decided to take IBM's offer. I joined the PC business in 1982 when it was not yet a separate division but simply a small unit of about a hundred crazy people in IBM's Boca Raton, Florida facilities. I started as a design engineer on the PC XT, the first IBM PC with a built-in ten-megabyte (MB) hard disk. The excitement of that project has stayed with me throughout my entire IBM career.

"During this early period, I experienced the core tenet of IBM beliefs—respect for the individual. Through the actions of Joe Sarubbi, the product manager responsible for the PC XT development, I learned that this premise should be the basis for any personnel decision that I would ever make as a manager. Sarubbi was a big influence on my career and demonstrated the value of a mentor. He recognized that I had above-average skills and put me on IBM's fast track. He guided and coached me. I was really sorry when he left in 1986 to start the Panda Project. I have always tried to use his approach throughout my career, and it proved extremely valuable in my various management assignments."

From 1981 through 1984, revenues grew from approximately $43 million to greater than $4 billion. The IBM Personal

Computer business unit not only grew in numbers—both employees and products—but also became a new division, the Entry Systems Division (ESD). The expansion led to increasing political battles, almost directly proportional to the press exposure and kudos attributed to Estridge's efforts. Even Estridge himself commented in the spring of 1984 that the team had been allowed to follow its own path for too long without the normal corporate intervention. Continual executive reviews had been kept to a minimum, except for the traditional mid-February executive trip to Boca Raton from the winter-ravaged Northeast.

Product development efforts during Estridge's reign included the IBM PC XT (*XT* for *Extended Technology*), the PCjr (IBM's home computer), and the PC AT (*AT* for *Advanced Technology*). Each product had certain elements of success, as well as its own set of problems. Each had its own unique story and set of players. The product managers sometimes forgot that they were part of the same business unit, vying for resources and funding. These conflicts were often resolved with little regard for the future. Strategy decisions sometimes affected resource allocations, which later stymied IBM's leadership in the personal computer market. The strategy was to invest in products that would grow market share versus investing in the emerging technologies necessary to grow the business.

Despite internal conflicts, IBM worked hard to create a solid business in personal computers and to build a skilled organization. However, Compaq Computer Corporation had started to hire key IBM personnel away from Estridge's team. This newcomer's story was beginning to influence the future direction of the IBM personal computer effort. By 1984, the IBM PC unit knew that Compaq was a competitor to be reckoned with, but IBM had yet to make the decision to seriously fight Compaq on its own turf—portable computers.

The Authors' Insights

Estridge staffed a team committed to "do it right." This commitment derived not only from sharing Estridge's vision but also from his tremendous care of people. Much later, some of Estridge's initial team—Winston, McHugh, Dell, Suarez, and Sanchez—brought his visionary concepts to the ThinkPad effort. Vision and commitment came together within a renewed operating model to fuel tremendous market growth.

The original personal computer team demonstrated the value of a self-contained unit spanning market analysis, development, manufacturing, marketing, and service and support. Unfortunately, early success and staggering growth overshadowed some underlying foundational problems and blocked the insights necessary to maintain a market lead.

CHAPTER 4

IBM's Losing Streak

IBM didn't come out with a decent portable until years later, in 1990, long after the PC market had moved to the much smaller laptops and was well on its way toward the even smaller notebook computers.[1]

—Paul Carroll

At the start of a journey, we always ask Where are we going? How are we going to get there? What are we going to do along the way? It is no different in business. The IBM personal computer business was at a crossroad in its early history. IBM was encountering a new kind of competition. It was now time for management to get some answers to some very basic questions such as Why did IBM let Compaq get such a head start in the business of portable computers? Why did IBM let that Houston upstart company build a multi-hundred million dollar business in portables and then allow a similar success in desktop computers? Why did IBM lose its market edge?

A contributing factor to IBM missing new PC markets was the constant demand to prove to executive management that the desktop market was every bit as important as mainframes, if not more

1. Ibid.

important than mainframes. This ongoing argument took precedence over any attempt to even show portables as a part of the growing PC market. Significant political battles occurred almost daily, obliterating forward thinking and planning. Emphasis was on the battle at hand, not future challenges.

Many of the original team, disgusted with the IBM corporate executive team's lack of vision, found success and monetary rewards by joining other companies. H.L. "Sparky" Sparks, who was key to the initial PC marketing programs, James D'Arezzo, who was responsible for the Charlie Chaplin marketing campaign, and Max Toy, who was responsible for IBM's PC sales effort, joined Compaq Computer Corporation, IBM's fiercest competitor in this market space. IBM had yet to realize that allowing employees to pursue emerging markets and participate in the company's financial success was fundamental to retaining its strongest contributors. The Boca team was unsuccessful in its efforts to challenge corporate decisions in regard to strategy and compensation.

Additionally, the PC business unit had its own internal problems. Significant turf wars, battles among egocentric executives, and space and resource constraints added to the tension at the Boca-based operation. During its growth period, the PC operation was relegated to numerous off-site buildings, including a vacated department store where employees joked about holding meetings in *Lingerie*. The PC employees were often treated as second-class citizens by the controlling Boca Raton site management. Before the PC operation *became* the Boca site, the hosting division controlled all facilities and operations. Support was allocated after the site's needs were satisfied, despite the significant revenue that the independent PC unit was already bringing to IBM. This location struggle, coupled with the political climate, consumed the valuable time of many key PC managers.

If the truth be known, efforts were underway to address emerging markets, but these were generally hidden within the operating budgets of authorized projects. IBM's PC team had actually started work on a portable computer well before Compaq emerged as a leader in this market segment. According to Paul Carroll in his book *Big Blues: The Unmaking of IBM*, "IBM did a few portable prototypes, showed them only to other IBMers, got an indifferent response—and Compaq produced a portable that not only secured its future but showed legions of other companies how to compete with IBM."[2]

IBM did eventually enter the portable market. On February 16, 1984, IBM announced its first portable machine, a thirty-plus pound "luggable" that weighed more than the competition, was late to market, and was too expensive. Even the name, *IBM Portable Personal Computer*, coupled with award-winning Charlie Chaplin ads, could not work magic on this less-than-stellar offering. A lack of market acceptance and an ever increasing inventory level drove the division's executive team not only to reduce its investment in the fledgling portable segment but also to delay additional product development until the market established itself.

An important lesson was learned from this initial portable endeavor and reinforced over the next decade: Manufacturing expertise is a critical component of the formula for success. Bob Kanode captured this lesson in his retrospection on IBM's portable story. Kanode had worked in a number of manufacturing positions, including the plasma display division. He then migrated from subsystem component manufacturing to system manufacturing. His first portable assignment was the IBM PC Portable, an AC-powered portable that included an amber orange display. Kanode's recollection of this box agreed with industry reaction: "We had a product that was the laughing stock of the industry. It was too heavy and too slow. The display was terrible. The fit, feel, and ergonomics of that box were terrible. It didn't look good, it

2. Ibid.

didn't feel good, it didn't work good. It was too late, too expensive, just too everything. It wasn't something that you wanted to take with you. It was a disaster." Making note of these mistakes, Kanode's on-the-job experience later influenced the manufacturing decisions determining IBM's mobile journey.

The IBM Portable PC.

This first portable fiasco contributed to the division's turbulence from 1983 through 1986. In August 1983, the entry systems unit was given the mission for not only the Personal Computer but also the System/23 Datamaster, the IBM DisplayWrite, the IBM 5520 Administrative System, the IBM 5280 Distributed Data System, and all the software related to these products. Now, the unit's product managers were fighting not only with one other for resources but also with the newly acquired groups included under the banner of *entry systems*.

No longer a start-up operation, the IBM PC was generating more than a billion dollars in annual revenue and had become a major part of IBM. As a separate division, the Entry Systems Division (ESD) was an operation of 10,000 employees selling PCs to customers around the world. The division had expanded beyond Boca Raton to include a major part of IBM's Austin laboratory. Estridge was no longer just the division president; on January 31, 1984, he was elected an IBM vice president.

The organizational turmoil, delayed product announcements, and quality problems diminished the Management Committee's support. In 1985, Estridge was reassigned, and William (Bill) Lowe, the original concept man behind the IBM PC, returned to the PC effort as ESD division president. Lowe encountered employee resistance to his role, which only increased with the untimely death of Estridge and his wife, MaryAnn, in an August 1985 plane crash. Estridge became the legend, the measure of what was essential to lead a nontraditional IBM organization. Lowe did not have the charisma or time to challenge Estridge's legacy—nor did he attempt it. After all, Estridge had been his choice to lead the PC effort.

Lowe was fighting numerous battles, in both the product and personnel arenas. To assist Lowe with development, Dr. Robert Carberry was brought in as the head of technology. *Dr. Bob*, as he was known by the troops, was an extremely creative thinker. Forcing new projects almost on a daily basis, his technical creativity contributed to the division's growing problems. Dr. Bob often killed products already in testing for ones that looked better on charts, the perennial "chartware." Specifically, a project code-named *Caribbean* was one of the projects cancelled well into the development process.

Caribbean integrated personal computer functions in a color television form factor with built-in home automation. The system controls and a phone were embedded in the television remote control, which could also manage a home-based local area network

(LAN). Caribbean was a concept well ahead of its time. It was killed because of an unrealistic assessment that the 1984 market required a price point less than $1,000 for such a full-function unit. It also went under the cost-cutting knife because of the need to balance resources across both laboratories, equitably spreading the available development dollars. The investment was not a total loss because the team learned about the wants and needs of the consumer and some of the technologies were the basis of several IBM patents.

The two laboratories, Boca Raton and Austin, seemingly could not find a way to work together or to make their product plans jive. Neither Lowe nor Carberry were able to bring the laboratories together. Compounding the problem, projects were no longer self-contained units as in the initial days of the personal computer. Within each site, hardware and software were managed by separate organizations with little cross-talk and minimal product testing. The product or system manager no longer controlled all aspects of his or her business. On September 19, 1985, another realignment attempted to reunite hardware and software at each of the sites. It created lab directors, more clearly defined the Boca Raton and Austin missions, and increased site decision-making responsibility.

A matrix approach to development within each laboratory was established versus self-contained product development organizations. Product teams were composed of employees from vertically aligned hardware, software, planning, and marketing organizations. Their primary mission was to recapture the eroding PC market share. Ironically, amid this chaos, the IBM executive team began to accept the personal computer as essential to IBM's future, lessening the pressure of executive battles and interference.

Interestingly, one of the first products to emerge from this reorganization was a portable. In April 1986, the Austin team announced the IBM 5140 Convertible PC. Code-named *Clamshell*, IBM's first laptop weighed twelve pounds and was extremely portable with its built-in handle. The system could also be used as a desktop computer by adding an external monitor and attaching an expansion box. Containing 256 kilobytes (KB) of memory and two 720KB diskettes, the Convertible replaced the PC Portable in the family line. In August 1986, at the fifth birthday party of the PC, the Convertible had its own placard and was described in the following anniversary marketing deliverable:

> The IBM PC Convertible.
> One computer for people who really need two.
> Here's a powerful computer
> that's both a portable and a desktop.
> When you travel, the PC Convertible works
> with a flip-up screen.
> Back at the office, it works
> with an optional desktop monitor.
> It's light (just over 12 pounds),
> but a full-fledged member of the IBM PC family.
> With PC-sized keys and a 25-line display.
> And there's really nothing lightweight about that!

Although different teams developed IBM's two entries into the portable market, the Convertible exhibited some of the same problems as the luggable, but with additional technological deficiencies. Using an Intel 8088 processor at a time when the 286 was the norm, applications ran slowly. The liquid crystal display (LCD) blurred text and was initially monochrome. Critical to portable operations, the modem was not available when the system announced, preventing the much needed communications capability for mobile users. Finally, although technologically advanced and a leadership feature, the Convertible's 3.5-inch drives were incompatible with the industry's 5.25-inch standard drives and resulted in a dearth of software. The team immediately went to work on an external 5.25-inch diskette drive.

The IBM PC Convertible.

This fix, as well as efforts to improve the Convertible's display, arrived after the market had moved beyond the "clamshell" form factor. IBM missed the opportunity to be a significant player in the portable arena because the marketplace turned to competitors' products such as Compaq's Lte and Apple's PowerBook. In addition, because the division's executive management was in the process of moving from Boca Raton to its new headquarters in Montvale, New Jersey, products announced in this timeframe did not receive the marketing communications attention necessary to combat the poor press. Distribution centers filled with both the initial Convertible and its refreshed successor. Shortly before his 1988 departure, Division President Bill Lowe, not known in the media for his sense of humor, when asked how the Convertible was selling, deadpanned to the press, "If you'd like one, I'm sure we can get one for you."[3]

ESD's biggest challenge was not just the internal struggles and main competitor, Compaq. It was also how to keep IBM, with its higher operating margins, competitive against a rash of clone companies making basically the same desktop computer at a much lower cost. As these companies figured out how to make quality products certified as compatible by the trade magazines, businesses began to buy them in lieu of IBM's products. Once again, a little upstart Texas company, Dell Computer, was making matters even more difficult. When someone ordered its PC, Dell would assemble it and ship it directly to the user. By completely bypassing the dealers who were then selling most of the world's personal computers, Dell could offer personal computers to the masses at significantly lower prices and configured to individual specifications.

IBM was forced to focus on the clone competition in the desktop business. Its growing billion-dollar business was threatened on all sides. Its approach—to redesign the personal computer with a proprietary internal bus called *Micro Channel*—made sense, at least to IBM. These Micro Channel systems would still run all-compatible software and the MS-DOS operating system, so the user would not know that it was internally different from any other PC. The primary difference was that the system would work with only IBM-licensed or internally built expansion boards, making it almost impossible for any other company to build a truly IBM-compatible PC unless it licensed IBM's Micro Channel circuitry.

IBM, in effect, created a new personal computer system—one that protected IBM more than the original PC with its proprietary BIOS. IBM now defined *compatibility* as both hardware and

3. Ibid., 135.

software, something that would make it much more difficult for clone vendors to copy. In April 1987, the Personal System/2 family of Micro Channel personal computers was announced.

IBM's Micro Channel strategy might have worked except for the users who, for the most part, found that the clone companies were now making such good personal computers, they did not need to switch to IBM's Micro Channel personal computers. "Why should I pay IBM a higher price for the same basic capability?" was argued by many MIS [Management Information Systems] managers. If IBM had offered Micro Channel from the onset, the story might have been different. The clone market was now many times that of IBM's sales and had become the measure of true compatibility. Thus, in an effort to raise the bar and create a new standard of compatibility in personal computers, IBM had made a personal computer that was incompatible with the industry.[4]

Timing was not the only problem with the introduction of the Micro Channel. Had IBM initially done a better job of marketing this new technology and describing its benefits, the market might have accepted Micro Channel. In addition, had IBM invested in the development of adapter cards that exploited this technology at the onset, third-party support would have pushed the market. Instead, IBM made it difficult for other equipment manufacturers (OEMs) to do business with them. Not until almost a year later did the PC Company announce a program to support Micro Channel card developers.

When you consider the competitive environment from November 1983 through the Micro Channel announcement in April 1987, it's easy to understand IBM's reluctance to pursue the portable market segment. Why spend time and money on a new product line that was only ten percent of the larger PC business? On the surface, it did not make sense. Bill Lowe recently recalled

4. Ibid., 150.

that "We did not focus on portability early in the game because of our large system heritage. The original personal computer did not touch the heart of IBM—it caused a revolution. This revolution shook the company's foundation and challenged the core precepts. We had all we could do to maintain the flow in our desktop line, much less strongly pursue the portable market."

Although customers were asking IBM to add a viable, competitive portable to their product line, ESD's management faced too many challenges, both internal and external. Minimal resources were focused on this emerging market—the results were telling—and the IBM executive team was not pleased with the results. A major change was needed.

The Authors' Insights

What would have happened if Don Estridge had been left to manage the IBM PC unit? What if he had not been killed in that tragic plane crash in Dallas in August 1985, raising him to the status of a legend? Could his vision and leadership have helped IBM make the right decisions in the personal computer and, eventually, the portable computer marketplace? Clearly, Estridge and his original team understood the value of continuous market analysis and ongoing customer contact—a fundamental focus lost in IBM's late 1980s efforts in the personal computer market.

If we return to Professor Kosnik's Seven Qualities of Enduring Brands, we find that the IBM PC unit lost focus of basic business fundamentals. Although recognized for providing innovative technologies and world-class products in the growing personal computer space, it did not address the market shift to portable computers. After Estridge, no profound visionary emerged to propel the business through the uncharted waters of a dynamically changing market. Individual product houses, as well as the laboratories, operated as standalone units; no integrated strategy was ever really agreed on. A balanced investment strategy was lacking. Managers could not even get budgets at the department level.

Additionally, a truly devastating mistake was made. The team lost focus on the power of the IBM PC brand; it undermined its own brand. It introduced the IBM Personal Systems/2 and the IBM Micro Channel. It ended up "eating one of its own children." It failed to correctly evaluate the brand equity that had been established.

Finally, the IBM PC team forgot to leverage the power of its network. IBM needed the power of its network of dealers, vendors, and customers to fight the ever-increasing competitive tide. Compaq was no longer the only competitor to fear. Apple, NEC, and Zenith were delivering creative solutions to the changing requirements of both the desktop and portable markets. By establishing renewed contacts with the key members of its network and educating them on the advantages of working with IBM over its major PC competitors, IBM eventually turned around and established a new direction for its personal computer business.

CHAPTER 5

Zenith and NEC: Early Portable Innovators

Victory is in the quality of competition, not the final score.

—Mike Marshall

Compaq was not the only key player in the portable game in the 1980s. IBM faced strong competition from other companies such as Apple, Zenith, and NEC. Also, because the PC industry had spawned the trend of employees changing companies every few years, computer companies were able to add experienced personnel with minimal effort. Compaq had started this trend with its hiring of TI engineers and IBM marketing executives; other companies soon followed suit. Industry veterans were those individuals who accomplished a great deal in a relatively short period of time and then moved on; James D. Bartlett was just such an industry veteran. During the early portable years, Bartlett worked at both Zenith Data Systems and NEC, enabling him to provide insight into these companies. Later a member of the ThinkPad team, Bartlett provided a nontraditional IBM perspective.

Zenith Data Systems (ZDS) was one of the first companies to build a clone to the IBM Personal Computer. Back in the early 1980s, a company wishing to build a PC either had to have its own BIOS or had to license the BIOS, the proprietary part of the IBM PC, from IBM. ZDS had their engineers write a BIOS, an approach similar to the tack Compaq had taken. They also developed a lot of custom chips instead of using standard industry parts. It was an unusual combination at the time.

It was this type of unusual thinking that led Bartlett to join ZDS in 1984. He recalled, "Our first portable was the one we acquired from Morrow Designs. It was like a sewing machine with a flip-down keyboard at the front—very similar to the Compaq Portable. It had two 5.25-inch floppy disk drives and used a huge videotape-size cassette battery from a portable camcorder. It also had a black-and-white LCD display. Introduced in early 1985, this system was one of the first portable computers that would run without being plugged into an AC outlet."

ZDS focused on selling to the government, whereas its primary competitors focused on the business enterprise. Despite the size and somewhat archaic design of the Morrow-based portable, ZDS won many of the original government bids, including the first one with the IRS. These wins made it an early competitor in the portable market, following its initial offering with a line of portable computers under the Super Sports sub-brand.

In 1986, NEC recruited Bartlett to do product line management for a new line of portable computers. Bartlett reflected, "The opportunity to move from a marketing communications job to a line job at NEC was appealing. I had Profit and Loss (P&L) responsibility for their new line of portables. They had lots of internal resources we never had at ZDS. They built their own processors. They built their own floppy drives. They did miniaturization. They had vertical integration. I saw this as a company that could be formidable in the mobile business—and they were strong in data communications, which I felt was going to be very important for the future of portable computing. I thought these guys could really be hot. It was a great career move for me.

"Our first portable product at NEC was the MultiSpeed. We brought it to market in less than six months after I got there. It was the first portable product to have a multiple speed processor. It was lighter and smaller than the other luggables on the market at the time. We came in with a product that had a full-size keyboard and a numeric keypad. Nobody else had done that. We had integrated software, including personal information management [PIM] programs, in ROM [read-only memory] that popped up on the screen when you turned it on. It was really quite innovative."

To illustrate this innovation, NEC came out with an ad whose tagline read "We're not too big for your britches" and had a split screen below it. On the left side was a picture of a guy's legs with an IBM Convertible looking as though it was going to fall off his lap. On the other side was somebody with a MultiSpeed that fit very nicely and comfortably in the lap. The ad highlighted its bigger keyboard and larger screen.

Bartlett described the successful launch of the MultiSpeed product: "I'll never forget a very humbling experience at our press conference. Someone from the press asked me, 'Why do you think you are going to be successful in portable computing when IBM, with all its technology, hasn't done a product like this?' I replied, 'It's a better question for IBM than it is for me. However, portable computing hasn't yet become strategically important to them. I believe that if they wanted to be in the portable business in a big way, they'd be announcing products more like the MultiSpeed.' Of course, at the time, I never had any idea that I'd end up at IBM six years later helping make portables a strategic business for them."

NEC is perhaps best known for the development of the NEC UltraLite, its first ultraportable. Bartlett continued, "We had been sniffing around one of NEC's Communication and Computing centers, a thinktank for new development. We discovered a terminal they were developing that was thin, light, and had a large display. We thought it would make a great portable computer. I still have one of them in my office. I kept it because it looks so much like today's ultraportables. In fact, it looks very similar to the IBM ThinkPad 560 today."

The NEC UltraLite was one of the first solid-state machines, meaning that it did not have a hard disk like today's portables but had a ten-megabyte (MB) solid-state hard disk. It also used little cards much like today's PCMCIA cards. It had Lotus 1-2-3 built in to the system's ROM and ran MS-DOS. It weighed four pounds, including the built-in modem and a battery. The system used the NEC V30 8086-compatible processor.

"The UltraLite was way ahead of its time," said Bartlett. "People were leery of a portable that didn't include a floppy drive or a rotating hard disk. You could plug in a floppy using an external cable. It was an instant hit. I think we got on the cover of most major PC magazines. Everyone acknowledged the advanced technology, but we had a really difficult time getting them into production. There was all this hype from the promotions at the introduction, but it was many months before we got them into production. So, we ended up selling fewer of them than we anticipated. We really could have sold five times as many if we had just been able to get the manufacturing going faster than we did. By the time we got the first unit into production, we found ways to make the display better or add more storage. We went very quickly from the UltraLite to the UltraLite 286, which had a VGA display and a hard disk. It had a 286 processor instead of an 8086-compatible V30, so we moved up to a very powerful portable PC—with essentially the same rough dimensions.

"We also developed the ProSpeed family of notebook PCs. This was the first line of portables that included modular accessories you could swap out. We also put forth the whole idea of docking stations. The term *docking station* was actually trademarked, but no one pursued controlling the name. We used the analogy of connecting your portable in the office being like a space shuttle docking in space.

"About the time I decided to leave NEC, the company was developing a new line of portables called *Versa*. At first, the idea was to add it to the name *UltraLite*, but the name *UltraLite Versa* was too complex. Eventually, NEC dropped the UltraLite brand and branded all portables *Versa*. They actually lost one of the best names in mobile computing in *UltraLite*. It was a powerful name."

The Authors' Insights

Both Zenith Data Systems (ZDS) and NEC, major players in the early years of portable computing, brought their own visions and strengths to this emerging market.

NEC, in particular, taught portable market players several key lessons. First, it demonstrated that the correlation of announcement timing and manufacturing volumes was critical to a product's success. Second, NEC's marketing cemented the concept of the right name and the protection of that name as fundamental to brand management. Last but not least, NEC displayed the value of its tremendous vertical integration.

If we relate these points to Professor Kosnik's Seven Qualities of Enduring Brands, NEC balanced its development and marketing objectives, capitalized on the value of a recognizable brand, and leveraged its network through its vertical integration requirements. Unfortunately, like IBM, NEC, as well as ZDS, had lost focus on its vision. Perhaps like IBM, though, a new vision would propel them to the forefront of the portable market.

Function	NEC UltraLite	Zenith MinisPort
Processor	NEC V-30	80C88
Clock Speed	9.83 MHz	8/4.77 MHz
Operating System	DOS 3.3	DOS 3.3
Display	Electroluminescent backlit LCD	Backlit transflective
RAM	640 KB Standard	640 KB (1MB)
Floppy Disk	No internal	2" internal 720 KB
Hard Disk	1 to 2 MB silicon	360 KB/1.3 MB silicon
Modem	2,400 baud (standard)	1,200/300 baud (optional)
Ports	RJ-11 (phone) Serial Expansion	9-pin serial 25-pin parallel Floppy
Weight	4.4 pounds	5.9 pounds

This comparison of the NEC UltraLite and the Zenith MinisPort demonstrates some of the innovation found in products delivered by these companies.[1]

1. Andy Seybold, "Portable Computing in the 1990s—Part II," *Dataquest* (December 1990): 2–8.

CHAPTER 6

IBM Gets the Message

Like all great travelers, I have seen more than I remember, and I remember more than I have seen.

—Benjamin Disraeli

As the decade of the 1980s came to a close, competition had eroded IBM's market share in the personal computer industry. No longer were the IBM PC and the IBM PC AT desirable purchases in the desktop arena. IBM's attempt to replace these machines with the IBM Personal Systems/2 and the IBM Micro Channel had failed miserably, giving companies such as Compaq a chance to get a foothold in the desktop market. IBM had failed to deliver a portable computer that its customers wanted. For years, IBM did a terrible job of designing and building portable computers. It built portables, but they were not very glamorous and were always late to market. Luckily, one person at IBM had the vision for the company's future success in this market. That person was Jim Cannavino.

James Cannavino arrived on the Entry Systems Division scene in late 1988. Cannavino was born and raised on the West Side of Chicago and, like many self-made men, never went to college. He joined IBM in January 1963, eventually fulfilling his fifth-grade dream of running a part of the world's largest computer maker.

Insight into Cannavino's decisions as head of the personal computer business can be gleaned from a look at the IBM executives who affected his career. Shortly after joining IBM, Cannavino ran into an individual from whom he thought he could learn continuously for the rest of his career—an executive named Jack Bertram. Called *Black Jack* by his friends and enemies alike, Bertram was an outstanding businessman, a very good technical guy, and a man driven to succeed. According to Cannavino, "Jack was the first person that I felt was driven at the same level I was driven. He made a profound difference in my view of how business works.

"Besides Bertram, there were two more guys who made a big difference in the way I saw things. Jack Kuehler, then president of the IBM Company, was the first guy to teach me that good ideas were a dime a dozen. He knew the difficulties of managing an organization focused only on good ideas while needing to head in a different direction; he was a master of management. And, finally, Paul Rizzo taught me everything I needed to know from a financial perspective. Paul was one of the finest executives in the company, with his no-nonsense, financial background...We used to call him a 'shiny ass accountant,' because they sat in chairs for so long that their pants got that look to them. All three—Bertram, Kuehler and Rizzo—influenced my management style."

Until the end of 1988, Jim Cannavino's only involvement with personal computers was to influence their designs so that they could participate in the enterprise-computing model, which he was managing at the time. Cannavino, having largely grown up on the mainframe side of IBM, had once sneered, "If God wanted us to have distributed data processing, He would have put brains in our wrists." That perception changed when John Akers asked him to run the personal computer business. After his move to the PC side of the business, his quote was modified to "If God had meant for man to have personal computers, He would have built them in to our wrists."[1] Cannavino himself expounded on the quote, saying, "After taking the PC job, my wrists seem to have a mind of their own."

According to Cannavino, "I actually took the job between Christmas 1988 and New Years 1989. Bill Lowe had left the company, and in retrospect, it wasn't hard to figure out why. After working for three days, I got the chance to present 1988's results to the Board. It was a dismal presentation; the Personal Systems/2 line of personal computers wasn't selling, the OS/2 operating system was all over the floor, and the PC Company had incurred a 1.4 billion dollar loss. In fact, I almost got fired after that first presentation until Akers [then IBM Chairman] reminded the board that I'd only been in the job for three days.

"So, things were not going swimmingly well for IBM's personal systems hardware and software. If you looked at IBM's position at that time, we had a mess with our PC desktops, had virtually no servers, and had no portables at all. Our primary focus was on that part of the PC industry that had become a commodity, despite serious attempts to differentiate the mix. With the announcement of the PS/2 desktops in 1987, we officially entered a major battle between this thing called *Micro Channel* versus the industry-accepted EISA architecture. However, the architecture war actually started much earlier with the PC AT's 1984 introduction, which included a proprietary bus meant to give IBM a leg up against the fast amassing clone industry. The PC AT and the PS/2 line fueled the war between IBM and the major clone manufacturer at the time, Compaq Computer Corporation. My immediate

1. Ibid., 169.

challenge was to decide whether a strategy existed that could re-establish IBM as a leader in the personal computer market, from both a technology and share perspective.

"By the middle of March 1989, I was ready to present my assessment of where things were and where they needed to go. A prerequisite to understanding the report was the cost structure affecting the PC Company. During the 1980s, IBM's personal computers were marketed through its own sales force and the dealer channel. The dealer channel was established to reach those customers who did not have access to the IBM sales force. Unfortunately, the contracts with the dealers were not specific, and the dealers immediately went to the enterprises where all the money was and where IBM already had coverage. So, for all intents and purposes, we had the dealer channel and the sales force selling personal computers to the same customers at the same time. IBM's SG&A (Sales, General, and Administrative) costs at the time were forty-eight percent and the dealer channel costs were about twenty percent, so the PC business was seeing SG&A costs of about sixty-eight percent. Think about that for a second—how could any one make a buck with that kind of overhead?!

"So, my report back to the management team addressed not only this ridiculous marketing overhead but also significant product strategy holes. IBM, I believed, was a company that made 125 percent of its profits on server-related activities; thus, in my opinion, the PC Company not being in the server business was kind of silly. I also recommended that they get out of the desktop business altogether or, at a minimum, really slim down their efforts into this market. I strongly believed that an emerging technology referred to as *portable computers* would dominate where the desktop used to be viewed as 'king.' The high-premium, high-volume market would be mobile personal computers, and I had rationale to support this premise. However, I really felt that IBM would be better off as a company if it exited the PC business altogether.

"Besides these product holes, I did not believe that IBM had a model for delighting the customers within this market space. At the time, we made about eighty percent of our profits from 110 large customers who frequently paid five or six hundred million dollars a year to IBM. And, in my opinion, it was very hard to tell one of those customers who just wrote you a half a billion dollar check that they were going to get only ninety-day service on their PCs. Either we were going to have to spend a fortune to make the PCs better than the industry's average, which was almost impossible to do, or we were going to have to deliver support that matched the customers' expectations. Personal computers were not on the same scale of reliability, usability, and integration capability as other IBM products shipping at much higher gross margins, so numerous changes were going to be required in order to level the playing field."

The Board responded that it only wanted to see plans that kept IBM in the PC business. Cannavino reiterated his strong belief that the PC Company had to get back into the server market. The OS/2 plan had to be revisited, and some kind of relationship with Microsoft had to be established. Alternative channels needed to be developed to offset the decline in the dealer channel. Whereas in 1986 dealers delivered ninety percent of all PCs, by 1988 they were delivering seventy percent of all products, including desktops. Cannavino predicted that, in the near future, dealers would account for only a third of the product volume, whereas direct sales from companies such as Dell and Gateway would take a big slice of the retail market and, eventually, the business segment. IBM also had to reduce the expenses associated with its distribution channels. Finally, Cannavino stressed the need to reduce the amount of money spent on developmental engineering as the market turned quickly to clones.

Clones were not prevalent in the mainframe industry, and the concept was foreign to many of the Board members. However, in the personal computer segment of the late 1980s, clone-makers delivered sixty percent of the systems to the market. The aggregation of the clones was a dominant factor in this industry, growing much faster than any one brand name company, and this growth had to be stymied immediately.

"At the time, IBM had the rights to make derivative products from Intel's 386 processor," said Cannavino. "We put together a plan to make a series of IBM manufactured processors and products. However, after serious contemplation by the Board, we were told not to proceed. Tragically, at that same time, the CFO sold our twenty percent interest in Intel instead of taking advantage of the opportunity to grow our interest. It was an odd set of decisions—refusing to let me make some interesting products *and* walking away from the one company on which we were going to be 100-percent dependent. We lost the opportunity to increase our position in both Intel and in the personal computer market."

At this meeting, Cannavino also took a position on the Microsoft relationship, addressing the Board: "Look, OS/2—this joint effort between Microsoft and IBM—is a folly. The code generated by both companies is terrible. The teams aren't focused. They spend more time fighting about where they're going to go than working on the product. This product, this new operating system, was based on 286-processor architecture. An IBM executive decided that anybody who bought a PC AT would get the advanced operating system—a definite sales gimmick that probably killed OS/2.

"At the same time, IBM had another development group, much larger than the OS/2 development team, building something called *OfficeVision*. OfficeVision attempted to integrate the various business software—electronic mail, word processors, spreadsheets, databases, and graphics—in a way that it shared information effortlessly. Unfortunately, despite huge investments in

OfficeVision, the product design points kept changing based on the executive with the most influence at the time. If anybody had just sat back and looked at what was happening on the software side of the house, he would have laughed.

"I believe that several things were true. Had OS/2 been initially aimed at the 386-processor instead of the 286, it would be the premier operating system today. Had the OfficeVision guys aimed at a graphical product instead of a character-based product, the product would have had a chance. Remember that there was no clear leader in the market at that time. Unfortunately, both these products were wrong, and, therefore, my recommendation on OS/2 was to kill it. I firmly believed that OS/2 would eventually disappoint its customers. If they killed it immediately, the customers would hate them for having led them down the path and changed their mind. If they killed it later, the customers would hate them for having led them down the path, got their applications on it, and then watched it not be the industry standard. The feeling of IBM's senior executives was that OS/2 must succeed, and they told me to 'Build a world class operating system.' And, in fact, the team did. To the Boca team's credit, we trimmed the resources, took things back from Microsoft, and consolidated them into IBM. The team eventually delivered a version that won every industry award for operating systems.

"OS/2 required substantial memory over the PC DOS operating system. The OS/2 team was up against memory prices that were very high and hard disks that were sized very small. In the final analysis, customers had to pay a premium of five or six hundred dollars to run OS/2—the price of OS/2, plus four additional megabytes of memory, plus a PC substantial enough to run an advanced operating system. So, in my March 1989 report to the Board, I stressed the fact that OS/2 was virtually all but dead. I discussed the fact that Microsoft was building its own product, called

Windows, and that IBM had no participation in it. Windows was going to fit the client market much more adequately than OS/2. In addition, independent software vendors were hurting from their first attempt at OS/2. They got zero return for that effort and, in many cases, were financially troubled. Clearly, they would not be able to support two divergent operating environments; Windows would definitely dominate.

"We actually got very close to working directly with Microsoft for the development of an operating system (OS) that essentially merged Windows and OS/2. I could envision what was going to happen if we kept going on the same track. We had solid technology. They had the right strategy. So, I went out and met with Bill Gates. In spite of all the things you read in the papers, Gates and I had a number of very good meetings and shared a common vision on the future of the industry. Things went sour because I was not able to get the IBM Board to approve a closer relationship with Microsoft.

"As I recall, Gates and I had agreed that the world needed a true combination of the best of Windows and OS/2. For us to work more closely together, we had to find a way that both companies would have an incentive to make the resulting 32-bit OS successful. I got him to agree to—and you're not going to believe me here— IBM purchasing forty percent of Microsoft. If we had a vested interest in the future of Microsoft, we would both be motivated to make it a success. I was higher than a kite. I just knew that IBM would see the benefit of this strategy. Boy, was I wrong.

"I presented the option to purchase forty percent of Microsoft to the IBM Board, but they would have nothing to do with it. Man, there was so much not-invented-here [NIH]. They said things like, 'We're not going to have some upstart company out in Redmond, Washington, tell IBM what to do. We don't need to invest a cent in Microsoft.' The Board turned down the offer, and the days of our working closely with Microsoft went down the tubes. I wonder what forty percent of Microsoft would be worth to IBM today."

During this same period, Cannavino was also faced with key organizational issues. His primary laboratory, based in Boca Raton, Florida, was reeling from a lot of things. Personal computer manufacturing had been moved to Raleigh, North Carolina, and resulted in the first layoff in IBM's recent history. According to Cannavino, "That [the move] was something that had to be done. Trucking parts down to the tip of Florida and then trucking them all back out again was an expense that just didn't make any sense. The hardware development teams were split between Austin, Texas, and Boca, with quite a set of rivalries between the two locales. Adding to this fray, the development team in Japan was starting to come on strong. All three groups wanted to make personal computers. When coupled with the growing number of labs developing chip sets for the PCs, the complexity of the organization increased beyond anything ever experienced within IBM.

"With this backdrop, I now had my marching orders. I'm in the middle of 1989. Our development cycle time for a personal computer was more than three years, which meant that you had to see four years out to be able to build something you could sell for just a year, after taking three years to develop it. I knew that scheme was a death spiral! I decided to force the development teams to research how our competitors operated. I knew inherently that smaller, more focused approaches to the various segments—servers, desktops, and the emerging portables—could reduce the development cycle.

"The world was desperate for a desktop replacement laptop. I felt that portables had a chance to provide the PC Company with a sustainable foundation. My view was that the portable had a premium niche in the marketplace. It was going to address the business traveler segment, as well as the requirements of anyone operating where space was constrained. I knew that it would eventually be an individual's only personal computer. Instead of all the complications of trying to coordinate between your desktop and your portable, augmented by the then slow transfer rates, I thought there was a whole niche that would run with just portables. That has certainly turned out to be true."

At IBM's 1989 Annual Senior Management Meeting, Cannavino told the marketing team, "If you give me specifications for a portable, I will deliver that portable in a year." Marketing created a set of specifications that would provide the basis for IBM's next entry into this illusive market space.

After several months of evaluation and management reviews, the PC Company had a plan to address the portable game. By 1989, the office had become so automated by the personal computer that professional people out on the road found it increasingly necessary to take computers with them so that they could knock out reports in their hotel rooms.[2] Cannavino recognized this trend and asked yet a third team to define a product that would establish IBM's presence in this ever growing market segment, a market where major competitors were having great success and where IBM had been a nonfactor as the market grew to several billion dollars a year.[3] This third team, once again headquartered in Boca Raton, was self-contained and had its own hardware and software engineers, planners, and marketing support personnel. This organization was contrary to the lab's matrixed approach.

Cannavino selected Bob Lawten, the manager of Special Development Operations, to analyze IBM's previous attempts to develop a portable computer. According to Cannavino, "Lawten was a creative wild man who surrounded himself with some good talent like Leo Suarez." Lawten's craziness was founded on the original IBM PC management philosophy of forgetting how

2. J. Carlton, *Apple: The Inside Story of Intrigue, Egomania, and Business Blunders* (New York: Times Books, 1997), 104.

3. John Sculley, *Odyssey: Pepsi to Apple, A Journey of Adventures, Ideas and the Future* (New York: Harper & Row Publishers, 1987), 241.

things were supposed to be done and just doing it the way it needed to be done. He was a real risk taker.

Lawten started by looking into what was being developed by IBM Research and in Japan. Executives were finally asking, "What does the customer want in this marketplace?" According to an internal article written by Pete Leichliter, a member of this team, "This effort meant embarking on a new path—a new methodology—for developing a product. The developers were encouraged to continually go back and check with customers. Customers were asked about their reactions to development's progress and the decisions regarding form factor, keyboard, display, desktop functionality, and power. For the first time, a PC development team kept track of customer requirements in an online database."

Suarez, a member of this small "skunkworks" team assigned to develop the third IBM portable, provided additional insight into IBM's attention to portable computing. "Building a portable computer at IBM was like going from mini computers to the PC," said Suarez. "None of the people in the traditional desktop PC area wanted anything to do with developing a portable because, at the time, the [desktop] volumes were going through the roof. So, they decided to put a skunkworks group in place to figure it out. The basic idea was to see what this small group would come up with to allow IBM to play in the portable space. Because Compaq was now making a lot of money in portables and customers were asking for an all-IBM solution to their computing needs, IBM executive management acknowledged the need for a portable computer in their product line."

As a skunkworks operation, Suarez and the team were left to do what they could on limited resources. He continued, "I was working with a small group of engineers who were basically told to see what we could do. The group was designed to do the same thing the original PC team did—develop an entirely new computer system within a small, separate organization. Not many IBM PC managers actually knew what we were doing, because they had so many other issues to deal with—the growing clones and what to do about them. We were basically left alone.

"But, we didn't have enough engineers to actually do the work. After all, there were only four of us. So, we went to Japan, which at the time had an excess of engineers. We went shopping for resources, and IBM's Yamato lab happened to have the right resources at the right time. We started working with them. We came up with IBM's third portable, code-named *Aloha*. By the way, that's how the present portable computing development laboratory ended up in Yamato—how the group that does all the engineering on ThinkPad portables today came into existence. They did such a wonderful job on Aloha that we kept them working on one portable computer after another. They just had the knack for product innovation with a little direction from us.

"We got business direction from our executive, Lou Bifano, Lawten's manager. He told us to go off and build a truly great portable, something that would sell well against the Compaq portable. He anointed us to get it out the door, no matter what. I have to hand it to Bifano. He sold us on the vision that portables would be the next wave in personal computers. Companies like Compaq were doing a small but successful business in portables, but it wouldn't be long before portables would equal or exceed the sales of desktop computers. Sales are now in excess of five billion dollars a year."

This small team went off to develop a truly great portable. One feature they felt would make it great was a high-quality display incorporated in the portable. IBM Research had been working on a plasma display, which was thinner and brighter than a typical CRT display. It was not yet color, but it was a distinctive display none the less.

IBM's third entry into the portable marketplace, the Personal Systems/2 P70, was announced in May 1989. "From our perspective, the P70 was a huge success," said Suarez. "It was one of the most successful and profitable portables IBM had done to date. We thought we'd done a really good job. It was a solid portable with strong market demand."

The IBM PS/2 P70.

Market research supported Suarez's perception, indicating that IBM sold enough P70 portables in its first year of business to become the number two selling luggable in the market. In September 1989, *PC World* stated, "This time IBM did it right" and awarded the P70 its Best Buy award. Also, in March 1990, *PC Magazine* bestowed its Editor's Choice award with kudos of "wonderfully usable" and "the most thoughtfully designed of the 386 luggables." It was not enough to become the market leader, but it was the start of a great journey.

According to Jim Cannavino, "In 1989, the PC Company made 1.2 billion dollars in profit for the corporation. We went from a 1.4 billion dollar loss in 1988 to 1.2 billion dollar profit in 1989. So, the Board wasn't thinking that we were collapsing…although I was convinced that we were. The management team started feeling pretty good about themselves. We started making some money, and we were starting to make some—actually, we were making— price deals. We were back to winning big accounts. But, although we were doing all kinds of things that made sense, I still didn't think we had a sustainable strategy. The P70 contributed to some of the turnaround in 1989, but I was convinced that more effort was needed in the portable arena."

Lawten's team expanded and was chartered to begin working on successor products. It remained a self-contained unit within the Boca Raton laboratory, eventually causing some significant political problems. This did not deter the team from an eighteen-month development cycle versus IBM's standard development cycle of almost three years. In November 1990, the team announced the Personal Systems/2 P75 486.

As great as the P70 and P75 luggables were, all the team's work was for naught. Once again, Compaq changed the rules of the portable game, introducing the first notebook. The portable computer industry would never be the same.

The Authors' Insights

As the history of IBM's participation in the personal computer industry was explored, numerous errors in judgment were discovered. IBM's failure to exercise an option to purchase forty percent of Microsoft was likely one of the worst business decisions of the IT industry. Cannavino's realization that IBM's OS/2 effort was not going to succeed and that IBM needed to partner with Microsoft on Windows also made sense. Had Microsoft and IBM cooperated and used the OS/2 memory management, user interface, and architecture, the combined effort might have delivered something like Windows NT 5.0 in the early 1990s. Hindsight is cheap, though. It takes vision, skill, and luck to recognize and capitalize on opportunities ahead of their time.

Cannavino saw the future of mobile computing before others at IBM. He realized that IBM had the technical resources to become a leader in this emerging segment. Even while the various laboratory groups squabbled over ownership of this segment, Cannavino understood that mobile development needed to be focused and funded. Without his vision and sponsorship, IBM might never have ventured into the portable market when it did. Time and time again, such vision and sponsorship has changed the world in which we live and work.

Sponsorship comes into play in another arena as well. How does a company recognize and/or train individuals to be insightful executives? Cannavino mentioned key executives who mentored him throughout his career. Great companies take the process of mentoring and "sit beside me for a year" to the heart of personnel practices: planning the line of succession. A successful line is assured when managers select talent that is as good or better than they are and then stay out of the way. Learning from these assignments, as well as from product successes and failures, provides cost-effective lessons.

The Portable Forefathers: The Technological Advancements of IBM's Early Portable Computers

System	IBM Portable	PC Convertible	PS/2 P70	PS/2 P75
Form	*Sewing Machine*	*Clamshell*	Luggable	Luggable
Processor	8086	80C88 4.77MHz	80386 20MHz	80486 33MHz
Memory	128KB	256KB/ 512KB	4/ 8MB	8/ 16MB
Storage	(N/A)	(N/A)	120MB	160/400MB
Display	Amber/ orange plasma	Detachable LCD	Hi-res plasma (VGA)	Hi-res plasma (XGA)
Operating system	DOS	DOS 3.2	DOS 4.0 /5.0 OS/2 1.3 /2.0	DOS 4.0 /5.0 OS/2 1.3 /2.0
Weight (lb.)	29	12.2	20.8	22.1
Other		Internal modem	Micro Channel	Micro Channel
Announced	2/16/84	4/2/86	9/89	11/90

As the story progresses, some terms need clarification. *Portable* computer describes a personal computer that can be carried by an individual from place to place and operated on battery power. Different form factors have evolved over the years:

- *Transportable*—Referred to as a *luggable*, it weighed fifteen pounds or more, did not fit in a briefcase, and normally ran off AC power. It is no longer in production.

- *Laptop*—Refers to the original portable that used a "clamshell" design. It weighed more than seven pounds and ran off battery or AC. *Laptop* is now used in the press as a generic name for portable PCs. The more accurate term for today's portable PC is a *notebook* PC.

- *Notebook PC*—Weighs five to eight pounds, with maximum dimensions of nine by twelve by two inches. The more popular ones are "thin and light," weighing less than five pounds, and are less than 1.5 inches thick. Notebook PCs have a bay in which multiple devices can be inserted and removed. Typical bay options are a CD-ROM, floppy disk, and battery.

- *Tablet*—A portable system that does not include a keyboard and uses a stylus for input. Larger tablet systems are used in vertical markets, whereas small tablets such as the Palm Pilot and Palm III are used by general business professionals.

- *Subnotebook*—Weighs four pounds or less. It might require an external diskette drive or port replicator to achieve the full function of a notebook. Generally, the keyboard is small, with less than 17mm between the keys.

- *Ultraportable*—A notebook PC that does not have an internal bay but does incorporate a standard keyboard with 19mm between the keys and a large 12.1"–13.3" display.

1990–1992:
THE TIME OF CHANGE

The 5th Wave   By Rich Tennant

"OF COURSE IT'S PORTABLE SIR, LOOK, HERE'S THE HANDLE."

CHAPTER 7

Birth of the Notebook Computer

And the Little Blue Engine smiled and seemed to say as she puffed steadily down the mountain, "I thought I could. I thought I could. I thought I could."

—Watty Piper, *The Little Engine That Could*

The rules of the portable game had changed again. Compaq aggressively pursued its vision to be the industry leader in portables with its 1987 introduction of the Portable II, which was lighter than twenty pounds, and in 1988 with the "lunch box" Portable III, a svelte fourteen pounds. IBM's portables response was the solid "lovable luggable" known as the *P70*, equal to or better than some of market leader Compaq's portables. If the size and shape of portables had continued as luggables weighing between fifteen and twenty pounds, IBM's P70 might have had a long life. But, just when IBM thought it was in the game with a solid line of portable computers, Compaq redefined what it meant to be a "portable computer."

Meetings with portable purchasers always told the same story: They wanted a smaller (and lighter) form factor. Questions such as

"Can you guys make it smaller and lighter? Can you fulfill our dream of a computer no bigger than a notebook?" were pervasive. Clearly, users wanted a box about the size of a spiral notebook (8.5"×11") and weighing less than ten pounds.

A significant technological advance was required to make this happen. Until 1989, all portables had a built-in small CRT that occupied a lot of space, added weight, and required lots of power. Industry talk of a Japanese advanced display technology foreshadowed a flat screen display called the *super-twist neumatic* (STN) liquid crystal display (LCD) to market. This new technology, if rumors held true, would immediately allow the portable computer to be much, much smaller and weigh less than ten pounds. Expected to use less power, new portables would be able to run on batteries longer. The personal computer was approaching a major breakthrough, and it would stimulate the entire industry.

In October 1989, Compaq introduced its first notebook computer, the Lte (pronounced *Lite*) and the Lte 286, joining the ranks of portable manufacturers such as Data General and GRID. As the first implementation of the notebook form factor, this portable broke the ten-pound barrier with a weight of six pounds. The industry press was ecstatic. Once again, Compaq had done what no one thought was possible: It made a computer that was the size of a notebook. The headlines from the industry trade magazines heralded the introduction as an innovative move within personal computing. Users said, "Finally, Compaq has developed exactly what we have been wanting for the past five years—a thin, light, portable computer that can actually run on its own internal power."

By today's standards, it was underpowered. It had a 286 processor, a 40MB hard disk, 4MB of memory, and an 8.5-inch monochrome display (at a time when everyone was converting to color monitors on the desktop). It also included both a hard disk and a floppy drive.

Compaq Lte Notebook PC	
Processor	286
Memory	4MB
Disk	40MB
Display	Monochrome LCD
Weight	6 lbs.
Other	Full-size keyboard
Power Source	Battery with AC adapter

By now, IBM realized that Compaq was a threat. Leo Suarez related IBM's reaction to Compaq's announcement of the Lte notebook that occurred only five months after the successful launch of the IBM Personal Systems/2 P70. "It seemed that right after we introduced the P70, Compaq announced their original notebook. Man, did the world change on us almost overnight. Here we had just developed a portable computer that was clearly competitive with its advanced plasma display. But, it was shot right out of the water when Compaq announced the Lte notebook."

The customer base no longer wanted luggables. From now on, it was notebooks, notebooks, and more notebooks. The demand for the Compaq Lte was great, and customers were asking their IBM sales reps when IBM was going to come out with a notebook PC like Compaq.

The world was desperate for a portable from IBM. More emphasis on the product area was needed, and Jim Cannavino stepped up to the task. Cannavino told the executives at IBM's 1990 Annual Senior Management Meeting and the marketing team that if they gave him specifications for a laptop, he would deliver that laptop in a year. And they did! They created a set of specifications, eventually announced as the L40SX laptop. Also, before finalizing the product design, Cannavino insisted that Lawten's team spend time with the customers who were requesting IBM's participation in this market. After meetings with hundreds of customers, the team produced its set of concept drawings.

Unfortunately, it was a laptop, not a notebook.

Suarez remembered the situation quite well. "Our CEO, John Akers, kept getting calls from customers, 'When is IBM going to deliver its laptop?' We continuously got notes from Akers office, 'Where's the laptop? Where's the laptop?' So, our team was asked to go forward on the first laptop. It was a crash project. We decided to develop a laptop that was slightly larger than a notebook. The reason may surprise you. It wasn't because we couldn't build a portable as small as Compaq. Rather, it was because of IBM's bad experience with the PCjr keyboard. The PCjr keyboard used tiny button keys (referred to in the press as *chiclets*) rather than full-size. The reason for this design was to accommodate various keyboard overlay templates, which would describe the keyboard actions for a particular application. This was necessary in the pre-GUI (graphical user interface), mouse-driven applications days. Back then, everything was accomplished at the keyboard. We decided that, whatever small portable we developed, it had to incorporate the best keyboard possible.

IBM PCjr chiclet keyboard.

"This requirement drove us to use the slightly larger laptop form factor, even though Compaq had just come out with a notebook platform with a smaller keyboard. In hindsight, it was probably a mistake. But, there was such a build-a-great-keyboard mentality at IBM, we didn't think that a slightly larger form factor would make any difference." On March 26, 1991, IBM delivered its laptop, the PS/2 L40SX.

The development team had addressed the marketing requirement for a full-size keyboard, which the L40SX incorporated. However, it announced at the same time that the notebook form factor was taking over. The world said, "No, full-size keyboards are not that important. I'm more than happy to use a smaller keyboard if you can reduce the size and weight of the total machine." So, although the product was initially a market success, the form factor was too big. It did, however, receive numerous awards for its industrial design, high-quality keyboard, and look and feel.

According to Suarez, "We developed a lightweight, durable, battery-operated 386SX full laptop with a great keyboard called the *PS/2 L40SX*. The product was not necessarily a major success story in the sense that it was a laptop in the timeframe that the notebook was really taking off. But, although we might have sold more units if we had built a notebook instead of a laptop, we managed to sell more than one hundred thousand L40SXs, which in those times was fantastic. We had projected to sell only twenty or thirty thousand units. We never considered the L40SX a true market success when compared to Compaq's Lte, but we beat our projections. Our customers got a laptop with a monochrome LCD display, adequate processor, memory and storage—and a really good keyboard. The L40SX was also the first system to use liquid crystal display (LCD) indicators to provide essential system status to the user. LCDs were used instead of LEDs because they used less of the system's battery power.

"Throughout this project, the team's motto was 'We know we can.' At the announcement celebration, Bob [Lawten] presented each of us with a copy of the book *The Little Engine That Could*, along with a train model mounted on a plaque inscribed with the motto. It's one of the few mementos I still have at home.

"Many people don't know it, but we used the L40SX as a 'test bed' in our labs for many of the leading edge technologies that ended up in the ThinkPad. Some of the patents on the L40 for power management are still used on ThinkPads today. We tested both the TrackPoint cursor control and the 10.4-inch color TFT display to see how they would perform. We never sold them to the public, but we did test the concepts with focus groups.

"By the way, we also built an L40SX colored all black. We wanted to go with a black cover, but the IBM executives thought that was just too wild and out of character for the personal computer market. It was not the IBM soft off-white pearl that was on the minicomputers and mainframes. Even though we were doing all sorts of innovations in the lab, the linkages to traditional 'big blue' just couldn't let us go. So, we used off-white pearl instead of black."

Tom Hardy, then corporate manager of the IBM design program, offered a different perspective on the color decision: "I was one of the 'IBM executives' who made the decision that black not be used on the L40SX product design. By 1990, Richard Sapper, an influential design consultant, and I had already concluded that black should be the 'personality' color for IBM's new line of mobile tablet, laptop, and notebook products. However, the application of black was to be in conjunction with the specific new design concept and detailing that Sapper was developing based on the Japanese 'lunch box' concept.

"The L40SX design did not follow Sapper's concept direction. I escalated this issue to Cannavino because so many concerns existed with the L40SX design. We initiated some work sessions to see how the L40SX could be adapted. Sapper even made some mock-ups that were sent to Boca Raton. However, Lawten refused to implement any changes to the team's base design. Therefore, I held to my position that the L40SX did not meet the corporate brand design criteria required to be the first IBM laptop to introduce the dramatic black color.

"Introduction of the color black on an IBM product was an important brand image statement. We wanted to ensure that all aspects of the product design were at a certain level of design concept and detailing excellence. Unfortunately, Sapper and I had some serious design problems with the L40SX that could not be resolved. So, although it might have appeared to the development team to be an arbitrary decision tied to tradition, it was an action to protect a design element that would be influential and important to the mobile brand."

Tom Hardy.

Design was not the only aspect changing the portable arena that Lawten's team wanted to address. Cannavino offered a marketing view of the portable program: "We tried different marketing programs with the L40SX. Working with Harvard University, the plan was to seed incoming MBAs in the fall of 1990 with IBM's newest laptop. But, the box was delivered too early in its development cycle, and there were lots of problems. We were very concerned about the issues hitting the press before we were ready—despite the nondisclosure agreements each student and the University had to sign. The system was just not ready for prime time.

"As it turned out, the Gulf War and other economic pressures obscured these problems from the press, preventing another black eye in the portable market. We never made the papers! But, I also had a team of fifteen people resident at Harvard so thatpeople having problems could get immediate support. The support was way, way beyond anything a company could afford to give, but I was more interested in the long-term effect on the product launch. Winning Harvard was a way to get the portable business re-energized. It was a good starting place, with its reputation for delivering future decision-makers into large enterprises. The students actually liked the box after we resolved the initial development and manufacturing problems."

The final success aspect of the L40SX program was its reduced development cycle: only an eleven and a half month development cycle, compared to the PC Company's normal three-year cycle. A shorter development cycle was the only way the PC Company could get back into the market as a major player. Cannavino started to have serious meetings with the key management on this topic. He recalled telling them that if a shortened cycle can be done with portables, it surely can be done with desktops. These discussions would lead to significant changes within the Boca organization.

It was, in fact, a time of change and uncertainty within IBM Boca Raton. Following the first voluntary separation program in 1988, which offered employees two years' salary and $25,000, two years of health benefits, and a $2,500 education allowance, 1991 brought another significant headcount reduction objective. This employee separation program was neither as lucrative nor as voluntary as previous programs. Executive management tried to improve the morale of the remaining employees and to soften the realities of these actions by concentrating on an organization high point—the tenth anniversary of the IBM PC.

Pulling the employees together and celebrating the tenth anniversary became a site focus. Debi Dell and Dr. Dave Bradley took the lead on documenting the first ten years of the PC's history. Employees were asked to contribute their precious mementos to product displays, which were part of the coordinated Boca site celebration. A questionnaire was developed to see how many employees remembered the key executives, code names, and office locations involved in the first decade of operation.

Jan Winston (on right).   *Debi Dell with Dr. Dave Bradley.*

Employees were provided mementos, flyers, and a single red rose to remember the day. On one of the flyers was a comparison of how far the technology had come since the IBM PC announced. The growth was exponential but did not nearly reflect the advances the industry would see in the next ten years.

Features	August 1981	August 1991	Difference
Processor speed (MHz)	5	50	10x
Instruction execution rate (MIPS)	.25	25	100x
System memory	16KB	16MB	1000x
System storage	160KB	1.6GB	10000x

The past was not the only focus of the celebration. As part of the August 12, 1991, press release, IBM discussed its thoughts on the future:

> In the coming decade, pen-based and wireless computing devices will bring computing to an entirely new class of user—the mobile worker. The mobile worker is someone who does most work standing up or moving around, such as car insurance adjusters or repairmen or someone who meets with clients face-to-face: architects, lawyers, reporters, and so on. Pen-based computers will need to be able to function indoors and out, be lightweight and rugged, having no moving parts such as spinning disk drives that could be damaged if the system is dropped when moving about. Pen-based computing will also move to the desktop but will differ significantly from mobile computing, acting as a replacement for a mouse and an adjunct to the keyboard.

The good news was that the direction was on target, although a little premature. The bad news was that the executive team behind this direction would soon be changing, both in the United States and Japan. Bob Lawten, who led the L40SX effort, took an encouraged early retirement. Unlike Estridge, who had to spend time in the penalty box, risk takers in the early 1990s were encouraged to leave or face the prospect of being "shot." Lawten realized that it was time to move on and use his experience in other venues.

With Lawten's departure, the team became slightly confused and had little development direction following the L40SX. Cannavino pushed the introduction of IBM's notebook products to replace the L40SX, but they also fell behind schedule. In March 1992, IBM announced several notebook products: the N51SX, the N51SLC, and the CL57SX. Despite its innovative color, IBM's first black notebooks still trailed the industry leaders and were pronounced "me, too" products by the press.[1] The market did not react favorably to these products, and today few industry pundits could probably even

---

1. Carroll, *Big Blues*, 258.

name them. According to industry observers, IBM's portable plan was catastrophic at best!

The whole area of portable computing development was coming under the scrutiny of senior executives inside IBM. Customer pressure, supported by the sales organization, was pushing IBM to do a good notebook computer. After all, if Compaq could do it, why could not IBM with all its resources?

During this period of introspection, strong marketing programs were required to push the portables currently in IBM's product line. These programs were developed and driven by two individuals who later had major roles on the ThinkPad brand team: Scott Bower and Maurice Fletcher. Fletcher reflected on IBM's general view of the mobile market and why a good notebook computer was absolutely necessary: "The Boca portable team and Yamato development drove the product specifications. Mobility had taken off, especially in the U.S. After the L40SX, products developed by Japan for the Japanese market were retrofitted for the U.S. Because these systems were originally designed to be used in Japan as desktop replacements, little attention was paid to the weight or battery life. The weight and battery life were unacceptable in the U.S. market. So, once again, IBM faced inventory excesses of unmarketable products.

"The ESD business strategy at that time noted that worldwide notebook sales opportunity was growing from 2.6 million in 1990 to 5.6 million in 1993. It was a market that deserved attention. I spent the next month analyzing the notebook market and developing our competitive methodology. We started to use something called *Price-Function-Value* (PFV), which represents the relative market value of the product.

"If the PFV equaled one hundred percent, the product equaled the competition. In late 1991 and early 1992, all of our notebooks were significantly less than one hundred percent. We developed a detailed *foil* (IBM's term for transparency or overhead) presentation on our positioning and took it to the president of IBM's marketing division. When we compared our proposed product plan against thirty-five notebooks by key competitors, we were way behind competition with the present product line. Even worse, our analysis showed that we would still be behind in 1992.

"Within two years, we felt that notebooks would be twenty to twenty-five percent of the PC business. The only product on the drawing board that appeared to meet the U.S. market requirements was a product code-named *Nectarine*. It had an internal ship date of September 1992 but no external announce date. We offered the team several recommendations to strengthen the portable plan: (1) keep the U.S. volumes low on all other products except Nectarine and emphasize Nectarine as the premier offering, (2) enhance Nectarine specifications to leapfrog the competition, and/or (3) get a third party to develop a product for the U.S. as a potential alternative development and manufacturing source. The development team in Yamato was beginning to get the message that we were serious about this market and the U.S. was going to be in the driver's seat. The U.S. requirements were to be the basis for the next portable product."

Pressure was not coming just from market requirements but from many directions, especially the competition. IBM did not merely want to "meet the competition" by doing a copycat notebook. The team's decisions to try to leapfrog the competition would end up having a greater effect on the portable computer market than even the introduction of the original Compaq Lte notebook. Although the Lte was truly portable, it was not a state-of-the-art personal computer. Yet, it was perceived as the best and most innovative notebook you could buy. The market wanted something more, something that would provide users with an experience closer to what they had in the office.

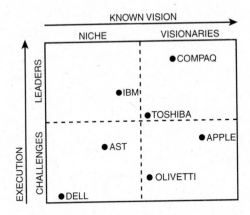

IBM was not yet a leader. Its portable products were perceived as niche, "me, too"
products.

The IBM team knew that it could deliver what the market wanted. They reviewed the L40SX laptop and its follow-on black notebooks, finding them a poor excuse for notebook computers. They documented what was competitive and what was not. They projected where the technology was going. This escalating energy within IBM was counter to the almost "we're on top of the world" attitude at Compaq. Compaq no longer worried about IBM affecting their leadership in portable computers.

That was probably a mistake.

The Authors' Insights

The creation of the Lte notebook sparked a fire under IBM's portable team. Mobile computing was becoming a larger share of the personal computer business, on a trajectory to become a multibillion dollar segment. Compaq's Lte notebook, the measure by which analysts evaluated most notebook computers, drove customers to demand that IBM produce a high-quality notebook. The Compaq Lte enabled users to fulfill their dream of using their computers whenever and wherever, within certain technological limits.

Compaq's notebook success drove IBM to acknowledge this market as a strategic battleground and to focus on leapfrogging the competition. IBM could not just play catch-up on this road to industry leadership. It might have been Compaq that invented the notebook PC, but it was IBM that would perfect it. IBM would soon not only surprise the competition but also surpass it.

The 5th Wave   By Rich Tennant

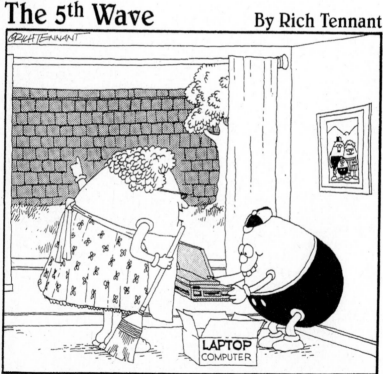

"WHY DON'T YOU TAKE THAT OUTSIDE, HUMPTY, AND PLAY WITH IT ON THE WALL?"

The Pre-ThinkPad Family: IBM's Initial Notebook Offerings Before the IBM ThinkPad

System	L40SX	N51SX N51SLC	N45SL	CL57 SX
Form	Laptop	Notebook	Notebook	Laptop
Processor	386SX 20MHz	386SX 386SLC 16MHz	386SLC 25MHz	386SX 20MHz
Memory	2/18MB	2/10MB	2/8MB	2/16MB
Storage	60MB	40/ 80MB	80/ 120MB	80MB
Display	10" VGA display	9.5" LCD	10" LCD	10.4" TFT color
Operating system	DOS 3.3/ 4.0	DOS 3.3/ 4.0/5.0 OS/2 1.3/ 2.0	DOS 5.0 OS/2 2.0	DOS 3.3/ 4.0/5.0 OS/2 1.3/ 2.0
Weight (lb.)	7.7	6.2	6.9	11
Other	Micro Channel Integrated fax/modem TrackPoint (opt)	Micro Channel Nondisruptive battery xchange Communications cartridge	ISA bus Power management	Micro Channel Trackball
Announced	3/26/91	3/24/92	3/24/92	3/24/92

CHAPTER 8

The ThinkPad Before ThinkPad

Whoever doesn't know the past must have little understanding of the present and no vision of the future.

—Joseph S. Raymond

Before IBM made its mark in notebooks, another IBM mobile product laid the foundation for its renewed portable focus—a focus that eventually resulted in the ThinkPad brand. Interestingly, if asked to describe the first IBM ThinkPad, most people familiar with the portable industry might respond with something like "Well, it was a notebook computer with a large display, a black case, and that funny red stick in the middle of the keyboard." Although a good guess, it would be totally off base.

The first ThinkPad was a pen tablet (that is, a portable computer with a stylus and no keyboard) that IBM showed at Fall Comdex 1991. This product demonstration was the culmination of a small Boca Raton advanced technology team's efforts. IBM's pen venture, started in 1989, continues to this day in an IBM branch office in

South Florida. The original team's approaches, even some key personnel, are still part of the current pen development and marketing processes. It is, however, the initial pen project that deserves further reflection.

IBM's venture in pen computing was closely tied to events happening in the industry. The industry's pen computing journey had begun when Jerry Kaplan set out to revolutionize personal computing.[1] With the initial backing of Lotus founder Mitch Kapor, he founded GO Corporation, a company developing a new operating system dedicated to stylus-based tablets instead of keyboard-based laptops. Because the idea was so revolutionary, yet niche-focused, the product was not viewed as a threat to Microsoft's operating system dominance. Investors viewed this undertaking as a worthwhile endeavor, and Kaplan secured the resources necessary to move forward.

GO's initial plan included both hardware and software products. Initially, it developed its own hardware and delivered a working prototype in June 1989. GO eventually realized that the hardware was not the driving force behind the evolution and focused its efforts on the operating system and some key applications. Given the functions expected of the pen operating system, GO worked with AT&T on a line of processors called *Hobbit*. In addition, GO asked Intel for processor enhancements to enable GO's operating system, named *PenPoint*, to run on Intel-based machines. Then, to complement its operating system, GO approached hardware companies such as IBM to build new personal communicator products.

Before deciding to become involved in this part of the portable market, IBM needed to be convinced, and it took several factors to influence IBM's decision to pursue the pen market. First, according

1. J. Kaplan, *Start Up: A Silicon Valley Adventure* (New York: Houghton Mifflin Company, 1994).

to Jerry Kaplan in *Start Up: A Silicon Valley Adventure*, State Farm issued a Request for Pricing (RFP) in March 1989 that jump-started IBM's initial interest in the pen market.[2] Four companies were asked to respond: IBM, Hewlett-Packard, Wang, and GO Corporation. The RFP requested details on hardware that could support an auto claims estimating application for State Farm's field personnel. Having successfully worked with State Farm in the deployment of IBM's Series/1 minicomputers, IBM wanted to be State Farm's personal computer vendor of choice.

Fueled by this real customer demand but not quick to jump into unproven markets, IBM had to validate the total pen market opportunity. The market intelligence indicated tremendous potential and spurred IBM to enter the pen market. Throughout 1990 and until Fall Comdex 1991, numerous articles appeared on pen computing hardware, applications, and the market potential. Analysts predicted exponential growth for vendors who designed digital writing capability, either hardware or software, so that users could electronically record data and execute formulas as if using pen and paper. An article in *Portable Office* in October 1991 stated that

> The pen interface is likely to be to portable computers what volume and channel dials were to radios: the non-technical person's key to a powerful new technology. And it will become that because it's the first computer input device that most people already know how to use.

Comdex articles were filled with numerous projections, but that of International Data Corporation (IDC) was quoted the most:

IDC	1991	1993	% Change	1995	% Change
Unit shipments	28K	250K	793%	850K	240%
Revenues	$80M	$540M	575%	$1.56B	189%

2. Carroll, *Big Blues*, 319.

IBM tied these first two factors, customer demand and healthy industry projections, to some advanced technologies that were under development. From this analysis, the Boca Raton executives became convinced that it was time to pursue the pen market. They asked Sue King, a long-time IBM development manager, to head this effort. She wanted her team to include not only product and market planning but also hardware and software development. Such an integrated approach was contrary to the laboratory's structure at the time. However, because the L40SX had recently succeeded using the same organizational construct, King's request was approved. She then enlisted key managers with proven track records in IBM's personal computer division to work on the project. Her first choice was Patty McHugh, one of the twelve engineers who developed the original IBM PC. The combination of King's extensive experience in advanced technology development with McHugh's engineering and planning skills resulted in several innovative approaches that would later affect the development of the ThinkPad brand.

Mike McHugh, Sue King, and George King.

King expounded on these approaches: "Because experimental development was so expensive and funding always in question, we knew it was important to validate the product offering. I insisted that our *budget be set up as independent* of the Boca lab so that it could not be cannibalized to fund other mainline projects that were short-funded. This budget was very specific so that we could clearly demonstrate to IBM management that it was a relatively modest expense.

"We also decided to work with a limited number of customers as part of the *requirements validation process*. We informed these customers that this was a prototype effort. We would do a second version if we decided to go forward to the mass market. We established an early pilot program in which the customers paid for the chance to use prototype systems. While this helped us to validate the product's features and functions, it also gave the customers a jump-start on developing enterprise-specific applications.

"We also used the *House of Quality* concept to track the feedback from our pilot customers. We systematically reviewed the proposed product changes with our PC marketing team and pen application development vendors. We balanced the customers' feedback, the field expectations, and the operating system requirements before making any changes to the product design.

"Finally, as part of the Boca Raton laboratory development process, we were required to track the project in the lab war room. Each product under development was summarized on a single chart and reviewed on a monthly basis by the lab director—Paul Mugge at the time. In the case of our product, code-named *Whitestone*, our chart was a sea of red ink. Red ink designated the high-risk factors of the project. We were pushing the envelope in regard to the number of emerging technologies to be integrated. This first pen tablet used a new digitizer, pen, operating system, industrial design, and magnesium casing, just to name a few.

Because of such dramatic innovation, we were under constant scrutiny."

If the war room had been the only bureaucracy with which the pen team had to contend, its creative approaches might have been enough to ensure limited market acceptance. Unfortunately, King was "virtually" managed by three executives. Paul Mugge, the Boca Raton lab director, needed to make schedules, stay in budget, and deliver in volume. Jim Cannavino, the general manager for the Personal Systems Line of Business, wanted to establish a strong presence in the portable market; he had assigned Kathy Vieth to oversee this Boca Raton operation. Fernand Sarrat, director of the Personal Systems Line of Business, desired a product that the marketing teams could sell, priced to make money. Each had his own objectives for this project, and they were often diametrically opposed. Little attempt was made to resolve these discrepancies because no centralized investment or development review board existed.

King and her team worked diligently on their plans throughout 1990. They chose GO's PenPoint operating system as best of breed for pen systems. They made significant decisions regarding the product's design. GO's prototype system was the basis for product concept testing. Field test results indicated the need for a transflective display with an etched glass digitizer. Durability requirements suggested the use of solid-state files and magnesium casing. The end users wanted a "pen-to-paper" feel when using the system. The team also viewed silicon disks for storage and the advanced handwriting recognition engine as key technologies to this project. Each requirement added to the complexity of the effort, increasing the focus by the various executives interested in the program's progress.

In January 1991, Fernand Sarrat established a pen-based project office to "assist" King with her marketing and announcement plans. Debi Dell and Pete Leichliter, assigned to this project office, worked closely with McHugh's planning team to educate IBM's executives and industries on the viability and importance of this endeavor. In March 1991, George H. Conrades, senior vice president and general manager, IBM United States, wrote to the executive in charge of the industries, requesting support for the pen effort:

> Jim Cannavino and I have been discussing our opportunity to not just be market-driven with our PS/2 technology, but to be market "drivers." We have concluded we have such an opportunity utilizing pen-based technology.
>
> I would like you to conduct an effort with your industries to prioritize market segment opportunities for pen-based solutions.

Following this "request," the industry executives designated contacts to work with the Project Office and the pen team. In May, these representatives met to document product requirements and to determine the special efforts required for market success. The attendees benchmarked the Whitestone product against various IBM products and their marketing practices. By reviewing the AS/400, PS/1, PS/2, RS/6000, and S/390 programs, they discovered deficiencies in Whitestone's plan. Recommendations from the meeting included an application development center with hot line support, early customer disclosures, and a "shadow" announcement to determine market acceptance. They also requested funding to establish these programs.

An individual who worked on the benchmarking, Bob Sztybel, then a marketing manager for IBM's manufacturing industry, offered this reflection: "This was a very exciting time for us. We were watching dramatic developments in workforce mobility. We saw novel solutions like Frito-Lay's implementation of handhelds for route delivery as a portent for an upcoming industry revolution. I saw Whitestone as the first and best alternative to address the changing workforce. It was unique, simple to use, easy to explain, and, most importantly, it had the focus and endorsement of senior executives. Unfortunately, sometimes too much focus is not a good thing."

Yes, despite everyone's best efforts and the approval of a subset of the work group's recommendations, the project started to fall behind schedule. Increased executive interest only compounded these delays during the summer of 1991. This interest manifested itself in IBM's favorite method of self-investigation: task forces.

The task force started in June when Mugge, the Boca lab director and King's immediate manager, requested a peer audit of the project. The outcome was 123 action items, a reduction in projected volumes to 27,000 from 100,000, and more people assigned to track the action items than to track the project's technologies. The next month, Cannavino ordered a review of the entire mobile product line. He wanted to know whether pen systems should be a key player in the future of IBM's portables. In September, Corrigan, PC Company Division president and Mugge's manager, reviewed the results of the June and July meetings. He reduced Whitestone's volumes to 5,000 and insisted that, if this program was to survive, it needed to be shown at Fall Comdex as a technology demonstration. Corrigan wanted to gauge market reaction to IBM's pen prototype at the industry's biggest event before committing to a final announcement plan.

According to King, "That summer was ridiculous. More people reviewed the project than worked on Whitestone's actual development. But, the team didn't get discouraged. Patty [McHugh] was not only an effective product planning manager but also an extremely strong people manager and a regular cheerleader. She was always working on ways to keep the team motivated.

"When the going got tough, the tough got going. We got the product ready for Fall Comdex, and our pedestal was constantly crowded. We followed this demonstration with disclosures to more than sixty-five customers. These disclosures, coupled with the early pilots, resulted in special bid orders for one thousand units. In addition to gauging customer interest, this special bid process was also a great requirement-gathering mechanism. It helped us to determine the product's strengths and weaknesses. It laid the groundwork for our announcement, press messages, and marketing deliverables."

While the Whitestone team worked on the product and addressed an onslaught of problems, IBM executives were tackling even bigger issues. Kathy Vieth offered another executive perspective on this pen effort. In January 1989, just a short time before State Farm issued the RFP, long-time IBM veteran Vieth started working in the IBM PC division.[3] She reported directly to Cannavino, who was responsible for not only personal computers but also displays, adapters, and monitors.

Recalled Vieth, "I honestly think that Jim [Cannavino] was impressed with my management skills, but he didn't have a senior position open at the time. He asked me to run the display and graphics adapters business. I ran it for a year, making or exceeding our business plan. It wasn't a glamorous role, but it was a solid, profitable business for IBM.

"In January 1990, Jim called his group executives to a planning session in Somers, New York. At this conclave, Jim summarized my success and announced my promotion to vice president. With the promotion came a move to Boca Raton and responsibility for all graphics products. Two development teams, portables and pen, were part of this group.

"Cannavino planned to move all pen and portable computing development to Japan by yearend 1991. Because I worked well

3. Ibid.

with the Japanese display group and had garnered their respect from my work with them on displays, I had a good rapport with them. So, in addition to continuing my monitor and display activities, I was asked to coordinate the transition of the mobile effort to Japan. We were to downsize the Boca effort and move development to Japan within the year. Cannavino's plan continues today in IBM's mobile effort; portable development is still done in Yamato, Japan. That guy had a real knack for seeing before others how things should be organized to succeed."

Some interesting reasons were behind Cannavino's decision to move mobile development to Japan. He was frustrated by Boca's long development cycles. Ideas went into this mill and never came out. Plans were made and then changed numerous times; shades of Bob Carberry and "plan du jour" still permeated the Boca site. Change was the only constant! This lab already had difficulty delivering servers and desktops. Cannavino knew that he couldn't give Boca the added responsibility for mobile products, an ever increasing market segment.

The argument to move the mobile effort to Japan was also strengthened by its success in the PS/55 (Asian) market. When Hajime Watabe, the Japanese development manager for the PS/55, visited Cannavino, he indicated his team's willingness to assume a significant role and responsibility in the PC Company. Because many portable components such as displays came from Japan, Cannavino believed it was logical to align Boca planning and the Yamato development teams.

Vieth continued her retrospection: "I came to Boca on a two-year assignment. My acceptance of the assignment was contingent on a deal with Cannavino that would eventually allow me to relocate to San Francisco. He agreed because he honestly believed that I would love Boca and would want to stay instead of moving to San Francisco. During this discussion, Cannavino also indicated that he expected Mugge to become president of the PC Division and that he wanted me to consider becoming Boca's lab director. Although I was flattered, I wasn't really interested.

"My Boca agenda was simple. I picked a small team to transition pen and portable computing to Japan over the next twenty-four month period. Seemed like a slam-dunk job to me, so I accepted it. It certainly turned out differently than anticipated!"

The plan was never executed as originally mapped out. The development for portable computers did shift to Yamato on schedule, and it resides there today. However, before it could move, the pen development activities exploded like a nuclear bomb. What was once a small pen computer effort became a black hole that sucked people into it. No one ever dreamed that this little "side initiative" in pen would become such a big deal.

The project became highly political because it was not an OS/2 project, and IBM was pushing OS/2 to the max. An OS/2 version of a handwriting operating system was too large to fit on the silicon disks, which the team had determined were critical to the mobile environment. But, despite its political and technological challenges, the project stayed within budget and within three to six months of the original schedule, a relative success in terms of resource management.

This success was tightly coupled to what was happening with the GO Corporation. As previously explored, IBM became involved with GO Corporation and its innovative PenPoint operating system. When Kaplan approached Cannavino in 1990, he had been seeking both capital and a partner that would build a pen computer acceptable to State Farm Insurance.[4] Norman Vincent of State Farm told Kaplan that they would commit to using the PenPoint operating system only if it came in a tablet made by IBM, their primary supplier of information technology. In his book, *Start Up*, Kaplan documented his belief that IBM was the

4. Ibid.

last company in the world with which his team would ever deal. However, a real customer interested in GO's software required a deal with IBM.

Kaplan called Cannavino and set up a meeting. It was a long process that took almost three months to finalize, but IBM finally agreed to invest ten million dollars in GO. In addition, IBM committed to develop a tablet system (Whitestone) that would run PenPoint. IBM would then market the system to its major enterprise accounts.

Vieth was GO's primary executive contact at IBM Boca Raton, and King managed the operational activities. The Boca team worked to convert PenPoint to run on the Intel processors that IBM used. This was quite a challenge because GO's development had been focused on AT&T's Hobbit RISC architecture. GO had to continue Hobbit development and add staff to do the Intel port. Working with State Farm and IBM, GO wanted a real PenPoint licensee, hardware partner, and investor for its company launch on April 16, 1992.

IBM did some trials with State Farm and other customers using PenPoint. Because the software was still not ready for general release, IBM had to wait to sell a complete system. GO ran out of money again, and AT&T and IBM invested more to keep the effort going. A false hope surrounded PenPoint. Billed as the next revolution in computing technology and Microsoft-independent, PenPoint was for everyone. GO and its partners counted on PenPoint becoming a general-purpose operating system selling multimillion licenses each year.

Why did IBM continue to invest in GO? Remember that Cannavino was committed to expanding IBM's role in portable computing. He wanted IBM to be recognized as a premier leader in portables. He knew inherently that a dramatic technology leap was necessary to do this. GO's PenPoint and the concept of pen computing appeared to offer this potential. Also, to be fair, one's first experience with PenPoint was quite addictive. An October 1991 *Portable Computing* article describes the experience:

> To someone who has computer experience, the first encounter with a pen computer such as the 286-based, non-backlit portable that GO uses to demonstrate PenPoint, is a strange and exhilarating experience. Despite time lags and minor bugs, the PenPoint device manages to create the illusion of liquid paper.[5]

But, it would take more than an operating system to drive success in this market.

King summarized the decision to go with GO: "IBM went with GO because (1) it was conceptually and technically superior as a solution, (2) OS/2 did not fit in our configuration and was not going to at any time in the near future, (3) Microsoft was playing catch-up with GO at the time and did not have a viable product, and (4) GO potentially represented a major new software technology standard that, if successful, would have made those sponsoring it important in the eyes of the industry. It offered us a chance to establish ourselves in a new segment for a relatively cheap investment."

But, just as GO and its operating system had captured the interest of the industry, King's team knew that it would need something to make its mark. Throughout history, product naming had proven to be an important aspect of a product's life cycle and its market success. Just as the myth of the IBM PC's original Dirty Dozen has evolved over time, the creation of the *ThinkPad* name has several versions.

During 1990, while the pen team was trying to get a user-friendly name for its tablet, a new naming strategy for personal computer products was underway. In February 1990, a *Business*

---

5. David Essex, "Pen Portables Prove Puzzling," *Portable Computing* (October 1991): 27.

Month article by Laurel B. Calkins states that "IBM has a new corporate department whose mission is to kill the acronym. Simply put, all new products must actually be meaningful to customers." John Akers, then IBM Chairman, realized that he had no idea what the letters and numbers on many of his company's products meant. And if he did not know what the acronyms stood for, surely his customers would not either.

Of course, a group within the laboratory has to work with Corporate Naming. Before joining the pen project office, Debi Dell, as manager of market planning for the Boca Raton laboratory, had responsibility for product announcements. Part of this responsibility included product naming, which Dell had assigned to thirty-year IBM veteran Denny Wainright.

Wainright joined the pen development, planning, and marketing team in their naming discussions. According to Sue King, "The team had gathered to discuss the name. We knew we wanted something that would not intimidate the novice user. We wanted a name that reflected the system's purpose. We had a contest to find a name, but nothing jumped out at us."

At the next staff meeting, Kathy Vieth asked Wainright to report on his progress in naming the new pen tablet. He took the small leather pad with the word *THINK* embossed on the cover and simply tossed it onto the table. All eyes followed the little black think pad as it sailed through the air, almost in slow motion, and landed—*PLOP*—on the conference room table.

The team was very excited; everyone was talking. No one was sure whether it was Sue King, or Kathy Vieth, or Patty McHugh, or someone else, who first declared, "Denny, that's a think pad—a tiny tablet. It's the perfect name. We'll call it a *ThinkPad*."

Although everyone thought that the *ThinkPad* name was a winner, they also realized that obtaining the approval of the naming committee would be difficult. Because names were so closely tied to IBM's core value system, *ThinkPad* would certainly be scrutinized.

With the team's approval, Wainright took the name to the lab management. They rejected it numerous times because it did not fit the current naming scheme that included model numbers (for example, *IBM Personal Systems/2 Model 90*). The product group rallied around the naming effort. McHugh decided that it was time to take the name to the real decision-makers—the customers—primarily through customer briefings at Boca and focus groups throughout the U.S.

Customers were captivated with the name *ThinkPad* and wrote letters endorsing the name. Armed with these letters, Wainright persisted in explaining that this new product needed a name that would not intimidate the novice computer users or unskilled field personnel. Luckily for Wainright, the corporate naming committee was getting behind more personalized names, so most of his effort was concentrated on the Boca lab management.

Heinz Hegmann was part of this new endeavor, and he recalled how pro-active Patty McHugh was in getting the ThinkPad name approved for the tablet. It was not easy changing the IBM naming traditions but Hegman said the new team was committed to the effort. The submission of the name 'ThinkPad' eventually made it to this group, and the going got easier. The group got the necessary executive approvals and then submitted it for legal clearances. A massive undertaking by IBM Intellectual Property Law (IPL) to clear and trademark the name was undertaken in 60+ countries. Hegmann cited this as "one of the most exciting moments of his career" because he played a major role in getting the ThinkPad name approved as an integral part of the new IBM naming strategy. On March 28, 1992, Hegmann wrote to the development team "ThinkPad is the new exciting IBM brand name for most all portable PC products. The name ThinkPad has been successfully tested, legally cleared, and registered as an IBM trademark."

Unfortunately, local management remained uncomfortable with the idea of a product without the *Personal Systems* designation and wanted the name to be *IBM Personal Systems/2 ThinkPad*. Corporate Naming took a middle-of-the-road stance and, acting as Soloman, approved IBM's first pen system as the *IBM 2521 ThinkPad*.

The development team had not sat idly by while the name was being decided. They worked to reflect the name modification on the product before the GO press conference. However, it was too late to change the industrial design on the nameplate. The logo had been designed on the diagonal similar to the PS/2 "racetrack" and contained only the words *IBM ThinkPad*. This racetrack logo is still used today without any model designation. Luckily, the press decided to shorten the name to the desired *IBM ThinkPad*, and corporate naming began to see the value of personalized names.

As the time approached for the joint GO press conference, Vieth wanted to announce the product's name with a memorable flourish. Dell and Wainright recommended that Vieth use two transparencies (overheads) to contrast the traditional think pad and the new ThinkPad.

Vieth recalled, "At the April 1992 GO press conference, we announced the first ThinkPad tablet computer. I brought along a little pocket think pad that I held up at the press conference. I said, 'This is the think pad of today,' and then I took the wraps off our new tablet computer and said, 'This is the think pad of tomorrow. It's called the *IBM ThinkPad*.' That's how we formally introduced the name *ThinkPad* to the market."

In addition to this innovative naming and a distinctive announcement, the pen team undertook some imaginative marketing activities. Under McHugh's leadership, early customer pilots, widespread customer disclosures, and an extensive loaner program showed the product's strengths and weaknesses before its announcement. This knowledge led to the decision to announce the initial tablet as a "developer's release" on April 16, 1992, rather than as a full-fledged product. This developer's release, known as the *IBM 2521 ThinkPad*, received quite a welcome.

The early customer pilots also highlighted another area to which the PC Company had paid little attention: the customer's out-of-box experience. Because the primary handlers of this tablet were expected to be mostly novice users, straightforward directions were necessary. Instead of a manual, marketing designed a nine-page glossy package. Pages were color-coded to the information the users would need—at the touch of their fingertips. It proved to be one of those approaches that would not be lost on future products and with which the press fell in love.

Another creative marketing ploy, which turned out to be a field test as well, occurred later in the year. Debi Dell, now project manager for market development activities, worked with Joseph Rickert to field test the ThinkPad tablet during the excavation of the ancient Egyptian city of Leontopolis. Through the efforts of Rickert, she was put in contact with Carol Redmount and Rene Friedman of the University of California. A ThinkPad was loaned to the archeological team for a summer dig in the Nile Delta. The resulting report documented the ThinkPad's excellent performance under intense conditions, as well as provided the basis of the Fall Comdex presentation by then PC Company president, Bob Corrigan. The final report stated that

> The ThinkPad is an impressive machine, rugged enough to be used without special care in the worst conditions that Egypt has to offer. Although improvements are possible, its ease of use approaches the goal of a clipboard replacement. Pen-based computing is a reality. It promises to be an enabling technology that will bring benefits of personal computing out of the office and into the field.[6]

6. Joseph Rickert, "Field Test of the IBM ThinkPad," *Tell el-Muqdam* (August 1992), 5.

The press also judged the tablet as more natural to use than a Macintosh. *InfoWorld* declared that "ThinkPad, PenPoint Make a Natural Pen-based Team." *PC Week*, in its April 27, 1992, issue proclaimed "IBM's ThinkPad: Cream of the Tablet Crop" and stated that

> If PCWeek Labs had to decide on hardware to run pen-based software right now, the choice would be IBM's ThinkPad, a sturdy but somewhat bulky tablet sporting an innovative display screen and superior ease of use.

(Photo provided by IBM with permission of Joseph Rickert.)

Shortly after the announcement, Sue King left IBM to take the lead in Apple's experimental development projects. Discouraged by the politics surrounding the project and the lack of executive support, King decided that it was time for a change. As a result of the Cannavino task force, Patty McHugh had already left the pen effort to become the planning manager for the entire portable line. The loss of the team's cornerstone managers resulted in a lack of focus, eventually affecting the product's competitiveness and longevity.

(Photo provided by IBM with permission of Joseph Rickert.)

With growing confusion from changing management and mission changes, the developer's release of the 2521 ThinkPad did not become generally available until October 1992. In the six short months between announcements, the technology curve had taken another twist. New players had entered the market with faster processors and larger storage. Microsoft and IBM had decided to develop their own pen operating systems. Industry consultants were reducing their volume projections and questioning the viability of this market.

IBM's own tablet product added to the questions of market viability. When compared to the tablet competition in October 1992, IBM's first commercially available tablet was not technically competitive. Competitors used the more powerful 386SL processor, included memory caching, and generally offered at least one PCMCIA slot. IBM's first pen tablet ran PenPoint using an Intel 386SX 20MHz processor and did not offer any PCMCIA slots. Most pen players offered users a choice of PenPoint, PenDOS, or

Windows for Pen versus IBM's decision to offer only PenPoint. Also, despite claims of three-hour battery life and built-in power management, IBM's Nickel Cadmium (NiCd) battery actually ran for forty-five minutes, compared to competitors' Nickel Metal Hydride (NiMH), which touted three to four hours of actual use.

The nine-by-twelve inch tablet weighed 6.3 pounds and had built-in serial, parallel, external fixed disk drive, keyboard, and RJ-11 ports. Designed for the field worker, the transflective display was a ten-inch monochrome LCD with an electromagnetic digitizer, thus providing use both indoors and out. The magnesium case was hardened and could withstand a three-foot drop. Debi Dell demonstrated its durability by dramatically dropping the system during customer disclosures and sales training sessions. She recalled, "When I presented the ThinkPad to our customers and field reps, I would always talk about the casing and its durability. I would then 'accidentally" drop the system while it was running. In every demonstration I did, the machine never failed after it was dropped, but I'll admit that I always held my breath as the system left my hands."

Another advantage of the magnesium case was its capability to limit radio wave emissions, a problem encountered by several tablet manufacturers. Despite the positive attributes of its screen and casing, though, it was too heavy to carry for an eight-hour shift, adding another insurmountable deficiency.

Ongoing market analysis and customer testing indicated pen systems were desired in specific vertical markets such as insurance, finance, and home health care. However, because the vertical market was substantially smaller than the broad-based business market, the underlying financial model did not support the significant development investment required to modify the product. Too many manufacturers, too few customers, limited applications, and high prices stymied this market in 1992. Also, the eventual purchase of GO's reference design by AT&T and Microsoft's investment in

Windows for Pen sounded the death knell for IBM's first ThinkPad. However, pen computing did not die; it simply migrated to a totally different form.

To understand this migration, as part of the tablet project and in conjunction with the portable team, a technology roadmap for portable computing was put together. This roadmap forecasted the key technologies important in portable computing for the next four to five years. Developed in conjunction with IBM Research, the roadmap was updated regularly and eventually served as the foundation for the ThinkPad effort known as *Headlights*. Perhaps the most successful of long-lasting portable strategies, McHugh, in her new role as Portable Planning Manager, used this effort to push the portable product line forward.

IBM had spent an inordinate amount of time, money, and human energy on something that became a failure instead of the anticipated resounding success. Individuals either distanced themselves from the effort or denigrated the team trying to make it work. With the transition to Japan underway (announced internally but not yet implemented), Veith received external and internal criticism for the pen project, as well as employee resistance to the development move to Japan. In a 1994 meeting with Debi Dell, Vieth recalled, "From being upbeat when I arrived in Boca to the time following the GO press conference, I felt like one of those square pegs in a round hole, and this peg just kept getting pounded farther down in the hole. I didn't feel as though I was having any impact in Boca. With so much executive attention on the GO alliance, PenPoint, and IBM's new notebook, I wasn't able to concentrate on anything else—particularly my primary mission of the Japanese transition.

"Following the GO announcement, I went to Japan with Cannavino and his whole team. While there, I received a phone call informing me that my father was terminally ill with cancer. At dinner with Cannavino, Paul Mugge, and Jan Winston, I found it difficult to concentrate on the development move and work items; I was pretty upset. After dinner, Paul showed a compassionate side that was unfamiliar to me and asked whether I wanted to talk. So, we walked around this Japanese garden talking about my father's illness, how upset I was, and how things were not working out in the pen area. Paul reminded me that I wasn't in this alone, that the concept of family was not lost in the current turmoil within IBM. He was one fine person to treat me that way."

"During this trip," continued Vieth, "management made the decision to accelerate the move of product management responsibility for pen and portable computing to Japan. I didn't think we were ready to accelerate the transition. Japan didn't know what they were going to do, and I didn't think adequate leadership was in place. Although we had Hajime Watabe on assignment in Boca working on pen and mobile activities, his activities as a liaison with the folks in Japan left something to be desired. In my opinion, he was [like] a skin graft that never took. When the decision was made that Watabe would run the Japanese mobile product development effort, I strongly opposed it.

"Teamwork did not yet exist between the two locations. We did not have a process for how products would be defined in Boca but developed in Japan. The pieces just weren't in place. I felt strongly that accelerating the transition would cause the pen effort to fail and would, most likely, affect the emerging portable computing products as well."

Shortly after this meeting, Vieth was relieved of line responsibility and started her personal move to San Francisco. She worked closely with the GO Corporation through the termination of the agreement with IBM.

The alliance with GO Corporation and the pen tablet development were not viewed as successful endeavors for IBM and, in fact, resulted in talented people leaving the company. But, the pen venture positively influenced the future direction of IBM's portable strategy. According to Cannavino, "The pen effort was an area of research. It was a new technology area to me, and I don't believe we thought about it very carefully. IBM was trying to figure out what was going to happen, what was going to play in this market space. The pen investment was insignificant compared to the profits we were beginning to realize in our renewed portable focus. In the two years I was there, we did the entire pen effort, started the ThinkPad notebook line, and still delivered significant profit, in the billions, back to the company."

The pen effort was part of the transition of product development to Yamato, Japan. It profiled the processes necessary to make a multicultural relationship work. It planted the seeds for a worldwide team focused on the mobile market. Finally, it provided the foundation for a line of follow-on products that, although never widely successful, enabled IBM to remain a player in the pen market. Follow-on products such as the ThinkPad 710T, ThinkPad 730T, and ThinkPad 750P continued IBM's participation in various industry vertical markets. It continues yet today with focus on new interfaces (voice and pen) and form factors (handhelds).

Most importantly, IBM's pen tablet spawned the name *ThinkPad*. The first IBM ThinkPad enabled users to focus on the work they wanted to accomplish and not on the technology. Users could work with it, write on it, and think with it.

The Authors' Insights

IBM had started its ThinkPad journey. In addition to creating a very descriptive name, the pen team developed and implemented numerous innovative planning and marketing concepts. The technology roadmap was in place with its guide, Patty McHugh, moving from the pen project to the mainstream portable product line. She would take the lessons learned from this effort and apply the best ones to the development of IBM's new line of portables.

On the technology front, in the not-too-distant future, we will be using a thin pen computer tablet instead of a paper writing tablet. GO Corporation's vision was not wrong; it was simply premature. In the early 1990s, technology could not deliver a pen solution that combined price (hundreds instead of thousands of dollars), form factor (5"×7" or 8.5"×11"), and applications so that the user had a truly enjoyable experience. A sophisticated pen tablet will succeed when it works better than paper. Can you find the meeting minutes from six months ago? Can you correlate your notes over the past year on a given topic? Can you easily manage these documents, as well as access and interact with documents taken off the Internet? Can you easily draw on a notebook? Can you insert electronic ink anywhere in a document? Sooner than you think, a pen tablet will be able to perform these functions and more.

We are headed in that direction. IBM and A.T. Cross have a joint venture called *CrossPad* that allows users to record their notes using a standard pad and an active pen. Digital ink is recorded in a tablet that sits underneath the paper tablet. You then migrate the digital ink and keywords to a notebook (or standard PC) for future reference, eliminating the need to keep reams of paper lying around. Someday, this logic will be embedded in a flat panel color display so that the ink can be recorded "in place." Our grandchildren will ask us whether we wrote on paper with a pen "the old fashioned way."

Pursuing the "bleeding edge" of the technology curve, such as pen computing, requires executive support and significant funding to stay the course. Not many companies have the resources or commitment to do so, but those who desire to be market leaders will invest in such ventures. The IBM tablet team thought that they were building the next "big thing" in computing. But, the technology was not ready to be deployed on a broad scale; it was not ready for prime time. As Professor Kosnik pointed out, all elements must come together to build an enduring brand. ThinkPad did an enduring portable computer brand, but only when the name was reapplied to a new generation of notebook computers.

The following table describes the products that comprise the IBM pen family. It demonstrates the movement from form-based tablets to multiapplication convertibles.

The Pen Family

System	700T	710T	730T	750P	360P
Form	Tablet	Tablet	Tablet	Convertible	Convertible
Processor	386SX 20MHz	486SLC 25MHz	486SX 33MHz	486SL 33MHz	486SX 33MHz
Memory	4/8MB	4/12MB	4/20MB 8/24MB	4/20MB	4/20MB
Storage	(2) 10MB cards (Solid state)	60MB (3) Type II PCMCIA slots	105/210MB (2) Type III PCMCIA slots	170/340MB	170/250/340 540/810MB I/II/III PCMCIA
Display	10" Trans-flective LCD	9.5" Mono LCD	9.5" STN LCD	9.5" Mono STN LCD	9.5" Dual scan color pen
Operating system	PenPoint 1.01	PenPoint 1.01 PenDOS 2.0	PenDOS 2.2 Pen for OS/2 Windows for Pen 3.11 PenRight!	DOS 6.1 OS/2 2.1 PenDOS 2.2 Pen for OS/2 Windows for Pen	DOS 6.1, 6.3 OS/2 2.1 PenDOS 2.2 Pen for OS/2 Windows for Pen
Weight (lb.)	6.3	3.3–5.8	3.5–3.9	6.1/6.6	6.8
Other	Electro-magnetic digitizer Data/fax modem RJ-11	Detachable handle Password security	(2) batteries Ext. drive Port replicator	Audio on planar	Dock II Value pricing AT-bus
Announced	4/16/92 ISV 10/5/92 GA	3/2/93	5/17/94	9/8/93	
Withdrawn	3/30/93	2/22/93		8/30/94	

CHAPTER 9

IBM Gets Serious

We must rekindle the spirit of teamwork and empowerment that produced the first personal computer.

—Paul Mugge, August 1991

As Sue King and her team readied their pen tablet for announcement, Patty McHugh moved in the notebook development organization as its planning manager. McHugh had realized that there was a broader market that needed strong product and market planning. She also knew that IBM's strengths emerge when put to the test. IBM needed to muster all its resources to make a major run at countering the notebook mania Compaq had recently created.

By 1992, portable computing was big business. According to IDC (International Data Corporation), the U.S. industry was selling two million portables and generating revenues in excess of $4 billion. The U.S. market was projected to double again by 1996 to four million units ($8 billion) and to grow to eight million units ($15 billion) by 1999. In that same year, worldwide sales would exceed seventeen million units ($34 billion). Customers who were now buying portable computers for employees working outside the office fueled this growth. Customers wanted these adjunct PCs to provide the same kind of computing capability that users had in the office. Such comparable desktop performance required faster processors and larger storage than customers had previously been able to get in portables. Customers were no longer willing to compromise when going mobile.

The IDC Shipment Review and Forecast (Thousands of Units)

Year	U.S.	Worldwide
1992	1,976	4,832
1993	2,527	6,273
1994	3,200	7,365
1995	3,563	8,919
1996	4,949	11,824
1997	6,000	14,192
1998 (estimated)	6,608	15,427
1999 (estimated)	7,988	17,793
2000 (estimated)	9,367	20,385

IBM knew that it was time to get serious. Then IBM CEO John Akers wanted IBM to develop a truly great portable—something that customers would die for. He directed Jim Cannavino to "go make it happen." According to Cannavino, "After the announcement of the L40SX laptop, it became clear that a major shift was occurring in the form factor desired by the market. In my opinion, standard paper sizes defined the PC form factor more than anything else did. An 8 1/2"×11" sheet of paper, known as *A4* within the industry, was the form factor people would use. If there were a machine smaller than that, it would follow the paper size down because that's where everything fits in the world. That's also the way briefcases are built—to accommodate standard and legal size pads! Desk drawers are also built for paper-size things. Everything is built around paper sizes —A4, A5, A6. So, if we wanted to make something that people carried around and used, we needed to follow the paper size. This concept was behind the various form factors of the ThinkPad line. I called Nobi Mii, head of our advanced technology, to see whether he could help us do something revolutionary in portables, keeping this form factor concept in mind."

Nobuo "Nobi" Mii studied engineering at the University of Japan, where he graduated in 1955. He moved to the U.S. to do graduate studies at Columbia University and then joined IBM in 1969 in the Federal Systems Division, where he worked on NASA projects. He later moved to Raleigh, North Carolina, to help start the Communications Division, until Jack Kuehler asked him to start an advanced technology laboratory in Fujisawa, Japan.

The advanced laboratory at Fujisawa focused on terminals, developing the famous IBM 3270 terminal. The IBM 3270 became the standard for how people interact with mainframe computers and influenced the development of some technologies that would be used in later products. Mii-san also helped to create the Yamato development lab that was eventually responsible for the IBM ThinkPad. Mii-san returned to the U.S. and continued to work in advanced technology.

Mii-san recalled, "I remember that John Akers was very unhappy with our laptop. He wanted to know why IBM, with all its resources, could not build a portable with any technical innovation. Akers put pressure on Jimmy Cannavino to see what he could do. Cannavino asked me whether we had any new ideas for a better portable computer. I told him we needed a smaller hard disk and better flat panel display based on TFT technology. He told me to get it done."

Mii-san decided that the best way to evaluate the situation was to get together the core portable team. The meeting was quite a cast of characters. In addition to Paul Mugge, the PC Development lab director, Hajime Watabi, representing the portable development lab in Yamato, Japan, and Maurice Fletcher from marketing, the planning team was also invited. Patty McHugh, Portables planning manager, along with Ron Sperano and Leo Suarez, was also present. The Yamato portable design team members participated via the conference room's speakerphone.

Leo Suarez described what it was like working in portables at the time: "We had all this technology sitting around—displays, pointing devices, form factors. It was all there, but we had not done a good job of bringing it together in one place and into one product."

Ron Sperano, a fellow team member of Suarez's recalled, "We weren't looking at customer requirements. We were too engineering focused. I had put together a huge database on all the customer complaints we had received on our luggables and laptop portables. It was the first true portable computing market research we had done at a customer level. I told everyone that we needed to review and learn from the customer complaints so that we could develop a portable that would meet user requirements."

Suarez continued, "It was all those failures that basically led us to one, very long meeting in early 1991. I called it our 'Come to Jesus meeting' with the entire portable development team. We had to get our act together in portables. We had to stop dickering around. We had so much technology that we should have been able to bring it all together into a single, really exciting notebook computer."

The meeting participants tried to figure out how to take the input from the customers and build what they wanted. Conversations were intense. The Boca team believed that customers wanted a small, light notebook with a large color display that could run for hours on its own batteries. Customers wanted performance equivalent to what was available on the desktop. The Japanese team said that it couldn't be done.

But, the Boca team would not give up. In unison, they stressed several critical points. The announced portable products had terrible battery life, and customers were continually complaining. Previous products had small, monochrome displays, and although the innovative 10.4-inch color TFT display was under development, it appeared to be too thick to use in the proposed notebook form factor. Present designs weighed in at eleven pounds, and the customer wanted less than ten! All the portables had great keyboards, but every machine had a different keyboard layout. Consistency was needed.

"We started putting all the product attributes that people wanted on the white board," said Suarez. "Customers wanted parts that were removable and/or upgradable. They wanted a desktop keyboard, yet smaller and with great typing action. We listed what ports were to be put on the back. Customers wanted a display port on the back in order to make presentations. We wanted to enable the user to easily switch from one screen to the other. We needed the largest hard disk available. We needed to rethink the form factor and make sure that it was a notebook and not just another laptop like the L40SX.

"But, our Japanese counterparts stated that it just wasn't possible to do all these things in a single portable computer. Remember the way this whole thing started. A U.S.-based engineering team under Bob Lawten and Lou Bifano had told the Japanese team what to do on previously announced portables. The Japanese team did not want to be told what to do by the U.S staff. They thought that they knew how to design the stuff better than we did. It wasn't a cultural thing per se. Rather, it was the classical IBM mentality where the engineering team knew better than the customer what the customer wanted. Japan was still in that mode. So, it wasn't arrogance on the part of the Japanese. It just happened that the Japanese were the development team, and they were just propagating traditional 'big blue' philosophy.

"The Japanese team present in this meeting was now headed by a Japanese executive. The Japanese team liked having a Japanese executive in charge of development and became more reasonable. They felt that they were now in control and were not being told by the U.S. team what to do. A member of their team whom they respected, Hajime Watabe, was assigned to work in Boca Raton and manage the portable development. Although resident in the U.S., he reported to the Japanese lab management. Educated in the States, Watabe-san was very Western minded and familiar with the concept of 'The customer may not always be right, but he is always the customer.' He realized that, although he had a great engineering team, they had no clue as to what customers wanted. He dealt with a lot of resistance from the Japanese engineering team."

Watabe-san's personal history helped him to develop a Western attitude while keeping a traditional Japanese outlook. His parents emigrated from Japan when he was young and settled in Jamaica, a neighborhood of Queens borough in New York City. After completing high school there, he attended Adelphi University in Garden City, New York, majoring in math.

After graduating in September 1961, he visited the United Nations in New York. While there, he noticed the IBM building across the street and went in without an appointment. He introduced himself and asked for a job, explaining that he spoke fluent Japanese. He spoke with a personnel representative who expressed interest in him not because he spoke Japanese but because he spoke English. On returning to Japan, he was invited to visit the IBM Japan office. He was offered a job as a systems engineer to help develop IBM's Japanese business by communicating with the U.S. organization.

Watabe-san had numerous assignments in Japan and the U.S. throughout his career. He worked in programming for the IBM 360 mainframe and worked in development under Nobuo Mii in the seventies. In the eighties, he took the portable development assignment in Boca Raton coordinating efforts between the U.S. and Japan. He is credited with getting the Yamato team to understand the importance of listening to the market requirements rather than building something from an engineering perspective.

Tom Hardy, intimately involved with the notebook design, reflected on the efforts to get Yamato to consider customer requirements in their design: "A little-known event occurred during 1990 in the Yamato lab that deserves mention. The industrial design group could see that local product development lacked sensitivity to customer needs, especially for a notebook-size product. Led by Kazuhiko Yamazaki, the designers initiated and produced a 'concept video' in which they posed as customers with notebook models in various environmental scenarios—such as in an office, home, car, park, lobby, and airplane—and while carrying, storing, and transporting the notebook. The video emphasized the importance of the notebook size (designated as A4) and many ease-of-use concerns. It also highlighted that a notebook has social status implications because it is a 'personal accessory.'"

The video was the start of a cultural change, a realization that customer needs might or might not be addressed by the technologies the engineers wanted to use. The shift was happening, but it was very gradual. Suarez continued, "We seemed to be at a standoff in this meeting in 1991. Watabe was highly respected by the Boca Raton development engineers because of his Western approach. He came across as very un-Japanese to us. Yet, he was highly respected by the portable development team in Japan.

"After he listened to this bickering, Watabe stopped the meeting. He actually told the Japanese team in front of the U.S. team, 'Listen to what these guys are saying. They know what the customer wants. They know what they're talking about. They understand the customer. We don't.' It was the first time the Yamato team had been told, 'You're going to design what these guys tell you to design.' I was totally awed by that statement. It was really funny. The whole tone of the meeting instantly changed from confrontation and disagreement to one of trying to figure out, as a team, how we could build what the customer wanted. I'll never forget that meeting as long as I live."

At that point, the Boca team asked Yamato to rethink the possibility of putting a 10.4-inch color active matrix TFT display into their new notebook. Suarez and Sperano remember taking a sheet of paper and a ruler and marking off a rectangle with a diagonal of 10.4-inches. They then put it against the mock-up of the new portable, where it appeared that it would, indeed, fit. They asked the Yamato team to reevaluate the manufacturing process and determine whether the electronics could be rearranged. Doing so would provide this new portable with a revolutionary 10.4-inch display, something no other company was expected to have.

Maurice Fletcher, the portable segment marketing manager, offered this perspective on the display request: "Yamato had started to listen to us. They already knew that we were getting a third party to manufacture the value systems in the portable line. This decision resulted in reduced development funding and builds, except for the premier notebook code-named *Nectarine*. A little-known fact was that Nectarine was always planned to have a 10.4-inch screen. IBM had already invested in a joint venture with Toshiba on color active matrix TFT panels. In fact, we were dealing with an inventory exposure of twenty thousand panels that had been ordered for the CL57SX, a less-than-stellar market performer. Yamato development had decided that the next product would include a 10.4-inch display but had not figured out the packaging. The packaging needed to be more innovative than the L40SX or CL57SX, both of which had already proven that a screen that size had market value. The new packaging had to include upgradeable hard files, a sleeker industrial design, and easily removable batteries. These requirements, when coupled with the 10.4-inch display, caused the Yamato team to initially balk at Boca's requirements. Watabe helped to reshape their thinking."

The Japanese team documented the requirements and accepted the assignment to come up with a design that would meet the customer requirements—and to do it in a few months. Several months later, Ron Sperano returned to Yamato and drilled these engineers on the design details. From that initial passionate meeting in late August 1991 and over the course of the next three months, the Japanese team laid out the design for what was to become the ThinkPad 700C. This plan incorporated the best technology of the time into a notebook form factor—a feat that months earlier they didn't believe could be done. They found a way to make the 10.4-inch display fit into the new notebook. Sperano and the Boca team were ecstatic.

On returning to the States, the Boca team reviewed the market requirements against the technical specs. For the first time, IBM had the makings of a portable computer that would leapfrog the competition. The team was certain that they had a winner in this new design. They told the Yamato team, "Yes, this is exactly what the customer is looking for." It was the beginning of a powerful partnership—Yamato development and Boca Raton planning.

The players were finally lining up for something that Compaq never thought possible in its ten-year history: IBM was going to use all its capabilities to find a way to develop and market a competitive notebook computer.

The Authors' Insights

Under the sponsorship of Jim Cannavino, the IBM PC Company started to "get its act together" in 1991 and build a unified portable team. Cannavino understood that, fundamental to winning in the mobile market, new systems had to meet known customer requirements. Even better, he knew that IBM would have to anticipate what the customers wanted before they realized it. By using the development resources in Yamato, Japan, the best technologies and engineering resources were coupled with the excellent planning skills found in the Boca Raton laboratory. Cannavino leveraged each unit, recognizing its differences, playing to its strengths, and building a superior team. Professor Kosnik pointed out the importance of strong management and technology leadership in developing an enduring brand. Cannavino's leadership, along with the portable team and the technology innovations of the Yamato Lab, were essential to steering IBM on its portable journey.

CHAPTER 10

Jim Bartlett: Improving the Bench

An expert is someone who knows some of the worst mistakes that can be made in his subject and how to avoid them.

—Werner Heisenberg

IBM had many capabilities and resources to bring to bear on its renewed portable effort. However, its history of hiring young college graduates, grooming them for management positions, and keeping them onboard for their entire careers had not prepared IBM, and particularly the PC Company, to be responsive to a dynamically changing market. Established "good old boy" networks had caused an inbreeding of ideas and stymied the changes necessary to not only fix the business but also change it—and fixing the business was a maniacal focus in the early 1990s. Within the hallowed halls of IBM, executive management acknowledged that there were industry professionals who could make significant contributions because of their experiences and skills. Specifically, given the emphasis on the portable segment and with the challenges facing IBM to energize this effort, Personal Systems management wanted a seasoned marketing executive who knew the mobile market. An extensive professional search resulted in the hiring of James (Jim) Bartlett.

Although his roots were in Indiana, Bartlett attended Northern Arizona University and majored in marketing. In his spare time, he built home computers via Heathkits. This hobby laid the foundation for his interest and skill in the area of high tech marketing.

Commenting on his early technical endeavors, Bartlett recalled, "As product review editor for an electronics journal, I helped to write a product review for the first TRS-80. Because it came without a user's manual, I didn't know how to use it. I stayed up until 2:00 a.m. figuring out how to program this thing. I didn't even know BASIC at that time. It was a frustrating but exciting experience.

"From that point on, I knew that personal computers were going to be a huge market. A few years later, I heard Ken Olsen, then C.E.O. of Digital Equipment Corp., say, 'No one should ever have a need for a computer in the home.' I just knew that it wasn't true. I knew that everybody would eventually use a personal computer for writing letters and all kinds of things."

Bartlett, now a skilled computer industry marketing professional, actively participated in several portable computing programs before joining IBM. Bartlett managed several key programs, first at Zenith Data Systems in the Chicago area and later at NEC in Massachusetts. During this period, Bartlett worked with a number of industry pioneers developing a sixth sense of what was required to market mobile computers.

"In the early 1990s," said Bartlett, "I went to Philips because they wanted to get into both the mobile computer business and the communications products business. I relocated to Tennessee, where this new PC business was headquartered, and I developed the business plan for this endeavor. We began to develop a line of portable computer products, bringing our first portable products to market in about nine months. We sold our first portable under the Magnavox umbrella using the Metalis sub-brand. I actually wanted to bring them out under the Philips logo, which I thought was much stronger from a technology perspective. But, the division's president wanted to leverage the Magnavox name to increase the perception of technology in their television line. I tried to convince him, based on the market research, that Philips was actually a much stronger brand for us to leverage in conjunction with a notebook computer. I lost the battle. I believe that the branding contributed one of the reasons why the products didn't do as well as they could have."

Before Bartlett left the company, Jan Timmer, the Chairman, put out a new branding policy: Any new technologies would be brought out under the Phillips brand. It was bittersweet vindication! Despite some innovative things in the portable arena, the entire operation eventually closed because of, in part, huge losses in its desktop PC business.

In 1992, after his brief stint at Philips, Bartlett was looking for an opportunity to do something significant in mobile computing. He interviewed with IBM in April 1992 meetings with Bob Corrigan, Personal Computer Division president and Fernand Sarrat, vice president of the Personal Systems Line of Business. He was told that he would be working in IBM's refreshed mobile computing organization. Corrigan and Sarrat, in conjunction with Jim Cannavino, had decided to bring in an experienced general manager named Bruce Claflin to head this effort. Claflin knew IBM. Bartlett knew mobile computing.

"When I started the conversations with IBM, they asked, 'Where do you want to live?' said Bartlett. "I responded that I was currently in Tennessee and liked it there. They countered with Raleigh, North Carolina, or Boca Raton, Florida. Raleigh held PC manufacturing, and Boca was the center for its product development.

Personal preference and two children who were intrigued with the ocean and proximity to Disney World led me to choose Florida. With that decided, we continued the interviews.

"IBM was not terribly experienced in the hiring of outside executives, so the interview process felt like I was joining the CIA. As we were about to finalize the deal and they were putting the offer letter together, a fly appeared in the ointment. I was asked to move to New York instead of Florida because the new mobile business unit was to be headquartered in Somers, New York. I took my wife there in May. It was a pretty nice place at that time of year. Everything was green and in bloom. We made the move. About two and a half years later, we were thrilled when the entire PC Company moved to Raleigh, enabling us to get back to a more reasonable climate."

Upon accepting the employment offer, Bartlett reported to John Patrick, marketing vice president for the Personal Systems Line of Business. Patrick reported to Fernand Sarrat, who reported to Jim Cannavino, head of IBM's Personal Systems Line of Business. Cannavino's responsibilities included the PC Company, OS/2, and other software and services within one big amorphous organization. At this time, the business unit concept did not exist within Personal Systems. Organized functionally, all marketing people supporting the IBM PC Company were grouped together under Patrick. But, Bartlett had been told that they were going to create this new mobile business unit and that he would have a significant role in it.

Bartlett continued his reflection: "A task force was chartered to answer the question 'What should IBM do in mobile computing? Is this something IBM should be in?' Of course, the study came back with 'Hell, yes, you'd better be in mobile computing because it's going to be big.' This task force drove IBM's decision to create a mobile business unit. It was designed to be a separate, strategic business unit, not just a department within the desktop division.

"Rumors abounded that a strong manager, Bruce Claflin, was coming back from Japan to head this new mobile business unit. Claflin was a well-respected executive inside IBM. When I talked to Corrigan, he had nothing but glowing reports on this guy. Corrigan felt that Claflin and I would get along famously. He was right. We hit it off well. It's funny, but Bruce and I got into a debate early on in our relationship over which one of us knew less. I'd say, 'I don't know anything about IBM,' and he would reply with, 'Well, I don't know anything about mobile computing.' We realized that we needed each other in order to succeed in our jobs.

"Bruce was a fantastic mentor and a very capable marketing guy. He also had a lot of intuition about the other parts of the business in which he wasn't an expert. But, he knew that he needed expertise in areas that were not his specialty, like knowledge of the mobile computing industry. I provided that knowledge for Bruce and for IBM."

When asked to recall his early days at IBM, Bartlett said, "I think that one of my personal accomplishments was just surviving the IBM culture. I struggled for a long time. I felt like I was a fish out of water. I remember telling somebody that it felt like I went to the moon. I was eating green cheese and speaking alien. Almost every other word I heard was an acronym I didn't understand. I would ask somebody what an acronym meant, and oftentimes people did not actually know. They used to know but had forgotten. All they could try to do was describe what it meant in the context of the discussion. But, nobody knew what the letters stood for anymore.

"I was also trying to learn the IBM management process. I inherited a team of bright people who certainly knew more about IBM than I did. I struggled with how to manage these folks who were in Boca Raton while I worked from Somers. Our computer systems couldn't even talk to one another. At one point, I had to give a Boca

Raton secretary authorization to sign all the electronic forms that needed to be done on a regular basis because I couldn't do it from New York. I called someone in IBM's Information Technology group saying, 'You mean we make this stuff and we sell it to our customers, but we can't make these two computers talk to each other?' I remember him saying, 'Well, we're working on it.' To which I responded, 'Well, how long is it going to take to get if fixed?' And he said, 'About two years.' Two years! Can you believe it?!"

Bartlett's Boca-based team was staffed from the pen project office, which had had responsibility for the portable requirements process and marketing programs. Bringing varied skills to the project office, Pete Leichliter, Leo Suarez, and Debi Dell comprised Bartlett's first IBM team. Dell recalled, "Jim was not only an unknown entity to us, but he was an outsider. None of us had ever worked for a manager within IBM who hadn't been grounded in its basic beliefs. It was quite an experience!

Pete Leichliter, Bruce Claflin, Jim Bartlett, Scott Bower (left side of table), and Mark Hofert (right).

"I remember my first one-on-one meeting with Jim. He had come to Boca to meet the team and discuss how he wanted to organize it. After the team meeting, he had individual meetings with each of us. I am sure that mine was quite different from Pete's or Leo's. Jim was a technology 'bigot,' and it was apparent that he really respected engineers. Because my background was business management, I'm not sure that he was comfortable with how I was going to fit into the group. We discussed the marketing support programs I had put in place for the IBM ThinkPad tablet and, previously, for Boca's product line. He seemed a little more at ease, but there was something else, an underlying attitude.

"When he asked about my marital status, children, and whether I could travel, I got the feeling that these were not routine questions of interest. Perhaps it was just his way of getting to know me. Luckily, my work was perceived as having value. I also had the support of the Boca management team, particularly Patty McHugh, the Portable planning manager. Otherwise, I might have missed out on the opportunity to work on the original ThinkPad team. Jim and I eventually developed a mutual respect for each other; much of what I learned from Jim has proven valuable in follow-on assignments. His non-IBM perspective taught me to look at things differently."

Bartlett's perspective was a major contribution to the early ThinkPad efforts. He related his previous portable experiences at Zenith, NEC, and Philips, as well as an in-depth knowledge of the mobile industry. Bartlett reflected, "I remember some early meetings with planning and development. I asked, 'Is the parallel port bidirectional?' and they asked me what I meant. After I explained that it was necessary for things like file transfer, they'd go off to make sure the parallel port was bidirectional."

Questioning of the development team to such a level of technical detail by a member of the marketing team was not standard practice within Boca, or even within IBM. It caused quite a shift in how product features were decided, how they were validated. To capture this shift, Bartlett assigned Leo Suarez to develop and execute a program called *Headlights*. Headlights, grown out of the requirements work sponsored by McHugh, brought together the best technologists within the company twice a year. The objective of Headlights was to highlight the shifts in technology and applications, demonstrate research projects that might have value in future projects, and review competitive information. Headlights had such an effect that other Boca development teams soon established similar programs.

Bartlett's contributions and ideas would permeate ThinkPad development and marketing through 1997. Luckily for IBM, Bartlett did not follow his career habit of changing companies; he instead followed the typical IBM practice of moving to another organization. According to Bartlett, "Basically, in the summer of 1997, I felt that I had done what I had gone to IBM to do—be a key part of the team to make something from nothing and grow it into a successful line of portables."

The Authors' Insights

Adding individuals to a team is never easy; adding an industry veteran to IBM's culture in the early 1990s was almost never done. IBM's PC division was staffed primarily with career IBM employees. Employees were not exposed to individuals who frequently changed companies. They were used to managers grounded in the company's basic beliefs: Respect for the Individual, Best Customer Service, and Pursuit of Excellence. But, IBM's employees were in for a surprise. Things were changing at IBM.

Jim Bartlett challenged traditional management stereotypes and attitudes. He brought an outsider's view to the newly formed portable group. He demonstrated to PC Company executives that they would have to become familiar with and adapt to the new dimension of adding outsiders to the various teams.

IBM, like many large companies, did not know how to absorb outsiders. IBM did not, in the early 1990s, have an orientation program for professional hires, especially those who would be IBM managers. Professional hires such as Bartlett had little assistance in figuring out the policies and practices with which long-term employees were so familiar. Individuals like Bartlett were used to companies that did not have IBM's bureaucracy. Adding individuals like Bartlett was a true measure of the portable's executive team because they capitalized on his strengths; Bartlett got things done despite cultural and personality differences. Together, they realized that a new perspective at the right time could significantly enhance a business's direction—and this fresh perspective would bring with it a *built-in network of industry contacts.*

CHAPTER 11

Bruce Claflin: Mobile's Change Agent

The very essence of leadership is that you have to have a vision. You can't blow an uncertain trumpet.

—Reverend Theodore Hesburgh

Although the addition of Jim Bartlett to the mobile team was course-altering, the single most important person recognized for the rise of the IBM ThinkPad is Bruce Claflin. He did not know that he would have such an important role when he accepted the assignment in 1992. But, history has proven that Jim Cannavino, head of the IBM PC Company at the time, made a masterful decision in selecting Bruce Claflin as the first general manager for mobile computing.

On his early portable decisions, Cannavino reflected, "I believed that this new line of portables could not just look like a small personal computer; I wanted something more innovative, yet personal. I had already asked Nobi Mii to look at the technologies because he had the technical skill and personal relationship with the Japanese development team. I now needed someone who would figure out what *personal* meant in terms of this emerging market. That was when I decided that Bruce Claflin should run the operation. Bruce was one of IBM's best marketing executives. He had presence. He had the thought process. He understood about an industry and how to make things occur. I knew Bruce would handle the complexities of large-volume shipments for a world-wide customer set, while I guided him on the development issues.

"Because Bruce was working in Japan at the time, my intention was to hire him back from IBM Japan. I wanted him to get the portable business running because, over time, it would be the biggest part of IBM's PC business. Bruce wrestled with this proposal because he thought portables were a niche market. He was coming from a significant marketing job to run some single product in the PC business. I convinced him that he didn't want the entire PC business—desktops, servers, and the rest—but that portables were the business he should drive. Bruce did a spectacular job, and the line of business was soon successful. I had had some ideas and a basic vision for what needed to happen, but I'm not so sure I would have got it done without him. Hiring him was a pivotal moment in the ThinkPad history."

Bruce Claflin grew up in a nice suburb just outside Philadelphia. His father and mother, John and Elizabeth, had three boys; Bruce was the youngest. His parents taught him good values and a strong work ethic. He went to school in Radnor, Pennsylvania, for elementary, junior high, and high school. He then went to Penn State, where he majored in political science. He wanted to be a lawyer, but he was tired of school. He was also in love with the girl who would later become his wife.

Bruce Claflin, IBM ThinkPad's first general manager.

Claflin recalled those formative years: "I was more interested in socializing in college than I was in academics. Toward the end of my junior year, it all started to gel. That summer, I bought an old pickup truck and put a camper shell on it. I threw a foam rubber pad in the back and took off west by myself. I lived out of this truck for the summer and had all kinds of adventures. When the engine broke down, I rode freight trains. I met lots of different people along the way. But, when I got back, I swore the next time I went anywhere, I was staying at a nice hotel. That summer adventure shaped my thinking on the need for work. I knew that I wanted to have a steady income and live a more regular life than the one in the back of a truck.

"In the spring of 1973, I decided to get a job instead of entering law school. I interviewed with eight different companies; IBM was the only one that offered me a job. So, I took it. I wanted to go into sales. My father had told me that if you were in sales, you didn't have a boss and you could make more money. Both ideas were very appealing.

"I joined IBM in the Office Products Division. I thought that meant selling computers to offices. When I showed up the first day, I discovered that we were selling typewriters, copiers, and dictating machines. I thought, 'Why in the world would I want to work here? I want to work for the guys who sell those big mainframe computers.' One of the senior salesmen walked me to the back door and into the parking lot. He said, 'You see all those Fords and Chevys?' I said, 'Yeah.' He said, 'That's what they drive upstairs in Data Processing.' He then said, 'You see the Cadillacs and Mercedes?' I said, 'Yeah.' He said, 'That's what we drive here in the typewriter division.' So I said, 'Okay, I want to be in the typewriter division.' I became a salesman, selling the low end of IBM's product lines that didn't have anything to do with computers. I fell in love with it. I just loved working. I just loved selling. IBM was just an incredibly stimulating environment. They trained me well. High-powered people surrounded me. I loved every minute of it. I married that college girl I fell in love with, and then I got a house, a mortgage, and kids. Man, I was hooked.

"I remember going out cold calling. I had two counties, York and Adams, in south central Pennsylvania. There wasn't much of anything in them, but I was out there cold calling and canvassing, selling typewriters, copiers, and dictating machines. And you know, I saw in action those lessons I learned in sales training: Calls plus demos equal sales. The more calls you made and the more demos you gave, the more sales you made. It wasn't particularly sophisticated, but you had to pound the pavement to make sales in those days.

"I recall going into a firm called McCall Insurance. I saw the name *McCall* on the sign, so I went in and said, 'Hello, may I see Mr. McCall?' The receptionist asked, 'Well, who's calling?' I proudly responded, 'Bruce Claflin from IBM.' I was twenty-one years old, and I had two whiskers on my face. But, for some reason, probably because I was from IBM and I think they were intrigued by me, they allowed me to see this guy. He was probably fifty years old, and he ran an independent insurance agency. He might have had ten employees. Even to this day, I remember this call because I don't know why they let me in to see this guy. But, there I was, sitting in his office. During my entire presentation, he had a bemused smile on his face. He bought an IBM Mag Card II typewriter, which was considered a big sale. The order was $12,320. I was stunned. I was a hero in the office. Two weeks into my job, I had landed one of the top sales in the office.

"I went back two months later because I needed one more sale to make my full year quota in only three months. I sold him a bunch of dictating machines. To this day, I'm grateful. I'll never know whether he bought them because he wanted the machines or he bought them because he wanted to help a young guy get a start. Regardless, I remember him vividly because he was my first big sale. He was the guy who gave me the order that put me in my first 100% Club, IBM's most prestigious recognition event."

Claflin added to his retrospection: "A lot of factors influence one in the early days of his or her career. Mr. McCall was one—my first big sale where someone who did not know me had given me a chance. Dick Eldridge, my first branch manager, was another. As my hiring and second-line manager, Eldridge influenced my early career. An IBM branch manager was a God-like creature whose comments were to be taken seriously. Eldridge was a 'wise old man' of probably forty, which seemed quite old to me at the time, and he was a brilliant sales leader. He was a fantastic motivator of people. He was extremely driven, very results oriented. I learned a tremendous amount from him about selling, about people management, about motivation, about good hiring, about firing. He provided me with the foundation to be successful within IBM.

"I'd been selling about a year and a half and was twenty-three years old. About that time, Eldridge called me in for a career discussion. He said he thought I was one of the brightest, most talented people he'd ever met. He believed I could run IBM someday. Remember, a year and a half earlier, I was a dopey college kid just getting by. This was heady stuff. He encouraged me to pursue an active career through IBM management. He planned to support me for very rapid advancement from my current job. I went home all starry-eyed that day. I knew that he probably said that to twenty other guys every year to get them motivated, but it really lit a fire under me. Wow! I could be something more than a salesman.

"Eldridge recognized me as one of his up and coming sales execs. He put me on the executive fast track. He promoted me into positions that you normally got in three, four, five years. I got them in nine months. He gave me territories that veterans of ten and fifteen years wanted; I got them in twelve months. He constantly threw me in over my head. His philosophy was that good people will rise to the occasion. He took huge risks with me. In a very short time, I had the largest territory in the Philadelphia office."

Claflin started down the path of a traditional IBM marketing career that was soon refined to include a senior management career track. He did a marketing job, went to headquarters, and came out as a branch manager. At that time, branch manager was a good job, one to which many sales people aspired. It carried a significant amount of responsibility and a high degree of autonomy. Claflin became a branch manager when he was twenty-nine years old, young for an IBM branch manager. Within a decade of his first sales job, Claflin progressed from branch manager to regional manager, ending up as an executive assistant in the Chairman's Office.

A stint in the IBM Chairman's Office provided a chance for a young executive on the fast track to observe the company's operation. In addition to participation in meetings that affected the company's overall well-being, it provided insight into the responsibilities and roles of a senior executive. The Chairman's Office also benefited from this arrangement because many special projects needed the attention of sharp IBM executives. This practice provided a pool of resources for special projects where decisions had to be made irrespective of organizational structure.

Kathy Vieth, the executive who announced the original ThinkPad pen tablet, knew Claflin from his stint in the Chairman's Office. According to Vieth, "Claflin was assigned to the Chairman's Office just as I was leaving it. He was a whipper-snapper Office Products (OP) branch manager from the Midwest who sold typewriters. He was the only OP guy who successfully made the transition when the various field divisions were consolidated. As a National Marketing Division (NMD) branch manager, Claflin was one of the most successful in the country. That's what got him to the Chairman's Office."

Said Vieth, "During this period, Claflin and I recognized each other's capabilities. When he left the Chairman's Office, he often called to ask my opinion about jobs he should take. He once told me, 'If I'm going to make the transition and be successful in this company, I've got to shed my image of being a typewriter sales-man. I've got to make everybody forget that I'm an OP-dopey guy.' It's probably too strong a term, but it was like a mentoring relationship between us. I enjoyed these conversations and felt for-tunate that he valued my thoughts and recommendations. Claflin was the single reason that I stayed with IBM as long as I did. He did a good job of making the transition from an OP-dopey guy to stellar executive."

Claflin was thirty-nine years old when he had another huge break in his career. He was asked to be an assistant group execu-tive, and although that was a lousy title, it was a big deal in IBM. Basically, the position was general manager running Asia Pacific South; every country in Asia but Japan reported to him. Claflin had responsibility for ten thousand people and a few billion dollars of business.

According to Claflin, "I knew it was a significant job when I had to sign an agreement indicating that I would turn over the position when I was sixty years old! I laughed about it at the time. Even though I was only thirty-nine, I had reached one of those positions known as a *turnover* position. It meant that you had the job for life, like tenure in a university, but you had to turn it over to someone else when you were sixty. And what's my reward for all this 'fast track' career activity? I got called back to the U.S. to run a new mobile computing group of fewer than two hundred people with, at best, two hundred million dollars in revenue. My first reaction was to think, 'What in the world have I done wrong to deserve this?'

"At that time, my career manager was Jim Cannavino. A career manager was someone who made sure that you didn't get lost while on assignment. He was the guy trying to get me back to the U.S. Along with Ned Lautenbach, my boss in Asia Pacific,

Cannavino stressed that this was a really important job. It was a piece of a rapidly growing market where IBM had had terrible performance. They told me that IBM wanted to rapidly make a mark in this market. They wanted me to take the job and make it succeed. They kept telling me that I shouldn't view this move as a comedown. To make sure I understood just how important the job was to IBM, they sent me to meet with John Akers, IBM chairman and chief executive officer at the time. At the meeting, Akers told me, 'Bruce, you're free to do whatever you want. You've earned the right to pick your spot, but I want you to go do this job.' And so I said, 'Yes sir.'

"This job was completely out of character for me. I'd never run a research and development group in my entire career. I'd never run a product group. I didn't know what a portable computer was. I'd never been associated with anything like this. I was a field general with experience in running large sales organizations. I felt no one was less qualified than I was to do this job."

With Claflin's agreement to become general manager of Mobile Computing, the executives decided to expand the mobile computing group beyond notebooks and pen systems. Cannavino wanted to include a project code-named *In Touch* under the mobile banner. A wireless networking system, In Touch was to use IBM's mobile products within a broadened set of mobile services. On his arrival back in the States, Claflin asked Cannavino to put In Touch on hold. Claflin felt that it was absolutely critical to establish a strong mobile computer business first before coupling it with the technology challenges associated with wireless. He was also convinced that getting in the services business was diametrically opposed to getting a product out. In short, he wanted to concentrate on developing a decent portable computer line. Cannavino immediately acquiesced to Claflin's request.

Claflin described the elements of the mobile effort in early 1992: "Different groups were working on various aspects of the portable product line—but I use the term *product line* loosely. My predecessor, Hajime Watabe, managed the laptop, tablet, and display activities. While he provided functional guidance to the teams, the Boca Raton laboratory director, Paul Mugge, controlled the underlying development processes. When I accepted the position, I was given total autonomy to drive the mission as I saw fit. Although resident in Boca, we were no longer required to operate within the site's processes. We established processes and procedures that the desktop and server teams eventually emulated."

Claflin decided that his first management action was to stabilize the team because the mobile team was fragmented and receiving direction from all sides. Enormous distrust of the Personal Systems Line of Business executives and their directives existed. Before his official announcement as general manager, Claflin went down to Boca and met not only with the management team but also with a subset of the employees. The employee meetings took the form of round tables, one for the engineers and one for the planners.

Debi Dell recalled the planning team round table: "As a senior member of the mobile team, I participated in one of the first employee round tables. Bruce arrived on the scene with no official announcement, although rumors abounded that he was to take over the mobile effort. We weren't sure what to make of this IBM executive who was asking for our opinions on the state of the mobile effort. After a significant pause following his brief explanation of his soon-to-be announced role, I decided someone had to break the ice. And there was one topic that was near and dear to my heart.

"At the time, the naming of our upcoming notebooks was under discussion. Pressure was intense to take the name *IBM ThinkPad,* which was originally approved for the pen tablet, and use it across the product line. Because I had a vested interest in both the name and the pen products, I felt strongly that this was a mistake. I remember sitting forward in my chair and asking, 'Well, Bruce, I guess I'll go first. Because rumor has it that you will be taking over the mobile effort, perhaps you can help me to understand what idiot made the decision to use the name *ThinkPad* for notebook computers.' Bruce leaned back in his chair and folded his arms across his chest, a gesture that would become very familiar to the team, and responded, 'Well, I guess I'm that idiot.' I always gave him credit for accepting responsibility for the decision, even though he had been in the job only a month and had yet to be officially announced as the general manager."

The team never knew the details behind Claflin's decision to use the *ThinkPad* name across the product line. Claflin later provided this insight: "IBM was test marketing a tablet device under the name *ThinkPad*. Now, the ThinkPad tablet computer was a wonderful concept with a very advanced design, but it was an idea way ahead of its time. Customers were not ready for this type of device, and its operating system scenario was a horrible disaster. One of the first things I had to do when I got there was kill the first pen product. It's a long story, but we had to write-off tens of millions of dollars and cancel parts for twenty thousand units. But, all was not lost. Everyone—customers, the press, IBM management—loved the name *ThinkPad*. The name was brilliant. One of my first decisions was to use *ThinkPad* as the name for our upcoming line of notebook computers.

"Almost as soon as I took the job, I had to review the naming for our new line of portable products. Bartlett and I sat down and discussed the name under consideration: *PS/2 ThinkPad*. We both decided that we wanted nothing to do with the *PS/2* name because the industry associated it with the Micro Channel. It was a radical departure, but one that was sorely needed.

"I remember enormous pushback on this decision because a whole constituency who loved that tablet viewed ThinkPad as a perfect name. They wrote letters to Cannavino saying, 'This is an outrage. How dare you let them expropriate this name.' Cannavino just didn't even bother. He sent them to me and said, 'This is entirely your call.' I talked to Jim Bartlett, our mobile computing marketing manager and a recent addition to IBM, saying 'You know, I believe *ThinkPad* is a great name, but it's going nowhere on the tablet. Let's just take it and use it as the name for our entire portable computer brand.' There wasn't a lot of research over it. It was a great name, and we expropriated it from a product that was dying."

Claflin followed the employee round tables with a general mobile meeting attended by Patty McHugh, the planning team, and the Boca Raton engineers. Claflin recalled the meeting: "It reminded me of a union hall meeting where I was management and they were the union. They were really frustrated over our lack of success in portable computing. They had no confidence in the Yamato team and were very outspoken about it. They believed that they had been given nothing but product failures in the early notebooks delivered from Yamato. They were also extremely distrustful of the field sales organization. Their view was that even if we had a good machine, field sales would never sell it. And the biggest distrust of all was for senior management. They viewed IBM senior management as intrusive and not helpful. They gave examples of product plans where the specifications were set. Then, a senior executive would come into town, start criticizing it, rip it up, and then change it. The products were then late to market and didn't get a chance to be successful.

"So," said Claflin, "here I was at my first team meeting. It was a horrible experience. I had no idea what they were talking about. I had never run anything like this. The meeting finally came to the end, and I said, 'Look, you've given me a lot of information here. I can't comment on much specifically, but let me make a few points. I came here to build a successful mobile computing business. I need to know which of you are in and which of you are out.' By the way, the timing of this meeting coincided with the announcement of a special early retirement plan. Everyone was saying, 'If you don't make decisions, we're all leaving.' So, again, I said, 'I need to know. Are you in or are you out? You're going to have to take my commitment to mobile on faith. I can't give you the answers to your questions in the time frame you need to make your decision, so you've just got to decide. Do you want to be a part of a winning team, or do you want to leave? So, make your decision now and let me know whether you're going or staying.' It really shut them up. I believe they realized that this new guy was going to try to do something. It was a very important meeting. I think it quickly brought the group together."

Kathy Vieth, operating in the role of consultant to Claflin, offered this perspective: "Bruce had the ability to draw consensus among warring factions and make everybody believe that they were on the same team. Bruce eventually set up a culture so that everyone looked good. He made order out of chaos."

About thirty days into his new job, Claflin met with Jim Cannavino on where the team was going and why. He informed Cannavino that this was not going to be a standard strategic review because the team felt it needed the next six months to get the plans right. Cannavino was encouraged by what he saw and requested an update again in three months. Claflin suggested that there should not be another review until the following year. Cannavino took a moment and then agreed. Although a small victory, it was very significant to the mobile team. The group got the necessary breathing room to do whatever was necessary, without excessive levels of review. This incident added to Claflin's credibility and helped to create a team atmosphere.

The Authors' Insights

As Bruce Claflin's career clearly demonstrated, careers can be made (or broken) by one small, unexpected event. The decision to choose Claflin to head this renewed focus on portable computing was the culmination of good management practices. Early recognition of good talent, combined with the right mentoring and developmental activities, significantly strengthens a company's ranks. Cannavino knew Claflin's strengths and weaknesses. He planned to supplement Claflin's lack of development experience while he positioned him (and his new organization) for growth.

Claflin proved Cannavino's decision was a good one. Building on his reputation as a consensus builder, Claflin was masterful in his first personnel actions. Much can be discerned about a manager from his first decisions and how they are presented to a new organization. As Professor Kosnik pointed out, to create an enduring brand, you need consummate leadership. Who can question Claflin's leadership and sincerity when he not only met with the Boca personnel but also acknowledged his part in what was considered by many to be a questionable decision—using the *ThinkPad* tablet name for the soon-to-be-announced line of notebook computers.

CHAPTER 12

Building a Winning Team

[We] quit squabbling about internal issues and worried instead about beating the competition and winning customers.

—Bruce Claflin, *IBM Think Magazine*, December 1993

IBM was accelerating its foray into mobile computing. The PC Company president, Bob Corrigan, and his immediate manager, Jim Cannavino, head of the Personal Systems Line of Business (PSLOB) had recognized that mobile computing was going to be an integral part of its future strategies. The product strategy was to take the best that IBM and the industry had to offer and design a leapfrog development plan to position IBM as number one in this segment. The resources necessary for this plan were being made available and included many of the most skilled engineers and planners in Boca Raton and Yamato, Japan. The executives even challenged IBM's tradition of promoting from within and hired a strong industry veteran, Jim Bartlett, to head its brand management. Also, by convincing Bruce Claflin that this was a management role critical to the survival of IBM, the portable effort now had an energetic, charismatic leader to pull the plan together.

Claflin went after his new role with a vengeance. With his arrival in June 1992, he started by gauging the attitude of the Boca team and reviewing the key managers under his auspices. He quickly realized that he had to cement the relationship between the Boca planning community, the Yamato development team, the Raleigh manufacturing group, Somers marketing, and key field sales personnel. He knew that he needed to address underlying communications problems and territorial attitudes.

Claflin decided to hold a business review meeting in July 1992. It was held in Building 3 at the Somers, New York, IBM facility, which housed Claflin and the other top IBM PC Company management. Somers is an architectural marvel located approximately twenty miles north of White Plains, with its pyramid towers visible from I-684. The height of this magnificent structure forced IBM to install special lightening rods on the rooftops because the buildings towered above anything else in the area.

The various groups supporting the mobile venture were invited to review the business plan. The Yamato development team was to describe the features and functions of the upcoming portable products. Manufacturing was to assess its ability to build the products. Field sales was to commit to a product life forecast. Marketing was to describe its communications and public relations programs for the soon-to-be announced portables. All factions of Claflin's "virtual" team were represented at this key meeting.

According to Claflin, "We started with development. By this time, Hajime Watabe had been replaced with Koichi Higuchi. Higuchi-san was working hard to get the Yamato team to respond to the planning requirements agreed to earlier in the year. This was Yamato's finest hour. Higuchi-san and his key engineers came in and demonstrated the first working notebook in the new line of

IBM portables. This product had a 10.4-inch color display. Everyone in the room was really turned on! Development then gave a very credible presentation on how they would meet their schedule. Finally, they committed that this product could be announced on time. Confidence started growing in the room; you could feel the excitement building. I hadn't yet polled the room for official positions, but excitement over this innovative notebook was evident."

Scott Bower, one of the marketing representatives at this meeting, would eventually work for Claflin directly. However, at this meeting, Bower was offering the field perspective on the notebook products under review. Said Bower, "I saw the first model of this innovative notebook. The Yamato team presented a notebook that was black in color. Truly sharp. Truly unique. The prototype had an interesting approach to the mouse problem facing mobile travelers. Developed by IBM Research, it was a little button in the middle of the keyboard. The crowning feature was the 10.4-inch display, which fit into this under-eight-pound notebook. To say the least, my reaction was very positive."

Bower continued, "After reviewing this revolutionary notebook design, field sales stated that they could sell fifteen thousand units over the five-year life of the product. All that could be heard was dead silence. Shock at the possibility of a market failure replaced the positive excitement that had just filled the room. During this time frame, successful portable products sold hundreds of thousands of units. Claflin was certain that sales estimate was ninety percent below what the market would want.

"Sales felt that most of the units sold would be monochrome, despite their excitement over the new display. At that time, color displays in the mobile market were relatively untested and just too expensive. Based on Sales's volumes and the product mix commitment, the business plan did not make sense. This exciting portable product was likely to be killed. The team was on the verge of 'torpedoing' the entire mobile computing program if we couldn't get together."

Scott Bower portrayed these forecast discussions: "The product forecaster came into the room and saw the product prototype. Around this time, IBM was doing about two thousand notebooks a month, selling them at basically fire sale prices. We were going to announce a four-thousand dollar-plus notebook. The forecaster said that we would be lucky to sell maybe seventy-five hundred units in the United States and another seventy-five hundred throughout the world. Claflin and I looked at each other and couldn't believe it. Here we were sitting with this unique 10.4-inch display, which, we were sure, no one else was going to fit into an under-eight-pound notebook. We had a sleek industrial design in a sharp black color unlike anything IBM had ever done before. We had been given the directive to make a big splash and make a name for IBM in mobile computing. There was no way that was going to happen with a product forecast —worldwide—of fifteen thousand."

Claflin decided that he needed to know everyone's position regarding this product. In classic IBM bureaucracy, Maurice Fletcher, representing the field, said, "I non-concur with development," and he would not commit to greater volume. Marketing wouldn't support such a low-volume product. Development was frustrated because they had delivered a product that met the design criteria and no one wanted it. Manufacturing didn't trust the Japanese development schedule and design, so they weren't going to build any more than Sales wanted. Despite what appeared to be an award-winning innovative portable sitting on the table, everyone was non-concurring.

Fletcher recalled the tenor of the session: "Prior to this meeting of Claflin's new management team, Claflin had told Scott Bower and me that we were going to head U.S. marketing as brand managers. So, we were prepared to offer our positions on the proposed product line. Unfortunately, Jim Bartlett had not been informed that he was not going to head the worldwide marketing effort for mobile; the other countries were also going to have brand managers. Bartlett's role was to be more of an advisor to Claflin on the market than a line executive."

"In classic IBM form," continued Fletcher, "I did non-concur with the product specifications and proposed volume. I'll never forget the look I got from Bruce as he stated, 'From this date forward, the ThinkPad team will not have another non-concur. We will agree to discuss, we will solve the problem, but we're not going to hold up development, manufacturing, or announcement because one of the geographies does not concur.'"

Claflin reflected, "I turned to my left toward Maurice Fletcher, Scott Bower's right-hand man, and said, 'I don't recognize that word *non-concur*. You don't have the right to non-concur. This team makes the final decision about the product—as a team. We're either going to do this product, or we're going to kill this product. No one else is developing it. No one else is manufacturing it. No one else is marketing it. And no one else is going to sell it but us, the people in this room right now.'"

"We were about to kill it," continued Claflin. "IBM's business review process would have mandated killing it because the business case didn't make sense. The forecast was simply too low. And marketing just wanted to say, 'I non-concur.' They wanted other people to make the decision and, in so doing, relinquish any responsibility for the fate of these portables. I saw what was in front of me, and I just wasn't going to let that happen."

Claflin realized that he was fighting an uphill battle. The sales field team did not work for him. Manufacturing did not work for him. Marketing at the time did not yet work for him. Plans were in place to change all that, but, at the time of the meeting, only a few engineers and planners actually reported to Claflin. The meeting was stymied by each area's classic functional position based on business as usual and the historical perspective of portable computer products.

At this point in the meeting, Claflin showed his level of frustration and simply repeated, "I don't care whether you work for me or not. We're making this decision right now. There's no one else in IBM who's going to make this decision except for the people in this room." Although Claflin did not say it, the implication was that he had the full authority to decide this matter. Everyone in the room knew that Claflin had a mandate from IBM's chairman, John Akers. No one doubted that he was not going to play the functional game of "passing the buck." He made it abundantly clear that he did not care who reported to whom. He was responsible for this business, and the meeting participants were the senior management of the *virtual* mobile team. No one was leaving the room until a go/no go decision was made.

Claflin reflected, "I told them that if it was a no-go decision, I would leave the room, kill the product the next day, and all of them would be gone. They were either going to be out of a job or doing something else in another part of IBM. They knew I was serious. It was a binary decision. We were either doing it, or it was over."

Claflin got everyone's attention in the room. You could almost read their thoughts: "Uh oh, I can't just pass this up the line anymore. This is *my* problem." All of a sudden, the enormity of the decision was clear. The decision was not passing to someone else. According to Claflin, "I think they found it energizing. I know they found it sobering."

The group decided to throw caution to the wind and to take the volumes up, nowhere to the levels that actually sold, but significantly more than fifteen thousand over five years. Development agreed to deliver the product on schedule to Manufacturing.

Manufacturing committed to build it on time in the quantity required for announcement. Field Sales said they would sell sufficient volume to justify the product. Marketing talked about the program they would put in place to position the new product line. Everybody left the meeting committed to doing this new portable computer product. It was another step in the right direction. The decision was reconfirmed when Corrigan later raised the volumes more than enough to keep the project alive.

The Yamato team was the hero in this meeting. They delivered on their commitment from the meeting months earlier. They met the schedule critical to this product's announcement timing. Without the working prototype, no one in the meeting would have budged from his or her functional position. Yamato's efforts were the foundation for IBM's renewed commitment to the portable market.

Claflin summarized this pivotal moment in IBM mobile history: "From that meeting—and I honestly believe that meeting was a turning point—we got ourselves focused on success, not past failures. The sales team, headed by Scott, changed their attitude and became the strongest proponent of our new portable line. I'd love to tell you that everyone was a team after that meeting. They weren't, but they began to work as a team at that watershed meeting. I think it helped to have someone running the show who believed in the team's ability to do the job."

"It was probably the most memorable meeting of my IBM portable computing career," said Claflin. "I am proud of building a team and getting everyone focused on the job, as opposed to tearing each other apart. When I arrived, the base technology was already there. The design was already there. We just lacked confidence. What I did was build confidence within the team that this product could be a winner. Then, the team and I built confidence across IBM and the industry. That's probably what I contributed most to the mobile effort."

Claflin's approach to building his team was a step ahead of the rest of the PC Company. In the September timeframe, the business decided to follow suit and formalize the brand concept. Each major product area—desktops, servers, portables, and options—would have its own brand. The brand team concept eventually challenged the traditional IBM contentious approach to development. Everyone was part of the same team and had a voice in all decisions affecting the brand.

Everyone had a role and provided a specific expertise. Patty McHugh had a great set of planners headed by two strong managers, one with sales experience and the other with business sense. Higuchi-san staffed his Yamato operation with the most talented engineers available in Yamato who brought forward the best in leading edge technology. Jim Bartlett and his team were always thinking "outside the box" when it came to brand management programs and customer satisfaction.

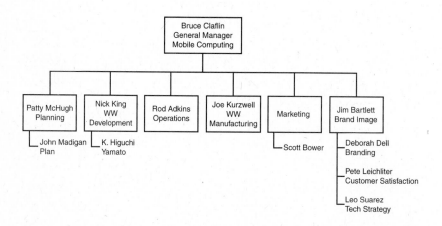

Claflin had no trouble recruiting the cream of the crop to join the portable brand. His reputation as a strong marketing manager who was open to new ideas and listened to everyone on the team drew employees to the team. His direct approach and grounding in IBM's basic beliefs allowed the management team to bounce ideas off one another without repercussion. Claflin's high energy level was contagious, and his attitude made it a fun place to work.

Said Scott Bower, "We worked our tails off, but we were learning. We were growing as a team, and it was a very, very positive experience. How many times does a person get the opportunity to grow a business? When I took over notebooks, pre-ThinkPad, IBM was doing $120 million in sales worldwide while losing $240 million. We were overpriced, under function, and always late to market. In the next two years, our portable business grew from $120 million to $3 billion. Even today, I don't think anybody—not Microsoft, not Dell—grew to $3 billion in such a short period. And we had fun! The whole team worked together ironing out the problems, which were inevitable. Bruce had communicated where he wanted to take the business, and you were either on the team or off."

The Authors' Insights

Pivotal moments. Crossroads. Watershed times. We remember those moments in our lives when turns in the road could have drastic results. Think about the decision to make Bruce Claflin the general manager for ThinkPad. Think about the implications of that July 1992 business review meeting led by Claflin. Imagine if there had been a breakdown in communications. The ThinkPad could have been killed just months before it was launched.

Claflin knew when to "bet the farm" and when not to. Although he did not have all the decision "influencers" reporting to him, he had the implied authority to do whatever was necessary. Claflin got everyone focused and steered the group towards success instead of failure. Billions of dollars were at stake. Strong leadership was necessary to steer this burgeoning business in the right direction. Claflin provided it, and all of IBM would eventually benefit from it.

CHAPTER 13

IBM ThinkPad 700C: In the Game

We compiled a very comprehensive list of customer requirements, put them in order of priority, and went to work on meeting them. From initial concept to the ship date took less than one year. The portable team has the right to be very proud of this effort.

—Bruce Claflin, November 1992

A core component of IBM's mobile effort was the Yamato portable development team. Yamato development had been extremely successful in delivering products for their own geography, driving a strong design reputation. This reputation encouraged Cannavino to transition mobile development to Japan. It was not an easy decision nor an easy transition. Just like one of their major competitors, Toshiba, the IBM Yamato development team was not initially open to the product requirements provided by U.S. marketing. Because Yamato had the technology, they felt that they knew how to put the parts together in a portable the market would want. What the Yamato team learned was that each market—each geography—had a slightly different set of requirements. Yamato needed the planning and marketing teams to balance the myriad of worldwide requirements into a product line acceptable to all geographies.

According to Leo Suarez, one of the original members of Boca's portable effort, "During 1991, Hajime Watabe was the chief liaison between the Boca team and Japanese development. He encouraged the Japanese team to build a great portable computer. But it wasn't enough! We needed a more formal structure and someone who could enforce a requirements process. When Koichi Higuchi was assigned to head the mobile computing effort in Yamato, Japan, we asked him to listen to the U.S. requirements and build something of which IBM could be proud.

"Higuchi-san turned around the indifferent attitude displayed by the Japanese team during Watabe's Boca assignment. Resident in Yamato, Higuchi-san encouraged the Japanese development team to listen to what the U.S. planning and marketing organizations said. His actions enabled the U.S. organization to focus on market requirements, marketing, and sales and the Japanese organization to focus on technology and development. Putting Higuchi-san in place enabled us to introduce the first IBM ThinkPad notebook one year later."

Suarez painted a picture of Boca's concern over the development transition: "We were worried about who would replace Watabe when he left Boca. Although the process wasn't perfect and the announced products were marginal performers, Watabe had the respect of the Japanese organization. Compounding the fear of losing Watabe was the fact that mobile development was moving to Japan. The Boca group was extremely concerned that they would lose what little control they had over what went into the products. Luckily, Higuchi turned out to be fantastic. He was very Western minded and open to what we had to say about what the market needed in a notebook computer. Higuchi garnered our trust. We knew that he was committed to giving us what we wanted."

Higuchi-san himself reflected on this change: "In IBM, I could use the early [leading edge] technologies. That's critical in the personal computer industry because speed of development is very important. I knew that it was fundamental to listen to the planning team while taking advantage of the technologies found at home [Japan]."[1] Higuchi-san and his group concentrated primarily on display and pointing device technologies combined with excellent industrial designs.

Kathy Vieth, continuing as an executive advisor to the mobile team after Bruce Claflin's arrival, augmented Suarez's views: "Having someone from the Yamato team assigned to 'make it happen,' and who understood the need to address the U.S. market requirements, was a masterful ploy. Higuchi-san recognized the absolute need for leading edge technology delivered on a consolidated schedule. He knew inherently that the Boca planning team had a good grasp on what needed to be done. He also knew that Yamato engineering could deliver if they really believed in the product."

Even Higuchi-san's own managers complimented his approach and the teamwork that ensued from this crucial transition. Toshiyuki Ikeda discussed his view of how the process needed to work: "We came to realize that in order to create a successful product, you had to be close to the market. You had to understand the users, their needs and desires. That's the number one principle. On the other hand, in order to create a good product, you must also be close to the technologies available for use in the product. It's very difficult for the same team to address these two principals at the same time.

"We were developing a notebook product for the United States, our biggest and most important market. We expected the U.S. planning and marketing team to define the market requirements for the development effort. The Yamato team was the best resource to gather the best technologies from the Far East or wherever. I was

1. The *New York Times* (June 1993).

able to call any company and get the information I needed almost immediately, usually on the same day. Every month, I summarized this information, went to the United States to attend the mobile brand meeting, and presented the latest technology updates. Development, planning, manufacturing, and marketing met every month to review the status and plans for any new portable computer product. Although the process started with the arrival of Higuchi-san on the scene, Claflin formalized the process when he became general manager for Mobile Computing in June 1992."

Now responsible for development, the Yamato team wanted to develop a truly exciting portable product. This computer not only had to equal the other portable players (Compaq, Toshiba, and Apple) but also had to give IBM customers something that met their needs. An assessment of the customer requirements indicated a growing interest and desire for large, color displays in a mobile package. Thus, the single most important technology in IBM's latest portable was the innovative 10.4-inch color display.

Joe Formichelli, an individual who later had a significant role on the ThinkPad team, was instrumental in mobile's display decision. In 1992, Formichelli took over the Visual Products business, becoming the first operations manager in IBM's history to become a division general manager in charge of a major product line. According to Formichelli, "Visual Products was a two to three billion dollar business, but it was scattered across IBM. Every division built monitors and displays. I gathered it all up and brought it together into a single operation in the PC Company. I got support from Cannavino, one of my mentors from my days in Poughkeepsie [one of IBM's oldest plants].

"I soon realized that we had significant untapped opportunity in monitors. For example, when Tech Data bought two thousand PCs from IBM, they only bought one thousand monitors; our attach rate was less than fifty percent. I wondered why we couldn't get our attach rate up. I didn't have the answer, but I soon discovered that our monitors weren't multi-synced. Our monitors worked only with IBM computers. Can you believe it? So, in order to sell them in the open market, we made them multi-sync like the rest of the industry.

"Another problem was the thousands of different models. The next thing we did was to get rid of all those models. I just scrapped all of them. I put together a strategy for monitors and displays. We had one monitor for the low end of the market, another for the middle, and a third one for the high end."

Formichelli then simplified the components for these monitors. He told his team to build one motherboard for all three monitors, that is, put the same components on everything and then simply turn off features for the mid- and low-end products. The high-end monitor would have power management and better controls. This strategy was cheaper to implement than keeping track of three motherboards and manufacturing lines. Visual Products started to make money on monitors. Formichelli's management of visual displays led to his critical role in the creation of the 10.4-inch TFT flat panel display. The decision to develop TFT displays had come earlier when Cannavino asked Nobi Mii to figure out how to get a 10.4-inch display in a notebook.

According to Mii-san, "Although IBM had developed a lot of advanced display technology at its Yorktown Heights research facility, it had limited display manufacturing expertise. Toshiba, on the other hand, had experience building TFT displays but didn't have the advanced display research necessary to build active matrix color TFT panels. I went to Toshiba and proposed that we combine our efforts. They agreed that it was a good idea. We formed a new joint venture called *Display Technology, Inc.*, which was equally owned by Toshiba and IBM.

"The original plan was to produce a 9.5-inch display. However, when I reviewed our progress with Cannavino, he told me that he wanted a 10.4-inch display. He was certain that it would fit in our new portable and give IBM a competitive edge. I did not think it could be done. After many long meetings with the team in Japan, we figured out how to package the electronics to fit in the notebook mechanical design. The difficulty was not in building the actual display, but in the electronics that controlled the display. We found a way to wrap them behind the panel. Our team was very creative and worked very hard to solve what was, at the time, a very difficult problem."

According to Cannavino, "I felt strongly that a high-quality screen was fundamental to the portable computer. Unlike the display business that ran for fifteen or twenty years with black-and-white tubes, portables—whether for business or home—were not going to run off of black-and-white. I firmly believed that monochrome displays would make up a minor portion of the portable volume. I stood alone in that debate. My own people didn't agree with me on that subject.

"I eventually managed to convince them. We did the joint venture with Toshiba, investing in active matrix displays. IBM put five hundred million dollars into that venture. It's paid off handsomely! Not only did we get our supply of active matrix displays, but it was also foundational to building the mobile line."

After Mii-san established the DTI partnership, Formichelli started to focus on this investment. Formichelli reflected on this responsibility: "In the beginning, I had to read a book to see what a TFT or LCD was. Greater minds than mine had figured out that we needed to make this investment. Much of the credit for the initial success of the portable line actually goes to Nobuo Mii. Mii-san had the wisdom to recognize that large color active matrix thin film transistor displays were going to be important technologies in the mobile space. Mii-san convinced Cannavino and a few other key executives to make the investment with Toshiba to build color TFT displays through the joint venture known as Display Technology, Inc."

When the factory was ready, a critical decision faced Formichelli and the portable team. What size should they make their portion of the display production? Initially, the team was comfortable with an 8.1-inch screen. Toshiyuki Ikeda, engineering manager working for Higuchi-san (and later the director of Mobile Development, replacing Higuchi-san), related the background to this decision: "Let me tell you why we did the 10.4-inch display. In 1991, the best LCD in the industry was the 8.1-inch, although it was really small. We knew the industry was considering a 9.1-inch or maybe 9.2-inch for the next generation of portables. The team had lots of discussions about display size. We were certain that it would be the one area in which users would appreciate an improvement. It was also an area in which we had advanced resources via our new partnership with Toshiba.

"During one of the Yamato product reviews, we showed a mock up of our design. Jim [Cannavino] stood up and said, 'This machine is big enough to fit a 10.4-inch display.' So, we immediately measured out a display with a diagonal of 10.4 inches on a piece of paper and put it on the machine. He said, 'It will fit.' But, no one was building a 10.4-inch color TFT display in a notebook, or anywhere else for that matter. He challenged us to go out and get a 10.4-inch display and put it in the new notebook. IBM had managed to use a 10-inch display in the L40SX. Remember, however, that the L40SX was a laptop not a notebook. We got very excited about the concept because this would allow us to be the first in the market. But, we had more work to do to make it a reality."

According to Cannavino, "I made the technical team a bet that we could fit a 10.4-inch screen inside a 8.5"×11" notebook. In fact, I still have the five dollars hanging on my wall that I won from Ikeda-san. Within a relatively short time, his team came back sheepishly and said, 'He's right.'"

Cannavino and Mii-san then met with Toshiba. The team had done some arithmetic on the panel sizes, and it looked like the panel sizes would yield IBM two up and four up of the 10.4-inch screens. By producing four panels at the same time through the assembly line, instead of one, the yield and profitability would go up. Cannavino convinced them to modify the tool set to actually get the 10.4-inch screens. Luckily for IBM, Toshiba chose not to do the same thing.

Mii-san reflected, "Because Toshiba owned half of DTI, they also had access to the 10.4-inch display production. However, they didn't think the yields would be good enough and focused their production on 9.5-inch. So, part of DTI was set up to produce 9.5-inch displays, and the other half was set up to produce 10.4-inch displays. IBM acquired one hundred percent of the 10.4-inch panel production for the next eighteen months. We were lucky because it was almost two years before DTI could start producing enough 10.4-inch displays to satisfy both partners. By the time that happened, we were already building larger 11.3-inch displays and had plans to develop 12.1-inch displays. Needless to say, Toshiba wanted to share the capacity of these larger displays when they came online."

Cannavino added more detail to Mii-san's remarks: "Our display team told us that they could do it and have panels ready by fall 1992. We decided to produce about two-to-three hundred thousand panels in their first year of production because we felt that the market would really like our display. That decision, coupled with Toshiba's lack of interest, gave IBM the lead on screen size. No one was able to introduce a notebook with a 10.4-inch display until almost eighteen months after we introduced our new notebook." Toshiba didn't offer a portable with a 10.4-inch display until 1994.

Scott Bower recalled the display activity from the marketing perspective: "The press didn't realize that we had actually used the 10.4-inch display on a product called the *CL57SX*. As a twelve-pound notebook, it did not sell very well—even with the 10.4-inch display.

If the truth were known, IBM was worried about the multi-million dollar investment that had been made in DTI. The Yamato design team was the hero of the hour when they rose to the occasion and were able to reduce the weight, incorporate the display, and provide an intriguing industrial design. Finally, our labors bore fruit."

When asked about the display decision at the time of product announcement, Bruce Claflin gave credit where credit was due. According to Claflin, "This decision goes back to Higuchi-san, Ikeda-san, and their team. It was one of their finest moments. The Yamato team decided that they could design a notebook that would accommodate a 10.4-inch screen with an acceptable thickness and weight. The packaging allowed the display to fit in a pretty standard-size notebook. It was brilliant engineering!

"Toshiba also had the chance to do the 10.4-inch display, but they viewed it as too risky. Furthermore, they were concerned that their manufacturing yields would be too low and that they would not get enough good displays to use. As a result, Toshiba took a more cautious route and requested that their fifty percent of the panel production be 9.5-inch instead of 10.4-inch. Higuchi-san's engineers said, 'We can make it work,' and they were right. Eventually, the line got the yields up on the 10.4-inch display to almost exactly the same as the yields for the 9.5-inch. This, of course, allowed us to become an instant hit in the market and keep the competitive advantage for quite awhile."

The display was not the only major decision the mobile team made. All development decisions that affected the form factor and packaging had to be made in conjunction with the IBM design community. Tom Hardy, the corporate manager of this group, oversaw the coordination of the IBM ThinkPad design process. Hardy worked closely with designer Richard Sapper, IBM's corporate industrial design consultant from Italy, and Kazuhiko Yamazaki, IBM Yamato industrial designer.

Tom Hardy shared the process by which the various elements of the ThinkPad came into being: "During the 1980s, key elements of the IBM industrial design program were lost. We lost touch with the total customer experience and with innovation and unity. The product line was in disarray. Working with Sapper, we introduced a structured 'personality' approach in contrast to the traditional 'systems-thinking' common inside IBM. We felt that the personality direction was capable of differentiating IBM and adding excitement while providing product line unity and a revitalized brand image. The ThinkPad was the first product to emerge from the personality design effort. We wanted a design that expressed the four universal characteristics of *reassuring, caring, exciting*, and *inspiring* so important to our customers."[2]

Hardy continued to equate the value of this differentiated approach to product design: "This effort by the company's industrial design teams added value to the portable product line. At the point of purchase, perceived quality affected the buying decision. A product's appearance that pleased and informed or that presented an image of user friendliness and innovative characteristics was sought after. This design approach also added value during the product life cycle where customers were interested in ease of use, ease of repair, status conveyed, durability and expandability.[3]

Said Hardy, "By addressing these two aspects early in the cycle, the team made changes to the preliminary ThinkPad design that set the product line apart from the competition."

Although Hardy headed the corporate design program, Richard Sapper was the individual most directly responsible for the actual industrial design of the IBM ThinkPad. Throughout development, Sapper collaborated with Yamazaki to blend their ideas into a final product. According to Hardy, "Sapper designed the original ThinkPad. He was a preeminent industrial designer with an international track record of market success. Since 1980, Sapper had been

2. Tom Hardy, "design saves the brand," *Innovation* (Summer 1998): 39–43.
3. Kiyonori Sakakibara, Ph.D., "IBM ThinkPad 700C Notebook Computer," London Business School (September 1994).

IBM's corporate design consultant. It was clear to everyone that mobile products would be an important image-building product line for IBM. I knew that Sapper needed to be intimately involved."

Hardy arranged for Yamazaki to meet him in Sapper's Milan, Italy, studio. The objective of the meeting was to work on the mobile industrial design strategy and tie it to the upcoming portable products being developed in Yamato, Japan. Sapper had already built a basic black model to illustrate the Japanese "lunch box" approach, a simple black box like a Japanese Bento box. It was a perfectly crafted black lunch box, completely enclosed so that you had no idea what it was until you opened it. Sapper believed that the new mobile line of products should be completely devoid of any signal as to what the box contained. The only interruption to that form on the outside was the angled, multi-colored stamp of the logo treatment.

John Wiseman, the industrial design liaison for headquarters, Boca, and Yamato, joined the Milan meeting. The group discussed conceptual direction and product details. At the end of the meeting, they were all in sync. Yamazaki returned to Yamato with specific directions and Sapper's model as a guide.

Hardy relayed a little-known fact: "The day-to-day developmental collaboration between Sapper and Yamazaki was facilitated by a high-resolution digital imaging system. I had established an internal design network of Sony imaging systems at several IBM locations, including Sapper's studio in Milan, the Yamato design center, and the corporate Design Program headquarters. This system transmitted color photographs rapidly over telephone lines and enabled notes and sketches via a digitized tablet. The tool allowed rapid visual communication across three continents and permitted Sapper to interact on a daily basis with Yamato. Given time differences, it created a virtual twenty-four hour design development process."

The beauty of the ThinkPad was its simplicity, restraint, and elegance coupled with a feeling of excitement. Hardy summarized the design activities: "Designing something to be simple and not simplistic is no simple task. An approachable 'personality' can be achieved through sensitive use of form, color, finish, size, ease of use, materials, technology, and detailing. The first ThinkPad notebook design utilized all these characteristics to perfection, including details such as tactile finish and multi-colored IBM logo. Such perfection required early and cooperative working relationships among industrial design, research, engineering, and manufacturing. A great deal of credit goes to the collaborative effort of these disciplines during the notebook development process. We tried new ideas and attained high quality as a team."

Although the ThinkPad's smart, all-black color and overall industrial design seem so natural today, it was a big issue in the early 1990s. According to Hardy, "Despite the fact that within IBM, long before ThinkPad, black and colors other than gray and off-white had been used on typewriters and large computer systems, this had changed. In the late 1970s, Germany initiated workplace standards that required 'light-value' colors on office computing equipment; these standards were soon picked up by other European and Scandinavian countries. Then, during the 1980s, any offerings other than gray and off-white were virtually eliminated across the computer industry because of cost and the European workplace standards.

"During the 1980s, human factors scientists debated the validity of the initial German research premise, although the standards remained. Considering that 'color' was a very important design element, we knew that, in order to differentiate IBM products, we needed to break away from the dogmatic gray and off-white syndrome. I commissioned a well-respected Swiss ergonomist to conduct an objective study on the state of global workplace standards and to declare which were valid and which were flawed. The final report concluded that, although some aspects of the standards were valid and necessary, the aspect of 'light-value' product housings was not, except where glare was concerned. I sent the report to the IBM international standards group to argue in various country standard meetings. We pursued our strategy to introduce black on new mobile products, as well as to consider black and other colors across varying IBM product lines.

"Although we had credible data, I knew that we were in for a debate with the IBM Germany standards authority. I asked Yamakazi to add a pebble-gray color option on the ThinkPad drawings that would meet German standards. This enabled the worldwide ThinkPad offering to be black while providing an acceptable solution for Germany and countries with standards issues. IBM Germany objected to this solution because the pebble-gray increased product cost. A lot of pressure was exerted to make the entire product line pebble-gray to increase the volume of standard gray parts and, thus, reduce the product cost. I remained adamant that black was to be the ThinkPad color. Eventually, Germany could not afford the higher product cost and capitulated to the use of black, but with the condition that the German user manual covers be boldly printed *This product not for office use.*"

David Hill, another IBM industrial designer, added to Hardy's historical perspective: "There were a lot of barriers to getting the original IBM ThinkPad design approved. Many were opposed to using black as the color of the notebook. At the time, black was very radical in personal computing, even though it was accepted in earlier computer products. If you went back and looked at the IBM System 360 mainframe from the 1960s, it was primarily black. It was in the computer room behind glass windows and was supposed to look outstanding. The black color allowed clients to show off their prize possession to visitors.

"But personal computers weren't black at the time. That's because we wanted to make PCs fit naturally into the office so they wouldn't be noticed. So, we made all of them in pearl white, a sort of cream color that no one would notice. But, then along comes the ThinkPad, and we wanted to make a bold statement that was just the opposite. We wanted everyone to notice it, so we adopted black. A lot of people objected to our using black as the color of ThinkPad, thinking it wasn't like 'IBM.' Eventually everyone saw it as something that would really differentiate IBM."

Whereas the corporate design team was happy with the move towards black, the Yamato development team felt the black finish was quite a challenge. Ikeda-san expressed his concern: "First of all, black was very difficult to do. You had to manufacture the case in a dark color and find a paint-like cover in which to seal it. Painting plastic was very difficult because it could easily peel off. And to make matters worse, it was nearly impossible to get an exact color match between parts. We worked really hard on this, trying out many different shades of black and different kinds of paint. Eventually, we found that we could do it. We were pleased when we showed it to the planning and marketing contingencies, who reacted quite favorably."

Tied to the industrial design and packaging was the disk drive. At the time, the 3.5-inch disk drive affected the overall size of the notebook, forcing a more laptop form factor. During the planning stages for its notebook, the team realized that a high-capacity but miniscule disk was needed for the desired form factor. Mii-san related his recollection of how IBM developed its 2.5-inch disk: "I went to Fujisawa and put together a team to build a 2.5-inch, despite the objections of Mike Armstrong (now CEO at AT&T) who managed the storage systems group. But I went forward with the approval of Cannavino. When Yamato began the ThinkPad development, I showed them the results of our efforts. Our exciting 2.5-inch disk drive provided lots of storage in a smaller space than previous 3.5-inch disk drives. This was an important technological advance for the mobile market. The first 2.5-inch disk was only 120MB. Although the capacity seems small today, at the time [1991/1992], it was a lot of storage to put into a portable computer."

The Yamato development team now had a new industrial design, color, larger display, and smaller disk drive. The team knew inherently that there was one thing that they would not be allowed to compromise: the keyboard. IBM has always been known for its keyboards. Fortunately, most of the time, it is for having the best keyboard in the industry. In general, IBM keyboards have a better tactile response. Typically, the keys are positioned "better" than other manufacturers. Of course, it wasn't always that way. One particularly unpleasant keyboard experience caused Ikeda-san to concentrate on getting the keyboard "right" on the first ThinkPad notebook.

Ikeda recalled, "Because of my PCjr experience, I knew that you couldn't make any keyboard compromises. It couldn't have a smaller layout. It had to have the same tactile feel. The inverted-T cursor area could not invade the keyboard space and, therefore, invade the area designated for the Shift key. You needed to provide separate Home, End, Page Up, and Page Down keys. It really had to be right! And because my reputation had recovered from having developed the 'chiclet' keyboard for the IBM PCjr, I was not going to take any chances. I would not accept any compromises with the keyboard going into this new portable."

The IBM chiclet keyboard.

The result was a winner. The keys had great spring to them. The inverted cursor control keys were placed slightly down under the right Shift key. If they gave out awards for keyboards (they don't), it would have won first prize. Although one of the more significant things associated with the ThinkPad creation, it didn't get much attention. The keyboard was overshadowed by a new cursor control device.

The Yamato team developed most innovations attributable to the new line of portables, with one notable exception. The IBM TrackPoint was conceived at IBM's Almaden Research Laboratory, an ergonomic laboratory in San Jose's foothills. Its brilliant but somewhat eccentric creator, Dr. Ted Selker, was director of the ergonomic lab and had been studying man-machine interaction for years. He evaluated software user interfaces and hardware while trying to figure out ways to use machines more effectively.

The 5ᵗʰ Wave   By Rich Tennant

"YOU KNOW, IF WE CAN ALL KEEP THE TITTERING DOWN, I, FOR ONE, WOULD LIKE TO HEAR MORE ABOUT KEN'S NEW POINTING DEVICE FOR NOTEBOOKS."

In the late 1980s, Dr. Selker was working on a way to improve the mouse, an accepted method of input familiar to desktop users. Because the mouse took the hand off the keyboard, the hand moved independently of the cursor on the screen. Selker figured that there had to be a better way to combine mouse-like capabilities with a portable computer.

Dr. Ted described his development of the IBM TrackPoint: "We knew that we wanted to establish a means for people to control the cursor without having to move anything across a large desktop space like when using a mouse. So, we used a small pole that sensed pressure instead of motion. It was an isometric class device, sort of a joystick that didn't move. We fiddled with it for a long time. Eventually, we got it working in a standard desktop keyboard. We recommended that it be included in IBM's desktop keyboard as an alternative to the mouse. We felt that it would give us a competitive advantage in the market. But, marketing didn't feel it was wise to go up against the mouse because millions of people had gotten used to it. The project was about to be cancelled."

About this time, Tom Hardy heard about Selker's invention through one of his team members, Sam Lucente. Part of Lucente's assignment was to search the halls of IBM Research so that industrial design could stay on top of emerging technologies. Hardy recalled, "We were very excited about the invention because it clearly provided a differentiated IBM feature. Selker's prototype was a crude-looking stick wrapped with masking tape and protruding from a very large IBM keyboard. I think that Ted simply used a keyboard he found laying around the lab. However, I told him that such a demo model did little to show off the concept advantages. I suggested that we place it in the smaller notebook model then under development. Industrial design would help him promote the idea by showing the invention on a high-image product that could benefit from it.

"We sent information to Yamazaki-san, who put the pointing stick in one of the portable models after he and Sapper improved the stick design. Then, we altered our model so that we could help Selker push the concept simultaneously in Yamato and the U.S. I remember showing it to Bob Corrigan, PC Company president, while Yamazaki was discussing the idea with Yamato engineering. Meanwhile, Selker was going around selling the idea, as well as interacting with executives and the team in Yamato. Between all these parallel efforts, the TrackPoint was thrust into the product plan."

As with any product to be announced, the naming process had to be invoked. Heinz Hegmann had actively pushed the *ThinkPad* name. He was asked to complement this work by naming the small erasure-tipped pointing device that Selker had developed. According to Hegmann, Selker had nominated *Pogo Stick* or *Whiskers* (like cat whiskers, instead of mouse). Because of the time constraints, these names could not be cleared worldwide, and Hegmann brought forward *TrackPoint*. This name would prove as long lasting as ThinkPad and clearly demonstrated IBM's move toward personality-based names.

The renewed focus on the portable segment and the involvement of the industrial design team gave Dr. Selker's project a stay of execution. "I went to Yamato and worked with the development team," said Selker. "We found that the little pressure stick could be placed between the G and the H key because, when typing, the fingers don't actually cross over that area. We thought it might make it distinctive to put a little red eraser-like tip on the pointing stick. The rest, they say, is history."

According to Ikeda-san, "TrackPoint was another difficult feat for us. The TrackPoint technology existed before we started ThinkPad. It had been tested in the prototype of the L40SX, but unfortunately it had yet to end up in an announced product. While developing the original notebook plan, we asked Dr. Selker to run some human factor tests. We wanted to evaluate whether we should use a mousepad or the isometric pointing stick. Selker's results demonstrated that the isometric pointing stick could move the cursor faster than either a mouse or a mousepad. So, our team started thinking about how we could get this little pressure stick inside the notebook. We tried it in a number of locations. Then, working with Dr. Ted, we found a perfect place for it—right there on the keyboard itself between the G and H keys."

Claflin recalled the marketing team's reaction to this innovation: "Here's this mad scientist, Ted Selker, running around demonstrating this pointing stick used to control the cursor. Controversy surrounded every aspect of this feature. The portable team finally made the decision to incorporate it into its new line. Marketing finally agreed. Because the new portable was so good in so many other ways, the team rationalized that the notebook would overshadow the TrackPoint's other innovative features if it proved a failure.

"One of our early smart decisions was to put the TrackPoint across the entire brand. It became a distinguishing characteristic of the ThinkPad line. It distinguished the product visually, being a little stick in the middle of the keyboard and being bright red. We built on the concept of the TrackPoint's red dot and distinguished the ThinkPad name by using a little red dot over the *i* in *ThinkPad*. It was a design aspect that helped to pull the ThinkPad personality together."

Sapper influenced this decision just as he had the industrial design and the color. He wanted customers surprised when they opened a ThinkPad and suddenly saw what was inside—a bright red dot. Before Sapper's involvement, the TrackPoint was to be blue. Blue was chosen to remind people of IBM (Big Blue), as well as that blue, within IBM, was the color denoting "normal" control functions. But, Sapper felt that TrackPoint should be red because red would provide much more of contrast against the black keyboard. It could certainly be showcased as an IBM differentiating feature in advertisements and at point of purchase.

Hardy described the argument against red: "The problem was that red was the IBM Safety Standard for 'emergency power off' controls. It was not to be used for anything else. We knew that a *red* spec for the pointing stick tip would not get through the IBM standards maze. Sapper asked Yamazaki-san to make the tip magenta, which is a reddish-pink color. Yamakazi-san also labeled the parts drawing *magenta*, not *red*. It sailed right through the parts procurement process. Not too many people knew what color magenta was, but it sure wasn't the word *red*.

"Eventually, hundreds of magenta parts arrived and began to be assembled on the notebooks. IBM Standards went ballistic when they saw what appeared to be red controls in the middle of the keyboard. Yamazaki-san was immediately contacted, and he said that the Corporate Design Program had approved the color. I received a call regarding this non-standard red control issue. I stated to the caller that the part was not red. It was magenta. The Standards person was not buying my opinion and insisted that the parts were indeed red.

"We discussed the visual differences between magenta and red. I finally stated that the Corporate Design Program has color expertise, as well as adjudication responsibility, for such aesthetic issues. Therefore, magenta was different than red, and I would prove it if he wanted to escalate me to my management in Armonk. Realizing that to escalate my decision meant debating subjective opinion in front of senior management, the color magenta prevailed. Of course, over time, the color spec was gradually refined in Yamato to a richer color, very close to red."

With the major debates regarding the physical design resolved, IBM process required one final review. The pieces were in place: the innovative 10.4-inch display, a keyboard with TrackPoint, a 2.5-inch disk drive, and an innovative black industrial design. Adalio Sanchez, a future ThinkPad general manager, recalled the final design review meeting: "Mii-san held a major review meeting in Boca to ensure that the next IBM portable would give Compaq a run for their money.

"Mii-san was interested in this line of products for a variety of reasons. First, he thought that IBM should be the market leader in portables, just as they were in desktops. Second, he was the mastermind behind the formation of the Toshiba/IBM venture, Display Technologies, Inc., that was created to build color active matrix color TFT displays. Third, he had been pushing the storage group in Fujisawa, Japan, to develop a low-power, 2.5-inch disk because he saw that size as the future of portable computing. He needed IBM to deliver a credible offering that took advantage of these technologies.

"This meeting was held at a critical stage in the development cycle for the ThinkPad portable. Ikeda-san entered carrying a bunch of flip charts and proceeded to place the charts around the room. He had specifications on all the different sub-systems for this portable, including requirements for the 10.4-inch color TFT display and 2.5-inch disks. Mii-san was quite interested because this portable appeared to be the solution to finding homes for his pet projects. But, just like the Boca planners, he was doubtful that the design could be built, given the lack of success of past portable computers.

"Mii-san, in his typical Samurai warrior style, tortured the hell out of Ikeda-san. He challenged everything Ikeda-san said. Having just gotten off the plane from Japan, Ikeda-san tried valiantly to stay awake and to convince Nobi Mii that this was, in fact, the real thing. And, of course, it turned out to be the real thing. It was the design for what was to become the IBM ThinkPad 700C.

The IBM ThinkPad 700C: The machine that started it all.

"Mii-san forced the team to review its ability to deploy this new portable. Ironically, Ikeda-san had already done the work. It was a brutal meeting! But, at the end of the day, that meeting helped to ensure the quality of what we now know as ThinkPad.

"Why did we succeed this time versus our other attempts in portables? In the past, we undershot the target; we tried to match what the competition was doing, not leapfrog it. Now, we were trying to become a major player, to lead the market as we had done in desktop PCs. We knew that this time we had to overshoot the present target. In fact, when the ThinkPad actually announced, it was ahead of market expectations. By pushing IBM's technology in the storage area, in the cursor pointing area, and in the display panel area, we achieved our objective to deliver a portable computer that wowed the market. We leveraged IBM technology in a creative package that fulfilled the vision of where we believed the industry was headed."

Tim Bajarin, president of Creative Strategies and a premier mobile consultant, echoed Sanchez's comments: "When I met the group for the first time, they wanted feedback on their direction. Initially, I did not see product, but it was clear that they were considering mobile products as an important part of their overall strategy. At this point in the game, they had not evolved to the idea of a separate brand, but the people at the meeting convinced me that this was going to be a serious venture. This team was going to get everybody within IBM behind their effort.

"Although Toshiba and Compaq had significant leads in this segment, the group realized that IBM putting their label on a notebook machine was a very important statement. Portable computing had come out of the hobbyist phase. It no longer was an individual buy but instead represented more of an enterprise purchase. Corporate MIS who looked to IBM now saw this thing as a very legitimate tool and began bringing it into the enterprise as a part of their I/T strategy. By '92, two factors underscored this trend. Number one was IBM's logo and endorsement of the notebook platform. Two, this first ThinkPad notebook was very good. It was a solid system. It had some innovation. It hit a sweet spot in a market that was just starting to emerge, the mobile links to corporate enterprise.

"You know, the fact that they were able to get that first generation 10.4-inch panel was significant because it pushed them into an innovative state. More importantly, it gave them an exclusive on the world supply, which meant that they could bring out the products. One of IBM's problems, as in many of their product lines, is that they just have not had [the supply]...they were restricted by components. They didn't have everything necessary. By going to the 10.4-inch and getting the initial worldwide supply, it gave them a competitive edge, and that was really important because it gave them a statement."

Bajarin also offered his insights on the TrackPoint: "By 1992, Windows had finally started to be a serious operating system with a graphical interface that was best used with a mouse. One of the problems with portables, of course, was the lack of this device in a mobile location (for example, on an airplane) for easy input. So, to create something innovative for navigation on a portable was actually a very important part of the strategy. Even though some people still have trouble adjusting to it, the majority of the folks who use the TrackPoint adjusted to it very quickly. It became a very important part of IBM's integrated mobile solution."

The Authors' Insights

Taking the mobile journey required a great deal of planning. According to Professor Kosnik, establishing an enduring brand demanded addressing key fundamentals; IBM's renewed focus on portables met these demands. First, the executives cleared the path of obstacles by providing resources and the necessary empowerment to control their own destiny. Second, the warring geographic factions operated as a team and disregarded their cultural biases. Third, the product leapfrogged the competition. Through its 10.4-inch display, the TrackPoint, and its innovative industrial design, the portable achieved this monumental task. IBM's Yamato Labs were empowered to deliver the best portable product, and by their attention to detail, this objective was achieved. Fourth, everyone on the team was committed to its success. They met their schedules, the manufacturing volumes, and their costs. Finally, all these dimensions came together under one centralized focus—in this case, a newly established brand.

The ThinkPad 700C design resulted from a global collaboration across three continents and involving numerous design centers. The players [Richard Sapper, Kazuhiko Yamazaki, Tom Hardy, and Ted Selker] worked across cultures and time zones to drive a change that altered IBM's role in the portable market. When the stars line up in the sky at the right time and in the right shape, a clear image develops that everyone can see, and it lasts for a long time. Such a line up of technologies, personnel, and timing allowed the IBM mobile team to create a breakthrough in personal computing. It was not any one thing, but a constellation of circumstances that enabled ThinkPad to thunder onto the protable computing scene.

CHAPTER 14

Developing the Brand

Brand is the personality or identity of a product, range of products, or an organization, derived from consumer perception of both tangible and intangible attributes.

—David Arnold, *The Handbook of Brand Management*

As the product crystallized, the U.S. marketing organization realized that they needed a name for this innovative notebook, known internally by its code name, *Nectarine*. All reports indicated that IBM had a successful product about to be announced. Focus group results were positive. Confidential briefings with major customers and analysts were also extremely positive. The challenge was to find a name that was as innovative as the product itself.

The mobile team wanted a name that would denote the personality of its new line of portable systems. The name had to convey an image of friendliness, eliminating the non-descriptive nomenclature associated with IBM's personal computer products of the late 1980s. The name needed some pizzazz that would complement the new technologies accompanying the emerging product family. Finally, the name had to be recognizable on a worldwide basis.

Recall that the mobile team had already started to fight the IBM bureaucracy of product naming with its first pen tablet, the IBM 2521 ThinkPad, shortened by the press to simply *IBM ThinkPad*. Denny Wainright had no way of knowing that he was championing a brand name so strong that it would eventually overshadow its parent company. The press had rallied around the name, and it was gaining favor with the consultants and analysts. It did not take a genius to realize that maybe the name for this new notebook was already in hand.

According to Leo Suarez, "Debate was lively over whether we should use the name *ThinkPad*, because ThinkPad was, at least to this point, a tablet computer, not a notebook PC. There was a lot of resistance by the tablet group to use *ThinkPad*, because it was their name. Even as late as July 1992—less than four months to announce—the marketing team was still referring to this product line as an extension to the Personal Systems/2 family and batting around names like the *PS/2 486 33*, the *LP100*, and others that were even worse. Bruce Claflin showed his leadership and market acumen on this decision. He told us, 'Hey, look. *ThinkPad* is a great name. It sounds great. It tests well. We're going to use it. I don't care about the tablet group. We're going to use *ThinkPad*.' He just made an executive decision."

Kathy Vieth, one of the executives who claimed the name *ThinkPad* as hers, recalled the notebook naming debate: "When I thought about it, I got very excited. I obviously had thought it was a great name for our pen tablet, but it was being wasted on an unsuccessful product. After all, the word *THINK* had been IBM founder Thomas Watson's pet expression; *ThinkPad* would clearly come to mean a method by which people could do their thinking. It's funny, considering how big the mobile business has become.

The single most important thing the pen group did during that hell ride in Boca Raton was to come up with the *ThinkPad* name. It is now the most well-known and respected brand in the portable computer industry."

Maurice Fletcher, in his efforts to market the first truly innovative notebook, knew that this was an important decision: "I think the brand equity started with the name. The name was not going to be *ThinkPad*, although to be honest I don't remember what is was going to be. Scott [Bower] and I felt strongly, from the U.S. perspective, that *ThinkPad* was the name for our flagship product, as well as for the entire line. Realize that, at the time, the PC Company tended to name each successive product with some numbering scheme that was not always consecutive or tied to each other. A lot of fighting occurred over this decision. We went to corporate naming for assistance, as well as the requisite approvals. Corporate naming hired an outside consultant to conduct a bunch of focus groups with probably fifteen or twenty names. *ThinkPad* was almost the unanimous choice. After another round of reviews, everyone was behind the name."

After the name *ThinkPad* was locked in, a model number system was necessary. During an interesting discussion with Jim Bartlett and Pete Leichliter, Leo Suarez described how the numbering scheme emerged: "We worked with Jim on the model designations. We wanted a simple numbering scheme to complement the *ThinkPad* name so that we wouldn't lose focus on the brand name. I suggested to Jim that we consider a numbering system similar to BMW's. I had just bought a BMW, so their number series was on my mind. We wanted to assign 700 to high-end series, reserve the 500 series for the mid range, and use the 300 series for the low end. We'd figure out the rest as we went.

"Claflin didn't like that scheme at first. He wanted a four-digit numbering system like Toshiba was using on its Toshiba Satellite

1000. Bartlett offered strong arguments in favor of our proposed three-digit sequence by saying, 'Leo's recommendation makes a lot of sense. We need to enhance the image of ThinkPad in the market. Using a system similar to the BMW model number series will help condition the market to think of ThinkPad as a quality brand.' Bartlett continued to work on Claflin until he eventually gave in."

Claflin was eventually proud of the name and the associated numbering scheme. In fact, he recalled that "after the ThinkPad came to market, I received a personal letter from T. J. Watson, Senior. He wrote that he was proud that IBM had taken his original idea of people thinking and applied it to such an innovative product. As a veteran IBM employee, that letter had a lot of significance."

After the product design was finalized and the name approved, it was time to concentrate on the announcement support plan. Pricing of the product was a critical component to this milestone. IBM was desperate for a blockbuster success in portables. The word came down from the Chairman's Office: "Price this product at whatever level you need in order to be successful." Market research indicated that IBM's pricing had to be below the competition because the portable reputation was so bad. Customers were not going to pay a premium for a system that had not proven itself in the market. So, despite its innovative features, the new ThinkPads were priced fifteen percent under Toshiba's best system.

Claflin described the pricing discussions: "After we had decided our pricing strategy, I found out that the PC Company's chief financial officer [CFO] wanted to price the system even lower than our fifteen percent. He had already informed Cannavino about this change. Now, think about the hierarchy. Cannavino's CFO was higher than me in the organization, but I called Cannavino anyway. I told him that I was calling in my chit for taking this job. I reminded him that he had given me carte blanche to run this portable business. I told him to get his finance guy out of my business. This guy was giving the machine away and cheapening it. Based on our technology alone, I knew that it didn't need to be priced that low. Cannavino was true to his word. He said, 'Bruce, you make whatever decision you want on this price.' I really respected him for giving me that support."

These decisions were possible because the brand team had been given far-reaching responsibilities. As part of the pricing effort, for instance, Scott Bower not only had direct responsibility for the marketing programs but had matrix management responsibility for the financial community and the competitive analysis group. These linkages, when coupled with the executive support, shaped the ThinkPad perspective. It enabled quick pricing and marketing decisions because the team owned the P&L responsibility. The brand was the hardware. The brand was software. The brand was services and support. The brand was everything!

As the team prepared to announce the ThinkPad 700, they realized that they didn't have any money to fund advertising and public relations (PR). By late 1992, the advertising budgets had already been allocated to cover the other personal computer programs around the world. Simply put, there was no money for ThinkPad.

Claflin reminisced, "The people who controlled those budgets were field managers who didn't report to me. They reported to Bob Corrigan, head of the PC Company. Corrigan was under enormous pressure at the time to cut expenses because the PC business, overall, wasn't doing very well. We escalated our need to Corrigan, who said, 'We're not going to squeeze the introduction of this new portable computer. That would be penny-wise, pound-foolish.' He gave us ten million dollars to do the initial advertising and promotions. Corrigan gets high marks for mandating this incremental investment in advertising. In retrospect, we might not have experienced our initial success if Corrigan hadn't stepped up to the plate and given us the money. He is the unsung hero in the ThinkPad story.

"We took those funds and spent them wisely. I asked Bartlett to make sure we got the biggest 'bang for the buck' possible. Bartlett was very important to us at this stage. There were lots of comments about his personality at the time, but I can say without equivocation that he was an extremely important member of our team. He came in as an outsider and suffered from all the natural elements at IBM that were likely to repel him. IBM didn't hire outsiders at that time, and, frankly, Bartlett didn't have the best style to ingratiate himself into the IBM culture.

"But I recognized early on that this guy was a gem. In fact, I often told him that he was a 'diamond in the rough.' He knew the industry. He knew the influencers in the industry. He knew the people who could help us become a success or not. We were in the industry, but we weren't a part of it. Bartlett came in and quickly became my tutor. He explained the industry and the competitors. He explained who the key industry influencers were. He introduced me to the key consultants and analysts. Bartlett's greatest contribution was to bring us into the industry; he taught us how to work with the industry, as opposed to sort of sitting outside it. His efforts were every bit as valuable as the funding we had received. Without him, I don't think we would have had the great product reviews we had at the announcement of this product."

Bartlett took his role seriously and started to review all the marketing programs surrounding the upcoming product launch. His efforts started one of the great internal struggles between Bartlett and the marketing team headed by Scott Bower. Bartlett was not impressed with the marketing team's key messages and wanted the advertising program reworked. Bartlett won some battles and lost others. One of the scrimmages he won was increasing airport signage, because he knew that the potential customers for the ThinkPad 700 traveled frequently on airplanes. In comparison, he lost his bid to cancel the first advertising program.

Maurice Fletcher, who reported to Scott Bower, offered this insight: "We had a worldwide launch meeting in Boca Raton to review the October '92 products and marketing plans. We had decided earlier to do something that I don't think the PC Company had done before—use an outside agency to assist with the launch. We hired Jennings and Company. We also started to own the advertising and collateral materials for our products. We did everything as colorfully as possible, in contrast to other PC Company brochures, which were factual and practical and accompanied a bland product shot on a white background. If you looked at the first ThinkPad 'Facts and Figures' brochure, you would see color, pizzazz, and the *ThinkPad* name prominently displayed. We took a lot of risks in developing an advertising campaign that was very dramatic and put us head and shoulders above the competition."

Scott Bower told an interesting story about the initial ad campaign: "The first ThinkPad ad showed a picture of an IBM mainframe and a red Maserati. The tagline read, 'Its mother was the mainframe, its father was a Maserati.' We did a great deal of research and found out that we needed to put some fun into the advertising. IBM's persona was very stoic, straight-laced; this was the right time for an element of irreverence in the advertising. We thought this might help to highlight that we were something different but yet tied to our legacy of computer power.

"We went forward to Cannavino because he had asked to review the total marketing and advertising program behind this new product line. Quite honestly, he was underwhelmed with the ad. I responded, tongue in cheek, that I appreciated his input, but that we were going to run the ad anyway. Once again, Claflin's status and empowerment came into play. We ran the ad, and it was, by far, the most successful ThinkPad ad. We spent about seven million dollars in two and a half months at the end of 1992 and launched the ThinkPad line of products. Despite the success that accompanied this expenditure, I actually had to fight for funding the next year because we went to a two billion dollar backlog almost immediately. Of course, our rationale for continuing to advertise was that we were building a brand and that when we eventually caught up with demand, we wanted people to recognize us. Many of the executives at the time did not comprehend that there was more to a brand than just hardware."

The team augmented this print ad with an inaugural launch campaign that featured the theme line "Use it wherever you think best," thus associating the *think* part of the product name with the idea of portability.[1]

According to Maurice Fletcher, "We felt that this tagline was particularly applicable to the travelling professional. We developed a plan to build a diorama for airports to draw the attention of our potential customer base. Many of these individuals would be passing through the airport, and we wanted them to see the message about ThinkPad.

"We also developed a campaign called *Good News about ThinkPad*. The campaign was an internal crusade directed at the sales force. Every press release with good news about ThinkPad was packaged and sent to the entire sales force. This had never been done before. We were building, and building, and building the momentum and confidence around the mobile products. We knew we had to do it both outside and inside IBM; why not link the two? By increasing the sales force's confidence, they started driving the business with the customers. It got the product off to a quick start and was the impetus to the backlog state.

1. Marty Brandt and Grant Johnson, *PowerBranding: Building Technology Brands for Competitive Advantage* (San Francisco: International Data Group, Inc., 1997), 129.

The first in a series of innovative brochures for the ThinkPad brand.
(Photo provided by IBM.)

"We had the keys to the portable kingdom at our disposal. First, there was the display panel stock. Second, Claflin arrived from Japan and established a vision for the team. Third, this vision drove changes in the product plan that resulted in innovative products and ways of doing business. Fourth, we did not follow the accepted naming convention of the PC Company and went with something with personality. Finally, we augmented a strong advertising and marketing campaign with a very aggressive pricing strategy. We lowered the price to below the standard U.S. profit target in order to interest customers to buy the product. We made ThinkPad a very sought-after product. Now, we just had to let everyone know about our progress."

October 5, 1992, was the official announcement of the ThinkPad line of notebook computers. A press conference was held at 590 Madison in New York City, the traditional site of personal computer announcements since 1987. Scott Bower, as director of Mobile Computing, IBM Personal Computer Company, highlighted this event: "We wanted to drive home the naming of our new product line at this first announcement. We wanted to stress that the *ThinkPad* brand name combined the name of the device with its benefit.

ThinkPad 700 / 700C	
Processor	486SLC/25 MHz
Memory	4MB/16MB
Disk	80MB/120MB
Display	Mono/10.4" Color TFT
Weight	6.5/7.6 lbs
Other	Full-size keyboard
Power Source	Battery with AC adapter

"Consider the most convenient device a person uses to sketch out an idea, outline a plan—it's a pad of paper. Portable computers enable the user to think more efficiently, wherever he or she happens to be. It was our intention to make *ThinkPad* synonymous with easy-to-use mobile computing that merged the functionality of a pad of paper with the benefits of state-of-the-art technology."

Tim Bajarin, noted consultant within the mobile market, echoed this sentiment on IBM's mobile brand strategy and its first product announcement: "First of all, the team leveraged the IBM name, a powerful brand in its own right. Second, perhaps most important, they created very specific ads instead of just doing branding strategies or logo-type IBM strategies for advertising. These ads showed why and how the ThinkPad would make the individual more productive. I think those specific ads, focused on productivity, gave people an understanding of why they needed a ThinkPad and made the initial market acceptance so successful."

Unfortunately, the press was not that interested in the initial ThinkPad announcement. Stronger tactics would be necessary to garner the interest of the industry.

The Authors' Insights

The brand concept was re-emerging within IBM and, especially, within the Personal Computer Company. Claflin was acting as the change agent to get IBM's portable business going. He staffed qualified personnel across the organization who believed in the team's mission.

With everything in place—the people, the product, the promotions—this newly formed team delivered innovative, quality products that commanded a recognizable, standalone name. Capitalizing on a name well received by the press, the name *ThinkPad* became the focal point for everything that was to come. The management team favored the name because of its tie to the original *THINK* sign that was pervasive throughout the company under IBM's founder, T.J. Watson—a decision indicative of the team's need to be grounded in traditional, established policies while forging ahead into new business areas. The press liked the name because it broke the boring nomenclature associated with *IBM Personal Systems/2*. Consumers liked the name because it was friendly yet powerful.

The ThinkPad team was executing Kosnik's Seven Qualities of Enduring Brands without any formal training or past experience in brand development. Each member of the team contributed to the effort, instinctively aware that it would take a balanced approach to establish ThinkPad as the most recognizable brand in portable computing history.

Industry Advisory Council member Rob Enderle summarized the brand effort: "IBM did the proper amount of advertising and marketing and general investment to make sure that the ThinkPad brand was both visible and recognized as something that related only to mobile computers."

CHAPTER 15

Unveiling a Masterpiece

The principal mark of genius is not perfection but originality, the opening of new frontiers.

—Arthur Koestler

Since its inception in the early 1980s, Fall Comdex has been the launch pad for innovative products; Fall Comdex 1992 was no exception. IBM's introduction of its ThinkPad line of portables was the first of many strong tactics to garner industry support. In an effort to establish itself with the key press and analysts, a full-scale effort was put in place to inform these key influencers of what IBM was doing. Gerry Purdy, then head of Mobile Computing at Dataquest, was invited to meet with IBM's portable team. Purdy was told that he would be meeting with Bruce Claflin and Jim Bartlett. Although Claflin was a new entity, Purdy knew Bartlett from his portable days at Zenith and NEC. Bartlett had a decent reputation in the portable field, which caused Purdy to wonder whether Bartlett had lost his marbles going to work for

IBM. IBM had not produced anything outstanding in the portable arena during the past ten years.

Purdy was curious about this meeting. He knew that IBM had had serious problems in recent years. Their portable computer efforts were constantly out of phase with the market, delivering products that never measured up to what the industry leaders were doing. But, when IBM asks you to visit, you do not refuse. He figured that it would be one of those quick meetings where you smile, act nice, and then leave with a ho-hum feeling. He was hoping that the meeting would be brief so that he could get back to meeting with the more important players in the mobile market.

Purdy took a taxi from the main floor of Comdex to the Alexis Park hotel, a small facility located off the strip. The Alexis Park catered to those executives not interested in Las Vegas gambling and was housing IBM executives during the show. Arriving at the Alexis Park, he followed the signs to the designated IBM waiting area. It looked like a very busy doctor's office, with five to ten other press representatives and analysts sitting there. A cadre of IBM PR personnel paraded back and forth from the inner sanctum with their clipboards in hand, trying to keep order in this chaotic environment.

On checking with one of the PR reps, Purdy was informed that IBM was running behind schedule and was asked to take a seat in the waiting area. He knew that IBM had developed a new portable computer but had not yet seen the press release. Because IBM had never done anything outstanding in portables, he had not spent much time focusing on its newest entry; so much was happening with the main portable players. But, the buzz on the Comdex show floor was about IBM's exciting announcement in portable computing. He decided to wait. Fifteen minutes later, the PR rep ushered one analyst out and then said, "Dr. Purdy, Mr. Claflin and Mr. Bartlett will see you now."

"Oh my," Purdy thought, "they are so formal about all this. It's so different from just sitting down with an executive on the show floor and having a chat." He was led into a hotel room that had been converted into a mini-conference room. Purdy sat at one end of a conference room table, with Jim Bartlett on his left and Bruce Claflin on his right. After introductions and an exchange of business cards, Bartlett and Purdy talked about their past involvement in portable computing.

Bartlett initiated the conversation: "Gerry, you probably wonder why someone like me would work for a company like IBM. Prior to my accepting this position, IBM showed me some advanced technology that would allow them to make truly advanced portable computers—better than anyone else in the world. I joined IBM because I realized that they are getting serious about portable computing.

"We have something to show you that is going to catch your attention. I got to see what we're going to show you before I joined the team. In a few minutes, I think you'll be just as impressed as I was. I think you'll go away from this meeting with an entirely new impression of IBM with respect to portable computing."

Knowing Bartlett's background and his reputation for not being easily impressed, Purdy questioned whether his own opinion about IBM not doing anything outstanding in portables was a bit premature. Following Bartlett's brief introduction, Bruce Claflin discussed his background and his recent move into this arena. The immediate question that came to Purdy's mind was why someone with such a strong track record within IBM would have taken this job. Why would Claflin be involved with such a miniscule part of IBM after running an organization of more than ten thousand people?

Bruce Claflin, the visionary behind the ThinkPad brand.

Claflin shed some light on this unspoken question: "IBM has created the most advanced portable computer ever announced. We believe that it's a breakthrough product. It is going to raise the bar for what is accepted in the portable market. We're calling it the

ThinkPad 700." Bartlett removed the cloth cover to unveil a solid-black notebook computer. Purdy thought, "Holy cow, what is going on here? IBM products aren't jet black. They're pearl white. Is this some kind of a joke?"

Claflin continued, "We have designed a portable computer that's truly distinctive, one that doesn't look like any IBM product you've ever seen before. It has a distinctive industrial design. We even developed a special coating in jet black so that it won't show fingerprints." Purdy knew that he was in the midst of an experience that was going to be very important to the computer industry and one that he would not forget for the rest of his career.

Bartlett added, "We have done something that users have wanted in portables but no one, not even Compaq, has been able to do. We have incorporated the world's largest color display in this new product. At a whopping 10.4-inch display [measured diagonally], it's a full two inches larger than anyone else's in the industry." Bartlett then opened the ThinkPad to demonstrate this large display. Purdy couldn't hold back his reaction; he was half laughing, half in shock. "Oh c'mon, you guys. This can't be true. How did you do this? Are you serious? Does this thing actually work?"

Bartlett and Claflin smiled and did not say a thing. Bartlett reached over and flipped the ON switch. The size and color of the display were remarkable. Bartlett went on to describe the system's other features: "In addition to the 10.4-inch display, we have incorporated an entirely new way to control the cursor. It's called *TrackPoint*, and it sits right on the keyboard between the G and the H keys. We have also made sure that the keyboard is just what you'd expect from IBM. It has a 25MHz 486 Intel SL processor, 4MB of RAM, a 2400 bps modem, and a whopping 120MB of disk storage. And we're going to aggressively price it at $4,350."

Purdy was impressed. No, he was in shock. What he had thought was likely to be the least important meeting during Fall Comdex had turned out to be the most significant event. Obviously, this product was going to create quite a stir in the industry. Even more importantly, the product was going to sell extremely well. After some additional conversation on the product's features and functions, Claflin asked, "Gerry, what do you think? Has IBM arrived in portable computing?"

"Bruce," Purdy responded, "you certainly have the most impressive portable computer I have ever seen. The press will love it. Customers will love it. That's obvious. But, you really asked me a different question. You asked me whether IBM was now a player in portable computing. You have a long way to go to gain respect from analysts like me. Other companies like Compaq have been working with analysts for years. You're the new player on the block. Yes, you have a wonderful new portable computer, but I think it's going to take some time for you to become known as a credible player in this market."

Purdy feared that his reply might have upset Bartlett and Claflin. He then experienced the first of many thoughtful replies from Claflin, who leaned back in his chair, crossed his arms, and responded, "That's very interesting. I think you may be right. What do you think we should do in order to create credibility with key industry influencers?"

Purdy responded, "Well, you might want to develop a relationship with the movers and shakers in the portable market. Bring them together and try to 'get personal' with them. Demonstrate that you value their opinion. If you're doing a good job at product design and responding to their input, you'll get their support. If not, they'll tell you as much."

Purdy could see that Claflin was interested in his comments. However, he was surprised when Claflin replied, "Gerry, I like your idea. Would you be willing to work with us to put such a group together? I'd like you to work with Jim and make this happen for us. I want this to be your contribution to IBM and our new ThinkPad effort."

Purdy was thrilled to be asked to work with IBM to create such a group. Bartlett and he agreed to follow up the week after Comdex and put a consulting agreement together to cover the project. After the meeting, he was escorted out of the motel briefing center. Standing on the sidewalk in the bright Las Vegas sun, he stood there for a moment reflecting on what had just happened. He could not believe what he had just experienced.

Purdy was not the only one who could not believe what was happening at Comdex. All the Boca Raton portable team was in Las Vegas for the introduction of the ThinkPad line. In addition to the personal meetings with key press, consultants, and analysts, numerous product demonstrations were available on the trade show floor. Attendees were three and four deep at every ThinkPad pedestal, quite the opposite of the ho-hum interest in the other PC Company products. The ThinkPad products were also highlighted in the keynote address given by Bob Corrigan, PC Company president. Attendees were barraged with ThinkPad messages wherever they went. Clearly, the new portable line was a "New Shade of Blue" for IBM.

But, even in this new "blue" environment, Claflin's grounding in IBM's basic beliefs was evident. He had planned a dinner celebration of the ThinkPad's growing success and invited the entire team. In addition to the Boca planning team, key marketing and development employees were also in attendance. It was the first such event outside IBM's hallowed halls for the newly formed portable team. Because the team was dispersed across the U.S., not to mention the world, it was the first chance for many people to get to know one another on a personal basis.

Dolly Salvucci, Bill Bailey, and Jean DiLeo, members of the ThinkPad team, sharing good times.

Although IBM guidelines at the time did not allow for alcoholic beverages, wine and beer were permitted at the dinner. Needless to say, the libation loosened up the group, and some good-natured teasing ensued.

The evening happened to be Jim Bartlett's fortieth birthday, and much of the teasing was directed toward him. He had a reputation for clean-cut living; no one on the team had ever heard him use a cuss word or seen him take a drink. A bet was made that evening to see whether any one could get Bartlett to swear. No one won that night! In fact, it would take almost a full year before Joe Formichelli arrived on the scene and actually made good on this challenge. By that time, the team had grown to know one another's strengths and weaknesses, and the world had realized that IBM was in the portable market to stay.

Bill Bailey, Jean DiLeo, Scott Bower, Pete Leichliter, Leo Suarez, Maurice Fletcher, Mike Mullins, Chuck Pecnik, and Roseann Conforti.

The Authors' Insights

IBM's launch of the ThinkPad at Fall Comdex 1992 was as powerful as its design. By the end of the show, the crowds were so heavy around the ThinkPad that nearby vendors were upset because people lingered in their booths, waiting to see ThinkPad up close and personal. The IBM ThinkPad 700C was clearly the "Best of Show" by all measures.

After bringing the team together with the singular vision of delivering the best portable in the industry, Claflin brought them together to celebrate their success. The team was proud of its efforts on all aspects of the ThinkPad business—from innovative design, to manufacturing, to marketing, and, finally, to managing

the influencers so that they would become IBM ThinkPad emissaries. The ThinkPad team had begun to build its network of
influencers, a network fundamental to the brand's success.

CHAPTER 16

Influencing the Influencers

My view is that to sit back and let fate play its hand out and never influence is not the way man was meant to operate.

—John Glenn

In 1992, IBM's market image was that of a monolith with no personality and no linkage or sense of the market. Poor market awareness of IBM's offerings was rampant, and those offerings were given very low consideration rates. Bruce Claflin and Jim Bartlett realized that this position could easily cripple their emerging portable products and decided to create a focused market influencer program. The week after Fall Comdex 1992, Bartlett and Gerry Purdy met to discuss the objectives, deliverables, budget, and schedule for such a project.

Purdy had considered the brief discussion held in Las Vegas and brought forward his plan to create the Mobile Computing Industry Advisory Council (IAC). The council would have three objectives: (1) to increase market awareness and acceptance of the ThinkPad line of products, (2) to increase consideration rates, and (3) to provide the foundation for the re-engineering of the customer requirements gathering and market influencer process. Purdy felt that the council should meet twice a year, typically at an off-site destination for a day and a half. IBM should offer to pick up expenses but not pay any honorarium.

At this first meeting, Bartlett and Purdy reviewed a list of council candidates. Although many were competitors to Purdy's role at Dataquest, IBM needed to bring together the most influential and knowledgeable people covering mobile computing. There was one exception to this: Journalists who did not sign confidentiality agreements would not be invited. Because these were primarily editors who worked for daily and weekly publications, this eliminated about half the candidates on the list. After adding the editors from leading major monthly publications, the candidate list was about twenty people.

Working together, they added a personality profile to each name, taking into account personal interests and backgrounds. A projection was made on how each might interact with the other leading influencers on the list. This exercise narrowed the list to fifteen. To be conservative, Purdy recommended an initial goal of getting half the targeted individuals to attend. After all, there was no known history that any one had ever put a group of analysts and long lead press together in the same room for this type of meeting. Bartlett was concerned that the attendees might not be willing to share their thoughts and recommendations when their peers were present. Because Bartlett was fairly new to IBM, he was not as familiar with IBM's non-disclosure agreement (NDA) process. Purdy felt that by running the meeting under strict NDA, whereby everyone would be bound to maintain the confidentiality of the topics and opinions, open discussion was likely to occur.

Purdy then recommended that IBM present its confidential product plans. At this point, Bartlett said, "Wait a minute. We can't go in front of a bunch of analysts and editors and tell them our confidential product plans. They'll go public with it, or even worse, they'll tell our competitors what we're doing. No, that just won't work. I don't think there's an executive in IBM that would agree to that."

"Jim, I appreciate your position and concern," replied Purdy, "but I have to tell you that if you bring such a group together and just sit there and ask them to tell you what they think, they are going to feel used. They will think that you're only interested in getting free consulting. For this to work, you have to share your plans. This group will respect IBM for trusting them and wanting them to be a part of your future."

At this point, Bartlett indicated that he wanted one of his people, Debi Dell to join the meeting. Dell, as product marketing manager in Boca Raton, was a part of Bartlett's three-person team. Bartlett got Dell on the phone, brought her up to speed on the development of the IAC, and asked her to work the details as the program manager.

Bartlett, Purdy, and Dell discussed the issue of presenting confidential information at the IAC meeting. Purdy felt strongly that they should. Bartlett felt that they should not. Dell thought about it and then proposed a compromise, recommending that IBM "scrub" its confidential product plans, using different code names from the ones used internally and deleting non-essential product specs. Thus, if the code name for one of the future products showed up in the press, they could pinpoint the source as the IAC. They agreed that it was a workable alternative.

The next issue, after the attendee list and agenda topics, was the logistics. Purdy proposed that he initially contact the candidates to "sound them out" on their reaction to such a gathering. Dell said that she would manage the meeting logistics, including a personally signed invitation letter from Bruce Claflin. They set mid March 1993 as the proposed date for the first meeting. Early January, the team met via teleconference to review progress. Purdy reported unanimous support from everyone on the list. Even better, everyone said that they would personally participate if they were invited.

Overwhelmed with this response, the group was convinced that the first meeting had to be held somewhere special. Purdy recommended that the first IAC meeting be held at the Phoenician in Scottsdale, Arizona. Dell recommended that the meeting be referred to as "THINK Tank." This name was not used after the first meeting, however, because the corporate naming committee got wind of it and found that it was not available for use.

The year 1992 was not a stellar financial one for IBM, and the ThinkPad team had not had enough time to prove its viability. Despite financial restrictions, Claflin authorized the initial IAC meeting. He sanctioned the activities and logistics because of his inherent belief that ThinkPad would benefit from this effort. No expense was spared to make the founding members feel that this was, indeed, a unique opportunity. Claflin recalled this decision: "I thought that creating the IAC was an important thing to do. However, I was really opposed to holding the meeting at an expensive resort. Jim and Debi bid hard to hold the initial meeting at a very nice place because IBM had to make a strong statement to the analyst community. They knew that it had to be more special than just flying people into Boca. I'm glad they persevered; it turned out to be the right decision. And I even learned something in the process."

Unanimous support from the industry community for this event indicated the following:

- Meeting with IBM on a regular basis had value, especially because IBM had just announced the most exciting new portable computer in the market.

- Being part of the IAC enabled the attendees to enjoy an important "club-like" aura—an exclusive chance to meet with their peers at an event from which they would not want to be excluded.

- Seeing and critiquing IBM's future plans in portable computing was something they had never had a chance to do before.

- Meeting the management and development team responsible for the launch of the ThinkPad 700C portable computer, with its 10.4-inch display, would provide insight into one of the industry's most exciting milestones.

The team decided that the initial charter members of the IAC would be invited to participate for two years. This group included the following people:

- Bill Ablondi (BIS Strategic Decisions, renamed Giga Information Group as it operates today; now in his own venture, MarketMap)

- Tim Bajarin (Creative Strategies)

- Kim Brown (InfoCorp; now with Dataquest)

- David Coursey (*P.C. Letter*; now with Coursey.com)

- Bill Howard (*PC Magazine*)

- Leslie Fiering (Gartner Group)

- Jim Louderback (PC Week Labs; now with ZDTV)

- Peter Otte (*Portable Computing Magazine*, later acquired by Mobile Office)

- Gerry Purdy (Dataquest; now president of Mobile Insights)
- Andy Reinhart (*Byte Magazine*; now with *Business Week*)
- Andy Seybold (*Seybold Outlook*)
- Bruce Stephen (IDC)

The meeting went off without a hitch. The analysts and editors signed their confidentiality agreements and shared their thoughts and ideas. IBM shared its plans. A bonding occurred between the IBM management and the members of the IAC. Many of these influencers are still on the council today.

At the conclusion of the first IAC, Claflin, Bartlett, Purdy, and Dell held a debriefing. Dell was asked to manage the future meetings and council strategies, which she did from 1993 until 1995, when she transferred to IBM Global Services.

However, the IAC spawned interest in other affinity groups. Following the success of the initial IAC, the ThinkPad team created councils to focus on customers and the scientific community, as well as on brand management.

The Customer Advisory Council (CAC) started approximately six months after the IAC and was managed by Pete Leichliter. This effort consisted of two audiences of purchasers: road warriors and major accounts. The road warrior council focused on high-profile individuals who purchased for themselves or for small organizations. They were the mobile computing zealots. The major account CAC included large corporate MIS managers who purchased portable computer products. Participants for this council were recruited via personal contact, marketing team recommendations, user groups, and the Internet forum. Like the IAC, these members were required to sign non-disclosure agreements (NDAs) and were strongly urged not to send substitutes to the meetings.

Corporations involved in the early CACs included Bell South, Coopers and Lybrand, Chemical Bank, Eastman Kodak, Glaxo, General Motors, I.D.S., International Monetary Fund, J. C. Penney, Merrill Lynch, Nationwide Insurance, New York Life, Nike, Procter and Gamble, Spring, State Farm, Travelers, USAA, and Whirlpool. Participation by these companies in the ThinkPad CAC in no way implied endorsement of the product or supplier. In fact, because of the company policy of not appearing to publicly endorse a product or supplier, only Frank Wilbur, a professor at Syracuse University and associate vice president for undergraduate studies, offered his insights into this ThinkPad practice.

A member of the IBM Mobile "Road Warrior" Customer Advisory Council, Wilbur was invited to participate because of his documented interest in mobile computing and its security aspects. He was intrigued by the concept of small computers. He recognized that within a university environment, the broadest number of applications probably existed. Geologists doing field experiments used computers. Nurses used them to take bedside notes. Professors exploited them to do their lectures and presentations. The list was endless and, thus, so were the technology requirements.

Wilbur recalled, "I saw one of the first ThinkPads and remember thinking how well engineered it was. I knew that I wanted the University to hook up with this IBM mobile group because everything—the systems, the presentations, and the meetings—was done with such care and precision. Finally, IBM was getting it right. They were building something technologically sound.

"Just as people were beginning to admire what IBM had designed and produced, they were also becoming angry because the ThinkPads were generally not available. The council highlighted the frustration to the mobile team. They're doing better by introducing products with enough initial volume to meet demand.

"A diversity of ThinkPad models provided the appropriate price/performance point, whether for a student, a faculty member, an administrator, or an executive. They have never produced a 'clunker.' The engineering, the packaging, and the testing that went into every ThinkPad gave me the necessary assurance that I could recommend these products with confidence. I knew that it was money extremely well invested.

"I knew that if a faculty member or student bought one, IBM's renowned service commitment was behind it. They always supported their products. No matter what model you bought, when you could get one, if anything went wrong with it, the turnaround time on service and repair was superb.

"There was a downside to the diversity of the ThinkPad line. I think they got themselves into supporting more products and models than was wise or financially affordable. At one time, it seemed they had something like twenty-seven different products with hundreds of different model configurations. Now, they have honed that down to a much smaller family of five basic Think Pad models (IBM ThinkPad 300s, 500s, 600s, and 700s and the iSeries).

"Over time, the team developed a reputation for developing a jewel of a computer, something that was beautifully engineered, that worked, and that was supported. They also offered innovative, integrated solutions as part of the ThinkPad experience. When you bought a ThinkPad, most of what you needed to do your job was already built in. It was a very workable package out of the box.

"The mobile team was customer oriented from the very beginning. They were receptive to creative ideas and solutions. They were customer oriented before customer orientation was the prevalent culture within the PC Company. IBM's mobile group seemed to have a culture of its own.

"The percentage of PC sales at Syracuse University has increased every year for the last three years in favor of notebooks. Students are simply bringing portables to campus directly from home and using things like port replicators to attach to the campus network. The idea of throwing their portables into their backpacks is very appealing. Unfortunately, IBM hasn't paid much attention to young people in their marketing. I think that's a mistake. IBM should pay attention to the next generation of potential users by having products that perform well, are rugged enough to stand up to the use of young people, and create brand loyalty."

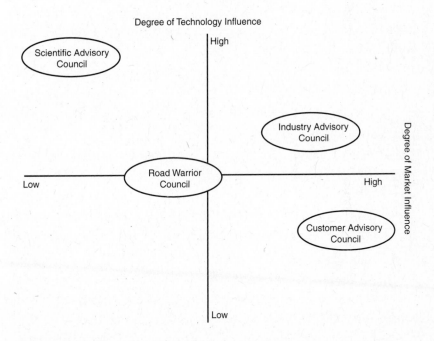

Advisory Council Positioning
IBM Mobile Computing

In 1994, IBM extended the IAC franchise to other geographies, including Europe, Japan, Latin America, and Asia Pacific (South).

It followed the original councils with the Scientific Advisory Council (SAC), which was composed of recognized scientists from business and academia. SAC's purpose was to provide longer-term potentially paradigm-breaking perspectives on technology. More recently, the Brand Management Council (BMC), managed by Kevin Clark, brought together consultants and consumer packaged-goods experts in brand management.

The ThinkPad management took these councils very seriously. The participating team always met before the meeting to contemplate the personalities and changing interests of the participants, as well as to review presentations and ensure message consistency. The team reminded itself that council meetings were not times to preach, sell, and convince; they were to be a dialog with the participants to understand their opinions. At the preliminary meeting, the management team reviewed the number of IBM attendees and restricted access. Too often, in the early days of the councils, there would be more IBM participants than council members.

Before arriving, each council member received a letter personally signed by the current ThinkPad general manager, an agenda, and information about the meeting logistics. Meetings alternated between the East and West coasts. The room was configured in a big U shape to maximize the interaction and dialog with the staff and council members. The intensity of the day's interactions was mitigated by an enjoyable entertainment activity in the evening, encouraging frank personal discussions with the key influencers.

To develop a sense of belonging, the participants received mementos at each meeting. Gifts included a Lands End–style logo'd jacket, a leather carrying case, a quality desk clock, book ends, and a crystal candy jar—each tied to the meeting's theme. Often, the gift was tied to the location of the meeting, for example, wine from the Napa Valley. Every member received a plaque for display in his or her office to promote the "special affiliation" the council member had with IBM. Also, every member was provided with an IBM ThinkPad, which was traded out once a year for the latest and greatest IBM had to offer.

Different councils changed the agenda and the evening entertainment. The fall 1993 meeting was held in the Lincolnshire Marriott Resort, outside Chicago. For entertainment, a bus ride into the loop for dinner and a night at Second City were arranged. A key lesson learned from this particular evening was to ensure that the entertainment was easily accessible *and that the bus driver knew how to get to the destination.* The council members and attending IBM executives ended up with twenty minutes to eat dinner and make the show on time! If it had not been for the beer and wine on the bus, the evening would have been a disaster.

Another revealing evening occurred in April 1994 when the council meeting was held in Boca Raton, Florida. Because the agenda was packed full, Jim Bartlett decided that he wanted to present the current brand awareness study at dinner. Dinner was usually preceded by a hospitality hour, so attendees were quite relaxed and in good humor. After the main course was served, Bartlett stood up to present. It was impossible for him to garner anyone's attention, especially after the management team had a birthday cake delivered to Joe Formichelli in the middle of Bartlett's most insightful chart. All focus was lost. The entire group began to laugh and talked of not having to do homework after a hard day's work. Bartlett realized that it was a hopeless cause and eventually sat down. Everyone, including Bartlett, laughed. Needless to say, no future evening presentations were ever scheduled!

Learning from experience, IBM adjusted the logistics over time. Attire moved from business to business casual. The addition of a telephone line at each seat so that each council member had access to the Internet during the meeting was a major improvement. Despite initial reservations that providing Internet connections would be a distraction, the ThinkPad team and council members found that there was actually more communication and listening than without the connection. Providing a means of confidential communications, council members and IBM staff often exchanged emails during the meeting about the topic being presented.

The IAC has existed for six years, meeting twice a year. Even with the changing players on both sides of the equation, a surprisingly strong sense of community has developed between the management and the council, who often act more like a single body. Meeting summary reports have indicated major consensus on many critical issues. Management knows the council members, and the council members know (and have access to) ThinkPad's senior management. Trust has developed between the groups and among their members. As Bruce Claflin remarked, "The advisory councils gave us better advice than expensive, formal market research. They were enormously important to us, worth more than we spent on them when compared to the results from many of the market research projects."

The Authors' Insights

The introduction of a product or service dictates the need to "take the message" to the market. Through the normal PR process, the press, industry analysts, and potential buyers want to understand what the product or service is, how it's positioned, and its pricing and distribution. The depth of knowledge required to answer such questions results in an "expert opinion coefficient."

Portable computers have a high *expert opinion coefficient*, which means that experts greatly influence the purchase decision. Because portable computers have ever changing and sometimes hard-to-understand technology, experts must describe the features and functions in terms of benefits to the purchaser or end user. By developing a close relationship with key influencers, IBM ensured that the feature/function, price, and benefit relationship was clearly articulated.

An important, often forgotten quality of enduring brands is the orchestration of a network of industry influencers. These influencers not only know about the product or service but also act as emissaries for the company. By cementing relationships with council members, IBM garnered ideas for new products and services. External to IBM, these relationships influenced mind share, generated positive press, and acted as an extremely inexpensive form of promotion. An additional benefit of these symbiotic relationships was a significant information source on major industry trends because council members had the "inside scoop" on the entire personal computer industry. Finally, IBM effectively managed problems arising with the ThinkPad product line because council members were immediately briefed on the situation, thus increasing their understanding and helping with IBM's "spin control" on the situation. Maintaining this approach has allowed IBM to build an enduring brand in ThinkPad.

GOOD THOUGHTS ON THINKPAD

LOOK MOUSE, NO HANDS

The IBM ThinkPad 700C has pizzazz! The 10.4-inch diagonal-active-matrix screen is 50% larger than most other notebook screens and offers resolution as crisp and clear as some color desktop computers... The TrackPoint looks like a pencil eraser but acts like a mouse, allowing the user to manipulate it while hands never leave the keyboard.

BusinessWeek

January 11, 1993
Best New Product Award.

The best notebook I've ever used. Clearly the product of the year.

IBM ThinkPad

IBM has finally hit the bull's eye. The new line of ThinkPads offer a splendid combination of performance, expandability and overall high quality .. In addition, IBM's service and support policy may be the best anywhere... We're greatly pleased to be able to say such good things, and are certain that they will be echoed by anyone who buys one of these perfectly dandy computers.

December 22, 1992

LAPTOP

Buyers Guide and Handbook
December, 1992

Speed, beauty, hard-nosed practicality and yes, grace make 700C an easy choice for an MVP.

December, 1992
1992 MVP Award.

IBM has finally come to play in the portable market... not only with a new portable computer, but also a whole new company-- The IBM Personal Computer Company... The colorful ThinkPad 700C offers the largest color screen of any notebook, plus a powerful processor, removable hard drive-- and a reasonable price... If you're looking for an outstanding laptop computer, it's time to think ThinkPad Time to think --IBM.

PC LapTop

February, 1993

I was blown away by the quality of the color display and the speed of the (ThinkPad 700C)... This is the computer to buy.

The Washington Times

December 21, 1992

Pound for pound, IBM's new 700C color ThinkPad may be the best notebook computer money can buy. The 700C could easily double duty as a desktop system. You'd be hard-pressed to find a better value.

The Seattle Times

December 15, 1992

Original permission to reprint granted to IBM for marketing use.

1993–1995:
THE BRAND EMERGES

The 5th Wave   By Rich Tennant

CHAPTER 17

Errors in Judgment

Never let the fear of striking out get in your way.

—Babe Ruth

After the 1992 Fall Comdex show, the ThinkPad line received significant press coverage and several key industry awards. Orders piled up, and the demand exceeded the product's lifetime forecast. IBM had made an impact on the portable market.

As a well-directed manager, Bruce Claflin did not just sit on his laurels after the successful product launch. In January 1993, as Claflin sat with Scott Bower, head of U.S. ThinkPad marketing, they reflected on the months since they had joined the portable team. The ThinkPad product line had announced the previous October and was enjoying enormous market success. Claflin and Bower decided to make a list of everything they thought had been done right in launching the ThinkPad 700C. Then, they made a list of everything they thought they did wrong. The list of what was right had five line items; the list of what was wrong was considerably longer.

Claflin commented, "This exercise demonstrated that, in order to succeed, you only had to get the basics right. We had a great product. We priced it right. We promoted it properly. The channel was ready to sell it, and they were trained. That's what we put on our list of what we did right. By comparison, the things we did wrong were less important. We recognized that, by doing the basics right, it did not make a big difference if we failed with the little things.

"So, there we were in January 1993. We had this runaway best seller, and we were short on supply. Absolutely nothing on God's green earth could be done about it. Only one place in the world made that 10.4-inch screen, and it was the DTI factory in Japan. There was nowhere else in the world we could go to get that critical part. We had been pumping lots of money into the plant and taking up capacity with the 10.4-inch displays. We couldn't keep up with demand. Things started to get ugly! Our major accounts became really upset with IBM for not fulfilling their orders."

According to Claflin's right-hand man, Scott Bower, "Momentum was building. People were starting to say, 'I have to have a ThinkPad.' We kept promoting the line to highlight the new brand. However, because product was in short supply, customers felt that we were holding back inventory and only sending systems to our key accounts. Every quarter, we built more ThinkPads. We kept taking the numbers up. We couldn't catch the demand. Although manufacturing was running as fast as it could, the demand remained unsatisfied. At one point, the backlog was more than two billion dollars. With customers waiting for the product, it was the first time in a long time that the PC Company did not take a price action on its portables." Both Claflin and Bower knew that, at this point, the display was the underpinning to most of their problems.

Joe Formichelli, in his role as vice president of monitors and displays, offered this perspective: "As for DTI, I was the guy blamed for not supplying Claflin with all the active matrix 10.4-inch panels needed for those new IBM ThinkPad 700s. Back then, those little suckers [displays] cost more than a thousand dollars apiece. They eventually went down the price curve, but the starting cost for each version, whether it was 10.4-, 11.3-, or 12.1-inch, was always about the same. I made a lot of trips to Japan to figure out why we couldn't produce more. I wanted to know whether it was Toshiba's problem or IBM's problem, or something else. Claflin and I joined at the hip really fast.

"Over time, we slowly increased DTI's capacity by an order of magnitude, as well as produced larger size displays. Claflin did a fantastic job, not only with ThinkPad but also with containing the image problem that could have arisen because of this supply problem. I was so envious of him and ThinkPad because nobody really cared about monitors. Monitors didn't have the sex appeal that the ThinkPad had. They had that great ad with the headline, 'Its mother was the mainframe, its father was a Maserati.' I was really jealous. What could I do to advertise a monitor?"

Claflin added detail to the supply problem story: "It was a worldwide problem. I remember a meeting in Germany with customers. Our German management was hosting the meeting. While we were sitting at lunch, our IBM ThinkPad marketing manager said, 'IBM has really screwed up the ThinkPad. We can't get any units, and our customers are screaming for them. Why can't IBM do anything right. This is disgraceful!' Of course, I'm a little embarrassed personally. But, I turned to him and said, 'Well, we certainly are having difficulty producing enough ThinkPads, but let me put this in perspective. Last year, IBM sold two hundred million dollars in portable products and lost two hundred million dollars doing it. This year, we're going to sell more than a billion dollars and be profitable. IBM could probably do with a few more failures like this.'

"You've heard the expression that too much of a good thing can be bad. Well, we were experiencing that with ThinkPad. The mood inside IBM was getting quite ugly because of the ThinkPad's success. Typical of IBM, the political battles were starting, and the jealousy of less successful organizations was impacting strategy decisions. The field was also growing ugly because our customers were getting frustrated trying to get this innovative product. You'd think it would have been a euphoric time, but it was really horrible. For about a minute, I was giddy as a school kid, but then, reality sunk in. We had to do enormous amounts of damage control. We even introduced a ThinkPad that used a 9.5-inch screen in order to try to balance the demand. We did everything we could to try to capture the demand. Unfortunately (yet perhaps fortunately), almost two years passed before we could satisfy the demand."

As was Claflin's style, in the spring of 1993, he held a meeting at the Hilton Hotel in Danbury, Connecticut. The whole team convened to review ThinkPad's status, including Scott Bower, Jim Bartlett, Patty McHugh, Nick King, Higuchi-san, and Bob Kanode. Kanode, responsible for total manufacturing, recalled the meeting: "Bruce brought in two facilitators who led us through a total assessment of our efforts with the ThinkPad 700C. We learned about the concept of branding. We explored such questions as where were we going, what was the business model, what we had created, and what did we want to do next? We spent two intense days locked up with these guys. They were putting our ideas on three-by-five inch cards and sticking them all over the walls.

"We were really surprised when we realized just how successful we were. We came out of that meeting understanding that we had a tremendous responsibility to convert that initial success into a worldwide business for IBM. It was a humbling experience. We knew that we could not just sit there and bask in the glory of what

ThinkPad had already become. We had to come together as a team to leverage our initial success into an enduring brand."

In April 1993, IBM voted in Louis V. Gerstner as its chairman. Gerstner, a strong financial executive, brought his own team, a team driven by dollars and cents, to drive the company's re-engineering program. The Personal Computer Company, of which ThinkPad was now just one brand and Mobile Computing was just one brand team, was initially affected by the decisions of this financial, non–computer industry literate management committee.

After numerous reviews, the committee acknowledged the portable market's expanding opportunity and associated profitability. The mobile team did not experience resource reductions as severely as the rest of the brand teams. What the ThinkPad team could not avoid, however, was the effect of the committee's decisions on such items as product naming, advertising, and even the pre-loaded operating system software. This management team also changed the rules of empowerment under which Claflin had accepted his role as general manager.

Shortly after Gerstner came on board, Claflin got word through the grapevine that IBM's chairman was very upset about the ThinkPad supply situation. The chairman viewed it as the number one customer satisfaction issue because so many top customers were complaining that they could not get any ThinkPads. He felt IBM had a huge failure on its hands. He wanted to know who was running the ThinkPad operation so inadequately and why customers could not get any units. The supply problem was becoming so intense that Gerstner even received a ransom note from some unidentified individual who craved a ThinkPad. The note was delivered in a brown envelope, and the message was created using words cut from newspapers and magazines.

OK ! **Listen** & listen Good ,

You Have WHAT I NEED

and I Want it NOW !

I'm DESPERATE !

This is *The* ONLY chance I have to

PROVE to You I *mean* BUSINESS .

So, put one of These

in a Brown Paper BAG

And wait Further Instruction

The ransom note.

Claflin heard that his job was at risk. Gerstner's new team brought forward well-intentioned suggestions for the ThinkPad team, but they were not really helping the situation. According to Claflin, "I was feeling particularly vulnerable over all this. I was hoping that senior management, those between Gerstner and me in the organization, would explain how we got to where we were. It was an amazingly good story, not a bad one. But, they didn't tell him the whole story."

Claflin continued, "I found out that Gerstner liked to read status reports. I sent him an eight-page history of the ThinkPad's creation: where we were, why we were proud of our success, and what we were doing to satisfy demand. This turned out to be an important document and a smart action on my part. All of a sudden, although Gerstner was still upset over not being able to meet customer demand, he was no longer saying negative things about ThinkPad or the team. He eventually expressed pride in the ThinkPad success. About this same time, the *New York Times* ran a front-page article saying that ThinkPad was one of IBM's big successes. Gerstner finally let us know that he thought that we were managing the ThinkPad operation and our short supply in a proper way."

Despite the lack of supply, the team announced new ThinkPad models. Advertising and promotion programs continued in an effort to build recognition of the ThinkPad brand. Then, the word came back from the executive committee once again, "How can you guys be so stupid? You're sold out. Why are you announcing new models?" Claflin told Cannavino, "Lots of ways exist to fix our supply problem. Becoming non-competitive is not one of them." Cannavino later told Claflin that he had said those exact words to Gerstner. It was enough to quell another inquisition.

The ThinkPad management was certainly not ignoring the supply issues. Another display source was added. Manufacturing was expanded under Joe Formichelli, an experienced plant manager. The problem was coming under control—or so the team thought.

Scott Bower, U.S. marketing manager, described the situation: "We were moving lots of product. We expanded the high-end notebooks from the ThinkPad 700 to the 720. We switched from Micro Channel to AT-bus (advanced technology–bus) because Micro

Channel got too expensive to develop and to support. Unfortunately, after we brought out the companion docking station for the 700C, which was Micro Channel, we were back in the demand/supply spiral. Everyone wanted docking stations for this product. Peripheral manufacturers complained about the use of the Micro Channel because they had to develop new cards and options for use with the docking station. Because it was Micro Channel, they had to do two versions—one for ThinkPad, one for other portable manufacturers. It increased their costs and development efforts for cards and options, causing business viability questions. The dilemma was even more complex because it was difficult to balance the demand with the available supply. Just about the time the supply would arrive, the demand would have dissipated. So, we reviewed what options were available. Because the AT-bus architecture was the industry standard, we decided to make the switch.

"This added another complexity to the picture. By switching to the AT-bus, the docking station for the original 700C didn't work on the follow-on 720. All of a sudden, supply of the Micro Channel docking stations arrived, but the demand had disappeared. Customers had moved to the ThinkPad 720. We ended up with a nice 'barrier reef' of docking stations that we had to write off.

"We learned a valuable lesson about demand forecasting in this market. Most parts required a six-month lead time, which meant that we had to peg the demand well in advance. Staying in touch with the market and our customers was critical to this effort. Unfortunately, when you chase demand and order parts to satisfy it, you usually end up with the parts or products arriving after you need them. The demand evaporates, and you end up writing off the costs and losing money.

"Of course, in an effort to deliver competitive products, we announced newer versions of the ThinkPads, making the preceding model obsolete before customers even got their orders. Where product had yet to be delivered, orders were cancelled or switched to the newer model in an attempt to stay current with the technology. This was a huge problem in the beginning because of the Micro Channel/AT-bus architecture. Many of the parts ordered for the 700C could not be used on the 720 when the demand shifted.

"I made some difficult sales calls during this initial period, calling on customers who were waiting for ThinkPads. I actually had to recommend that they buy a Compaq or a Toshiba. Now, from a salesman's perspective and as a marketing guy, those were the toughest calls I ever had to make. I couldn't lie to my customers and commit delivery when I had no idea if or when the systems would arrive. I knew some of my competitors were saying, 'We'll get you the same box,' but I couldn't lose credibility by promising something that I could not directly control. I believe that our honest approach on the supply status re-affirmed some of our customers' beliefs that IBM would recommend the best course of action for them, even if it cost us an eventual ThinkPad sale."

Simultaneously with the ThinkPad 700C development, Bower and the brand team were involved in another effort that, from a product standpoint, was sacrilegious within the hallowed halls of IBM. The portable team sought an OEM (other equipment manufacturer) to develop a lower function, more price-sensitive notebook. Eventually, executive authorization was granted to pursue the effort, but little latitude was granted on which company to use. Because of a pre-existing relationship with Zenith/BULL (ZDS), Bower and team met with Enrico Pasatori, who was then with Zenith. After long negotiations, terms were reached on a notebook design that would become the ThinkPad 300.

According to Maurice Fletcher, one of Bower's managers and a respected advisor, "We were given the go-ahead to address the value notebook space. Claflin authorized us to do whatever was needed. We sent some of the Boca planning team to Taiwan, an unprecedented action in the early nineties. We were close to a deal with an Asian manufacturer to produce a value portable. Unfortunately, at the same time, IBM Europe announced a partnership with Zenith. A mandate came down that any portable product, outside Yamato, had to be by Zenith. That's how a Zenith product became the ThinkPad 300."

Zenith was asked to deliver a unique model that met IBM's specifications. The portable team went through the design and was satisfied with the prototype. According to Claflin, "Somehow, Zenith had produced qualification units that passed our stringent qualification tests, but the line [production] units had a high failure rate. We cancelled the alliance with Zenith and their OEM partner, Inventa in Taiwan, because all their production units arrived DOA [dead on arrival]. The ThinkPad 300 never worked very well. The good news about the ThinkPad 700C overshadowed the 300's problems. It prevented the new brand from getting a major black eye in its early years."

Bower felt that this effort was important from a strategy perspective: "It sent an early signal to our Japanese development team. If we could not get our development act together and leapfrog the competition, IBM was willing to go outside and procure the necessary products. We would not wait for a long development cycle that delivered inferior products. At the time, the ThinkPad 700 was simply a concept on a piece of paper. By linking with Zenith, the Yamato team was forced to deliver something innovative on a very short schedule. We wanted a family of products, and they did not have the luxury of being late."

The IBM ThinkPad 300.

Claflin agreed, "Compared to the ThinkPad 700C, the ZDS machines were terrible. We included them as part of our ThinkPad line but only briefly promoted them. The ThinkPad 300 was positioned as a monochrome-only value product. When we realized that the ThinkPad 700 was a hit, we rapidly got out of the ZDS agreement. It was costly because we had ordered one hundred thousand units, but in the long run, it prevented an untimely stigma on the IBM-designed ThinkPads."

Fletcher summarized, "The ThinkPad 300 was a total disaster. It never really worked as Zenith claimed it would. We took back a lot of this product from our customers. There was even an incident in Europe where one of the batteries melted a terminal. We went through a full-court press to replace every battery in every ThinkPad 300 sold worldwide. We kept it very quiet. We had to report our action to the federal government within thirty days of the incident. We reported what we had done to find all the products, to alert customers, and to provide them with the batteries. We also took the time to inform our Industry Advisory Council and made sure that they were kept abreast of our action. Not one bad article was written about this problem! But, to be sure, the Zenith-based product had problems even before the battery incident."

The Authors' Insights

Ironically, the first major misstep on the team's journey was due to the ThinkPad 700's tremendous success. It has often been said, "History repeats itself"; in this case, the ThinkPad team experienced the same problem of poor volume forecasting as the first IBM PC contingent. More ThinkPad 700s were sold in the first year than the three-year forecast for the product. A good news, bad news situation, the team learned firsthand the importance of good product forecasting.

With the arrival of Gerstner and his minions, Claflin's position became shaky, but he did not wait for someone else to decide his fate. Claflin took direct action to get the real story in front of his new commander-in-chief and to educate Gerstner on the strong points of the portable activity. Although he could not immediately resolve the volume problem, he prepared a credible report, including action plans to address the segment's challenges.

These challenges included dealing with Zenith on a value line of portables. The ThinkPad team was new to developing a non-IBM product and was unfamiliar with the practices necessary to make such a relationship work. Similar to the pen tablet endeavor, this situation was one in which too many people were trying to manage the project. Line management had a vested interest, but their actions were subject to the direction of Claflin's advisor, Kathy Vieth. Also, adding another geographical location to the mix increased the project's complexity: Boca planning provided the requirements, Zenith developed and manufactured the design, and IBM marketed the product. The ThinkPad 300, subjected to IBM's stringent processes and quality measurements, failed to meet the market requirements and was quickly withdrawn.

In the Foreword, Professor Kosnik points out the importance of leadership and the ability to take swift action when something is not going right. IBM's management took quick and decisive actions regarding supply and the ThinkPad 300, so neither tarnished the emerging ThinkPad brand.

The Value Notebook Family Throughout Time

System	300	350/350C	355/355C	360/360C/ 360CE	380/380D
Form	Notebook	Notebook	Notebook	Notebook	Notebook
Processor	386SL 25MHz	486SLC 25MHz	486SX 33MHz	486SX 33MHz 486DX2 50MHz	Pentium 150MHz
Memory	4/12MB	4/20MB	4/20MB	4/20MB	16/80MB
Storage	80/ 120MB	120/ 250MB I/II PCMCIA	125/ 810MB I/II/III PCMCIA	170/340/ 810MB I/II/III PCMCIA	1.08/1.35/ 2.1GB II/III PCMCIA
Display	9.5" STN LCD	9.2" STN Color 9.5" STN mono	9.5" Mono STN 8.4" TFT	9.5" Mono STN 9.5" Dual Scan 8.4" Color TFT	12.1" TFT
Operating System	DOS 5.0 OS/2 2.0	DOS 5.02 OS/2 2.1 Prodigy	DOS 6.1, 6.3 OS/2 2.1 Windows 3.1	DOS 6.1, 6.3 OS/2 2.1 Windows 3.1	DOS 7.0 MS-DOS 6.22 OS/2 Warp Windows 95, 3.11
Weight (lb.)	5.9	5.2–5.8	5.6/6.1	5.6–6.2	6.6/7.1
Other	Std Ethernet ISA bus Port replicator TrackPoint II	Power mgt Preload SW AT /ISA bus TrackPoint II	VESA local bus Preloaded SW OnLine Housecall	EPA Energy Star compliant Preload SW AT(ISA)bus	CD-ROM Power mgt Preload Sw TrackPoint Enh
Announced	10/5/92	5/4/93	5/93	9/8/93	5/17/97

Although starting with a less-than-stellar product, the family grew to be industry recognized with its ThinkPad 380.

AWARDS

ThinkPad 300	*Portable Computing*	"Best of Our Comparison" Award"	1993
ThinkPad 350	*Consumer Reports*	"Excellent"	November 1993

CHAPTER 18

Building the Brand

While an original is always hard to find, it is easy to recognize.

—John L. Mason

The merging of computing, communications, and consumer functions spurred mobile growth in the 1990s. On one hand, multimedia became prevalent in the office (for example, CD-ROM). On the other, portables came "home," especially as office space became more expensive and telecommuting increased. A shift in emphasis from the rational sell to one focused on emotional and sensory appeal occurred. Even *Parade Magazine*, on March 14, 1993, recognized that mobile computing was part of a new wave that gave users the opportunities to finally get "personal" with their personal computers. In fact, users began to give their PCs personalities and pet names.

As this personal computer personality trend exploded, a brand name became important. These trends affected not only the physical but also the ease-of-use attributes critical to mobile's future design and marketing decisions. The ThinkPad team worked closely with industry consultants to monitor the changing trends and directions reflected in the following chart developed by International Data Corporation (IDC).

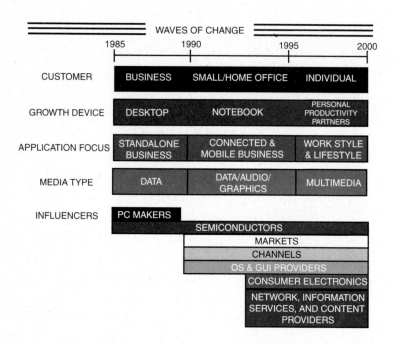

IBM's PC Company Mobile Computing team, as part of this expanding segment, established its vision as providing convenient, innovative access to and management of information—any time, any place. Key to this vision, the ThinkPad brand exemplified a personal and desirable personality. It personified such values as freedom, friendliness, simplicity, and familiarity. In driving to achieve the emotional rewards desired by purchasers—rewards resulting in personal or business success and status or ego confirmation—ThinkPad evolved a premium personality. This personality, both personal and desirable, attracted (a) individuals within medium to large businesses who were willing to pay a little more than industry standard prices to have their needs met and (b) individuals who were early adopters and innovators.

With four platforms in plan (notebook, subnotebook, tablet, and handheld), ThinkPads were used primarily by mobile individuals for business (organization, education, presentations, messaging, and computing), as well as for multiple personal needs (communications and entertainment). These platforms were designed for excellence in all dimensions: technical, customer satisfaction, ease of use, and service and support. As a result of focusing the development team on reducing weight and increasing battery life, almost every announcement after the ThinkPad 700 was lighter and had longer battery life.

ThinkPad's momentum was also accelerated by technology advances such as TrackPoint improvements, PCMCIA across all its products, standard infrared communications, universal docking, and no-compromise displays and keyboards. The products delivered in 1993 and 1994 were designed to address the customer need of convenience and investment protection. Through the proliferation of building blocks (processor, memory, PCMCIA cards, and universal bays), customers were able to choose the pieces not only before their purchase but also afterwards, achieving true modularity and investment protection.

All these advances increased the confidence of ThinkPad customers and the sales force in this new line of portables and in the new brand. The team never lost its focus on the product features recognized in that market, as evidenced in this quote from *Business Week's* Steve Wildstrom, a member of the 1998 Industry Advisory Council: "ThinkPads are very good machines. They probably have the strongest brand identification in the industry through their industrial design. From the brand point of view, this was very important. When you see a black machine with red buttons, customers know it's a ThinkPad, and that's a very powerful message."

Specific technology programs were established to recognize the mobile market acceleration and address the need for technology information transfer. Leo Suarez was assigned to develop and manage the primary program, called *Headlights*. A Headlights session was held every six months to update the team on future customer needs, technologies, and mobile applications. Information from IBM Research and outside consultants was combined with the knowledge and experience of the mobile team and incorporated into future product designs. The result of the analysis and feedback was then documented and circulated across the organization. The program became so successful that other brand teams incorporated similar programs into their development processes.

Jim Bartlett offered this reflection: "...what you have to do is determine what, from a technological standpoint, will be possible to achieve. Then you have to go and figure out which one(s) of those things will give you a substantial competitive advantage. And provide something that is attractive to the customer by testing some hypothesis with customer or industry insiders. We were actually driving it backwards and then getting feedback...rather than expecting them to come and tell us exactly what they want."[1]

The IBM team knew that staying close to the customer was not unique in the industry or even new to IBM's earlier portable efforts. According to Paul Carroll in *Big Blues: The Unmaking of IBM*, earlier efforts by IBM created a portable that was exactly what customers said they wanted. However, by the time it was released, better and lighter laptops were available, making IBM's offering no longer "what they wanted." The ThinkPad team did not want to fall into the same trap as previous portable teams and added Headlights in an attempt to achieve higher standards and more market-driven products. Headlights built on the technology roadmap first compiled by the pen tablet team under Patty McHugh.

---

1. Kathleen Riley, "The ThinkPad 750 Series: IBM's Comeback Kid," *The Best Practices Report* (February 1994): 5.

To drive the right technologies into products and to achieve high standards, the mobile team also listened closely to the "Voice of the Customer" through customer/industry advisory councils, customer call days, forums, and focus groups. According to Maurice Fletcher, who often bridged the marketing perspective to the Boca planning and brand management community, "The 700C was successful because the development group started being market-driven versus development-driven. By having the director of Yamato Development, Koichi Higuchi, present in the U.S., we got the Japanese engineers behind the real customer requirements.

"We involved the entire team in our Voice of the Customer programs. Engineers and planners were invited to present at the council meetings so that they could hear the input of key influencers and customers alike. Everyone on the team, from Bruce Claflin down, participated in monthly customer call days and made phone calls to recent purchasers to get their perspectives on the ThinkPad purchase. Can you imagine getting a phone call from ThinkPad's general manager, asking how you liked your ThinkPad and what needed to be done to make it even better in the future!"

The team verified their product designs through not only the councils but also focus groups. Focus groups were conducted around the world. Planners and engineers observed first-hand the blind input of real customers. Online forums were also established so that ThinkPad customers could communicate with the team directly whenever the need arose.

An early tenet of the brand development was that advertising dollars were sacred. These were the last dollars cut from the budget. This practice enabled ThinkPad to be advertised in places IBM had never advertised before—airports, pubs, buses, and trains—and to control its own destiny in regard to format and content. Significant dollars were spent to drive the ThinkPad image and name. The product was always to be visible to its customers.

Maurice Fletcher described some of the early ThinkPad advertising programs: "We did the first sports marketing that carried an IBM product brand. We sponsored Todd Martin, a young tennis pro, who wore ThinkPad on his tennis shirt sleeve. This lasted nearly a year, during which time Martin performed very well. So, we got exposure at a couple of Grand Slam semi-finals. The ThinkPad brand was seen by millions of viewers around the world. As a tie-in, we sponsored a 'beat the pros fastest serve' contest at the tournament sites. People attending each day of the event paid a small fee, which was donated to charities, to serve three tennis balls. The fastest speeds won the same tennis shirts that Martin wore. The fast serve challenge was a great success. It gave ThinkPad a lot of visibility while enabling us to make a contribution to the community. Unfortunately, after the U.S. Open where Martin had a very impressive run, an IBM corporate executive did not like the fact that it was a product and not IBM that was getting the visibility. We were told to shut down the program—in no uncertain terms.

"We also sponsored the National Basketball Association [NBA], which was another first for an IBM product. They are still running the slogan in some local arenas: 'IBM ThinkPad, the official computer of the NBA.' The slogan ran on a rotating sign under the scorers' table. It got visibility in the arena but, more important, it was seen during the sports highlight reports. We also had tickets to luxury boxes, where sales representatives brought their customers to enjoy the games and meet the coaches. We even supplied every NBA coach with a ThinkPad."

Combining the Voice of the Customer and the advertising programs, the team developed a campaign called *Thank You from ThinkPad*. It was the first time that anything from third parties (non-IBM organizations) was put into the ThinkPad box, the actual shipping box that went to the end user. The program was a means of saying thank you and offering opportunities to purchase additional value from third-party vendors. Thank You from ThinkPad was a coupon book with more than $4,000 worth of travel coupons. Coupons included airline discounts and even a discount on a Jiffy Lube oil change because if someone was moving, he or she could be moving in planes, trains, and automobiles.

Fletcher recalled, "We wanted the customers to know right off the bat that we appreciated their business and understood their lives. We also asked customers to complete a warranty registration card, for which they received a personalized nameplate for their system. We even put an indentation on the mechanical package to hold the nameplate. We felt strongly that our customers were proud of their ThinkPad investment, and we wanted to offer them something to 'personalize' their purchase. An added advantage was that the registration card provided the foundation for the customer call day program. We worked hard to link the various programs to get the 'biggest bang for the buck.'"

Although Fletcher reported to Scott Bower, they operated as the "dynamic duo" in establishing this new brand. Bower was excellent at rallying the troops, getting them pumped up and excited to sell ThinkPad. He was also experienced at fighting battles with executive management and holding his ground. Fletcher complemented Bower's style by ensuring that the troops had the information necessary to move forward on product design and marketing programs. Fletcher drove the advertising and PR agencies to constantly exert influence over the industry's key consultants, analysts, and press. He also made sure that the various communication campaigns were consistent from one source to another.

Unfortunately, as part of his responsibilities, Fletcher also had supply management and allocation. According to Fletcher, "We did everything possible to provide our large customers with product, but when the brand took off, we almost immediately went into an allocation mode. I would receive ten to fifteen phone calls a day from sales reps who had customers wanting to order but needing to know when they would get delivery. I spent fifty percent of my day balancing allocation and the other half promoting the brand."

The marketing dynamic duo worked closely with Jim Bartlett and his brand management team. Bartlett's team consisted of the program managers for many of the Voice of the Customer programs. The programs were designed with input from Bower and Fletcher, but Bartlett was the force behind their execution. Bower reflected, "Based on input from the Voice of the Customer programs, it didn't take us long to realize that we needed to center on the entire packaging concept. Bartlett eventually agreed."

The brand success had resulted in everyone, both inside and outside IBM, wanting to add flyers and promotional materials to the shipping content. At one point, there were more than forty items inside the shipping container, which declared "Read Me First." Debi Dell, one of Bartlett's senior program managers, was asked to address this problem by bringing together the worldwide packaging teams and deciding on a new out-of-box concept.

Dell, Sam Lucente, and the worldwide representatives designed a product map that would act as both a checklist and a diagram of the system's major components. According to *Portable Computing* magazine, July 1994, "Moreover, for novice users, IBM has developed a clever aid called the 'Product Map'—a large sheet of paper at the center of which is a white rectangle on which you place your ThinkPad. Whatever else can be said of IBM, it puts its users' needs first—a fact underscored by such attentive details as the product map." Accompanying the product map was one envelope designed to hold all the miscellaneous items the team was pressured to include in the box. To further clean up the unpacking experience, only the most critical information, as decided by the brand team, was labeled as "Read Me First." The team then documented these decisions in a process guide that detailed the worldwide standards, as well as the exceptions required in each geography. This process guide was another first for the brand team and was copied by other groups within the PC Company.

This effort also resulted in the ThinkPad being the first portable manufacturer to bring out a small box with a handle on top similar to the appearance of a notebook. The graphics on the box reflected usage scenarios of ThinkPads in different environments; the same graphics were then used on the manuals, packaging materials, internal envelopes, and preloaded images. It was the first coordinated effort of all items shipped to the end user. The acceptance of the program was so high that other brands eventually used similar approaches to their out-of-box efforts.

One negative surfaced from this effort. According to Bower, "At one point, we were pressured to take the name and icons off the box—to ship ThinkPads in plain brown containers. We had the hottest products being stolen in New York City. You knew you had arrived when you were number one on the hit parade for theft prior to delivery to your customers. However, we didn't give up! Our strategy eventually won a design award for usability and creativity. Even today, the consistency in packaging makes the systems easier to set up."

Packaging was not the only ease-of-use advance the ThinkPad team pioneered. Another program, quickly copied by both portable and desktop competitors, was software pre-load. Bower described the program: "We loaded 'applets' on ThinkPad, software vignettes for the notebook user. Again, because of the popularity of the emerging brand, the effort didn't cost us any money. Companies were willing to pay us for the privilege of having their products associated with our brand. We didn't just load the operating system, but also software that mobile users could use immediately. Imagine getting a system that is usable as soon as you turned it on!"

Bruce Claflin, supporting these ease of use programs, commented, "About the timeframe of the ThinkPad 750, we started to get in a grooved swing, to balance technology advances and customer programs. I would love to tell you that we had this brilliant plan on how to get ThinkPad to appeal to different market segments from the very beginning. We didn't. We announced the ThinkPad 700 with a whole bunch of neat technologies in it, and it did well.

"Even more important, however, was what we did well after that first announcement. We started listening to the individuals who actually used the product. We found out, for example, that our customers were using ThinkPads for multimedia presentations. Because there was this presentation segment, we customized our approach and machines to address it. This discovery led us to developing a portable docking station and a multimedia load. But, we primarily went on gut feel. We watched carefully what the industry valued and what they didn't. We dropped what they did not value, and then we exploited what they did. I wish that we had been smarter, but, in hindsight, perhaps listening was the best thing to do."

The ThinkPad brand team also concentrated on service and support for the mobile customer. EasyServ, first announced by the portable team, was the capability to get a notebook back from service within forty-eight hours. Through a partnership with Federal Express, if a customer had a problem, he or she simply called the EasyServ 800 number, and technicians arranged to have Federal Express pick up the defective unit. A customer could arrange to have the unit returned to whatever location was desired. For a fee, the system could be returned within twenty-four hours, depending on the urgency of the situation.

Another program was ThinkPad Proven. Concerned that customers would install non-tested hard files, PCMCIA cards, and memory, the planning team decided that it would be better to test and authorize third-party devices for the ThinkPad product line. ThinkPad Proven not only ensured the quality and compatibility of the peripherals used with ThinkPad, but also provided an additional revenue stream to the company. The program allowed approved vendors to use the ThinkPad logo with their products for a fee and provided them with a strong channel.

Scott Bower offered another example of understanding the mobile customer and tying that to the brand: "When we first started with ThinkPad, we offered one poorly designed carrying case. It was boring in design and had little affinity to the image we wanted to create for our new brand. At the time, PORT was a start-up company interested in doing business with IBM. We struck a deal with PORT to build a product catalog with offerings segmented to our ThinkPad customer profiles. The catalog was put into every shipping box and contained an 800 number that would allow customers to order an upgraded carrying case. PORT handled all the calls, took the orders, shipped the merchandise, and billed the customers directly. They went so far as to connect the ThinkPad carrying case to the original IBM PC advertising by including a silk red rose with every purchase. The red rose had been used in the original IBM PC ad featuring Charlie Chaplin.

"So, we were trying to create a brand, yet remain tied to the legacy of IBM. The secret to branding, in my opinion, was to have more than just technologically superior hardware. Hardware was going to trend up or down, depending on the current hot features and functions. No one vendor was always going to be in the lead. But, if you developed other brand attributes that customers desired, you offered the potential of a total solution, not just a piece of hardware. We were certain that our customers wanted the total experience from the best hardware, to an easy-to-set-up and easy-to-use initial encounter, to pre-loaded software with immediate utility, to the comfort and guarantee of post-sale service and support, coupled with the best peripherals in the industry. The success of the brand confirmed our beliefs."

The Authors' Insights

The development of the ThinkPad brand was just as important as the development of the ThinkPad product. Although significant focus was placed on product innovation, the work done by Bower's, Fletcher's, and Bartlett's teams created ThinkPad's brand equity. Completing a situation analysis of where the brand was in regard to market positioning and product recognition provided the foundation for the brand plan. The team then proposed a strategy of where they wanted to go and the marketing programs for how they wanted to get there. While paying attention to the attributes of an enduring brand, ThinkPad mastered the magic of the right name with the right product at the right time. ThinkPad was defined as something to be desired, something sought after by successful individuals. Because of its innovative features and the difficulty in buying one during the early years, the brand signified *exclusive* and *desirable*—and everyone knows that people want what they cannot have, at least for awhile.

While building the brand, the team did not overlook a very important aspect: service and support. Great strides were made in considering the wants and needs of the ThinkPad customer set. According to Chris Shipley, a member of the ThinkPad Industry Advisory Council, "The team continued to build on its initial success. They focused on usability from the mobile professional viewpoint. Mobile professionals who are on the road and need technical support do not have an IS department following them around to help service or reconfigure their systems. Successful companies will continue to do more for this customer set from a services perspective."

The ThinkPad team also created several innovative marketing programs. One of these programs included PORT as ThinkPad's first major outsourcing project. By the time Bower left the ThinkPad team in 1995, PORT was sending the brand more than a million dollars per quarter in royalties from carrying cases alone. The team had broadened its ability to make money by obtaining royalties from not only PORT but also ThinkPad Proven program participants. They had discovered a way to have an annuity stream tied to the brand but yet independent of the actual product technology. Given the ever increasing trend toward personal computers becoming commodities, this was a very strategic move by the ThinkPad organization. It also strengthened industry interest in partnering with ThinkPad, creating an affiliation with IBM that had not existed in almost a decade. These actions, as part of the emerging network surrounding the ThinkPad brand, remain an important element in its current strategy.

CHAPTER 19

Entrenching Success

A position is not established unless and until the market agrees it is so.

—Karen Kang, Regis McKenna Inc.[1]

The network supporting ThinkPad had many constituents, but the customer was the most important. The ThinkPad team realized early on that customer satisfaction was a critical underpinning to building a successful brand. Every brand program was focused on building and retaining customer recognition and loyalty. Unfortunately, for a time, the PC Company lost focus on these measurements. Pete Leichliter, one of Bartlett's program managers, was asked to develop and track key customer satisfaction indicators for the mobile brand. His first step was to establish a process so that the measurements had validity and could be gathered on a quarterly basis. A closed loop process was established and communicated across the worldwide team. This five-step process included

- *Listen to the customer*—Know and understand customer wants and needs.
- *Identify issues*—Provide a consolidated view of customer concerns and complaints.

1. Karen Kang, "The Corporate Positioning Myth," *Technology Marketing Insights* (December 1993).

- *Advocate change*—Anticipate and fix causes of dissatisfaction.
- *Measure performance*—Create common and consistent worldwide customer measurements.
- *Administer feedback*—Execute a closed-loop feedback program.

The team saw the results of the customer satisfaction program at the quarterly measurement meetings. In 1993, the key factors and attributes were measured against the top competition at the time. The following table documents the ThinkPad's third quarter (3Q) 1993 results for the U.S. market; to show change over time, the ThinkPad column's second number reflects 4Q 1994 results.

Customer Satisfaction Center (Percent Favorable)

Factor/Attribute	ThinkPad (3Q93 / 4Q94)	Compaq	Dell*	Apple*
Product reliability	86/90	88	72	87
Easy to use	87/89	88	90	100
Sales experience/ image	61/85	73	83	83
Compatibility	89/93	81	83	85
Speed/capacity	90/90	87	76	95
Product cost	44/63	66	76	40
Service/support	67/80	71	76	68
Features/design	96/94	89	88	91
Responses	176/97	80	25	22

* Insufficient responses to be statistically sound

The customer satisfaction measurements continued throughout the ThinkPad program. The factors changed, as did the competitors against which the team compared. With each quarterly report, actions were taken to address any decline in ratings or total customer satisfaction. The *ThinkPad Information Package* (*TIP*) was the result of one of these action plans. *TIP* was a newsletter sent to customers to help them with commonly encountered problems or little-known facts about the ThinkPad brand. Ongoing communications with the ThinkPad team seemed to be a consistent requirement voiced by customers, whether via focus groups, surveys, or forums.

As part of the ThinkPad network, communication was necessary with more than just customers. Jim Bartlett recognized that catering to influencers and customers was only part of the equation for a successful brand. From his past experience, he knew that IBM needed an aggressive outward stance to reach the media, who, in turn, would disseminate the ThinkPad message around the world. Although the PC Company had a media relations group, in the early 1990s, their focus was abysmal. Getting sample machines to the media was a nightmare. Engineers would not make themselves available to the press reviewers to answer questions, and the IBM PR people were PR specialists, not technologists. The few machines that would find their way to the reviewers did so months after announcement. By the time a story went to press and reached the newsstands, IBM was already planning to scrap the platform. If IBM was to build sales fast, it would have to get to these media influencers faster and more comprehensively.

Bartlett realized this and took action. In April 1993, he recruited Bob Sztybel to set up the PC Company's first product review program. Sztybel came to the PC Company with eight years of IBM experience. He had started in Owego, New York, with the Federal Systems Division (FSD), where he learned cradle-to-grave responsibility for projects, from development to sales, from manufacturing to test, from stocking for production to stocking for end-of-life support. Five years later, he moved to a staff marketing management position in White Plains, New York, which laid a great foundation for the position Bartlett was filling.

Catering to the media required an understanding of their motives: (1) to present timely stories with (2) meaningful content for their audiences. Unfortunately, some of the bigger magazines in the industry have three to four months lead times, so the story they are writing today might not hit the streets until three months later. Because the best time to have press is at the announcement of a new product, IBM had to be talking to the press and distributing examples well in advance. The ThinkPad team began to schedule and fund the building of additional prototypes (early working models) early in the production cycle for the sole use of product reviews.

Recalled Sztybel, "It was an exciting time. Yamato had been rumored to be on schedule for our first AT-bus notebook. Scheduled for announcement in September 1993, I had two units show up in my office in July! Granted, the plastics were warped, there was no paint, and jumper wires were everywhere. But, this was the platform that development was using to test out the final functions. By making this machine available to the press on a controlled basis, we could create a buzz and get stories started. Every magazine could actually have relevant stories at announcement time."

Sztybel became very close to the geographically dispersed teams in Yamato, Boca, and Raleigh. Each machine arrived without documentation, sometimes without critical operational software. Sztybel would build a disk image master during the day, spending hours testing features and identifying defects for planning and engineering. He also learned why things sometimes had to work the way they did. He would take other machines home and do LapLinks (file transfers) at night to get multiple units ready for the press. He kept modeler's glue and paints so that he could touch up the raw units for magazine photography. He often reattached doors with tape.

Sztybel usually had only a few days for preparation before the machines had to go out to a particular magazine. Early machines went out with a list of "warts" identifying known imperfections and problems. According to Sztybel, "If you told the reviewers up front about the pre-production glitches, they would not ding you for them later."

Sztybel also wrote reviewer guides that put the features and functions of the machines into terms the customer (user) would understand. Continued Sztybel, "Although improved speeds and feeds were propelling us, IBM had never been able to communicate why speeds and feeds were meaningful to business users. These reviewer guides bridged that gap, which helped reviewers understand and communicate the real message. That message was that ThinkPad was the most usable and thoughtfully designed machine on the planet."

IBM was not the first company to institute such a program, although ThinkPad was the first brand to do so. Gerry Purdy recalled that October 1992 day when he became vice president and chief analyst for Dataquest: "When I showed up at Dataquest, a Fed Ex box was sitting on my desk. I opened it up, and the note inside said, 'Congratulations on your new appointment at Dataquest. Use this PowerBook to give you the power to be the best analyst in the industry.' I was blown away. An hour later, Keri Walker from Apple's product evaluation department called to make sure that the PowerBook had arrived and to see whether there was anything I needed. Now, that was paying attention to an influencer! I later found out that Apple did that for a significant number of people they considered influencers. How could I not use the PowerBook when I was treated like that!"

Apple also went to great lengths to get each new PowerBook sent to the leading magazines ahead of their publishing deadlines. It also orchestrated the launch of each new PowerBook with widespread, simultaneous coverage in all major publications, no matter how much lead time the specific publication required. Press support was fundamental to the building of the PowerBook brand.

Media programs such as Apple's and IBM's provided information that enabled magazines to rank the various competitors. In 1995, *PC Magazine* rated the top desktop and notebook vendors against four factors: reliability, repairs, technical support, and buy again. In this survey, IBM ranked with the leading contenders. These contenders had changed since 1993 and now included Hewlett-Packard (HP) and Toshiba. But, like its reactions to industry awards, the ThinkPad team was extremely pleased about being in the top ranked category and the buy again rating—the highest of all the notebook vendors. The following table shows the grades of selected leading notebook vendors from February 1993 to January 1995.[2]

Vendor Grades: Past and Present

Vendor	1/95	7/94	1/94	7/93	2/93
Apple	A	A	A	B	C
Compaq	A	A	A	A	A
Dell	D	C	B	A	B
HP	A	B	(N/A)	(N/A)	(N/A)
IBM	A	A	B*	A	B
Toshiba	B	B	B	A	B

* Affected by the L40SX recall and poor performance of the ThinkPad 300 and 500

Articles such as the one in *PC Magazine* were fundamental to the brand's equity. The team spent considerable time on various communications programs to garner print space. Early samples allowed for media tours months before launch rather than immediately after, as was the norm elsewhere within IBM at the time. Bartlett and Sztybel worked closely with Jonathan Gandal, then of Brodeur and Partners, who was retained as the PC Company's media representative for ThinkPad.

---

2. Rachel Derby Teitler and Carol Venezia, "Desktop and Laptop PCs," *PC Magazine* (January 10, 1995): 166–167.

"Gandal would be on the phone at all hours with all the major editors, consultants, and reviewers," said Sztybel. "We would be juggling the few assets I had, depending on whose deadline was when. We personally visited these luminaries with machines that were technological marvels and really impressed them when we left machines behind for their hands-on evaluation. What other competitors did with a handful of machines, our deep pockets allowed us to acquire a larger number of early machines. The PC Company started to understand that the value and power of PR was far beyond any print ad we could muster. Bartlett championed the funding to protect this program during the financially challenged times at IBM."

Reaching the market took on other forms in the months after announcement. In his role as worldwide mobile executive, Jim Bartlett took it upon himself to become the unofficial spokesman for ThinkPad. He spoke at every industry conference that he could. Bartlett shared his passion for the brand and evangelized countless audiences.

"It seemed like every week we were up all hours customizing presentations for various audiences," remembered Sztybel. "I became an expert in multimedia presentations to support his [Bartlett's] frequent changes. It was hard not to succumb to the passion Bartlett felt for the brand; every hour spent meant we were closer to the customer and to market success. The work was addictive because we saw the results whenever we saw someone look at a ThinkPad for the first time. We wanted everyone to know about our products."

Soon Bartlett and Sztybel were showcasing other innovative IBM technologies, such as voice recognition and infrared communications, as part of their presentations. These demonstrations only advanced the wonderment surrounding the ThinkPad name.

These actions also led to recognition by magazines with industry awards for technical design, innovation, quality, and the out-of-box experience. Pete Leichliter successfully garnered a J.D. Powers award recognizing ThinkPad's service and support. Sztybel submitted nomination forms for most major industry awards to extend ThinkPad bragging rights even further. Corporate Design submitted the ThinkPad 750 platform, and later the 755 and 701, for countless design awards worldwide. Debi Dell, through the Industry Advisory Council and out-of-box programs, reached influencers in other ways that improved not only brand awareness but also design consideration.

Each award captured by the team was announced on a poster board centrally located within Boca Raton, but the actual award was housed in PC Company headquarters in Somers, New York. Eventually, the number of awards exceeded the available space! By late 1994, the PC Company management quietly asked ThinkPad to reduce its share of the award display to allow for a fairer representation of the company's overall product line.

Of course, the path to greatness is not without its challenges. On July 14, 1994, new corporate directions directly affected the ThinkPad brand. From the office of the General Manager, Product and Brand Management, came the directive that IBM was moving to a single, global advertising agency. This new advertising partner was chosen to help IBM develop and run high impact, consistent advertising around the world. The directive also announced a strategic decision to realign the marketing mix to shift more marketing money to advertising. Teams were asked to redirect money from existing communications and marketing program budgets to advertising. A minimum of fifteen percent of the full-year non-advertising communications budget was to shift to advertising. Such a move would result in the canceling of current plans for shows, promotions, and deliverables.

This was the first concrete example of other people stepping into the brand management and starting to control things previously managed by the brand manager. According to Maurice Fletcher, "We were in the process of finalizing an ad about the ThinkPad having flown on the shuttle. The ad talked about 'If you ever needed battery life, here was the time,' and we were ready to go, ready to roll. But, with the new directive, we had to pull the ad and go with the centralized advertising program. Instead of letting us continue to build the brand, the separate programs died. It really diffused our enthusiasm."

ThinkPad on the space shuttle. (Photo provided by IBM from proposed ThinkPad advertising campaign.)

Scott Bower echoed Fletcher's sentiments: "In my twenty-two years with IBM, the experience of developing a product and an associated brand, especially the brand, was probably the most satisfying part of my entire career. I would still be there—and I think a lot of us would still be there—if the executives above us had continued to let us run the brand worldwide. If there was anything I would change, I would change the fact that there were too many people who jumped on the successful band wagon and made the brand toe the party line."

The Authors' Insights

To sell a product requires demand. Demand is driven by awareness. By placing such a critical focus and investment on product reviews, the ThinkPad team effectively brought the media into the picture. By involving the media in the marketing launch process, the awareness of the ThinkPad brand was accelerated. The media was handed the tools they needed, the way a good sales organization might deploy to its staff. By allowing time and sensitivity to the press influencers, the press, in turn, helped to advance the success of ThinkPad. In an effort to draw attention away from leaders Toshiba, Compaq, and Apple, this zealous approach to the review process and public speaking succeeded in shifting the buying marketplace rapidly to the ThinkPad line.

As the mobile business expanded, the brand team worked hard to appeal to a broader audience through a comprehensive communications program. The message was that the brand was migrating away from "exclusive" to "affordable" and "available." This, combined with "desirable," led IBM to achieve something almost unheard of in the annals of IBM: The ThinkPad brand generated a higher positive opinion than IBM for people who were considering the purchase of a portable computer.[3] Remember that this was a time when IBM was rebuilding itself under a new chairman who knew the power of branding.

Like the IBM PC before it, everyone eventually jumped on the bandwagon and tried to affect the direction of the ThinkPad

---

3. Brandt and Johnson, *Power Branding*, 128.

brand. The new corporate executive team reduced the autonomy with which the brand could operate. They also wanted as many product lines as possible to be associated with or mirror the programs of ThinkPad. The name started to become diluted, and there was pressure to use it on other IBM products—even to the detriment of the mobile program. When brand is king, the ThinkPad general manager must be able to protect and build the brand. IBM eventually looked beyond ThinkPad for other "super brands" that could develop their own equity value. Perhaps Netfinity and Lotus Notes are two future candidates, but, for sure, ebusiness is emerging as a premier IBM brand, capturing not only product but services as well. When coupled with the power of ThinkPad as the platform of choice for mobile customers, this could be the start of another brand journey for IBM.

CHAPTER 20

In Transition

A permanent state of transition is man's most noble condition.

—Juan Ramon Jimenez

Innovative product designs and creative marketing and brand programs resulted in ThinkPad providing a multi-billion dollar revenue stream for IBM, in spite of its supply problems. However, the mobile segment, beginning to be profitable, was operating within the troubled PC Company. While the ThinkPad business was growing, the desktop PC and server businesses were collapsing. Significant excess inventory problems existed, particularly in the U.S. ThinkPad's almost immediate success and the PC Company's problems catapulted Bruce Claflin into the role of president of PC Company—Americas on August 18, 1993. The PC Company problems eventually drove Bob Corrigan to retire and Gerstner to hire Rick Thoman and make Jerry York the chief financial officer (CFO).

Claflin remembered the day he left the ThinkPad team, recalling how thrilled he was to be taking over the PC Company—Americas: "We had this great success in ThinkPad residing inside a failing business unit. I thought I was going to a job where everything was great, or so it appeared on the surface. We knew that the desktop business was growing like crazy across the personal computer market. Unfortunately, IBM was not keeping up with this growth. It turned out to be a horrible period! I started to look underneath the company's facade, and it was truly crumbling. We had ordered enormous amounts of parts based on the expected sales during the second half of the year. But, the sales weren't happening. In fact, the very day I showed up, the CFO came to see me. He said, 'Bruce, we're screwed. We had forecasted a big demand, but we're now late to market. We have all these parts coming our way, and users just won't buy the products going out the door.'

"We had this new Personal Systems/2 desktop, code named *Laguna*, with some very unique features. Unfortunately, the product ran into technical problems very late in the development cycle. We had already committed to almost half a billion dollars of Laguna parts that were now sitting on our shelves. We also had Value Point parts purchased on the wrong assumption that the demand was going to substantially increase. Compounding the sheer inventory problems was a logistic system so poor, we could not shut it off. So, we had all these parts coming at us. We ended up building the systems and stuffing the channel. The systems did not sell through, and we had a huge inventory return problem.

"We had to get the PC business stabilized. We had to drive enormous cost out of our personal computer business. We had to dramatically improve our cycle times. We had to abandon some technologies like Micro Channel. In short, we had to gut the IBM PC business, even though the ThinkPad was totally successful. We consolidated our labs from nine to three. We moved the principal U.S. lab from Boca to Raleigh, where it could have close links with manufacturing and procurement. This move was intended to get costs down, cycle time up, and designs centered on industry standard components. We wanted to challenge Compaq, who was consistently blowing everybody away in PCs and servers, just as we had done in the mobile space.

"We made significant product line changes. We killed the PS/1, the Value Point, and the PS/2, as well as the Micro Channel. We adopted a new bus. We introduced Aptiva as our consumer desktop brand and the PC 300 and 700 in the server arena. These changes had a dramatic effect on our PC business. In 1993, the IBM PC Company lost a billion dollars. In 1994, it was profitable, but not by much, maybe fifty million dollars. Although fifty million dollars wasn't huge profit, it certainly was a step in the right direction. It was a turnaround of more than a billion dollars year over year. We did it in one year. It was terribly painful, but it turned around our entire business."

Claflin's perception was confirmed by Rick Thoman: "I don't think anyone understood the intensity of the PC Company's operational problems when I arrived on the scene. As I recall, I was hired in late '93 and came to work in January '94. I initially reviewed all the brands at the time and determined that only one brand, ThinkPad, actually worked for us. All the others were finished in one way or another. The PS/2 brand was Micro Channel, a sort of proprietary technology. I didn't think it would work in the market space requiring high quality with very low margins. The Value Point, a less-than-stellar brand name, was voted out because of its go-to-market strategy. We initially introduced a low-cost industry standard model, then tried to upscale it, trying to convince customers that the Volkswagen they were buying was actually a Lexus or a Mercedes.

Even the PS/1 brand had trouble because our customers believed that IBM valued the corporate purchaser ahead of the consumer buyer and provided indiscriminant levels of support. So, essentially, ThinkPad was the only brand that worked.

"ThinkPad was a very powerful brand. It had real life and an identity that stood for something. Our only exposure with ThinkPad was our reliance on display and other technologies that were duplicable over time. We knew that we needed to build brand equity around the name with things beyond technological feeds and speeds. Bruce Claflin (and later Joe Formichelli and Steve Ward) really understood the mobile market. They knew what motivated the 'road warriors' versus those individuals who used their portable as a desktop, yet carried it twice a week across the campus for a conference or something. We also invested in research to back up our beliefs, which gave us some interesting insights into how to think about the product line differently."

In Claflin's own opinion, his move to president of PC Company—Americas happened so quickly that he did not get the chance to leave the ThinkPad team gracefully. He moved so quickly that the ThinkPad's general manager slot was left open for nearly four months. And his departure was during a critical time in the planning cycle—during fall plan, when funding for the next calendar year was decided. Without its leader, the ThinkPad team lost some of its focus, and its key managers vied for Claflin's slot. Schedule problems surfaced, compounding the already high stress levels of the group, which could not meet the supply requirements for its line of very "hot" products. Despite valiant efforts by then Operations Manager Rod Adkins, the team was confused, and the individual functional areas were battling among themselves. It proved to be the worst fall planning cycle in the team's short history. Luckily, the technology roadmaps, which were treated as gospel, helped direct the plan and stymie any long-lasting effects of this turbulent time.

During this four-month period, the only thing on which the team agreed with no debate was that Claflin deserved a special going-away present. Remember that this was a time in IBM when most employees were unhappy with management because of downsizings and erratic product decisions. The entire mobile organization, every single individual on the ThinkPad team, contributed to the gift. The team wanted Claflin to have something special, something reflective of the quality with which he had led the initial ThinkPad effort. They gave him a Steuben glass sailboat, a team picture, and a collage of press clippings and ads from his brief time as general manager.

Claflin summarized his tenure as general manager for the ThinkPad brand from June 1992 until August 1993: "I think that it was honest-to-God teamwork that made ThinkPad successful. No one person dominated. Everybody contributed in his or her own way, and I think that's what made it click. Everybody on the team had strengths. Everybody on the team had weaknesses. But, we were able to minimize the weaknesses and accentuate everybody's strengths. Bartlett brought some level of controversy with him, but he also brought a view that was indispensable; he linked us to the outside. Higuchi-san compensated for the Japanese parochialism with the strength of his engineers. Bower and Fletcher drove innovative marketing programs. Everybody had something to offer. What was our secret to success? Simply harvesting the best skills.

"I am proudest of helping to build a team that stayed together until the move to Raleigh. I recognized good people and kept the bad to a minimum. At times, I even kept them from killing one another. When I arrived, all the ingredients for success were there.

The basic technologies were there. The basic design was there. The people were there. It was just a matter of putting it all together."

Claflin's involvement with the team was best summarized by some of his managers. Bartlett, often at odds with Claflin, offered this perspective: "Bruce was, and is, a master in terms of marketing and strategy. He really understood the customer. Although he did not always understand the technology, he understood enough to competently do the job. He surrounded himself with people who had complementary skills. He developed a really effective organization by motivating and recognizing the team. Unfortunately, he moved too quickly to a more senior position in IBM. Frankly, I was disappointed, just from a personal standpoint, that I didn't get more time working under Bruce. I think that I would have learned a lot more."

According to Debi Dell, "If it had not been for Bruce Claflin's leadership pulling the mobile team together, it wouldn't have mattered how advanced the technologies were. Claflin's impact on the ThinkPad success mirrored that of Don Estridge's on the original PC. Both were consummate people managers who let their teams drive the day-to-day business while providing them with the vision of where the business needed to go."

The Authors' Insights

Upon his arrival, Claflin was accepted as the leader for this journey to build a recognizable mobile brand. He approached problems along the way in novel and unconventional ways. His convictions established the direction and mobile vision, and his clarity and sense of purpose regarding the vision made enthusiasts of those around him. His self-confidence gave employees the stability and assurance that had previously been lacking in the organization. Claflin communicated to his organization clearly and often. He was not afraid to make decisions and was prepared to live with the consequences. Claflin was aggressive, took a firm stand, and held people accountable for their actions.

Claflin had a knack for recognizing opportunities, mobilizing the necessary resources, and then standing back and letting it happen. He was better than most industry executives at getting people to commit to projects. He even kept morale high when an individual's pet project was canceled. No negative vibes existed around Bruce Claflin. When Claflin leaned back in his chair to discuss something with you, you knew that he was giving the topic under discussion his undivided attention. And his response would be the best for the team and the business, in that order.

Postscript on Bruce Claflin

After his promotion to President, PC Company—Americas, Bruce Claflin was asked to manage the PC Company's worldwide procurement, development, product marketing, brand management, advertising, and promotion in May 1994. But, unfortunately for IBM, Claflin resigned in October 1995 after twenty-two years with the company. He related the rationale behind his decision: "I had been at IBM for half my life. I realized that the headlines on me read 'Industry veteran and youthful,' but I knew in a few years they were just going to read 'Made the PC industry better.' I said to myself, 'If I'm going to stay, I'm staying for the long haul. If I'm going to leave, now is the time to do it.' I was at a crossroad in my tenure at IBM.

"I had a great deal of respect for what Lou Gerstner was doing for IBM. I thought he was providing enormously positive leadership, and I thought that ninety percent of what he was doing made sense. The problem was that the other ten percent directly affected me. At that time, we were still doing anything we could to prop up OS/2, even if it meant doing things that were not competitive for our PC business. I wouldn't have minded if I thought it was going to help OS/2, but I didn't believe the things we were doing were going to do a damn thing to help OS/2. We were loading both OS/2 and Windows on every machine and providing a 'dual boot' procedure so that the user could decide whether to load OS/2 or Windows when he turned on his PC.

"Dual boot added to our development schedule, and ninety-nine percent of the customers were just deleting OS/2 when they got their systems. It wasn't adding any value to the company. In fact, dual boot hurt us. Our OS/2 efforts were actually helping Microsoft because they were paid a license fee on every unit shipped, even if the customer only wanted OS/2. Then, they got a second license fee when the channel or customers blew away the hard disk load and loaded their own copy of Windows. As a result, the dual boot process did nothing for OS/2, hurt our PC business, and helped Microsoft. I was extremely frustrated that senior management and, in particular, Lou Gerstner just didn't get it.

"About this same time, Digital offered me the opportunity to run their entire PC business end-to-end, from research and development to its sales, marketing, service, and support. The idea of running a business end-to-end was very appealing after years of dealing with IBM's bureaucracy. Digital wanted to make a major play in personal computers, and the company looked like a candidate for a turnaround. Feeling a little philosophical about my time at IBM, coupled with my frustration over some poor decisions like OS/2, resulted in the opportunity looking very attractive."

The Premium Notebook Family, Planned During Claflin's Regime

System	700/ 700C	720/ 720C	750/ 750C	755C/ 755Cs
Form	Notebook	Notebook	Notebook	Notebook
Processor	486SLC 25MHz	486SLC2 50/25MHz	486SL 33MHz	486 DX2 50/25 Intel DX4 75/25
Memory	4/16MB	4/16MB	4/20MB	4/36MB
Storage	80/120MB	120/160/ 240MB I/II/III PCMCIA	170/340MB I/II/III PCMCIA	170/340/ 540/810MB (2.5")
Display	9.5" STN LCD (Mono) 10.4" TFT LCD (Color)	9.5" STN LCD (Mono) 10.4" TFT LCD (Color)	9.5" Mono STN 9.5" Dual Scan 10.4" Color TFT	9.5" Dual Scan 10.4" TFT LCD
Operating System	DOS 5.0 / 5.02 OS/2 2.0 / 2.1	DOS 5.0 / 5.02 OS/2 2.0 / 2.1 Prodigy	DOS 5.02, 6.1 OS/2 2.1 Prodigy	DOS 6.1 / 6.3 OS/2 2.1 MS-DOS 6.2 Windows 3.1
Weight (lb.)	6.5–7.6	6.5–7.6	5.0–6.4	6.1/6.4
Other	TrackPoint II Micro Channel Exp Cartridge	TrackPoint II Micro Channel Docking station	TrackPoint II AT- bus Audio	TrackPoint II Preloaded SW Mwave DSP
Announced	10/5/92	5/4/93	9/8/93	5/17/94

AWARDS

ThinkPad 700C	*PC Magazine*	"Best Systems"	November 1993
	InfoWorld	"1992 Product of the Year"	April 1993
ThinkPad 720C	*InfoWorld*	"1993 Product of the Year"	May 1994
ThinkPad 750C	Fall Comdex	"Most Valuable Product"	November 1993
ThinkPad 755C	*BYTE*	"Best Notebook 1995—Reader's Choice"	May 1995

CHAPTER 21

Joe Formichelli: Back to Basics

To understand a man, you must know his memories.

—Anthony Quayle

Almost as soon as the ThinkPad 700 announced, the team was faced with supply problems. Initially, worldwide portable manufacturing was managed from Raleigh. In addition to parts procurement and integration for the U.S., the Raleigh manufacturing group provided functional guidance for plants in Greenock, Scotland, Guadalajara, Mexico, and Fujisawa, Japan. By 1994, supply was the critical issue stifling brand growth. The ThinkPad brand team realized that a new approach and a seasoned veteran were necessary to fix this ever increasing problem. And there was only one person the executive team thought was right for the job.

Joe Formichelli grew up in a small blue-collar town in Hudson Valley, New York. His parents and older brothers came from Italy before Formichelli's birth. He was the first son born in the States and the first in the family who spoke English. Formichelli recalled these formative years: "We were poor. With four brothers, everyone had to work to make ends meet. My father got me a job when I was in the fifth grade. He farmed me out to a bakery shop every day after school, 3:30 to 9:30 p.m. I worked there through high school. I couldn't quit because I had to make money for the family. I got ten dollars a week. By the time I finished high school, I was making eleven dollars a week. I started washing pans, got promoted to squeezing jelly into doughnuts, then to making bread, and finally to running the oven. After a few years, I was like the senior engineer who ran the oven.

"I learned the basics of manufacturing from my experiences making donuts. By the time you ran the oven, you had to figure out what donuts people wanted to buy and when they wanted them. You planned the baked goods production to meet that demand. So, although it might look as if I was sent off to some sweatshop as a kid, I actually picked up the skills, at an early age, that led me to become proficient in manufacturing.

"Not only did I have to work, but I had to make good marks in school. If I didn't, my father got after me. There was no concept of life after school. But, it eventually led to the biggest honor in the world—graduating high school. I was the first guy in my family's history to graduate high school. They were from Italy, where you raised pigs or whatever the hell you did in Italy, right? No one thought of getting an education. They worked. So, graduating from high school was a really big honor in my family.

"During this time, the biggest influence on my life was a guy named Sam, who ran the local Boy's Club. Sam kept track of each basketball game and each game of pool. He knew which kid played which sport. He scheduled us to death and managed it all on a big billboard. Today, we'd call it a *Gantt chart*. The whole thing fascinated me because the guy had the smarts to know how to do that.

I figured that, if you wanted to be successful in life, you had to know how to organize and schedule. I talked to Sam about his billboard and how he managed the logistics of it all. That billboard was probably another reason why I became good at manufacturing.

Joe Formichelli.

"When I graduated high school in 1960, the concept of going to college was totally foreign to my family. I wanted to go to college and succeed. I only knew there was such a thing called college because one of my high school friends went to Hamilton College. His family helped me to realize that if you wanted to succeed in life, you went to college. So, when I told my father that I wanted to go to college, he said, 'Sure, go ahead.' Now, that didn't mean he was going to help me go to college, but he just gave me the approval to do it. So, I enrolled in Hudson Valley Junior College in Troy, New York. I majored in electrical engineering, graduating in 1962 with a two-year junior college degree and at the top of my class.

"I got a summer job with General Electric [GE] in Burlington, Vermont, working on the Vulcan Gattling machine gun. I got the highest salary in my graduating class, one hundred fifteen dollars a week. My father thought I was rich. But, in the fall of 1962, I got a permanent job offer from IBM to work for the Components Division in Fishkill, New York. With funding by IBM, I completed college at Syracuse University through the IBM Union College Extension Program. You see, if your manager approved your getting a degree, IBM paid one hundred percent of the expenses. Most young people don't appreciate this benefit until much, much later.

"I started on the drawing board. Back then, every engineer had a drawing board. You didn't sit in a room and think about things like you do today. You had a drawing board because you had to design things. My drawing board was in the process engineering department, where they were trying to automate the one transistor per chip. We were trying to build a 1/32 of an inch square chip with three balls on it, called *solid logic technology* or *SLT*, that eventually went into the 360 mainframe. Although I had never done process development, I got some patents on how to put the copper pins in the ceramic automatically. But, I really became the group's hero because I was one of those guys who worked twenty hours a day.

"My first manager was Mr. Kaufman. You didn't say 'Bill Kaufman.' You said, 'Mr. Kaufman.' About six months after I started, I got a raise. Mr. Kaufman called me in and gave me a raise of ten cents an hour. That translated into four dollars a week. I was cheering. I felt rich until I got a car. Reality set in. I realized that to succeed, I'd need to get more than just a raise.

"My desire to get ahead and my ability to get people to work together got me into management. I always approached work like, 'What is the project? How are we going to get it done? Who's going to do what next? Let's do something.' I could get guys who were 180 degrees apart working together. I would chart the stuff out and determine what the project was going to cost. And, by the way, you always made the date that you committed."

Formichelli's management jobs included manufacturing, equipment, and process engineering. These assignments produced products for IBM mainframes. Remember, in the 1960s, it was all mainframes; the personal computer was not even invented yet. The mainframes fueled tremendous growth on the component side of the business. This growth drove significant hiring programs. A person just walked in and, in a nanosecond, was offered a job. If he could think, they made him a manager. When IBM hired Formichelli, they got a good worker and a thinker!

Formichelli reflected on those early days: "I had a motto: 'Never say no.' If I was asked to paint sixty walls a day, I got it done. I always equated every job to working in the bakery shop. I worked hard because I didn't want my father getting mad at me for not making enough money. Even though I was now married and in the Army reserves, my father was still a strong influence on my life.

"When I got to Poughkeepsie, they didn't have anybody like me there. They didn't have process, manufacturing, or mainframe assembly engineering. By the time I left, module manufacturing had grown so much that we literally owned the place. We were doing modules, power, logic, and memory.

"When I became a third-level manager, I owned product engineering for an entire product line for the first time. Then, in 1980, they added manufacturing to my responsibilities. I had never managed manufacturing, so it was a challenging new experience. Manufacturing was very comfortable for me to manage. It constantly brought back memories of making doughnuts.

"In 1983, I was nominated to be a Sloan fellow at MIT. The program allowed me to get my master's in one year. I didn't think it was a vacation like the other guys in the program because I still thought I was making doughnuts, right? You had to work hard. After graduation, I continued my career at IBM. Although it was common to follow the graduate program with a stint at headquarters, I returned to Poughkeepsie. After all, my family was there, so I went back. I went from being assistant plant manager to plant manager in a very short period of time. I reported to a division president and had six thousand people reporting to me.

"In 1986, I got a call from Jack Kuehler, my mentor at the time. Jack liked me because I made dates. I never bullshitted anybody. Whenever I presented to him and the division president, I told them the truth. I told them when I couldn't do it. I told them when I could do it. When I said I could do it, I delivered.

"Kuehler asked me to head up motherboard manufacturing for the IBM PC Company in Austin. I didn't know what a motherboard was. I didn't know what a PC was. I hesitated. I had to look at a map to see where Austin was located. It didn't take long to realize that my real job was to close the place down. The PC Company, headquartered in Boca, did not want to use Austin for their PC motherboards because they could buy their motherboards cheaper offshore.

"I decided to take a big gamble and drive Austin to be competitive. We worked around the clock and fixed the plant, rather than shut it down. We continued improving things until 1990. Managing through this, I became the number one quality manager inside IBM. I worked on Six Sigma quality before it was popular. It was just like making doughnuts! The right product, at the right time, at the right cost—perfection every time.

"Austin was in the dumps when I got there. They had major morale problems. It was a hot bed of personnel problems. I had to not only fix the PC motherboard manufacturing process but also address the personnel problems. The first thing I had to do was strengthen the team with quality high-end talent.

"In 1990, I was asked to be corporate vice president of manufacturing in Somers, New York. I didn't want to become the guy from corporate whom I hated, because I hated those corporate guys. The VP of Manufacturing would be the guy to come down and offer to 'help' when I was up to my ears in stuff. I did not need a guy coming down and telling me, 'Joe, you've hired too many temps and not enough regulars. And what are you doing to get your yield up? Oh, and tell me about your OSHA policies.' They had more guys up in New York asking me questions than I had in Austin trying to fix things. So, I hated these guys, and now they were asking me to become one of them. Naturally, I didn't want the job.

"But, there were some upsides to the position. After all, becoming VP of manufacturing for all of IBM is the job you always wanted. I worked on strategic issues that affected worldwide manufacturing. I worked on programs to improve efficiencies. And I decided what plants were going to be built, consolidated or closed.

"First, I cut my staff in half. We didn't need hundreds of people in headquarters thinking about manufacturing details. I knew, because I had been one of them, which of the plant managers needed to do the thinking. Within my first six months, I gave a pitch to the senior vice president, Pat Toole, and recommended that we close down some of our plants. No one had ever said anything like this out loud. It resulted in dead silence at the meeting. I had dropped the bombshell; I mentioned the word 'layoffs.' I didn't say it again for a long time after that. It was a horrendous, horrendous emotional meeting. Fortunately, my experience and track record eventually got people to listen to me. When Lou Gerstner arrived in 1993, we closed several plants, and IBM significantly downsized. I felt somewhat responsible for making the initial case. Despite the personal ramifications to many people, in the end, it made a tremendous positive difference to IBM."

From the corporate assignment, Joe Formichelli became division general manager (GM) for Visual Products. For an individual with a manufacturing background to head a major development effort was quite unusual within the PC Company. However, Formichelli had proven himself as a strong business manager, and these skills were needed to complement Kathy Vieth's marketing efforts. Also, as mentioned earlier, Formichelli's actions in this new role had a significant effect on the future of the ThinkPad line. He was instrumental to the DTI relationship and the display decisions. As a peer, Formichelli built a strong relationship with Claflin and, eventually, his brand team—actions that would prove fortuitous in his next assignment as general manager, ThinkPad.

During 1993 and 1994, the IBM PC Company struggled with the conversion to brand management. Jim Cannavino and Bob Corrigan viewed Bruce Claflin as the general manager, ThinkPad, and Formichelli as the general manager, Visual Products, with responsibility for their respective P&L worldwide. According to

Formichelli, "I was told I owned the brand, right out of Michael Porter's *Competitive Advantage*. I had to manage the products in my brand. I had to understand how the market was segmented. But, the struggle arose because the sales organization thought they owned the brand. The debate was consistently about who was in charge. The brand org chart said I was, but whenever I saw the sales org chart, they were always on top. Sales tried to force Claflin and me into the role of vice president of engineering for our products. Despite the move to brand management, only sales officially committed P&L for the company. It was a constant conflict.

"In 1993, Lou Gerstner, in his infinite wisdom, took his executive management team offsite for education on brand management. He focused us on brand management and set up the measurement system accordingly. After that, I presented to the chairman once a month. I had to know the status and plans for my brand. I had to talk like a brand manager and answer questions like 'What are your margins? What are your products? What's happening with your brand? What's your competition doing? Why aren't you doing it?' Again, right out of Michael Porter. But, Gerstner got us thinking and acting like brand managers.

"IBM truly got behind the brand concept, reducing the product lines to seven or eight brands. Each brand manager had to attend and present at an executive brand review meeting every month. Gerstner even had Nick Donofrio personally chair the brand management meetings, which typically ran a full day with the chairman, Rick Thoman, or Jerry York in attendance.

"One day in November 1993, I got a call from Rick Thoman, who had just been assigned to head the Personal Systems group. He had my background on a single sheet of paper; it simply said that I had never failed at delivering. Thoman went on to say that Gerstner was absolutely pissed because he was tired of hearing why customers couldn't get ThinkPads. He told me, 'Formichelli, you're going to make ThinkPads.' Now, I didn't know a bus from a battery about portable computers. I knew how the TFT worked that went into them, because I was in charge of Visual Products, but that was it. However, it was a proud moment in my life to be asked to manage the number one brand name in the PC Company, maybe in IBM. And we knew our biggest problem was that we couldn't deliver on ThinkPad. Thoman said, 'Formichelli, you now own the ThinkPad brand. Go fix it so that customers can get one when they order it.'

"Claflin had been out of the job for about four months, but he still took a lot of time with me. He brought me up-to-date on the things he had worked on. He told me I needed a good marketing guy to balance my manufacturing background. I found Per Larsen, former IBM country manager in Denmark, who drove IBM PCs to thirty percent market share, and made him director of Marketing. He agreed to move from Paris—where he was managing the European ThinkPad program—to Somers. The Yamato development team was doing great. I also had a small development team and worldwide manufacturing based in Raleigh, and the core planning team was based in Boca Raton. Pulling it all together was the most hectic time in my life.

"The Boca team was pretty well organized, but the group in Raleigh wasn't. So, I had a goat rodeo on my hands. I needed to round everyone up so that we could get manufacturing focused and delivering. We needed to produce the quantity of ThinkPads people wanted and sales thought that they could sell.

"The Japanese guys were getting the drum beat; they were getting in sync with the planning team and delivering what the market wanted. They were good at power management, battery life, little motherboards, and packaging in plastics. Some of their best patents were for hinges. Yes, hinges. The Yamato team figured out how to get the power from the main system through the hinge to the TFT display without the hinge wearing out from opening and closing. And they figured out how to paint the plastic so that it had a nice slick feel, a feel unique in the industry.

"The first rule I learned as ThinkPad general manager was that I could never change the paint color on the 700 family without telling headquarters. If I wanted to mold some alternative black colors into other ThinkPad models, I had to go see the Corporate Committee. At the time, it was their favorite brand, certainly the most successful.

"So, I spent a great deal of my time getting the team to work on the key problem—supply. But, I still had the other responsibilities of a general manager, including the monthly executive reviews. The most memorable review meeting was shortly after the first of the year, 1994. I had been the mobile GM for about three months. Not only were the brand managers there, but also the key sales executives. IBM's CFO, Jerry York, was also there. He hated the PC Company at the time because we weren't making any money. He ran this tedious, horrible meeting. Not horrible because he was bad, but horrible because he was asking the right questions. I watched people with the wrong answers get blown away."

When it was Formichelli's turn, he had one chart. Remember that this was a meeting with all the geographies and the top IBM management. So, Formichelli put up one transparency with a single curve, and the curve went from nothing to off the chart. It went from one inch up to five inches, a really sharp, nice round curve with an arrow moving up to the right. No one knew what it meant because there was no legend on the chart. Formichelli had an aversion to numbers recorded on a chart. He knew that he had to carefully phrase what he was about to say. Rick Thoman, Jerry York, and Bill McCracken, VP for sales, were at this meeting, and they had just finished shooting several brand managers. So, Formichelli began, "I've learned something very valuable in my first few months as general manager for ThinkPad. [significant pause] What I have learned is that the sales team in the PC Company can sell anything I don't make."

After Formichelli's opening remark, they sat there with their mouths open. He went on to explain what that curve on his chart represented: "This line represents the number of TFT screens that I have coming as the DTI yields improve. From today to the uplift on the curve is about three or four months. There's a lot of this stuff coming at you marketing guys. Do you understand what this chart says? I am your worst goddamn nightmare come true."

Formichelli recollected the moment when Jerry York stood up. He thought to himself, "I'm fired." But York went on to say, "Joe has just thrown down the gauntlet. Now here's what we're going to do. We're going to break this meeting. It's now 11:30. You're coming back here at 1:30. I want the geographies [United States, Europe, Asia, Latin America, Canada] to add up to that number, plus twenty-five percent for insurance. Do you understand?" Not a sound could be heard in the room.

Formichelli recalled, "Suddenly, some guy from South America had the nerve to say, 'Well, if we finally get those quantities, I think we should start lowering the price rapidly and take market share.' Jerry York's skin almost fell off his body. I had never seen a man explode like that in public. Needless to say, the geographies came back after lunch and had plans in place to sell the uplift in production."

Joe Formichelli's takeover of the ThinkPad brand was well received by many members of the team. Leo Suarez summarized the majority's reaction: "After the introduction of the ThinkPad 700, the market took off. We experienced the classic PC Company problem associated with a successful product—our customers could not get any. Availability was always six to twelve months out.

The demand was so great that we just couldn't manufacture enough. We didn't need to market these products; marketing was simply an allocation process. We didn't have to market anything because we had backlog for a year. We simply needed to fulfill orders.

"We needed a GM with a strong manufacturing background. Formichelli was brought in to get a manufacturing process in place and availability up. And guess what? He did a damn good job. When we designed a portable for the general business user, the ThinkPad 380 with built-in CD-ROM, floppy, and hard disk, he was at the helm. And we built them by the millions."

Suarez's manager, Jim Bartlett, echoed his sentiments: "Joe Formichelli came at an important time. Our demand was way up, but we had trouble making enough ThinkPads to meet the demand. If we were broken anywhere, it was in manufacturing. We could not make these things consistently at any volume level, no matter how hard we tried. This was throughout late 1993 to 1995. If Formichelli knew anything better than anybody else at IBM did, it was how to build product; he was a manufacturing genius. Formichelli brought his expertise to bear on our problems and focused us on how to build more ThinkPads. We made the most significant growth in the shortest period of time while he was here, in terms of trying to build systems at a consistent rate with high quality.

"However, Formichelli had a difficult time managing the rest of the brand elements as clearly as he did the manufacturing piece. He was much more comfortable working within the manufacturing element, compared to Bruce, who could put himself into the other roles more easily. But, he still made tremendous contributions to the brand."

Bruce Claflin, Bartlett's manager and Formichelli's predecessor, had this to say about his successor: "Formichelli increased the focus on the manufacturing side of the equation. From day one, our biggest problem was getting enough capacity to meet demand. Whereas my contributions were in building a team and promoting ThinkPad to marketplace, Formichelli inherited a team that worked pretty well and a product line that was selling. His job was to get more discipline into the process and get manufacturing to quickly increase production. He did a great job! Without delivering the product, customers would have eventually lost interest, and IBM would have had another failed portable attempt in its history."

During an October 1994 interview, Formichelli said, "When I came onboard, I was consumed with fixing the manufacturing problem. I assumed, based on the ThinkPad's resounding market success, that the team and organization I inherited from Claflin was right for the market. I failed to recognize the need to reorganize in order to be more responsive to the market, the changing demographics, and the employees' needs. I made some pretty significant changes shortly after I arrived. For one thing, whereas Claflin had experience in marketing and basically acted as the worldwide brand manager, I knew that I needed someone to pull the geography managers under one umbrella.

"I asked Per Larsen to head the brand marketing team. Per relieved me of a lot of stuff that I didn't really know how to do at the time. He was instrumental to the ThinkPad's success. He attacked the brand management side of marketing. He inherently knew why customers were buying and how the market was segmenting. He helped me explain the changing market to guys like Rick Thoman. This was particularly important as the market moved towards value portables and away from the premium boxes. Thoman did not want to see the gross margins come down, but, obviously, as our volumes moved towards the ThinkPad 3xx family, they had to come down. Remember that this was at a time when IBM needed all the profit margin possible. The change was not easy for him to accept.

"I also went back to my days in the Northeast and hired a former mainframe executive, Nick King, to head our development efforts. This change created some friction with Yamato, where Higuchi-san had been managing the operation for Claflin. I decided to make this change to try to integrate Yamato and Raleigh, but the graft never took. When we disbanded the Raleigh development effort, Higuchi-san was put back in charge of development. He and the Yamato management team deserved most of the credit for our technological successes. Those guys usually met their dates, something that was almost impossible for the U.S. development teams to do. Because delivering on time was my motto, the Yamato team earned my respect.

"I think that, without those two guys, Per Larsen and Higuchi-san, the ThinkPad team would have fallen apart. I think those two guys were the senior partners that made ThinkPad a success."

Formichelli did not change two key management positions inherited from the Claflin regime. He left Patty McHugh as the planning manager. McHugh had a proven track record for quality product plans and a total solutions approach to the product line. She had been with the mobile effort since 1990, when she was the planning manager for the pen tablet project. She was a cheerleader for the organization's morale and had the respect of the geographically dispersed team. Even Yamato, with a cultural distrust of women, listened to McHugh when she brought forward new ideas and concepts.

Formichelli also did not disturb the worldwide marketing strategy department headed by Jim Bartlett. He reflected on Bartlett's contribution to ThinkPad: "Jim had a different perspective on just about everything. He brought an outside view to IBM. He kept you on your toes because he asked interesting questions. Maybe five of twenty questions weren't necessary, but the rest got you to really think. He brought excitement to the process.

"Jim always had a million questions. He was the little kid you hated in the third grade who asked the teacher every question imaginable. And he usually tried to answer every question that was ever posed by others. If I brought in a nuclear engineering Ph.D. from Cal Tech to discuss batteries and someone asked him a question, Jim would try to answer it. Or if someone asked me a question in a meeting, Jim would always say, 'I can answer that.'

"But, because Jim came to IBM from the outside, the poor guy didn't know anything about how IBM worked. He stumbled and fell into walls. He thought he could just do x, y and z as he saw fit. I remember one time when he told Debi [Dell] to go ahead and get a membership to the Delta Crown Room because they were all travelling so much. He wouldn't believe that IBM just didn't authorize that kind of benefit for its senior-level employees! I'm not saying the IBM system was always right, but I told Jim to try to understand the system before he tried to go around it.

"Now, don't get the impression that Jim wasn't valuable to us. I'd rather have one guy like Jim working for me than one hundred guys or gals who didn't want to do anything or just wanted to go with the flow. Bartlett was the guy who wanted to do everything. Many times, he was the only guy who knew how to do it. So, he brought some spirit to the ThinkPad team that was essential to building a new business."

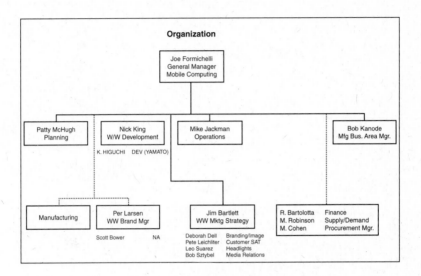

Formichelli had a strong team, one that knew, without a doubt, the premium mobile market. But, in 1994, the ThinkPad planning organization missed a major shift in the market, a shift to Pentium-based value notebooks. This oversight cost them the position of number one in the mobile market.

Formichelli recalled the impact of this faux pas: "Organization and bureaucracy aside, my biggest problem was Toshiba. We hadn't thought anybody was going to come out with a low-cost Pentium notebook for quite a while. At the time, we had forty percent gross margins on ThinkPad products and something like sixty percent market share of portables above five thousand dollars. The executives were thrilled and the market was buying. It was a great position to be in. But, I eventually put charts together and showed Rick Thoman and key PC Company executives that sales on premium ThinkPads were eroding. Customers wanted more value at a less-than-three-thousand-dollar price tag. It was a shock, but true.

"By the time I figured out what was happening, we were really behind the competition in getting a lower cost Pentium portable out the door. We were going to lose market share to Toshiba unless we acted quickly. We put every engineer into getting a good ThinkPad 3xx product out. But, I discovered that we were going to jury-rig a Pentium to get it out the door fast. So, we slowed down and did it right. Nobody was happy about it, but we had to do it right. By the time we recovered, Toshiba had stolen fifteen percent market share from us. It was our business to have, but we missed the boat. We finally got good value-based products into the market with the introduction of the ThinkPad 380, one of the most successful product launches in ThinkPad history. The ThinkPad 380 brought ThinkPad down into the less expensive, sweet spot of the market. We had to do this to compete on a broader scale and give customers what they wanted. Until the 380 line, we were primarily viewed as a 'high end' player."

Formichelli learned something else from this Pentium over-sight; sometimes the development plan did not tie to reality. Shortly after he had presented his product plan and forecast to the sales and executive management review board, he discovered a major exposure to the team's future. Formichelli had just com-mitted 1994 revenue and supply to the company. The sales guys were whipped into a frenzy to get the orders to make this forecast happen. However, when development reviewed their plans the following week, the products were delayed six to eight months. The update showed that the color displays were not going to arrive until after the product was scheduled to announce. In addition, the battery and hard disk did not fit the mechanical package, and the power management did not work. Formichelli also learned that a product, code-named Butterfly, that he had been led to believe would announce shortly, was way behind schedule. Formichelli had committed millions of dollars of revenue at an acceptable margin to the IBM Company, and the plans were in jeopardy.

Formichelli described the problem: "About a week after my executive review, I saw some development charts that indicated the revenue was never going to happen in the timeframe I had just committed. Never happen. This was a water shed discovery for me because I had assumed that the brand team was running smoothly. I could not believe that anybody was committing to plans they couldn't pull off. Remember that I'd never missed a date in my life on anything that could derail the business. Didn't anybody besides me think there was a problem? What were we going to do? We had this huge hole in our product plan. It was millions and millions of dollars. I told the product team, 'That's it. I don't trust anybody from now on, from this minute. We're going to review the plan by furlong, by fortnight, by acre, by part number, by minute, men, women, midgets.' That was the way I learned to manage from my doughnut-making days, right? Just do it. Don't trust anybody and just do it. We fixed it, but it took a lot of effort."

Formichelli continued, "I needed to pull together a team with a worldwide perspective if we were going to play in this market. We could have done all the PR in the world, and someday it would have collapsed around our ears. We needed to realize that we could not count on all the revenue showing up in the fourth quarter. We needed to start thinking about commonality in order to allow us some flexibility with model manufacturing. I needed the team to fix our inability to switch panels among the various models so that we could react to marketing's swizzle on the demand. During this timeframe, we were locked into panel A only going into box A, panel B, and so on; if Scott [Bower] needed to make a change on his demand, we were dead in the water. These meetings got the team running and looking at the business from a total business perspective. It took the heat off Bob Kanode and his manufacturing team. Until this point, development, planning, and marketing had given Kanode lip service on making this kind of change. I worked to fix this not only as part of building my team, but also to change the way we were doing business—to get to a commonality of parts."

Because of his manufacturing background, Formichelli often discussed with Kanode, head of the U.S. manufacturing based in Raleigh, the need for a better process and increased parts commonality. Kanode recalled, "I had been involved with ThinkPad from its inception because of my PC Portable and L40SX experience. The L40 was built in Raleigh, a manufacturing facility better designed for highly customized products. This line was better suited to manufacture a Rolls Royce than a laptop. It could never produce the required volume, cost, or quality we needed for the L40SX laptop, let alone the ThinkPad.

"We had a severe supply problem from day one. We had a forecast that no one believed because of IBM's past portable history. We needed to discard the automated L40SX line and design a facility to meet the higher volume, lower cost, and more repeatable quality line required by ThinkPad. In addition, Formichelli and I were concerned that a unique line built to fit each product would be totally out of date by the announcement and delivery of that particular product, given the nine-month development cycle. This drove severe limitations on what we wanted for our manufacturing process. No history existed on how to design a process that could handle large portable volumes over a short period of time and then be reconfigured for the next cycle. Coupled with the lack of a positive track record in delivering portables, the PC Company executives were reluctant to make a large investment in manufacturing ThinkPad portables. As a result, we were not able to catch up to the demand and build enough ThinkPads. By the time we made the investment to increase production, it occurred at the wrong time in the product cycle. But, we accomplished the required line transition just after Formichelli's arrival.

"We responded to the demand by constantly increasing production, which took a lot of time to implement. We would finally catch up in the fifth or sixth month of the product cycle. But, by then the product demand was not as high. That put us into a 'going out of business' strategy when we had reached the highest volume for that model. It didn't make any sense. In some cases, we ended up having to unload excess inventory even when we could not meet the demand for newer models.

"The only way to deal with this problem was to get the entire production process to be much more efficient and configured to match the ThinkPad product life cycles. We drove commonality into the design across the product line. This was particularly tough for a manufacturing guy who now had to do battle with the hardware designers. Designers don't like to repeat a design; they get high on designing new stuff. We began to standardize keyboards, displays, batteries, AC adapters, floppy drives, and hard drives.

"During Formichelli's regime, we developed a flexible ThinkPad manufacturing process in Raleigh. We were able to build a lot of products on it, and we could reconfigure it quickly for follow-ons. We began to use commodity components. But, the demand for ThinkPad was going through the roof. We quickly realized that we needed more plant capacity, and it had to be developed internationally.

"We decided to build major plants in Guadalajara, Mexico [for the Americas], Fujisawa, Japan [for the Far East], and Greenock, Scotland [for Europe]. Guadalajara, in particular, had manufacturing capacity and people that were not being utilized. They also had lower cost. I coordinated this effort, which proved very viable after the NAFTA agreement went into effect.

"I also managed the effort to get ThinkPad manufacturing in Greenock. I didn't have those people reporting to me, but I had the responsibility to roll out the new manufacturing processes. We created a truly international manufacturing operation for ThinkPad. Ironically, after we brought up our three regional manufacturing centers, we closed Raleigh because it didn't add any value to our worldwide operation."

In May 1994, Gerry Purdy interviewed Formichelli and Bartlett to get their perspectives on the mobile effort. Bartlett summarized the effect of Formichelli's actions up to this point, as well as the current elements of success: "Our success can be attributed to four factors. First was the organization established in 1992: the *structure of getting accountability and authority to execute as a multi-functional team*. Second, we challenged the team to *focus on excellence* in everything we did, the objective being total customer satisfaction. The *Voice of the Customer* was instrumental in shaping the overall direction of this business during the past eighteen months.

"Third, we developed a *fresh sense of urgency*. We recognized that sustained innovation in our processes and in speed of execution of what we did was going to be critical to our continued success in the mobile computing business. Before that we were late—with too little at too high a price.

"Fourth, we developed *an environment that encouraged people to really stretch*. In the past, we encouraged people to be conservative in everything, with very little risk. Now, we're encouraging people to take a reasonable amount of educated risk. That's a real departure from our past, when IBM was more risk-averse. We recognized that to achieve breakthroughs, sometimes you had to move fast, you had to make decisions, and sometimes some decision was better than no decision."

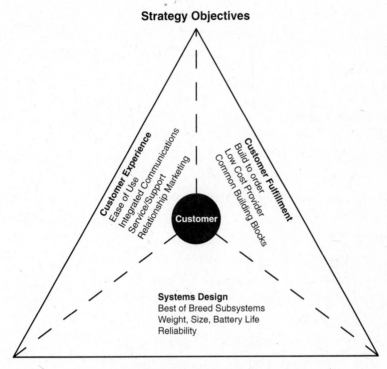

Strategy Objectives

Customer Experience
Ease of Use
Integrated Communications
Service/Support
Relationship Marketing

Customer Fulfillment
Build to order
Low Cost Provider
Common Building Blocks

Customer

Systems Design
Best of Breed Subsystems
Weight, Size, Battery Life
Reliability

Balance hardware requirements,
customer experience, and fulfillment

Formichelli added, "We focused our total efforts on the customer. If an action did not enhance the overall relationship, we did not do it. In addition to innovative system designs, we also worked on ease of use and the total customer experience. And, of course, my background drove me to focus on the customer fulfillment and supply processes.

"We began to recognize employees with changes, more than just the occasional award or salary increase. IBM changed its compensation plan. Employees and managers were compensated in the IBM PC Company for positive changes in both customer satisfaction and loyalty, as well as increased revenue. This was the first time that the average employee could feel that he or she was getting a payback for contribution to IBM's bottom line. This process, known as *variable pay*, continues today."

To assist with this process and garner the employee allegiance, the team met weekly to review the options and potential fixes available to them. As soon as Formichelli was convinced that every option had been explored and contingency plans were in place to recover, he instituted monthly meetings. These meetings became the only source of real information for the team. If an individual wanted to know what was happening with the brand, he or she had to attend this meeting. It got to the point where almost the entire Boca team went to this meeting just to find out current status. Something was lost in the day-to-day operations, and rumors were flying about the possible shutdown of the Boca site. Formichelli needed to rally the team.

With this in mind, he agreed to sponsor a barbecue for the Boca team and their spouses. The barbecue was held at Debi Dell's home, and almost everyone on the team attended. Formichelli hosted the event, and food and drink were plentiful. After turning a few slabs of ribs and flipping some burgers, Formichelli circulated throughout the crowd, thanking the team for their efforts. However, the atmosphere was guarded; everyone was pensive, tentative about the future. It provided a respite to long hours in the office and a brief interlude of fun. It was not enough, however, to change the undercurrent of uneasiness. Back at the office, communications improved briefly among the team members, but then deteriorated. Again, the only source of real information became the group meetings.

In the fall of 1994, the IBM PC Company lost twice as much money as projected. The inventory was up by a factor of two, and Jerry York was assigned to go to Raleigh every week to fix the problem. If you ran the PC business, you did not want Jerry York in Raleigh every week. York knew how to get to the bottom of an issue.

According to Formichelli, "Jerry York attacked manufacturing—I don't mean it in a derogatory way—but the group deserved it. After four weeks, he discovered the issue was not a manufacturing problem. It was a demand problem. Shortly after one of his sessions, he pulled me aside and told me that I was going to be the vice president of Operations. I agreed to do it if they moved Operations out from under Sales. York made it happen."

The IBM PC Company went through enormous change. Rick Thoman, Bruce Claflin, and Jerry York ripped the company apart and put it back together again so that it would work and make money for IBM. They needed someone to get manufacturing and operations working after they had corrected the basic product strategy. They truly needed Formichelli in this role more than as general manager of ThinkPad, at least in the short term.

Formichelli was allowed to hire whomever he needed. He went back to his strong manufacturing ties and captured the key skills of those individuals who had helped him to turn around the Austin plant. He also got Claflin and Thoman to agree to move Purchasing under Operations; it had reported to Claflin as part of Sales. During this period, the company made the decision to close the PC operations in Boca Raton and move the effort to Raleigh. It was an unpopular decision, and Formichelli was in the middle.

Formichelli knew that he did not want to do the operations job forever: "I realized that it was fun being the general manager of ThinkPad. After all, well-known people called me up and wanted my opinion, wanted to talk to me. Nobody called me when I was the manufacturing guy. I worked on the operations problem until mid-year 1995 and then returned to ThinkPad. Bruce was acting ThinkPad general manager during my absence, but we were really attacking major issues across the PC Company together. We made the decision to close the Boca operations and move the team to Raleigh. Patty McHugh, the planning manager, got a chance to drive ThinkPad, and she did a good job. When we started making the numbers in the second quarter of '95, they hired an outside guy to take over operations, and I took some time to train the new person. But, I was glad to get back to ThinkPad, at least for a while."

The Authors' Insights

With the success of the ThinkPad brand came unexpected demand and no way to fulfill it. A manufacturing guru who could cut through the process and make it happen arrived on the scene in the person of Joe Formichelli. Formichelli brought with him not only manufacturing expertise, but also the basic concepts of project management. A core competency within IBC, these project management skills enabled the team to gain control of an ever escalating supply problem.

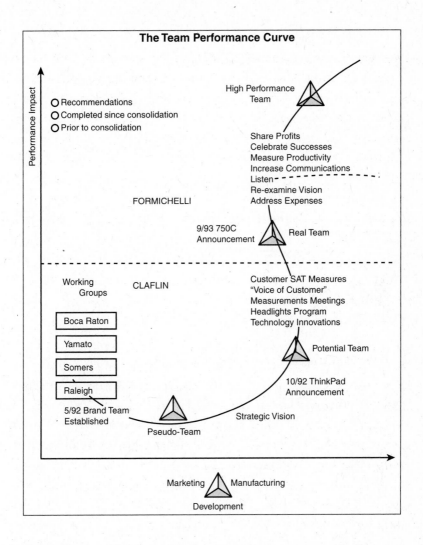

The success of the ThinkPad program can be tracked against the changing of its general managers.

In *Crossing the Chasm*, Geoffrey Moore states that new technologies that evolve from niche markets into large ones needed to cross a chasm. The key initiative that enabled IBM and the Mobile Computing team to cross its chasm was the huge investment in Mobile's brand identity, new products, channels, and updated fulfillment processes. This investment was critical to maintain the momentum of 1993's successes—market credibility through increased orders, press and industry awards, and brand recognition of ThinkPad.

Follow-on ThinkPad offerings achieved technology leadership on a consistent basis and expanded into new product categories. ThinkPads were no longer just premium notebooks and tablets but now participated as a player in the subnotebook and desktop alternative segments. Also, the team realized that key alliances and partnerships enabled them to expand ThinkPad's capabilities beyond the box and were instrumental to the successful crossing of the chasm.

Formichelli put the infrastructure and formal processes in place to make this crossing easier, a seamless effort to achieve greater volume and more timely product announcements. His efforts drove reduced cycle time and improved quality, factors critical to a player who wanted to be number one in the mobile segment. Formichelli was not the right person to launch the ThinkPad brand, but he certainly was the leader who could make the manufacturing changes necessary to meet customer demand.

CHAPTER 22

Butterfly: A Hit That Missed

IBM has blown the lid off the mobile computing market.

—Bill Ablondi[1]

IBM's portable journey was a checkerboard of successes and failures. Although ThinkPad successes far outweighed their failures, not every product was an overwhelming success. Sometimes, a system was viewed as a monumental success with no one distinctive feature other than that of fulfilling the ThinkPad brand promise. Such was the case with the ThinkPad 720. Other times, a system had innovative features that were well received in the market, but the total package missed the competitive mark. Such was the case with IBM's ThinkPad 701C, better known in the industry as *Butterfly*.

The ThinkPad 701C was an outgrowth of an early 1990s effort to create synergy between Raleigh manufacturing and Yamato development, sometimes referred to as *early manufacturing involvement* (EMI). The team based in Research Triangle Park (RTP),

1. IBM press release (March 7, 1995): 2.

North Carolina, started with a handful of engineers and managers with strong business sense. Working directly with Yamato, their mission was to increase manufacturing efficiency through mechanical and planar design changes. In the course of executing this mission, the group recognized unaddressed business and technical opportunities. A vision evolved—to deliver a value-priced notebook that was easy to manufacture and easy to use.

During this period, various IBM laboratories pursued mobile products without the sanction of a single brand manager because no centralized portable organization existed. Appealing to Personal Systems/1 (PS/1) Development in Lexington and using strategic assistance from RTP's Test Engineering and Austin's physical board design, the EMI team developed and shipped a "value" notebook on May 10, 1993. Because the PS/1 business unit funded the final development, it added the system to their line of retail products. Announced as the PS/1 Note, it proved a stepchild of the renewed portables focus and had minimum market success. But, the announcement of the PS/1 Note was one of several catalysts for the revitalized mobile effort. It also brought Scott Bower and Maurice Fletcher, strong additions to the brand team, onto the ThinkPad team. Bower and Fletcher had garnered a fundamental knowledge of the portable market through their work on the PS/1, which proved invaluable to the emerging ThinkPad brand.

A bed of critical engineering resources had amassed in Raleigh, and the then established ThinkPad brand team recognized this fact. Capitalizing on their "value line" experience, the Raleigh team was assigned the ThinkPad 350 for development. More was behind the decision to use Raleigh than just a core set of skills; the brand management wanted a development option if the Yamato team faltered—a poker ploy to keep the Japanese focused. Just as the team had used Zenith in its early years, management wanted to drive home the point that Yamato had to continue to deliver innovative, timely products or development alternatives would be sought.

The ThinkPad 350 team consolidated in the same building as the mobile manufacturing organization within Research Triangle Park. Raleigh management held the opinion that communications and teamwork would improve if the teams aggregated in the same physical facility. Because the staffing had increased the original team of nine to thirty-two engineers by the product's announce, the communications dynamics had greatly magnified. Expertise on the team now included electrical design, power design, physical layout, mechanical engineering, diagnostics programming, modem engineering, audio engineering, real-time operating system (OS) development, BIOS programming, and power management programming.

The Raleigh team proved their ability to develop special features specific to the value market, a focus of no interest to Yamato development and of limited interest to Boca planning. The ThinkPad brand management still wanted to keep the two development options viable, as well as utilize the Raleigh skills. Thus, the Raleigh team was asked to design a quite "different" ThinkPad, code-named *Butterfly*.

Butterfly was a product concept that incorporated a different kind of keyboard: a full-size keyboard in a subnotebook package. According to John Karidis, the chief engineer on the project, "The Butterfly concept was first developed in the form of a photocopy of a keyboard in spring 1993. We built various levels of prototypes during the summer and fall of that year, including a manually operated Plexiglas model with two shifting keyboard elements. The decision to fund the development of Butterfly came in the fall of 1993, with a planned introduction a year later. The development team felt that a one-year plan was extremely aggressive because twelve months was the standard time to develop a standard 'vanilla' notebook, without any innovations like the ones planned for Butterfly."

The 5th Wave   By Rich Tennant

"WHERE'S THAT FLAKE TEMPLEMAN? HE'S SUPPOSED TO BE HELPING US WITH THIS."

Butterfly was one of the early designs shown to the Industry and Customer Advisory Councils; the excitement of the council members drove the brand team to push for a quick delivery of this unique concept. Claflin, still general manager at the time, stood in front of the IAC and said nonchalantly, "I have something rather interesting to show you. For the past couple years, we have been trying to solve the keyboard problem associated with the subnotebook. Every time we tested small notebooks, the users expressed the need for a small, light portable with a usable keyboard. We figured that if we solved this problem, we would garner the sub-notebook market. I've invited Dr. John Karidis here to report to you on how we have solved the keyboard problem."

The council members looked around the room with skepticism on their faces. Surely, IBM could not be so arrogant as to think that they had figured out a way to put a full-size keyboard in a sub-notebook package. IBM had only been back in the portable game for a year!

Karidis stepped to the front of the room and uncovered a sub-notebook whose form factor resembled the ThinkPad 510C. He turned his back so that no one could see what he was doing. A few seconds later, he turned to face the audience and did not say a thing. He just stood there holding this new subnotebook with a keyboard that expanded, like wings, beyond the portable's edges. What was this, some kind of trick? Karidis smiled and explained that this subnotebook incorporated an expandable keyboard developed at IBM's Watson Research Center. He turned around, closed the cover, and turned back to show the unopened system.

"Do you want me to open it in front of you?" inquired Karidis of the group. At this point, the enthusiasm could not be contained. The IAC members jumped out of their seats and moved toward the front of the room. Everyone wanted to see up close IBM's latest wizardry. Slowly, Karidis opened the unit, and the group observed the keyboard expand and then lock into place. "No way!" yelled Tim Bajarin of Creative Strategies. "You've got to be kidding!" exclaimed Gerry Purdy. It drew them in just like kids wondering whether the light stays on when the refrigerator door opens and closes.

Karidis repeated the process a few times so that the group could see just how the mechanical marvel worked. "We've code-named this *Butterfly* because its keyboard opens like the wings of a butterfly. We think it's pretty innovative. What do you guys think?"

Dr. John Karidis.

Before articulating their thoughts, in the true spirit of fact-finders, the council wanted to know the history of the keyboard. Karidis explained, "I came to IBM's [Thomas] Watson Research Center right after getting my doctorate in mechanical engineering from Penn State. Because my dissertation had been on modeling and optimization of high-speed electromagnetic actuators, I initially worked on impact matrix printers and then on high-speed, miniature robotics. But, I quickly drifted towards consumer products. I started thinking about PCs and end user products, as opposed to manufacturing equipment or unique technical pieces such as actuators. As the market shifted, so did the Center's thinking. We looked at the notebook market and analyzed what had succeeded and what had failed.

"The ThinkPad 700 succeeded because of its large screen and full-size keyboard; other competitive units in the U.S. market had failed because of their cramped keyboards. The ThinkPad keyboard was a little wider because of the ThinkPad's more European design of 8.4×11.7 inches versus the competition's notebook size of 8.5×11 inches. That additional width provided a very nice keyboard layout that people liked.

"One day, I was staring at the ThinkPad 700 and thinking about subnotebooks. I observed that the machine's width was driven by the keyboard's width, but with wasted space in the front and the back of the keyboard. I also recognized that the system's depth was driven by the size of the display, but with unused space on its left and right. So, with the width being driven by the keyboard and the depth by the display, a bit of a mismatch existed. I did a quick estimate and determined that the total area of the keyboard was similar to the total area of the display panel; they just had different aspect ratios. The keyboard was wide and fairly narrow, whereas the display was more of a square. A definite mismatched aspect ratio existed.

"If the keyboard and display had the same aspect ratio, you could put them in a smaller box. There was little that could be done about the display's aspect ratio if you wanted to keep the standard 4×3 aspect ratio and have all the software work. But, there was at least a theoretical opportunity to change the aspect ratio of the keyboard.

"At that point, I flashed on the image of these wooden blocks I had bought for my three-year-old daughter. I compared the keyboard with this pair of triangular blocks I had. They mated along a diagonal slice that allowed you to slide the blocks together. When you did this, the combined width of the two blocks got a little narrower, and the depth increased. In a sense, a long thin rectangle turned into more of a square, and that was just what we needed the keyboard to do.

"But, you couldn't cut the keyboard on a smooth diagonal because it had overlapping rows of keys. I thought about cutting a stair-step diagonal. I made some photocopies of the ThinkPad 700 keyboard and thought about how much I needed to shrink it and where the diagonal had to be. I approximated the straight diagonal with a stair-step diagonal and started cutting up the photocopies. I rearranged them until I found a solution that let the keyboard match very nicely in the extended position. In the collapsed position, it was approximately two inches narrower, squarer, almost matching the width of the 10.4-inch display. So, this basic concept led to trying to find a thin inexpensive durable mechanism that reliably closed the keyboard and expanded it smoothly when deployed. With a small team of fellow engineers, we went through several iterations on the actual mechanism. The product evolved from there."

Although Karidis presented at the advisory council, the keyboard was the result of a team effort. Working with him were co-inventors Gerard McVicker and Michael Goldowsky, mechanical engineer Larry Stone, and manufacturing engineer Gary Friedly. These five individuals worked closely with the Raleigh development team to integrate their innovative keyboard design into the subnotebook form factor.

Despite their ebullience over the keyboard, the council members withheld their opinions until John Madigan, product planning manager, reviewed the product specifications. In addition to the innovative keyboard, this system included a 486 processor and the ThinkPad trademarks of a 10.4-inch display and the red TrackPoint. The group asked about the product's delivery schedule, and Claflin committed "before yearend." The IAC members encouraged the team to get the unit into production as soon as possible.

At the IAC meeting held in fall 1994, the group was given an update. Butterfly would not ship until the spring of 1995, much later than originally expected. The delays were due to the problems in getting the expandable keyboard to work properly. The members informed IBM that the industry was quickly shifting from 486 to Pentium processors and that displays were growing from 11.3 inches to 12.1 inches in full-size notebooks. The consensus was that the 10.4-inch display would be passé, potentially making the subnotebook form factor obsolete by the end of 1995. IBM had to deliver Butterfly in the fall of 1994, as originally planned, in order to have a full product life. Any later and the new "ultraportables" with larger displays and Pentium processors would squash the Butterfly.

The ThinkPad team pursued the product completion in earnest. The media review program was, by this time, fundamental to the launch cycle. Media representatives were hungry for the machines, teased for months by Bob Sztybel and Jonathan Gandal. "This was by far the most fun to present to the reviewers," recalled Sztybel. "Everyone was fascinated by the keyboard, although the unit was crammed with other winning features. To the media, Butterfly demonstrated that there might still be a future for the subnotebooks. We needed to hit key deadlines to make the right magazine issues for a big launch. The Raleigh team stepped up to the challenge in a big way."

According to Chris Farrell, one of the original Raleigh team members, the engineers worked obscene hours to complete the Butterfly on the schedule urged by marketing. Each developer, especially the mechanical engineers, took his or her craft to a new level. Together, they raised the bar on the technologies to be integrated in a ThinkPad: new BIOS architecture for docking and Plug and Play, ROM diagnostics, system-level power management with both hardware and software control, and interlocking dual-sided planars.

Farrell reflected, "Every person on the team was determined that his or her piece would be Best of Breed in the industry— *without question*. When the 701 shipped, it was on every magazine cover. The list of awards filled three pages, and they weren't just for the keyboard. At announce, the system had the maximum size display in the market, the fastest modem available, integrated telephony and sound, removable hard drives and infrared support. None were yet industry standard."

Of course, the design process was only part of what it takes to get a product announced; manufacturing Butterfly fell on Joe Formichelli's broad shoulders. Formichelli recalled, "Now, to be sure, Butterfly got a lot of accolades. We won product of the year. We won computer of the year at Comdex. Everybody oohed and aahed at that keyboard and wondered how we packed a 10.4-inch screen inside that tiny box. The consultants and analysts thought it was astounding. It was an absolutely exciting time. It would have been great if we only could have come out a year earlier, on the original schedule. When I got on board with ThinkPad in

November 1993, I was told that the design completion was imminent, with a planned product introduction in early fall 1994. Because of the delays in getting the engineering for the expandable keyboard worked out, the Butterfly actually announced on March 6, 1995.

"Shortly after arriving as general manager, I went to Raleigh and conducted a design review with the team. What did I find out? First, the plastics guys had not even talked to the display guys about whether the panel fit in the case. The display guys had yet to talk to the stamping guys to see whether all the pieces fit together. Metal shards were dropping off the trial production line. I certainly didn't want metal shavings inside my portables. And, by the way, I never told anybody this, but the thing didn't open and close without breaking. When you opened and closed the cover, the hinge would break. The total design was my worst nightmare. John Karidis, who got all the accolades for the Butterfly design, was off developing something else. I went berserk. I got him back and got him to focus full-time on getting it fixed.

"I flew to Raleigh and met with the team every single week. I had them show me the bolts, the screws, what they were doing on every little thing. I reviewed the dates. I scrubbed the actions of the stamping guys, the keyboard guys, and the monitor guys. That's what it took. But, it was so damn late. Although we had innovation in spades, by the time we introduced the Butterfly in March of 1995, everyone was talking about converting to Pentium notebooks, not 486s. We had ordered parts based on the preceding year's demand. The processor ended up being our most deficient feature. We couldn't use the Pentium in such a small package because it generated too much heat. We were stuck launching Butterfly with 486 processors.

"As a result, although IBM did have an innovative product, it was announced with a processor that was out of date and a display that was quickly becoming too small. IBM did the only thing they could at the time: They stopped ordering parts, reduced the price, and cleared out the inventory."

Claflin, still watching ThinkPad from his executive role in the PC Company, offered a marketing twist to this story: "From our previous subnotebook experiences, we knew that this was a niche category. We were enamored with the potential of a subnotebook because a sensational demand existed for *small* and *light*. Our first subnotebook, the ThinkPad 500, was mediocre. It wasn't a disaster, but it certainly wasn't a success. IBM learned a lesson from this first subnotebook entry. We should have built only enough units for the expected market, especially because our experience told us how many units we could expect to sell. This lesson was initially called into play when we did the famous Butterfly product. Although I was supportive of the innovative design with the expandable keyboard, I consciously kept the volume plan low. The team's goal was not to get so excited about the innovation that you bought a million parts, found out later that you had inventory everywhere, and then had to slash the price to cut the losses.

"Enormous momentum was building that this product was going to be a huge hit. In addition to the positive responses from the press and the analyst community, our large accounts thought it was wonderful. Our account managers were begging for it. Initially, I was successful keeping the volume plan relatively low. After all, this was a niche product. It was never going to be mainstream.

"I remember the day that I finally made a mistake; it was the day we announced the 701. Lou Gerstner called Rick Thoman and said, 'I am sick and tired of you guys being short on supply. Whatever you do with this latest blockbuster, don't get caught short on supply again.' In spite of research indicating that the 701 was truly a niche subnotebook, I made a dreadful decision and increased the volume plan on announcement day. We immediately qualified new suppliers for critical parts and our plant in Guadalajara, Mexico, as an additional manufacturing site. We decided to go for volume in a big way.

"The product was initially successful, but only for a narrow niche of users. The long-term demand was significantly less than the volumes to which we had just committed. We had to slash volume back and aggressively price to move it out of the channel. If we had kept the original volume plan, it would have proven a satisfactory product. It did well in its niche as an innovative product. Limited volume would have commanded a price premium. But, in trying to move Butterfly from niche to mainstream, we raised the volume and ended up slashing inventory and taking a major financial hit.

"In retrospect, we should have done a better job of target marketing. We should have targeted highly successful individuals with moderate demands for keyboard, screen, and technology, high requirements for small and light, and a willingness to pay a premium to meet their requirements. In fact, that was the original plan until the day of announcement. I'm the guy who caved on the demand. I said, 'Okay.' I should have said, 'No, we're going to keep this product as a focused product for a small segment of the market.' I blame myself for that mistake."

Rick Thoman, president of the PC Company during this juncture, echoed Claflin's sentiments: "Whatever problems we had with Butterfly, they were based on decisions that were a little bit of Claflin and a little bit of Formichelli. However, because I was running the organization, I have to carry the candle for any missteps more than anybody else.

"We should have capitalized on our ability to have the best mobile products and the best features like the Butterfly's keyboard. We should have planned in advance for processor changes so that we could have adapted our design more quickly, with minimum cost. Then, we should have had a quicker follow-on to the Butterfly product. Frankly, we were so focused on just making the company's turnaround work and getting the current product out that we forgot to focus on the follow-on. We died in the subnotebook market because it was too long between the Butterfly and the 560. We caught it back with the 560, but we shouldn't have had to run that kind of risk."

Technical risks were not the only challenges associated with this product; once again, product naming surfaced as a potential stumbling block. As a follow-up to their first collaboration on the Industry Advisory Councils, Gerry Purdy and Debi Dell were asked to work together on naming this subnotebook. After all, because Butterfly was considered the most unusual ThinkPad created to date, the brand team felt it deserved special attention.

The product code name was *Butterfly* because the keyboard could fold out into a standard keyboard from its small subnotebook case. It was a catchy code name; it really took off, becoming more popular than most code names or products do. About three months before announcement, the team was planning the launch and discussing how to expose the machine to key influencers to create a certain buzz about its innovative foldout keyboard.

Claflin reflected, "We immediately went into a debate on whether to name this product *Butterfly* and make it a registered trademark name of the IBM Company. We came to the decision that it would be a mistake to formally brand it *Butterfly* for several reasons. First, we already had a brand for the company, which was IBM. We also had the brand for the product category, which was ThinkPad. So, we asked ourselves whether we were now going to introduce a third layer of branding. Was this going to be the IBM ThinkPad Butterfly or was it going to be the IBM Butterfly? We knew that we could have only two major brand identities, and one was definitely IBM. If we went with IBM Butterfly, then we were not developing the equity around IBM ThinkPad. Or even worse, we might have ended up with ThinkPad Butterfly and might never have referred to IBM. That wasn't ever going to fly. We concluded that, although the name was seductive, having three tiers of branding—IBM, ThinkPad, and Butterfly—was one tier too many to invest in for the long haul.

"At the end of the day, after talking to everyone inside IBM and many consultants and analysts, we reaffirmed that there were only two brands. The company brand was IBM and the product brand was ThinkPad. We did, however, want to take advantage of this wonderful imagery around the Butterfly without registering it. Hence, we continued to use the butterfly icon as a part of the introduction to provide a symbol for what the keyboard did—it expanded like the wings of a butterfly.

"The week before the product announced, we started buying space in major newspapers, in the lower corner or on the upper-right side of a page. We used an iconic image of a butterfly and nothing else. A day or two later, we added *IBM* to the page with the butterfly icon. A couple days later, it said, *Watch for the announcement*. We built up excitement and buzz by leveraging the butterfly imagery to talk about the new product.

"An interesting thing most people don't know is that someone actually threatened us over the name *Butterfly*. Right after announcement, we received a letter from some guy named George saying that we were violating his trademark. It turns out that his company had a super computer product named *Butterfly*. It had nothing to do with the portable category at all. He alleged that we were at risk of violating his registered mark and suggested that we could have the rights to the name if we paid him many millions of dollars.

"Well, we had already concluded that it would be a mistake to use the name *Butterfly* as an official product name. I was called to headquarters to explain why I didn't accept George's proposal. I explained to IBM senior management about our brand strategy to stick to two levels: IBM and ThinkPad. Our brand strategy was endorsed, and we told old George to go take a hike. We never heard from him again.

"In a similar vein, I got a call from Jerry York, our CFO. He asked me, 'Why are you being so stupid? Why don't you register *Butterfly*? Don't you understand that this would be a smart thing to do?' And I remember telling him that I thought it was one of the stupidest ideas I'd ever heard. I then went through the issue of whether we were going to have a two-level or three-level brand. I asked him whether we were scrapping IBM or we were scrapping ThinkPad. Why spend money on a new brand like Butterfly when ThinkPad was already well known and, thus, would not require another nickel to promote the brand's equity? Why invest to build a brand for a technology you knew you were not going to sustain? I remember York saying, 'It sounds like a damn good reason to me. Why don't you tell more people that?' and hung up the phone."

According to Debi Dell, "We rejected the sub-brand concept after early discussions with the marketing team. No one wanted to diminish the emerging brand identity and awareness of ThinkPad. We did not want to change the established format of a *ThinkPad xxx*, where *xxx* represented the model number. We decided instead to name the underlying technology, similar to the way the ThinkPad used *TrackPoint* to describe its pointing device.

"We really thought that the exercise was trivial. Just call it the *ThinkPad 600* with the Butterfly keyboard. Job done. Go back to work. But, once again, the Corporate Naming Committee and IBM Legal raised their restrictive opinions. First of all, the designation of *600* was reserved for the upcoming Power PC line of portables scheduled to announce at the same time as Butterfly. Second, they did not want an IBM product or product feature named after an item in nature. Third, why officially use a name that had been used by another company, even though it was in a different product class. And, fourth, the name not only had to pass IBM stringent naming rules but also the language tests of the different geographies. We tried to fight the 'old guard' on both the model number and the keyboard name, but to no avail."

Purdy and Dell initially tackled the model number debate. They decided that, with its superior features and functions, it mirrored the premium 700-series. The product also had higher quality than the previous 500-series, so it was important not to taint Butterfly with some of the questionable impressions still lingering from that series. The product was better classified within the 700-series. Because the Butterfly had the same screen size and height as the original ThinkPad 700C, they recommended *701*.

The technology name was then undertaken. Approximately forty candidate names were created and evaluated against the ThinkPad personality and brand requirements. Evaluation variables included the name's emotional content, physical relationship to the expanding keyboard action, ease of pronunciation, capability to be trademarked, and overall appeal. An abbreviated list of twenty was presented to key influencers for their reaction. Their subjective input was then balanced against the scoring system reflecting the evaluation criteria. Because *Butterfly* was not on the list, the number one choice was *Expanza*, which accurately communicated the keyboard action.

Dell continued, "We were ready to finalize the name. We had the support of the analysts, product marketing, and the legal and corporate naming community. Butterfly would be known as the *ThinkPad 701* with IBM's new Expanza technology keyboard. There was just one problem: IBM Brazil recommended not using the name. *Expanza* had some kind of sexual connotation within their geography. We discussed going with it anyway if the meaning wasn't too objectionable. No such luck! After all this work and several weeks of effort, the name was killed because of some inexplicable 'sexual connotation' in a foreign country. It was back to the drawing board."

To circumvent the schedule problem now facing the team, the entire list was submitted to the corporate naming committee and to IBM Legal. The list included a previously approved name, *TrackWrite*, which had been used to describe the pen-to-screen feel of the original ThinkPad tablet. A name that had not received much play in the press, it certainly tied nicely to the TrackPoint pointing device. Purdy and Dell felt that perhaps *Track* could be part of the name for any input devices that would be associated with the ThinkPad in the future. *TrackWrite* finally won approval and was used in the launch materials.

But, guess what? The marketing team thumbed their noses at the corporate naming committee by having a colorful butterfly on the ThinkPad 701C screen in each and every print ad. The name and association of *Butterfly* was so attractive to the press that they made almost no mention of the name *TrackWrite*. They loved *Butterfly* and kept referring to the new product as "the IBM ThinkPad with the Butterfly keyboard." In the end, the team got exactly the name they wanted from the very beginning!

The executives ignored another underlying problem associated with the 701C story. Just before announcement, Raleigh learned that the Japanese development team had won the full support of the brand management. All future portables would be designed in Yamato. The Butterfly team was to transition into the desktop development when the group moved from Boca to Raleigh. In the ensuing weeks, pleas surfaced not only to ThinkPad's general manager but also to IBM's CEO. The team not only wanted to stay with mobile development but also requested to "keep the team together." The pleas were ignored. Today, Butterfly engineers and managers are dispersed from Raleigh to Seattle. They work for personal computer manufacturers and sensor, phone, chip, and biotech companies. Their jobs range from chip designer to development executive. Significant talent was lost over this management decision. This team, which grew from its initial core five members to more than thirty, had true esprit de corps. Through three development projects, no one left the team. In five years, the team spirit remained high—that is, until the team was disbanded.

According to Chris Farrell, "The team had a sense of itself. You know, the 1993-1994 Duke University basketball team had a poster titled "Defining Duke Basketball." To this day, that poster hangs in my office and makes me think of the Butterfly team." The poster states the following:

Commitment: A personal investment of time and self. A pledge of dedication to a common or individual purpose.

Honesty: Exhibiting fairness and straightforwardness of conduct.

Toughness: Uncompromising courage and tenacity. Character capable of enduring hardship. Stubbornness against opposition.

Friend: One attached to another by affections, esteem, and loyalty.

Pride: A reasonable or justifiable self-respect. Delight or elation arising from an act or personal quality.

Love: Affection based on admiration. Unselfish concern that freely accepts another. Steadfast devotion to a person or cause.

> Collective Responsibility: Individual accountability to a group and its goals without regard for personal accomplishment.
>
> Trust: Assured reliance on the character, ability, strength, or truth of someone or something.
>
> Integrity: Adherence to a code of values. A quality or state of being complete or undivided.

Farrell summarized, "From the first five to the last brought on board, every single member of our team lived these definitions. It was the purest team I have been a part of or have even seen, including the great sports teams in the Raleigh area. I am quite proud of the technical accomplishments we made in those five years, but those accomplishments pale in comparison to the feeling of pride from belonging to such a team. It was truly special."

The Authors' Insights

The ThinkPad brand team scoured the research labs for innovations to incorporate into its mainstream products. They started a trend that other PC Company's development teams followed. However, discovering these innovations did not automatically ensure easy integration into system designs. Such was the case with the Butterfly. Despite "innovation in spades," the team was not able to get the unit into production on a schedule that would guarantee its competitiveness. Butterfly was a textbook case of the need to balance product features with market timing. But, IBM did benefit from developing Butterfly. It received significant press and attention on its innovation. In essence, Butterfly represented more of an exercise of brand equity development than a revenue contribution to IBM.

The Butterfly was designed while the mobile market was in flux regarding portable positioning. A new category of portables, the ultraportable, replaced the subnotebook, and the ThinkPad 701C was obsolete within a few months of its introduction. Its timing to market had virtually destroyed the competitive edge of its innovation. As Al Ries and Jack Trout point out in their book, *Positioning*, a company has only one chance to make a first impression, and occupying first place in a product category is all that matters.

Perhaps the team should have done more market research or focus groups to properly position this product. Instead, the positioning was virtually dictated by the corporate naming committee and IBM legal. The resulting name, *ThinkPad 701C*, was one of the more confusing portable entries. The *700* designated its position as a premium portable, but without the latest in processor or display. Its overall size and the necessity of an external diskette drive clearly placed it in the subnotebook category. Luckily for the ThinkPad team, the ThinkPad 701C avoided a black eye because the press fell in love with the keyboard. But, like many love affairs, the infatuation was short-lived. Despite the market's excitement, IBM retired the Butterfly in 1995. The world was shifting to Pentium processors and larger displays that could not fit inside the Butterfly mechanical design.

Claflin offered the final perspective on this fleeting market entry: "We considered keeping the design alive by doing a refresh with the newer Pentium technology. However, we were going to be in the same basic dilemma. The screen was only going to be 10.4-inch; it was never going to be bigger. The product would have announced at a time when the average display size in note-books was already 12.1-inch and moving to 13.3-inch. The mechanical design was always going to be thick. We knew that it was time to cut our losses." That decision illustrated a valuable lesson for the team, one of cutting market losses and preventing a blemish on the brand.

The Subnotebook Family

System	PS/Note	500	510Cs	701C
Form	Notebook	Subnote	Subnote	Subnote
Processor	486SL 25MHz	486SLC2 50/25MHz	486SLC 50/25MHz	486DX2 25/50 486DX4 25/75
Memory	4/12MB	4/12MB	4/20MB	4/20MB 8/24MB
Storage	60MB	85/170MB I/II PCMCIA	200MB I/II PCMCIA	360/540/720MB II/III PCMCIA
Display	9.2" STN	7.4" Passive Matrix (Backlit)	7.7" Color STN	10.4" TFT/ Dual Scan
Operating system	MS-DOS 6.0 Windows 3.1	DOS 5.02/ 6.1 OS/2 2.1 Prodigy	PC DOS 6.3 Windows 3.1 OS/2 2.1	DOS/Windows OS/2 WARP
Weight (lb.)	5.1	3.4–3.9	4.0	4.5
Other	TrackPoint II	TrackPoint II 16KB cache	TrackPoint II Nameplate MultiPort Preloaded SW	TrackWrite keyboard Port replicator Integrated DSP Infrared
Announced	5/10/93	6/15/93	6/21/94	3/6/95

The Butterfly was the culmination of several early attempts in the evolving subnotebook. Its innovative design resulted in more awards in this category than IBM had previously received.

AWARDS

ThinkPad 701C	CES Innovation '96	"Good Design Award"	January 1996
	InfoWorld	"1995 Product of Year— Subnotebook"	January 1996
	Popular Science	"Best of What's New"	November 1995
ThinkPad 500	*PC World*	"Best Buy— #1 Value Mobile PC"	September 1994

CHAPTER 23

Per Larsen: Consummate Marketeer

Opportunities are never lost. The other fellow takes those you miss.

—Anonymous

The investment was paying off; ThinkPad was becoming recognized around the world. Now, after the departure of Bruce Claflin, Joe Formichelli felt the need to bring in a strong manager with worldwide marketing responsibility. After his manufacturing problem was fixed, a lot of ThinkPads would be looking for homes. Marketing would no longer be simply a matter of product allocation; a worldwide program would soon be required.

Formichelli's strength was operational, and he quickly sought someone to fill the role of worldwide marketing manager. Former GM Bruce Claflin had operated in this role because of his wealth of marketing expertise; he had taken a hands-on approach to developing worldwide marketing plans. Formichelli did not want, nor did he have the skill, to operate in such a role. After seeking the input of Claflin and such marketing-savvy individuals as Jan

Winston, Formichelli tapped Per (pronounced *pear*) Larsen to take on the ThinkPad marketing challenge.

Larsen grew up in Denmark in a commercial environment. His father ran a grocery store, and Per realized early on that he wanted to go into business. He got an accounting degree from a Danish commercial school. After meeting the one-year military requirement, Larsen worked for a Danish construction company. Dealing with branch offices throughout Denmark, he experienced all aspects of running a business.

When Larsen was twenty-four years old, he decided that the construction business was not for him. In 1975, he started with IBM as a typewriter sales representative. According to Larsen, "It was a fantastic life. I had my territory. I had my office in my home and ran my territory from there. I had a lot of freedom."

Per Larsen's early success led to fast promotions through the sales ranks. He followed the traditional path from representative to sales manager to a staff position in the Copenhagen headquarters. In 1979, he was appointed marketing manager, with responsibility for not only typewriters but also mainframes and MVS computers. Larsen reflected on this major career advancement: "I had to run this business that was really important to IBM. It was a big business. It made me realize that you can actually run a big business without knowing much about the products."

Eventually, Larsen was asked to manage the Customer Marketing Center. These centers were established to cover customer accounts where one-on-one sales teams were not cost effective. Larsen recalled, "Building that center was the biggest learning curve I ever climbed. Driving business from a pull rather than a push mentality was a new experience. I learned how to increase the sales force productivity using direct marketing long before Dell Computer started to use the same approach. We used direct marketing to leverage our sales force. We increased our productivity dramatically and grew that business in IBM. As one of the biggest success stories in IBM Denmark, the marketing center concept spread not only throughout Denmark but also around the world."

In 1986, Per Larsen went on assignment in the U.S. At the time, if an individual based in Europe wanted to succeed in IBM, he or she needed experience working in the States. Larsen transferred to the International Sales Office in New York, where he was the liaison to the U.S. sales operations around the world. He assisted these sales offices in getting access to the necessary IBM resources from the laboratories, development, and research. During this time, he visited almost every major IBM office in the world and met at least one new major customer every week. Larsen's hands-on approach broadened his knowledge about the computer industry and increased his understanding of how IBM supports international customers. He also experienced living and working in the U.S.

In 1988, Larsen went back to Denmark. The PC had become big business, and he pursued this as his new focus. He ran the PC Product Marketing group in Denmark until the Nordic countries were combined into one geography. In 1991, Larsen was promoted to general manager of the PC Company, Denmark. His team was very successful and, perhaps, just a little lucky. They realized a thirty-five percent market share in PCs in Denmark, the highest in all of Europe. Larsen learned how to build a solid team of dedicated professionals who worked together to become number one. He learned what customers liked and did not like about IBM.

In 1994, Larsen went to Paris as the European marketing manager for an exciting new line of portable computers called *ThinkPad*. His decision to take the job was based on an insight similar to the one he had had about the market moving from mainframes to PCs; Larsen truly believed that portable computers were the next big wave in computing. Formichelli gave him the chance to play in this emerging market while fine-tuning his skills as a marketing manager. Reporting to him in his position of worldwide marketing manager were all the geography marketing managers, including the U.S. managers, Scott Bower and Maurice Fletcher.

Larsen reminisced, "I felt that what we had with ThinkPad could clearly grow into something very big. It was a really different product for IBM. It had its own industrial design. It was solid black. It had panache. I knew that we would have to do things very differently for this line of products to be successful.

"The management team recognized that we needed to develop the ThinkPad brand and market it separately from other PC Company products. We wanted the ThinkPad to be viewed as something special, based on its own merits and not because of its ties to IBM. This, of course, was not a popular thing to do within IBM. You just didn't take a brand and elevate it above the rest of IBM's product line. But, the product stood on its own and provided us with this unique opportunity. We had something that was different and very special.

"You know, it wasn't the features that set ThinkPad apart. It was the emotion surrounding ThinkPad. Frankly, I don't believe that most of the people working on ThinkPad realized that the critical difference was the emotion encircling the brand. Every time the team was together, they sat around and talked about technology. Certainly, the technology was an important element to IBM's success. However, the most important thing in the minds of the customer was the emotional element tied to the purchase decision. We decided to try to describe what created this emotional appeal in terms of vital signs.

"Vital Signs"

■ THE **PULSE** OF THE MARKET (THINKPAD'S LIFELINE)
  ▬ Supply
  ▬ Quality and Reliability
  ▬ Cost Management

■ THE **VISION**
  ▬ Innovation
    ■ System Design
    ■ Customer Experience (e.g., Out-Of-Box, "One-Stop Shopping")
    ■ Customer Fulfillment (Build-To-Needs)
  ▬ Use technology to change the rules of the game

■ THE **THINK** IN THINKPAD
  ▬ Pre-Loads (e.g., Operating Systems, Software, Bundled Solutions)
  ▬ Software/Communicaton Skills
  ▬ Process Focus

■ THE **VOICE**-OF-CUSTOMER
  ▬ Brand Management (e.g., Influence Programs)
  ▬ Channel Expansion (e.g., Vertical Marketing)
  ▬ Alliances and Partnerships

■ **SMELL** THE ROSES
  ▬ Employee Morale
  ▬ Re-engineer the Culture

TASTE of
Success

Customer Satisfaction/Loyalty
Financial Results

During the Fall Plan cycle of 1994, the team tried to describe the appeal of the ThinkPad brand in terms of its "vital signs."

"When you described the elements that elicited emotions about ThinkPad, you had the key ingredients for the ThinkPad brand. Because the brand had such strong emotional appeal, people who used the ThinkPad tried to share their excitement with others. We often heard, 'Hey, let me show you my new ThinkPad,' or 'God,

I'm so lucky to have a ThinkPad.' It took quite a while to demonstrate the importance of emotional response in building brand equity versus promoting technical features. I knew it, and, in time, others on the ThinkPad team realized how important the emotional connection was in making the ThinkPad brand successful."

In the early 1990s, the success of laptops was determined by their technology; systems were viewed as business tools, as necessities. The screens tended to be monochrome and small, and battery life was almost non-existent. Early notebooks were not as useful as desktops, and sales were small. Overall, the lack of features and functions resulted in a negative emotional experience when using a notebook PC. Customers did not enjoy it. They tolerated the experience because notebooks allowed you to do some basic processing while out of the office.

However, the character of this segment altered with the technology advances, and the choice became more personal and more related to position and self-esteem. The emotional connection started with a strong set of features and functions that allowed the customer to achieve personal and business objectives. But, it was how the customer related to the 10.4-inch display that was really important. Larsen characterized the experience: "It brought people together just to see it. It was an exciting experience unique to ThinkPad. No other portable computer elicited such a reaction. By providing useful technology on these platforms, we learned that we could quickly grow interest in this business. Innovative technologies and immediate utility enabled us to foster the emotions necessary to brand recognition.

"Many difficult discussions centered on the paint for the ThinkPad line because color was one of the ways to influence emotional response to a product. If we had used the same off-white cream color employed on our high-end mainframe computers, the emotional reaction would have been totally different than if we had used black. During this timeframe, no other company had used black on its portables. The ThinkPad stood out. We had created a very positive emotional association.

"Another influential technology was the TrackPoint, the pointing device centered in the keyboard, with a little red cap. Many people wanted to use IBM blue for the top of the pointer, but red commanded a much stronger emotional reaction. When the ThinkPad opened, there was the black keyboard with a bright red dot on it. Again, no one had this feature. No one had a device that provided mouse-like function for the mobile worker. Travelers who owned a ThinkPad had a significant, positive experience compared to those individuals using other portables. The results were inevitable. People clamored to get one. Everyone wanted the same enjoyable experience as the person with the ThinkPad.

"In summary, the marketing team found ways to promote ThinkPad's positive emotional experience to others. We did it via testimonials. We did it via public relations. We did it in our advertising. We also had a big job inside IBM educating others on the importance of the emotional element key to the brand's success. This concept was new to IBM, and we educated many senior managers."

As the ThinkPad product line advanced, a number of trade-offs occurred. The ThinkPad marketing team headed in the right direction, balancing technology against the emotional attributes. They clearly differentiated the product lines: The high-end 700 series focused on performance; the 300 series focused on convenience and value; and the 500 series focused on portability. Even today, the positioning has remained clear. Most of the time, the right calls were made on what belonged and what did not belong in each product.

The team concentrated on refining the segments addressed by its product line, adding features deemed appropriate to a certain subset of customers. In November 1994, IBM introduced notebooks with greater storage, graphic, and presentation capabilities. The ThinkPad 755CD was announced as a complete multimedia system in a seven-to-nine pound package. Customers with intense data requirements benefited from the CD-ROM, stereo sound, and motion graphics in this portable for the road.

However, multimedia was still emerging as a segment. Simply adding a CD-ROM, as IBM did in the ThinkPad 755CD, was not enough. To be truly multimedia, a notebook had to include fast graphics refresh on the display and the capability to generate motion graphics. It needed to show video clips on at least twenty percent of the screen and provide stereo sound in support of the presentation. IBM achieved this combination when it announced its ThinkPad 755CV in mid-1995. According to Larsen, "The 755CV was an everyday portable while providing overhead projection capabilities. We expected that someday this multimedia feature would migrate toward the mainstream and not be perceived as a niche enhancement. Of course, this hasn't happened."

The ThinkPad team did not stop with the 755's multimedia features and functions. Guided by Larsen's understanding of the market and linked to Yamato's technological capabilities, another turn of the crank occurred in fall 1995. The team outdid itself with its new ThinkPad 760 notebooks. Containing the industry's first 12.1-inch SVGA display, this notebook set IBM apart from other high-end suppliers. IBM skipped right over other manufacturers and their 11.3-inch displays and went for leadership with this output of DTI, IBM's joint venture with Toshiba.

In October 1995, Gerry Purdy's *Mobile Letter* deemed the new industrial design the "sexiest in the industry." The keyboard was moved back, and the rest of the unit had sloping, rounded edges, similar to the newest cars on the road. Analysts commented that the whole experience of opening and turning on the 760 was reminiscent of the opening and closing of the ThinkPad 701C (Butterfly); they almost expected to hear trumpets sounding as the keyboard tilted up to meet their hands. Hearing the trumpets through the built-in stereo speakers with Sound Blaster quality would not have been totally unexpected! The team complemented the display and sound features by installing MPEG-2 hardware on the motherboard, thus providing flicker-free, full-screen display of video sequences.

Larsen described other areas where he was actively involved and which affected his ability to market these quality notebooks: "We established processes that allowed worldwide, simultaneous product announcements. For example, when we announced the ThinkPad 380, we introduced it not only in the U.S. but in Europe and the Far East as well. Before we created the concept of a go-to-market team, each geography fended for itself. Worldwide coordination was a cornerstone to worldwide brand acceptance.

"We spent a ton of money to create the ThinkPad brand. We didn't spend the kind of money that someone like Proctor and Gamble spends to develop their top consumer product brands, but certainly more than IBM had spent in a long time for a single product line. We created the ThinkPad brand not through advertising and promotion, but through a promise that the product would provide a positive emotional experience for the user."

Leo Suarez, a long-time team member who experienced every general manager and key executive, offered this perspective on Larsen: "It wasn't always easy for us to leapfrog the competition, but Per's overwhelming personality was partly responsible for our brand success. Per was like a big, gentle bear one minute and a raging tyrant the next. We knew that, in his heart, he wanted all of us to succeed, to be part of this exploding ThinkPad phenomenon.

By continuously playing the role of good cop/bad cop—all by himself—he somehow built an incredible loyalty within his marketing team. We loved to hear him argue. When someone challenged his position, Per would always retort, 'It's so because I am the goddamned vice (his Danish accent made it sound like *wise*) president and *say* it's so!' This was vintage Per. His tactics kept the team focused on the real issues at hand."

The Authors' Insights

IBM management was astute in its realization that a strong marketing executive was needed to balance Joe Formichelli's manufacturing experience. Per Larsen changed ThinkPad marketing from a group primarily managing allocation to a worldwide brand management organization that operated as a smoothly running machine. He knew markets, channels, brand equity, and the right product mix. Larsen drove the ThinkPad team and did not allow them to stand still, to rest on their laurels. The team continued on its journey, one step at a time. They moved forward in the minds of industry influencers and customers by building brand equity and adding to the brand's personality. The geographies were forced to work together on worldwide product announces and marketing programs. Larsen extended the original programs with creative new approaches and challenged his team to keep the brand in front of the customer on a worldwide basis. He helped to build a *global marketing network* for this dynamic brand.

Specialized Notebooks

System	755CD	755CV	760CD	Traveling MM(755C)	Traveling Exec
Form	Notebook	Notebook	Notebook	Notebook	Notebook
Processor	486DX4 100/33MHz	486DX4 100MHz	Pentium 90/120 MHz	486DX4 75MHz	486DX2 50MHz
Memory	8/40MB	8/40MB	8/64MB	8/36MB	12/20MB
Storage	540/ 810MB II/III PCMCIA	810MB/ 1.2GB II/III PCMCIA	720MB/ 1.2GB	540/ 810MB II/III PCMCIA	540/ 810MB II/III PCMCIA
Display	10.4" TFT	10.4" TFT	12.1" TFT (SVGA)	10.4" TFT	10.4" TFT
Operating system	DOS 6.3 MS-DOS 6.2 OS/2 .1 Windows 3.1	DOS 7.0 MS-DOS 6.2 OS/2 Warp Win. 3.1	Windows 3.11, '95 OS/2 Warp	DOS 6.3 MS-DOS 6.2, OS/2 .1 Win. 3.1	DOS 6.3 MS-DOS 6.2, OS/2 .1 Win. 3.1
Weight (lb.)	7.3	6.1/6.6	6.1–7.4	7.3	7.3
Other	Built-in CD-ROM PC Card Director Mwave DSP Infrared TrackPoint III	Overhead projection Infrared Mwave DSP Microphone Integrated SW	MPEG-2 UltraBay	Built-in Audio Fax Modem Dock I Preloaded SW	Microphone Audio card Preloaded SW
Announced	9/5/95	9/5/95	10/2/95	9/5/95	9/5/95

The specialized characteristics of IBM ThinkPads were directed at targeted markets and resulted in an ever increasing award portfolio.

Awards

ThinkPad 755CV	*PC '95* (Australia)	"Best New Hardware"	August 1995
ThinkPad 755CD	*PC Laptop Computers*	"Notebook of the Year"	November 1995
ThinkPad 760CD	*BYTE*	"Best Portable of the Year"	November 1995
	PC Magazine	"Technical Excellence"	November 1995

CHAPTER 24

Paying for the Journey

It's easy to make a buck. It's a lot tougher to make a difference.

—Tom Brokow

The team had real issues on which to focus. It focused on building and protecting the ThinkPad brand while developing its worldwide marketing network. The achievements in 1993 and 1994, as well as the 1995 plans, resulted from the combined efforts of numerous groups within Mobile and across IBM. Market planning and requirements definition were done in Boca Raton, Florida, and Somers, New York. The requirements were then forwarded to development teams resident in Yamato, Raleigh, Boca Raton, and Kingston, New York. The resulting designs were manufactured and distributed by teams located in Raleigh, Fujisawa, Guadalajara, Wangaratta, and Greenock. Research, sourcing, and suppliers throughout the world enhanced the entire process. The communication logistics alone, not to mention the actual costs associated with such a geographically dispersed team, represented significant financial challenges to the ThinkPad's management team—challenges requiring strong management actions in 1995. However, IBM had the insight to invest in the future by giving ThinkPad the development and the marketing support necessary to achieve market leadership. This eventually resulted in substantial revenue and profits for the company.

During the early 1990s, all organizations within IBM were affected by the increase in the cost of debt, some more directly than others. With IBM's debt, rating on bonds was lowered from AAA to AA in 1992 to A in 1993, the corporation was forced to reduce its expenses.[1] Dividends were reduced by eighty percent, making investors nervous about the company. To address this, for the first time in decades, IBM issued nonvoting preferred stock with a guaranteed return on investment. These actions dictated a twenty-percent expense reduction in research, development, and engineering, as well as a thirty-percent workforce reduction, driving employee morale to an all-time low.

In Mobile Computing, where development needed not only to keep pace with but to outrun technology, the brand management feared that cash would not be readily available for new or high-risk projects. However, in the fall of 1993, the PC Company acknowledged the initial success of the ThinkPad line; it committed much of the requested 1994 funding and did not reduce Mobile's headcount. In return, the Mobile Computing team accepted the challenge of becoming the number one player in the mobile segment while achieving 1994 revenue of two billion dollars, a sixty-six percent improvement over 1993's 1.2 billion dollars.

IBM unit sales were also a critical aspect of the plan, with targeted shipments of one million worldwide, more than double the four hundred fifty thousand shipped in 1993. Even more dramatic was the required profit turnaround. In 1992, Mobile lost two hundred million dollars and then broke even in 1993. In 1994, the

---

1. "IBM Annual Report to Shareholders," IBM Corporation (1993).

team planned to achieve in net earnings before taxes an amount equal to its 1992 loss.

Within an IBM that was re-creating itself, every action and investment counted and had to add to the bottom line. In an environment where headcount and Research and Development (R&D) expenditures were being reduced, Mobile Computing was funded to compete. No one was sure, at the time, whether the funding was adequate, given the push by its major competitors—Toshiba, Compaq, and Apple—to invest significant resources in development, key alliances, and tremendous marketing and advertising programs. Mobile's funding needed to keep pace and achieve a balanced investment portfolio, investing in products, future technologies, employees, solutions, and alliances.[2]

The ThinkPad's financial results during its first two years mirrored both its history and its successive leadership styles. In 1992, Mobile began with a committed plan projecting a yearly operating loss of fifteen percent. This reflected both its "start-up" nature and the substantial development, sales, and cost-of-goods investments required in an emerging business. During 1992, the team met most of its cost and volume targets. However, the delayed introduction of the N51 notebook and the overall mismatch of product functions to mobile market requirements caused a revenue shortfall that could not be offset by the fourth-quarter introduction of the ThinkPad 700. Early in the year, Mobile found itself in a fire-sale environment as it prepared to announce its new portable line. As a result, Mobile ended the year with an operating loss of more than fifty percent, not the fifteen percent planned.

Mobile's 1992 development expense was projected to be substantially high in relationship to its revenue targets; expenses actually ran even higher. This reflected the front-end investment in technical leadership that Watabe-san and Higuchi-san brought to the effort. It also highlighted the incremental expenses that

2. Boston Consulting Group (Spring 1993).

development incurred because it was spread over three continents and seventeen time zones, involving numerous languages and cultures.

Mobile exceeded its 1992 cost-of-goods target. Some of this expense can be attributed to investments in new technology to support the fall 1992 leadership products. However, much of it was due to the first-half inventory investments in obsolete technology. The cost of long supply lines between predominantly Japanese suppliers and the Raleigh, Guadalajara, and Greenock manufacturing sites also increased the overall expense.

In the spring of 1992, Mobile Computing became a standalone product brand team within the IBM Personal Computer Company; Bruce Claflin officially joined as general manager in June. Through Claflin's marketing leadership, he was expected to expand Mobile's participation in the exploding portable market. By August, Claflin developed and communicated a vision to Mobile employees worldwide. Key to the success of this strategy was defining and meeting customer requirements through focused development efforts. Clear development priorities, crisp roles and responsibilities, and the elimination of redundant efforts reduced the total cost of development expense. This was a step in the right direction of controlling expenses.

Establishing brand recognition was a key component of the total mobile strategy. As Per Larsen highlighted, a number of programs such as customer call days and industry council meetings generated more "face time" with customers to build brand recognition and loyalty. In 1993, customer shipments doubled, and revenue tripled from 1992. As a result, Mobile went from operating at a loss to becoming a modestly profitable business within one year. Although increasing revenue and volume shipments, the additional customer contacts and brand development programs generated incremental sales expense. In 1993, sales expense had doubled year-to-year in absolute terms but stayed constant as a percentage of total cost.

Unfortunately, Mobile did not reach its revenue potential because of supply constraints. Hampered by long vendor supply lines, the ThinkPad team struggled with communications and logistics problems while ramping its manufacturing capacity throughout 1993. They incurred premiums for labor, transportation, and components to meet scheduled production. Immediate action was required to turn this situation around if ThinkPad was ever to be a profitable business unit.

In August 1993, Claflin was promoted, and Joe Formichelli became the ThinkPad general manager in November. Formichelli was chosen with the express intent to increase manufacturing leadership for the ThinkPad brand. Formichelli inherited Claflin's team but left it largely intact while he concentrated almost exclusively on resolving Mobile's supply constraints. Formichelli's focus paid dividends. He succeeded in driving per-unit cost of goods down in 1994.

The emphasis on manufacturing caused neglect of other key business attributes. In 1994, ThinkPad marketing continued to grow the customer-interface and requirements-gathering processes initiated in 1993. Sales expense more than doubled in actual dollars because of, in part, the separate marketing programs of each geography. These expenses offset a substantial portion of the 1994 cost-of-goods savings. Although development costs grew in actual dollars year-to-year in 1994, they dropped as a fraction of both total cost and revenue. These changes, coupled with the cost reductions and revenue increase, indicated the onset of a positive financial trend for ThinkPad that continued through 1995.

In addition to its internal financial focus, the ThinkPad team monitored the competitive environment. As part of brand management, a market analysis group evaluated the current competitive environment, as well as attempted to predict future trends and directions. This group, headed by Lew Brown, with Gary Buer assigned to the Mobile segment, followed the major competitors such as Compaq, Toshiba, Apple, NEC, and Zenith Data Systems. They employed the Price-Function-Value (PFV) system to compare the systems by product line—700s, 500s, and 300s with comparable competitive boxes. In addition, they analyzed market position and forecasted the ThinkPad's chances to achieve the number one position in units sold and revenue.

According to *Computer Reseller News* (February 6, 1995), although Compaq Computer Corporation garnered the top spot in the desktop and LAN server market in 1994, the company lost significant market share with its notebook line. Toshiba Information Systems was expected to oust Compaq from its 1993 number one position, followed by IBM and NEC Technologies, pushing Compaq into the fourth position in notebook sales. Randy Giusto, an analyst for BIS Strategic Decisions, was quoted as saying, "Compaq has left a lot of opportunities on the table. Compaq is not a technology leader in the mobile market. It waits for the customer base to move to a technology—a good approach for the mass market but not for the notebook market."

During the 1993–1994 period, Compaq encountered several challenges in the notebook arena, including lengthened development cycles and product bugs. The development cycles drove Compaq to actually consider using a Taiwanese manufacturer for its next generation of product. The product bugs included a timing fix on its LTE Elite's communications port, as well as a recall of its LTE Elites in Europe due to faulty electric capacitors. Although IBM was not misled into believing that Compaq was on the ropes, it did provide a window of opportunity for ThinkPad.

Toshiba's history was not much different in that it moved up and down the positioning scale throughout this period. In 1995, Toshiba regained its top position by creating products that addressed specific needs, as well as creating high end systems for power users.[3] Its high-end notebook product line expanded to include the T4850TC, an active-color-matrix machine powered by a 75 MHz 486DX4 processor, one of the first systems on the market to adopt Intel's 75MHz Pentium processors for portable computers. Toshiba also revamped its subnotebook Vera S series while introducing the Satellite Pro line of entry-level offerings. In a move that would cause some reaction by IBM, Toshiba also expanded its one-year warranty to three years.

The competitive analysis team also positioned the ThinkPad in relationship to emerging trends and technologies. Combined with the financial analysis and the semi-annual Headlights and advisory councils, the team developed its roadmap for the next five years. Financial decisions were then based on the roadmap. Resources, both headcount and dollars, were tracked against these decisions and the brand's progress in the market. The team was gaining on the competition while building an enduring brand and turning around a less-than-stellar financial track record.

3. *Computer Reseller News* (February 6, 1995): 50.

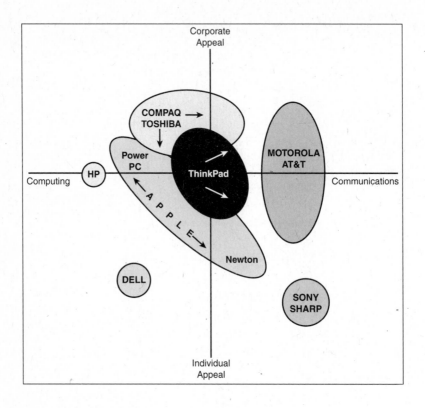

1994 competitive positioning.

The Authors' Insights

The Mobile Computing team was cementing a balanced approach to its business. By mapping trends and technological changes against its competitive posture, decisions were made to maximize the available development funds. In accordance with Kosnik's Seven Qualities of Enduring Brands, once again the team was on track.

The ThinkPad's success and financial accomplishments were the underpinnings to the PC Company's turnaround in the mid

'90s. The team's efforts, coupled with the business insights of individuals like Claflin and Formichelli, were instrumental to the reversal of fortune soon in store for IBM. The IBM executive team kept their fingers on the changing pulse of the organization required to drive this critical business endeavor. Their influence would not stop with assigning the right manager at the right time; soon they would make some fundamental changes to the underlying cost structure of this geographically dispersed team.

The 5th Wave   By Rich Tennant

CHAPTER 25

IBM (*I've Been Moved*—to Raleigh)

Change is inevitable in a progressive society. Change is constant.

—Benjamin Disraeli

During an executive meeting in the spring of 1994, Rick Thoman and his team reviewed Compaq's impact on the PC Company. Compaq was IBM's most dreaded competitor in the personal computer space, and it was ahead in almost every product segment. According to Joe Formichelli, "Thoman and his team knew every statistic about Compaq, but somehow the reality of why they were beating us just wasn't sinking in. I decided that I couldn't keep quiet any longer, so I said, 'Let me ask this team. Where does Compaq manufacture? Houston. Where do we manufacture? Raleigh, Austin, Guadalajara, Fujisawa, Greenock, and Wangaratta. Where are their sales decisions made? Houston. Where are our sales decisions made? In Boca Raton, Somers, Marietta, Bethesda, and Raleigh. Where's their development team? Houston. Where's our development team? Kingston, Boca, Austin, Raleigh, and Yamato.'

"That's when I used my all-time favorite phrase *It's a goat rodeo*, which means that you have to go all over the place to get the job done. I was on the phone from eight o'clock in the morning until eleven o'clock at night just trying to communicate with the different worldwide groups. At this point in the meeting, someone blurted out, 'What do you want to do? Move everybody to one site?'"

Claflin described his recollection of this same meeting: "Formichelli certainly understood the number of sites involved in the PC operations. But, it was Mark Loughridge who had earlier recognized that the cost structure of the PC Company didn't work and recommended laying off five thousand people. The move recommendation was just another step by Loughridge to improve the cost position. The PC Company had to drop people, decrease development cycles, and increase sales to survive."

This meeting was not the first time that site consolidations had been considered. It was, however, the first time that a study was undertaken to determine the feasibility. Unlike many of its competitors within the personal computer market, IBM's efforts were not centralized in one location. In the case of Mobile Computing, the geographical fragmentation had an even greater effect because mobile was the only organization with its key development arm in Yamato, Japan. In addition to the time zone difference, communication was difficult—both written and spoken. Cultural differences sometimes surfaced when females from the U.S. team traveled to Yamato to negotiate product requirements and development schedules. Of course, site consolidation within the States would not eliminate this problem for the mobile team. It would, however, reduce the number of sites working with Yamato and merge the U.S.-based operations. Some economy of scale would then be realized.

Formichelli recalled, "After the meeting, Thoman pulled me aside and asked me to conduct a feasibility study on moving everyone in the PC Company to one location. Because of the confidentiality of this matter, I was allowed to work only with Jan Winston, Thoman's operations expert. Winston and I sketched out the concept on the back of an envelope and then met late into the evening to develop the details on a blackboard in the meeting room. We reviewed the pluses and minuses of each PC Company location. I personally wanted the answer to be Austin because I liked living there. Our analysis quickly showed that moving everyone to Austin was comparable to a minnow swallowing a whale. At the time, Boca Raton had more than five thousand employees. Raleigh, on the other hand, seemed the logical choice. It was already home to the U.S. personal computer manufacturing effort, had an adequate physical plant already in place, boasted a temperate climate, and was halfway between Somers and Boca.

"After reviewing the site analysis with Thoman, we proceeded to analyze the employee population. We looked at their levels and classifications, salaries, and years to retirement. We conducted the old lifeboat drill: If you could put only ten people in the lifeboat, who would it be? We did this for every brand team, projecting who would go, who wouldn't go, and whom we wanted to go. Winston and I detailed the moving and living costs, as well as developed an incentive program for critical resources. We put this whole thing together in a week."

Jan Winston reflected on his work effort with Formichelli: "We worked hard to get all the information necessary to develop the right recommendation. Joe was tireless in this endeavor—I don't think he ever realized that there are only twenty-four hours in a day. Having worked with the PC Company almost continuously since its inception in the early eighties, this was a difficult task for me. I knew that many families would be disrupted by whatever recommendation we brought forward."

Cannavino recalled the executive attitudes concerning the closing of the Boca Raton site: "Boca was frustrated as hell. They had started an industry and were losing control of it. Their costs were out of control. They had lost their leader, Don Estridge, and his vision; that plane crash in Dallas really hurt them. They were struggling to make this business look like something they understood. And, of course, the PC, the whole PC environment was a big threat to the infrastructure of the IBM Company. The technology guys charged us a ten-percent tax to buy microprocessors from Intel and justified it by calling it a *qualification charge*. It was truly just a tax because these guys had nowhere to lay off their overhead. So, this was just part of a whole underground effort trying to suck this PC thing back into the middle of IBM.

"The original plan of manufacturing in Boca was a bad idea. I would have made the decision to move it out of there even sooner. The decision to move manufacturing out of Boca in 1988 had nothing to do with the capability of people. Combined with the limited IBM value-add in PCs, the lack of a high-volume distribution infrastructure made manufacturing at the southern tip of Florida totally unrealistic. There were no routes and no easy access. On top of this logistical nightmare, Florida's governor decided that he wanted his state to have a piece of the action and added a tax to all products shipped out of Florida. By the time the state realized its error, IBM had already determined that manufacturing had to go somewhere. If it had been me, I might have moved it to Austin, not Raleigh, but that was before my time. After manufacturing moved, it was only a matter of time before development would follow it. With the problems facing the PC Company, that time was now [1994].

"Why at this point? For one thing, we were driving to a reduced development cycle time. Think about the old three-year development cycle; early manufacturing involvement was the last year of the development cycle. Well, what do you do with a six-month development cycle? When does manufacturing development start? When does the last year start? Where were the boundaries and the blurs? You had to do end-of-life management before you could actually do a launch. So, when you had six-month development cycles, there couldn't be any boundaries between organizations. Everything had to be in one place. There was no question about that. The traditional manufacturing and development ways were gone. You had to lock in the form factor before you finished product development, because you had to order the power supplies. Power supplies required a nine-month delivery cycle for a six-month product development effort. You were ordering parts before you knew what you would be developing. The whole world of how things were developed and manufactured had changed. The handwriting was on the wall regarding the closing of Boca Raton after manufacturing moved to Raleigh; the development cycle reduction changed the writing from pencil to ink.

"I actually thought that Boca could stay in the server business, which required a slightly longer cycle. But, servers never got into the hearts and minds of the Boca team. They never had the passion. They never stood up and said, 'We are going to own the server business.'"

Kathy Vieth was on the fringes of the Raleigh decision and offered this perspective: "I'm going to be very harsh. Boca was a malaise. Boca was never going to bring back its glory days. It was an impossibility, despite the excellent people in Boca. To this day, I have never understood how so many excellent people, so committed, could not do anything well. It got to the point where everyone was telling us what to do and why we had to do it. The IBM executive team had lost confidence in Boca knowing what they had to do. The only apparent exception was the ThinkPad team, and no one was going to leave a portion of the PC Company in Boca. It was an excellent idea to get out of Boca, out from under the Boca stigma. In my opinion, Boca would never be viewed as a leader in IBM ever again. It had its glory days in the early eighties, and they could not be recaptured."

Formichelli and Winston presented their findings to Jim Cannavino, Rick Thoman, Jerry York, and Lou Gerstner. They told them that it would take about a year and a half to make the transition. Thoman responded that it had to be done within six months. Gerstner agreed, saying "When you're leaping the Grand Canyon, you can't do it in small steps."

Formichelli and Winston put transition teams in place to handle the move logistics. Given that he was still responsible for the ThinkPad brand, Formichelli retreated from direct involvement with the move over the next two months. In August 1994, the PC Company announced its intention to consolidate operations in Raleigh, North Carolina.

At the announcement, the details were not completely worked out. The initial employee information was sketchy. What was known was that some employees would get offers to move to Raleigh. Others were told that they were *surplus* (no longer required) and did not have positions in the relocated PC Company. Incentive programs were provided for a limited number of employees. Although all knew that these programs existed, no one knew what it took to qualify for the additional money or promotions. Employees had to commit within sixty days after visiting Raleigh and obtaining home appraisals. By November, the management team knew who was committed to the move and found out that they were going to lose much of the Boca team.

Patty McHugh, still in her role as ThinkPad planning manager, had several meetings with the Boca team to share information. Because of ThinkPad's market success, the team's affinity with the product line was growing. The executive team felt that fewer incentives were necessary for the mobile team because of its strong allegiance to the brand. Management felt that the pride associated with working on this team would propel most employees to move. To lighten the mood, McHugh not only made herself available for career discussions but also organized a HAT DAY, when the team members were asked to put on their "THINK-ing" caps and work on ways to make the transition smoother.

Bruce Claflin, in his role as president of the PC Company— Americas, visited Boca to explain the move. He held numerous roundtables to gauge the effect of the decision. One of the persistent questions that he and other mobile managers were asked was why the group that was developing and selling mobility had to be geographically located in the same physical location as manufacturing and yet would still be separated from Yamato development. The decision flew in the face of what the team was marketing to the industry. However, as much sense as this might have appeared on the surface to make, leaving the planning team in Boca was never an option. The entire PC Company was to be consolidated without exception—well, almost without exception. The only exception would be those executives who felt there was no need to move the headquarters operations and would not leave New York.

Debi Dell remembered this difficult period: "I was doing a job I loved with the ThinkPad team while completing a master's program at the University of Miami. My husband and I made the trip to Raleigh and were extremely disappointed. The builders took advantage of the situation, and housing prices increased dramatically after the IBM announcement hit the papers. For a house comparable to our Florida home, the price difference was more than sixty grand. Of course, the appraisals on our Florida home were depressed because the appraisers had to take into consideration the flood of houses that were going to hit the market. All in all, the financial impact in housing alone was more than one hundred thousand dollars. My situation was not much different from that of the other employees who had spouses employed by companies other than IBM. We had to balance the financial impact with the potential uncertainty of becoming a one-income house-hold for some period of time.

"Before making the decision, I had a great conversation with Joe Formichelli about the move and its effect on my career. He even offered to delay my move until the end of my master's program as an incentive to eventually make the move. But, unfortunately, there wasn't any way to make me whole financially. Probably the biggest mistake with the PC Company move was the limited number of incentive programs. IBM learned a lot from the Raleigh move. When the Boca programming lab moved to Austin the following year, the number of financial incentives tripled, as did the number of employees who actually moved."

Formichelli added to this reflection: "We did lose more key employees than our projection, but everyone was relocated to Raleigh on schedule. I was part of the team in charge of that death march for a little while. I guess you could say that I was partly responsible for the whole Raleigh consolidation process. My efforts certainly changed the complexion of the ThinkPad brand team, as well as other PC Company teams."

The ThinkPad team lost several of the original brand team members. In addition to Dell, Jim Bartlett lost his entire team; Leo Suarez went to work for IBM Latin America, Bob Sztybel went to work for PORT, and Pete Leichliter retired from the company. Patty McHugh, after she had convinced most of her planners to make the move, reneged on her commitment and left IBM to work for Motorola. According to a 1994 interview with McHugh, "We were the best in the PC Company, but this move definitely affected us. At the time, we had great products, a great team, and a great brand. It scared the hell out of my people that we would get swallowed up in the bureaucracy and politics of being in the same location as headquarters. That was one of the reasons I had a couple of turndowns for Raleigh. Even still, I had an exceptional accept rate overall. Those individuals who did not go truly believed that the PC Company was not going to survive. I know that was something everybody was considering."

Two ThinkPad team members who made the move—Mark Cohen and Dick Green.

The key ThinkPad marketing managers for North America, Scott Bower and Maurice Fletcher, also decided that Raleigh was not the place for them. Bower recalled his decision to leave ThinkPad and IBM: "I was one of the last to abandon the ThinkPad ship; in fact, I had bought land down in Raleigh. I had the best job in the PC Company, absolutely the best job. We had a good team. We were innovative. We were marketing almost everything we were doing from a ThinkPad perspective. It was a great part of the business in which to be involved.

"I had bought some land and sent my wife down to work with architects on a house. She came back in tears and told me that Raleigh just wasn't going to work out. She told me to start returning the calls from the executive recruiters, from headhunters. To be fair, I didn't listen to headhunters while at IBM. I was continually challenged and presented with great opportunities, especially after joining ThinkPad. But, at the time, my son was in high school, and we really did not want to uproot him. My wife had her own business, and we liked the Connecticut area. Even so, I think that I might have gone through with the move if the organization had stayed the same, but everything was changing."

Maurice Fletcher echoed Bower's sentiments: "I left the ThinkPad team in '95 for several reasons. IBM was going through a transition with Gerstner, who had, by then, brought in Thoman to run the PC organization. We were on a path to make the PC Company an independent company when Gerstner decided that this should not be the case. So, the management was changing, as was the freedom to do what needed to be done.

"This change in approach was demonstrated in other areas as well. For example, we worked hard to ensure that ThinkPad was part of the equipment on some of the shuttle missions. After the mission, one of the astronauts showed up at Somers headquarters to make a presentation to the team. Upon receiving the plaque, Gerstner stated that the only brand IBM had developed in decades was the ThinkPad brand. Yet, we would sit in meetings where we were told that we did not know what we were doing. Our decisions regarding marketing and advertising were being questioned at every turn. Despite the growing success and desirability of the ThinkPad brand, we constantly had to prove ourselves. The environment had changed from one of teamwork with the executive management to a very contentious atmosphere. It wasn't fun anymore!

"Couple that with Formichelli's push to consolidate everything in Raleigh, and you had a less-than-optimum work climate. Before making my decision, I went down the list of executives who had decided not to move from the headquarters in Somers, New York. That list told me that the move was not a good career decision. I started looking outside IBM. I knew that it was unlikely that I would find something within the company that would allow me to remain in New York and provide me with the excitement and freedom to develop a new business.

"If you ask me what the team thought of the move, just look at the number of people from the original group who left. We obviously didn't think much of the move in concept or design. Besides, it did not solve the problem. The move was a reaction by an executive that got picked up by other executives who did not know the PC Company history or its current situation. Getting the ball rolling to consolidate the sites was easier than admitting that we needed to abandon some of our product lines and concentrate on segments where we could be competitive.

"ThinkPad had the best-running organization IBM had seen in a long time. Despite the matrix management approach and the number of sites involved, we were delivering the vision of Bruce Claflin and the products our customers wanted. We accomplished something that had been done only one other time in IBM's history. Just as the IBM 360 changed the way computing was done, the IBM ThinkPad changed the personal computer market. ThinkPad made computing more personal."

The move to Raleigh caused ThinkPad team members to evaluate the various options available to them. Some—such as Bower, Fletcher, McHugh, Leichliter, and Sztybel—decided not only to refuse relocation but also to leave IBM. Luckily, for some employees, such as Debi Dell, another alternative existed that allowed employees to continue working for IBM without leaving South Florida. This alternative was the result of a telecommuting move started in IBM's Indiana territory under Michael W. Wiley.

Like most IBM managers in the early 1990s, Wiley was faced with significant staffing challenges as IBM tried to re-create itself. According to Wiley, "I knew that there had to be a better solution than continuing to downsize as we had had to do in 1992. I had just reduced the Indiana team by thirty percent. Through the foresight of my operations manager, John F. Frank, we came up with an alternative to doing the same reduction in 1993.

"Frank had recently stopped by a new building in Evansville, Indiana. As he toured the facility, he realized that most of the space was empty. He knew the reason: The sales personnel were out with their customers. On further investigation, he determined that we could probably save several million dollars each year by reducing our real estate holdings and allowing employees to work from home. On his return, he called me with his back-of-the-envelope sizing. I knew immediately that this was an alternative to eliminating more staff. I told Frank to go ahead and develop a proposal. Of course, in typical IBM fashion, he had three days to put together the details of such an alternative. I was scheduled to review my 1993 staff reductions with my management and wanted to present this proposal instead.

"We worked almost straight through the next three days. The outcome was a telecommuting project before *telecommuting* had emerged as an industry buzzword. We moved personnel who dealt primarily with customers into their homes and supplied them with the tools necessary to be productive: personal computer, fax, voice mail, and additional phone lines. Office [clerical] workers were not included in this initial proposal.

"We met with Personnel, now called *Human Resources*. They strongly encouraged us to ensure that these new 'telecommuters' had access to their managers, on-site space for the occasional in-office visit, and conference rooms for team meetings. The issues associated with this proposal were countless. We had to investigate tax and liability implications, process changes, and employee reimbursement guidelines. Working with Personnel, we developed a 'mobility guide' to assist both management and employees with the transition."

When Wiley presented the proposal to Midwest Area management, he informed them that this proposal would save about fifty IBM Indiana jobs annually. After much discussion, he received approval to go ahead. Frank and his team had informed Wiley that they needed nine months to implement the plan; Wiley gave them three. Through hard work, the team accomplished the near impossible, and three hundred Indiana employees were telecommuting within ninety days of the approval.

Wiley continued, "We started the project with PS/2 Models 70 and 80. But, in the fall of 1993, we found out that IBM ThinkPads, the monochrome versions, were available. We were able to financially justify the trade for laptops through the improved productivity that field personnel could get while on the road. We moved from the realm of telecommuting to the brink of true mobility."

The 5th Wave   **By Rich Tennant**

"Oh sure, it's nice working at home, except my boss drives by every morning and blasts his horn to make sure I'm awake."

Mobility represents an environment in which workers can access information and perform their work anywhere and at any time.[1] The mobility project saved IBM Indiana more than three million dollars in 1993 and was projected to save the territory an additional five million dollars in each successive year. But, even more important, it changed the alternatives available to employees who no longer supported the concept of *IBM* meaning *I've Been Moved.* By 1994, when the Raleigh move was announced, Dell was able to find another position within IBM and remain in Boca. She also found an opportunity to expand IBM's mobile efforts into the area of services and consulting. Working in Wiley's organization under Ken Stoffregen, she started to link services with the other areas of IBM that dealt in mobility, including her old ThinkPad team. According to Stoffregen, "ThinkPad had been a success with mobile professionals, but there was another segment—mobile field workers—that worked in environments where notebooks just did not work. Our services offering allowed us to fill in the mobile hardware portfolio with handheld and rugged devices from OEM partners, products that ThinkPad was not interested in developing at the time."

Another positive aspect of the move was the brand's ability to improve or update its skill base. Losing many of the original key managers allowed for staffing replacements. One of these was Kevin Clark, current ThinkPad Brand Steward. Clark offered this perspective on the Raleigh personnel impact: "At the time, I was still pursuing a career path in communications and felt that I wanted to get into management. My wife was from North Carolina, and we saw opportunity within the PC Company. People were dropping like flies because they did not want to move from New York or Boca to Raleigh. I went in, raised my hand, and volunteered to join the team. I had had some history with the PC Company and felt confident that there was going to be a positive reversal of fortune. I felt that I could

---

1. E.W. Martin, "IBM-Indiana, Case Study I-4" (1992): 179.

make a strong contribution because I understood the history of the product line. I joined the ThinkPad team on April 1, 1995. I have been working on the brand image and personality ever since."

The Authors' Insights

The move to Raleigh was not without its positive attributes. It provided the mobile group with opportunities for advanced education, a source of highly educated employees to increase the team's skills, and localized management communications. Yet individuals paid a high psychological price for the stress associated with either the move or being laid off. Mental problems, marital discord, and other signs of stress became more apparent each day.[2] These problems affected not only the team's relationships but also the competitiveness of the product plans under development at the time. No organization can effectively institute change if its employees do not, at the very least, embrace the change. No change works if the employees do not help in the effort, and change is not possible without people changing themselves. Any organization that believes change can take hold without considering how people will react is deeply delusional.

Change can be "managed" externally by those who decide it is necessary and who track its implementation. But, the outcome can be successful only when the employees accept the change internally. Regarding the Raleigh move, the management team, with Formichelli actively in the lead, needed to be in constant communication with the employees. Management, without exception, needed to personally experience the move to Raleigh and, thus, help the employees through the adaptation process. An example of this process working was IBM Indiana's telecommuting project and eventual move to mobility. According to Mike Wiley, the driver behind this program, "The team knew that I was moving home, just as they were. I was giving up my big office and the

2. Judith K. Larsen, and Everett M. Rogers, "Silicon Valley: The Rise and Falling Off of Entrepreneurial Fever," *Creating the Technolopolis* (Raymond W. Smilor, George Kozmetsky, and David V. Gibson, editors), 99–115.

trappings of my position. It helped them to believe that I was one hundred percent behind the change."

True to their own management styles, McHugh and Claflin were proactive in employee meetings and roundtables, as well as sending e-mail notes with updates on the move logistics. These actions moved the ThinkPad team through the change stages: shock (angry e-mails, requests for executive interviews), defensive retreat (denial, slow actions to schedule home appraisals), acknowledgment (putting money down on property in Raleigh), and adaptation and change (the number of employees who actually moved and severed their ties with South Florida). However, when Claflin and McHugh decided not to move, the actions conflicted with their message and undermined the employees' belief in the move. The psychological contract between executive management and the employees was broken. Employee morale and trust declined dramatically.

Was IBM right to consolidate into Raleigh rather than stay dispersed? Five years later, with the Internet, video teleconferencing, and telecommuting rampant, the decision might be different. In 1994, the PC Company had to get their costs under control in order to survive—and survive they have. No one will be able to quantify the effect of losing employees to competitors or other IBM organizations, but one has only to look at where members of the original ThinkPad team have landed to know that vital skills were lost. Ironically, the reason used to justify the consolidation— joining development with manufacturing—no longer exists. Raleigh has a very small part of the PC Company's manufacturing role because manufacturing is now primarily done in Greenock, Fujisawa, and Guadalajara.

CHAPTER 26

The Employees: ThinkPad's Backbone

It is only with the heart that one can see rightly; what is essential is invisible to the eye.

—Antoine de Saint-Exupery, *The Little Prince*

Most business chronologies are written from key players' perspectives, but such perspectives do not always tell the whole story. To tell the ThinkPad story, the key player perspectives can be balanced against a snapshot of the team's feelings at various times in its history. During the early ThinkPad years, team members were surveyed to gauge their feelings and reactions to varying management styles and decisions. These surveys were the basis for several case studies required for the master's degree in technology at the University of Miami.

A small team of IBM employees—Debi Dell, Steve DelGrosso, John Bilanych, and Nora Mosher—questioned the ThinkPad team on three separate occasions. The surveys were triggered at significant points in the team's history: March 1994, after six months of Joe Formichelli as general manager; November 1994, after the announcement of the Raleigh move; and November 1995, slightly more than six months after the team's arrival in Raleigh. The first two surveys were delivered in person, and the third was via e-mail (online).

During the emergence of the ThinkPad brand, IBM was undergoing significant infrastructure changes. In September 1993, Louis V. Gerstner announced a set of operating principles (published in *Think Magazine*) as the roadmap for the IBM revolution. The following eight principles defined how IBM and, in turn, Mobile Computing were to be managed:

- The marketplace is the driving force behind everything we do.
- At our core, we are a technology company with an overriding commitment to quality.
- Our primary measures of success are customer satisfaction and shareholder value.
- We operate as an entrepreneurial organization with a minimum of bureaucracy and a never-ending focus on productivity.
- We never lose sight of our strategic vision.
- We think and act with a sense of urgency.
- Outstanding, dedicated people make it all happen, particularly when they work together as a team.
- We are sensitive to the needs of all employees and to the communities in which we operate.

In December 1993, Gerstner took the principles one more step and asked for "a band of committed professionals—change agents" who, in their own way, were determined to return IBM to profitability and growth.[1] The Mobile Computing team was instrumental in this effort, responding to a computer market that was expected to experience greater than a thirty-five percent compound annual growth through 1999 and generate $69.6 billion in worldwide sales.[2] In fact, in Gerstner's March 24, 1994, address to the securities analysts, he cited the ThinkPad success strategy by stating that "we have to duplicate that success across our product line."

The survey coordinators felt strongly that the employees' feelings greatly influenced the brand team's effectiveness. They wanted to map these feelings against those held by the ThinkPad management team. Employees were asked to indicate whether plans were in place to address each of Gerstner's initiatives; the scale was from zero percent (no plans in place) to one hundred percent (plans fully meet the principle). The surveys were confidential and yet provided space for write-in comments. The survey outcomes were presented to the management team under Formichelli, although, disappointingly, no concrete actions resulted from the recommendations.

Gerstner's first principle, *The marketplace is the driving force behind everything we do*, was exemplified by the mobile organization. The mobile team verified how customers made their choices through Voice of the Customer programs. These programs led to the team's realization that the mobile computing environment was market-driven, not technology-driven.[3] It drove a reduction in development cycle time from a typical eighteen months to six-to-nine months, depending on the system's complexity.

1. "A Road Map for the Revolution," *ThinkTwice* (December 1993): 14.
2. Holly Hubbard, "Global Growth for Mobile Computing," *Computer Reseller News* (January 14, 1994): 44.
3. "Mobile Computing Guide," *Computerland* (June 28, 1993): 107.

The employee surveys indicated continual progress and positive agreement with this statement as a foundation to the ThinkPad team's approach to their business. Survey results exceeded eighty percent on all three surveys and were supported by write-in comments such as "Our industry and customer advisory councils provide great information for our future products" and "We now know what our customers want." In 1994, Bruce Claflin, then president of the PC Company—Americas, commented, "I still spend thirty percent of my time linked to customers—the greatest source of intelligence. I am concerned that the mobile team may be getting too arrogant in attitude and too cautious in execution."

Because of a multi-faceted market segment, "don't miss" technologies were fundamental to the ThinkPad's product plans. Various core technologies, often defined as "allowing people to stay connected to databases and networks via wireless workstations," were the genesis of the virtual office and drove many functional decisions.[4] Such technologies were often documented in the Headlights programs established early in ThinkPad's history.

When asked about the principle, *At our core, we are a technology company with an overriding commitment to quality*, the team expressed concern about quality problems that occurred in ThinkPad's early years. One employee expressed belief that the temporary/contractor population of the Raleigh manufacturing plant was the basis of the ThinkPad quality problems and parts shortages. Asking not to be identified, he wrote in that "the temporary personnel in the Raleigh manufacturing plant are sent home if they do not have the right parts for a particular product run. One of them admitted to me that they sometimes substituted

4. David Wiley, "Star Tech," *Journal of Business Strategy* (July/August 1993): 52–54.

other parts just so the line would keep running." This information proved invaluable to Kanode and key manufacturing management when they revamped the Raleigh facility.

Positive responses from the spring 1994 survey on this principle declined to thirty percent in the fall of that same year. But, by fall 1995, employees asserted that the quality problems had been fixed. This 1995 quality resurgence might be attributable to the team's geographic proximity to the Raleigh manufacturing team and ability to work closely with the manufacturing engineers earlier in the development cycle.

Tied to its Voice of the Customer programs and its Headlights technology updates, the Mobile team believed that *[Our] primary measures of success are customer satisfaction and shareholder value.* Customer satisfaction was tracked on a monthly basis and received worldwide focus; however, only 65 percent of the fall 1994 survey participants felt that the team had plans in place to achieve this objective, down from 77.3 percent earlier in the year. Employees commented that they were no longer aware of what was happening with the brand from an overall perspective. With Claflin's departure, information flow was short-changed, and individuals had to seek information that previously flowed openly. This communications degradation slowed slightly by November 1995 due, in part, to the Raleigh consolidation. Employees experienced daily communications with the key ThinkPad executives who had moved to Raleigh and were now seated right down the hall.

The brand team was established as a new cross-functional organization that would knock down the barriers between marketing, development, and manufacturing. *Operating as an entrepreneurial organization with a minimum of bureaucracy and a never-ending focus on productivity* was a critical objective for the mobile team. Claflin achieved the first part of the objective by getting the different factions to work together and to operate as an entrepreneurial organization. Where one would expect Formichelli's process-oriented approach to result in a consistent focus on productivity, the outcome was precisely the opposite. Employees felt that, under Formichelli, the monthly measurement meetings contained data that was usually two months old and that the rigid presentation format was unwieldy. The agenda was never followed and few decisions were made. Although discussions centered on controlling expenses better than the competition (Compaq) and on addressing supply and process deficiencies, a "goat rodeo" often occurred. Too many employees attended these meetings and often confused the issues by asking questions on irrelevant topics. But, because these meetings were the only source of information after Formichelli's arrival, one had no choice but to attend.

Throughout the survey's eighteen-month timeframe, this objective was consistently rated as needing the most focus. In 1994, Patty McHugh, the planning manager, stated that "Mobile is slipping in terms of execution. The measurement meetings are becoming less valuable. With four to five times the number of products and volume opportunity, fewer people are available to do the jobs, and they are spending too much time reporting on their progress." One employee wrote on the survey form, "We went from controlling our own areas of responsibility under Claflin to constantly reporting and justifying costs under Formichelli. All this detailed reporting started to slow us down."

Despite its six-year existence, even today, the ThinkPad team *never loses sight of its strategic vision*—to be number one in the mobile segment. The vision started with Cannavino and his belief in funding a mobile organization that was challenged to deliver a technologically advanced notebook computer. Claflin, in his role as the first General Manager—Mobile Computing, added to the vision by stating that the goal was to be number one in the mobile market. Formichelli built on the vision's foundation by stressing the importance of delivering the products when the customers wanted. Each progression was detailed in team meetings and written communications. Throughout his tenure, Claflin attended the monthly meetings personally and set the tone by inviting ideas and criticism from the entire team. Every person was encouraged to voice his or her thoughts. With his departure, the formalized communications suffered, but the team already had the vision and inspired each other to remain true to the objectives even when communications faltered.

Achieving the ThinkPad vision *required thinking and acting with a sense of urgency*. McHugh commented, "Sometimes I think that the team works with too much of a sense of urgency. It causes brain cramps. Sometimes, the urgency is simply panic, but urgency will never be a problem for this team." Throughout 1994 and 1995, eighty percent of survey respondents felt that the team operated with this sense of urgency in efforts to be number one in the market. When coupled with the premise that *outstanding, dedicated people make it happen, particularly when they work together as a team*, the achievements of this fledging group are easier to understand. Anyone walking the halls of the Boca Raton site would have found individuals working well into the night, conducting conference calls with Yamato or taking time, over pizza, to talk about the next iteration of ThinkPad. Although a small group, the results of their efforts were tremendous and continually recognized in the press and with industry awards.

Patty McHugh, Gary Buer, Gene Yaffe, Leo Suarez, Ron Sperano, and Jim Keitchens.

Pete Leichliter, Bruce Claflin, Jim Bartlett, Scott Bower (left side of table), and Mark Hofert (right).

The survey results on Gerstner's final principle, *We are sensitive to the needs of all employees and to the communities in which we operate,* were definitely reflective of the general manager in charge at the time. Certainly, the move to Raleigh was not perceived as sensitive to the needs of either the Boca employees or the community. If anything, more negative feelings arose from this single action than any other. Despite the picnics, employee roundtables, or one-on-one meetings with key executives, most respondents could not get past their feelings on the Raleigh move, documented as "strictly profit-driven" and "questionable with regards to employee sensitivity." Write-in comments also reflected that financial rewards were not commensurate with the turnaround effect ThinkPad had on IBM's overall image. Even the variable pay program, implemented in 1993, did not offset the belief that there should have been greater return for the greater risks taken by the ThinkPad team in doing business differently.

One other data point on the general population's attitude was undertaken as part of the University of Miami's student research. On January 13, 1995, a brainstorming session was held with a voluntary subset of mobile survey respondents. To facilitate discussion and to break the ice, the March and November 1994 survey results were presented. Ideas and comments were encouraged, with no judgments placed on individual observations. The following insights confirmed the state of the union entering 1995:

- Supply was still the biggest customer satisfaction problem.
- The team often acted with panic, which some equated to a sense of urgency.
- The move to Raleigh reduced productivity as individuals discussed housing appraisals and timing of their personal moves.
- A better heir apparent to Formichelli than Jim Bartlett or Per Larsen was needed in order to lessen the feelings of uncertainty over ThinkPad's future.

- The rest of the PC Company was pulling down Mobile, especially when it came to sharing the wealth (variable pay, move incentives, awards, and the like).

Despite these concerns and fluctuating responses to Gerstner's eight principles, 1995 proved to be a stellar year for the team, delivering innovative products such as the ThinkPad 701C (Butterfly), receiving numerous industry awards, and completing the Raleigh move with minimal schedule impact. One truism emerged that is still valid today: Employees were proud to be members of the ThinkPad team. Each felt that he or she had contributed to IBM's turnaround in the second half of the 1990s.

The Authors' Insights

Employees, the backbone of an organization, can positively or negatively affect business attainment. Throughout the early 1990s, the ThinkPad team was challenged on all fronts. IBM was not perceived as a player in the mobile segment, driving the absolute necessity of a recognized market success. The team was dispersed around the world without a centralized vision of the future. When the brand team was finally established and a strong manager put in place, the challenges of time, distance, and different cultures remained. The individual employees had to dynamically react to fluid product directions and technologies while adapting to a constantly changing management structure. The press interviewed the general, brand, and marketing managers but seldom cited the true unsung heroes of this business turnaround. Their numbers were few, but their contribution long lasting.

1996 AND BEYOND:
THE BRAND REIGNS

The 5th Wave

By Rich Tennant

"For further thoughts on that subject, I'm going to download Leviticus and go through the menu to Job, chapter 2, verse 6, file 'J.' It reads..."

CHAPTER 27

Steve Ward: Operations Master

When you contemplate giving battle, it is a general rule to collect all your strengths and to leave none unemployed.

—Napoleon

The ThinkPad team had contributed to IBM's turnaround in the 1990s despite a series of product introductions, organizational changes, human resource challenges, and general managers (GMs). Within its brief history, the team delivered a family of advanced mobile products and established the worldwide, recognizable ThinkPad brand. While expanding to include non-U.S. organizations, development was migrated to Yamato, Japan, and the U.S. effort was consolidated in Raleigh, North Carolina. The consolidation, as well as personnel downsizings, cost the team many of its original members. Also, during this relatively short period, the team had three general managers: Jim Watabe, Bruce Claflin, and Joe Formichelli. But, change is as much a part of this history as any other element.

With the team's arrival in Raleigh, the fourth general manager in ThinkPad's brief history, Steve Ward, arrived on the scene. Ward became the IBM ThinkPad general manager in January 1996 and brought a new perspective to the mobile team. Whereas Watabe was an innovative technologist, Claflin was a marketing leader and Formichelli was a manufacturing expert, Ward was a master at running a balanced, profitable business. At this point in its evolution, the ThinkPad business needed this kind of management talent.

Steve Ward was born in Pittsburgh, Pennsylvania, but spent most of his early years in California. His father had a contract with the Air Force, so Ward lived near almost every Air Force base in the western U.S. at one time or another. Moving as often as he did, Ward probably had a tighter relationship with his family than one might normally have. Until high school, he did not have any close friends, but he did get to know lots of people across the West.

Ward recalled, "When I was in seventh grade, my father decided to buy a gas station, and the family stayed in one place for a number of years. I grew up working in a gas station and became a gas station manager by the time I was fifteen years old. I put myself through college and went to Cal Poly in San Luis Obispo. While attending school, I managed a bicycle shop and worked for Peterbilt Motors until I graduated in 1978.

"After college, I joined the IBM disk division in Tucson. I had just spent five years learning that it didn't make any engineering sense to do what Peterbilt Motors wanted to do. They were talking about micron level tolerances, and I had just been instructed not to over-spec products. You need a balanced view of costs. You have to have a balanced view of quality. Those truck engineers spent all their time trying to make the perfect truck. It didn't make a lick of sense. On the other side of the spectrum, I figured that the one place where high tolerances had to make a difference was computers. So I joined IBM.

"I traveled frequently between the labs in Tucson, San Jose, and Boulder. During my first year at IBM, I must have spent one hundred nights in hotels. I worked on disk drives. I worked on flexible media. I moved into developing and managing test facilities for disk drives. I moved quickly inside IBM. I eventually ran a three-shift manufacturing and engineering operation in one of its disk drive plants.

"I left the plant to become one of John Aker's administrative assistants. This was a great career milestone and gave me a chance to see how the entire IBM Company ran. In the Chairman's Office, young executives were given staff assignments as administrative assistants reporting to a chief of staff known as the *Executive Assistant*. Three things happen when you work as an assistant in the Chairman's Office. First, you learn a lot. Second, you work a lot. For example, I must have reviewed one hundred 'open door situations' [an *open door* is a human resources practice in which employees can appeal management actions to a higher authority] in which employees requested the Chairman's attention to a specific matter. Third, each of the Chairman's administrative assistants had some technical responsibility. My responsibility was the worldwide manufacturing and development process.

"I was the first administrative assistant in the Chairman's Office with a hardware manufacturing and development background. Primarily, assistants were pulled from the marketing ranks, with the exception of some software developers. As a matter of fact, then Executive Assistant Bob LaBant, who has since left IBM, had breakfast with me my first morning on the job. He told me, 'Steve, I have to tell you that we've never had an engineer do this before. There's a lot of fear about whether an engineer will be able to handle a position like this.' My reaction was, 'How hard could this be?' When I left the Chairman's Office, about half the people on staff were manufacturing and development engineers. I felt some personal pride in being part of this transition."

From the Chairman's Office, Ward worked for Jack Kuehler. Kuehler was a big proponent of IBM getting into portable products. In 1986, Ward worked on the IBM Convertible, a laptop portable with features similar to the competition. According to Ward, "I got the job working for Kuehler because he believed in getting people into management within three years of starting with IBM. This was in total conflict with the accepted management mentality requiring a minimum of five years of IBM experience. Not only did I make it into management, but I also became a second-level manager with fewer than five years of manufacturing experience.

"Kuehler told me, 'If you do well in this job, you get to come back as my assistant.' A brief time later, Kuehler became a member of the IBM management committee. It all worked out fairly well. After working for Kuehler, I went back to the storage systems division and managed not only our tape products but also our entry into optical storage."

In 1990, Ward did an audit of IBM's personal computer business. This assignment led to his participation in the restructuring of all IBM plants, working with Joe Formichelli. From there, he managed internal software development, working for IBM's CIO. Ward eventually became the CIO (Chief Information Officer) for the IBM PC Company and often traveled to Boca Raton for reviews with Paul Mugge, then lab director. This relationship enhanced Ward's chances of taking over the portable business at some future date.

Ward's love for mobile computing germinated from his first experience in the 1980s; he knew that he wanted to run this part of IBM's business. Ward reported, "I was actually involved with mobile computing earlier than most people realize. In addition to my brief experience with the IBM Convertible, I became involved with the development of the PS/2 L40SX laptop in 1990. This project introduced me to Leo Suarez, who was a critical resource on the L40SX development team.

"Our chairman, John Akers, asked for an audit of this portable in what we called a Manufacturing Readiness Review (MRR). Alex Wilson, a Scotsman who two months later became head of the Raleigh manufacturing facility, conducted the audit. He brought in a heavy-handed guy who was carrying a Toshiba portable around IBM to enforce the audit results. That was me. So, in the first audit of the portable business, five years before I took it over as general manager, I tracked the development of one of our initial laptops.

"The audit results were predictable. We didn't think that the L40SX would be very successful. There were lots of risks, although, technically, it was a nice product. We didn't believe that the product would be as successful as the development plan said it would be. We were, however, impressed with Suarez; he was clearly the star of the group. The audit indicated that IBM still didn't have its act together in portables. Changes needed to be made."

After his participation on the portable audit, Ward went to work for Joe Formichelli on the worldwide restructuring of IBM's manufacturing plants. Working for Formichelli, Ward was involved with the decision to do business with Toshiba.

Steve Ward.

"We decided to do a joint venture with Toshiba to make active matrix TFT displays," said Ward. "It turned out to be a mutually beneficial partnership. Toshiba had excellent technology in making the glass, and IBM had excellent technology in packaging the circuitry around the glass. Thus, for any given display size, IBM has been one of the first to make the larger display. Why? Because we used less space around the display panel, which, in turn, means that we could allocate more of the total real estate to actual display glass. This packaging capability enabled us to use the first 10.4-inch display in our 1992 portable. We did this long before anyone else could figure out how to do it. With the exception of the 13.3-inch panel that we decided not to aggressively develop, we have been the leader in introducing larger displays."

In October 1995, Ward sat down with his new boss, Bob Stephenson, the head of IBM Personal Systems. Stephenson had replaced Rick Thoman, who left to become president of Xerox. Ward had brought a stack of things three feet tall to the meeting and was quite surprised when Stephenson stated that he wanted to discuss Ward's career. He sat there for a second and then responded, "I've got a ton of things that we need to discuss so that we can make some important business decisions. I need to get some things done. As for the career discussions, we can cut this real short. I want the mobile job. Whenever it's time, whenever that job comes open, that's the job I want. I love mobile computing. I was using a Toshiba portable long before we were in the business of making portables. I've had virtually every notebook we have produced, and I can't imagine working without a notebook. Mobile computing has become my lifestyle." Stephenson was taken aback but agreed to seriously consider Ward for the mobile job when it became available.

With the support of his former manager, Joe Formichelli, and the sanction of Bob Stephenson, Steve Ward realized his dream on

January 8, 1996, when he became general manager of IBM Mobile Computing. Ward reflected, "The difference between the past two mobile GMs [Claflin and Formichelli] and me was my experience running a number of different areas within IBM. I didn't have the marketing experience of Bruce Claflin. I didn't have anywhere near the manufacturing experience of Joe Formichelli. But, I did have more development experience than either of them, and I had a lot of experience in production control. My job was to take the mobile computing business to the next step beyond Claflin's and Formichelli's actions by refining and building a solid profitable business.

"I was charged with getting the business elements in mobile computing operating together like a well-oiled machine. Although the team had support throughout IBM because ThinkPad was its darling brand, mobile needed to refine its operational processes. In the past, they did whatever was needed to get the job done; it was now time to get the job done right. I expected the managers to set their objectives and then to deliver. I was fanatical about balancing accountability with the empowerment necessary to achieve our business objectives. I brought operational discipline to the mobile computing team."

Shortly after Ward's arrival, on February 20, 1996, IBM expanded its ThinkPad 760 family with the 760L and 760LD, models offering premium performance and design at mid-range prices.[1] His director of worldwide brand management for mobile computing, Per Larsen, stated that "The ThinkPad 760 series was extended to reach the broader, mid-priced market. These new models made ThinkPad notebooks more affordable for mainstream and fleet buyers."

In addition to Larsen and his marketing skills, Ward was fortunate to have several other veteran ThinkPad members on his team.

1. IBM news release (February 20, 1996).

Many of the employees had adapted to the Raleigh area and were pursuing advanced degrees at the surrounding universities. From a management perspective, Ward quickly learned to rely on Jim Bartlett's industry knowledge and Leo Suarez's technical expertise. In addition, he had Kevin Clark, who handled brand management through various industry and customer councils.

Clark reflected on Ward's arrival: "Steve came on board just as we were realizing significant market strides. We had a development team that had been together for a while and was now in sync with marketing and product planning. Ward understood the portable product line, and he forced us onto a quality track. His manufacturing background encouraged the simplification of our product lines. By knowing what we were going to make and putting the right processes in place, we achieved both the quality and business plan objectives. In my opinion, Ward could not have presided over the Claflin or Formichelli eras any more than those two personalities could have done what he set out to do. He worked minor miracles to grow the brand into a mature business that our customers both understand and respect."

Leo Suarez, a team member who bridged all three general managers' regimes (with a brief interlude in IBM Latin America headquarters), offered this perspective: "Three different eras were necessary for very different reasons. Bruce [Claflin] was brought in because we needed marketing leadership and guidance. We had to establish and take a brand to market; Claflin was excellent in that role. He was one of the best marketeers I've seen in IBM. It was a shame to lose him so soon after his arrival. But, he gave us the right marketing focus. Then, the market took off, and we just couldn't deliver. ThinkPad availability was always six months out—it became the ultimate, classical manufacturing problem.

Leo Suarez.

"Joe [Formichelli] arrived on the scene to drive availability up and to perfect our manufacturing processes. His efforts enabled us to build ThinkPads by the millions. Unfortunately, we built so many that we had inventory all over the place, just like the early days of the PC Company. The mobile team now had major business problems. Steve [Ward] was assigned to manage mobile computing as a business with discipline and auditable processes. He was put in place to make a dollar, to make a profit. We had a world-class portable line in ThinkPad, the best brand in the industry, and a strong marketing team. We had even figured out how to deliver high volumes. But, it was time to learn how to make money and do it in a repeatable, organized manner. Ward was excellent at doing just that; he was the right GM for the time. Where we had thought that Formichelli was tough, we found Ward even harder on the team. He came in and almost killed us. He kicked butt and took names. It was the best thing that could have happened to us because he got us running as a solid business for IBM."

What did his direct management reports think of Ward? Bartlett, another veteran of all three eras, expressed his thoughts: "Ward was an impressive IBM executive. I enjoyed working for him. He was the perfect blend of Bruce Claflin and Joe Formichelli. He came from a development background and was astonishingly savvy in marketing and customer satisfaction issues. He understood the marketing stuff with an intensity you would not believe for a development guy. He understood technology, manufacturing, and the entire business process. He drove us to fix things when the people surrounding him, who actually had responsibility for those processes, would not have fixed them on their own.

"His expertise helped us address, and even prevent, quality problems. He drove us to the top of the heap in terms of quality in portable computing. During Ward's regime, the Gartner Group made tremendous claims about IBM being the only guys who got the quality of portables right. Ward had the ability to manage all the functions reporting to him, including manufacturing, development, marketing, sales, quality, and customer satisfaction, and he made it look easy. He brought it all together and created a smoothly running business."

One of the things Ward would bring together was the worldwide announcement process. When Ward came on board, he was familiar with the team he inherited from Claflin and Formichelli. He quickly realized that Per Larsen was one of his strongest assets and a means to the end of effectively managing ThinkPad on a worldwide basis. According to Ward, "Prior to Larsen joining the ThinkPad group, the product was developed and launched publicly, with each geography managing its own execution. So, although the U.S. planning team worked with Yamato development to create a product, the various field organizations had to figure out what had to be done to manage the post-launch operation. What resulted was an international effort that looked disorganized and was extremely costly. ThinkPad ads in one country didn't even communicate the same thing as those presented in another geography. Products introduced quickly in one geography would be significantly delayed or, worse yet, never announced in another."

In their initial meeting, Larsen presented his vision of an effective worldwide business as a strongly linked process. This simplified flowchart highlights the development and delivery linkage.

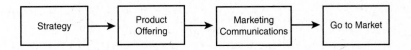

From this initial simple concept, Ward worked with Larsen to create a worldwide brand management process in which strategy led to products. The products resulted in a common set of messages worldwide. Both the product and the message were then implemented worldwide at the same time.

Under Formichelli (Ward's predecessor), Larsen spent the early part of his ThinkPad tenure getting the strategy piece right. A formal market assessment process resulted and ensured that the team know the customer requirements before product specifications were finalized. Marketing and development interlocked on the product roadmap and associated schedule. When Ward arrived on the scene, he worked with Larsen to create a worldwide marketing communications process. This process addressed the homologation issues (different AC adapters for the plugs in the various countries, and so on) early in the cycle and identified problems specific to the various geographies. The approach enabled the team to be proactive, instead of reactive, in its worldwide deployment; it prevented unnecessary development costs and schedule delays. The brand messages were the same, simply delivered in local country languages. Finally, the actual "go to market" process guaranteed solid execution from the brand team into the field.

During this period, Larsen selected Rick McGee, an IBM veteran with a strong operations background, to head the last two steps. After almost two years of effort, the process worked properly and the results were significant. McGee recalled, "My operations experience taught me to take tough issues and break them into bite-size pieces. By taking little steps, it was pretty straightforward to make a process work. I was not a strategy guy. I was not the guy who figured out what products to build. I simply knew how to make a process work on a worldwide scale. I jumped at the chance to set up this kind of process for the ThinkPad team. By setting up this process properly, I knew it would help an important part of IBM succeed.

"I spent a lot of time working with each geography to get a smooth process in place. I realized that they had the job of making it happen. I didn't want to be perceived as arriving from headquarters, giving a lecture, and then hoping that it would work out. I established individual geography marketing managers. We brought together the teams in the field and, together, planned how to make the 'go to market' process work. It was a joint effort. We got buy-in because we made them an integral part of the process."

This deployment was not always easy. First, McGee focused on the largest countries because the top eight countries accounted for eighty-five percent of the ThinkPad business. As the team developed and refined the management system, they spent a considerable amount of time in these countries learning the local market and creating relationships with the IBM regional and country teams. The approach was to listen and learn, as well as to include the regional and country personnel on the extended worldwide team. They recruited the right people on the local teams to execute the ThinkPad marketing plan around the world.

Then, he had to do the same thing in the developing countries. McGee continued, "We worked on developing our ThinkPad business in China by going to Shenzen to hold a Customer Advisory Council. We got a bunch of customers in a room with our in-country marketing managers so that we could learn what customers were expecting. We wanted to implement a joint process that would work for that geography.

"After about two hours, I realized that we had a major problem. Not one of the attendees had said a single word. We weren't learning a thing. I stopped the meeting and had our folks conduct one-on-one interviews with the customers. We used interpreters, which made understanding a little difficult at times. But, we finally got them to understand that we wanted their input and that we weren't there to lecture to them. When they finally understood, we couldn't get them to stop talking. We went beyond our scheduled times, but we learned what was important for this geography.

"After the customer sessions, we sat down with the local marketing team and put together a process tailored for China, slightly different from what we do elsewhere. For example, when we build a 'China' product, it really covers three areas: PRC [Pacific Rim Countries], Taiwan, and Hong Kong. About eighty-five percent of the customers wanted Chinese language systems, and fifteen percent wanted U.S. systems, particularly in Hong Kong, where customers conduct business in English.

"The management system and marketing processes we put together were not rocket science. They were basic fundamentals that needed to be executed on a consistent and constant basis. Repeatable, predictable, yet with plenty of room to allow the creative juices to flow and to keep it fun and exciting," concluded McGee.

This new worldwide announcement process would come into play several times during Ward's regime. Under Ward's watch, the first recognized successor to the ThinkPad 700 series was introduced in May 1996 as the ThinkPad 560. It was a new paradigm in portable computing. Before its introduction, small and lightweight portables were called *subnotebooks*. These systems had a smaller display, smaller screen, slower processor, and smaller hard disk. They were just *sub*-everything. But, IBM market research showed that, although users liked the idea of a very lightweight portable, they really wanted a thin form factor. They also wanted a traditional full-size IBM keyboard. Finally, they wanted a large display that they could easily read, coupled with the fastest processors and adequate hard disks. What they could live without was all the other accessories, such as CD-ROMs or diskette drives; these could be added when needed.

IBM responded to sore-armed, luggage-strapped business travelers everywhere when it announced the ThinkPad 560, an innovative notebook so slim and light that it fit into nearly any briefcase. It packed a 12.1-inch TFT display, full-size keyboard, and powerful Pentium processor in an ultra-thin 1.2-inch, 4.1 pound package. Before this announcement, the lightest notebook sporting a 12.1-inch TFT panel weighed nearly seven pounds. Also, for convenient computing on the road, the 560 featured an integrated infrared link for wireless file transfer, printing, and communications with other infrared-enabled desktop PCs and electronic organizers. Ward was quoted as saying, "The ThinkPad

560 changed the way people think of ThinkPads, and notebooks in general. The new design was extremely innovative, but the performance and price were equally impressive. For the first time, notebook users did not have to compromise in any of these areas."[2]

Jerry Michalski, a member of the Industry Advisory Council, described his reaction to the ThinkPad 560: "The machine I remember using first—not the first ThinkPad I had, but the first one I remember using—was the 560. It was quite an extraordinary machine. It was a big change for me because I had used a 760 for a while that was just overkill. Although the 760 was beautifully engineered, it was way too much machine.

"Once again, on the product front, the team had hit a solid combination of product features, price points, and functionality. There were no hidden killer flaws in the machines; the machines did what you wanted them to do and did it solidly. On branding, the black-and-red color scheme still worked. The general branding scheme of being a little bit funky and having good broadcast and print ads also worked in IBM's favor. When you open a ThinkPad on a plane, you can almost feel the envy. The branding scheme and design identity has played well for IBM over time."

July 1996 brought some organizational changes to the ThinkPad team. Ward announced that Koichi Higuchi had been appointed vice president of quality and alliances and would lead an extended cross-functional task force made up of development, manufacturing, procurement, customer relations, service, and the HelpCenter. The task force would work on improving overall mobile product quality, customer satisfaction, and customer service. Ward stated, "Koichi Higuchi's leadership in building the ThinkPad brand and his past responsibility for ThinkPad product development make him the perfect choice for this critical assignment."

2. IBM news release (May 21, 1996).

Succeeding Higuchi-san was Adalio Sanchez, named vice president of development, who would provide business direction to Ikeda-san, director of portable systems development, Japan. Between Rick McGee's efforts at worldwide branding and the newly established task force under Higuchi-san, the ThinkPad team had put in place some much needed updates to their processes and organization.

On October 15, 1996, IBM added additional systems to its ThinkPad line. It extended the 760 product line and enhanced the 365 series. Following the announcement, Gerry Purdy met with Steve Ward, Per Larsen, and Jim Bartlett at the fall ThinkPad Industry Advisory Council at the Aspen Institute. Purdy questioned them about the ThinkPad organization and its focus under Ward. Ward reflected on this time: "My group was organized along the new brand structure that IBM is now focused on. We tried very hard to inject classic brand management into the industry—this was something that had been lacking in the past.

"We also added a group called the *Integrated Project Management Team*, which included Per Larsen, head of Worldwide Marketing. Initially, the group managed our four manufacturing locations. However, based on the work of Larsen and his team, we decided to close the Raleigh, North Carolina, facility and manufacture in Mexico, Scotland, and Japan.

"Like the job, this decision was harder than you might think. I learned that it was tougher on the inside than it appeared from the outside. I learned that the ThinkPad brand, the strength of the brand, was heavily related to how we served our customers, the high quality of service, and the assurances of a low total cost of ownership and long-life products. Keeping that level of customer loyalty and satisfaction requires tough management to make sure that no compromises are made. The manufacturing decision was tied to this "no compromise" approach in determining our customers' wants and needs.

"As we made these decisions, the most important part of the process was to evaluate what promise of value we were giving to our customers. With ThinkPad, we always delivered a product that gave our customers a competitive advantage while providing them with a mobile solution that enabled them to manage mission-critical, network-centric tasks. We continued to evaluate our users' needs and document the attributes of the product—again, largely done by Larsen's group. Then, we developed these products in Yamato, Japan. Another critical component of this process was our research teams in Yorktown, Almaden, and Tokyo, who continually pushed us to go farther in what we provided to the customer."

Bartlett jumped in at this point and offered this projection: "Some of the best days for ThinkPad are still to come. People want to create the environment they like. If you have a favorite room in your house, for example, you really want to duplicate that wherever you are on the road. If you take that picture and drive it to the personal computing space, what we have to do is re-create the user's whole desktop or home environment and make it mobile. It's really a transparency thing. The user shouldn't have to think about any differences between the desktop environment and the mobile environment.

"In mobile computing, we are where the automobile was in the early 1900s. We had machines, but the roads were bumpy; the infrastructure wasn't quite there yet. Even if you had a Ferrari in those days, you couldn't drive it on the roads. You had to wait for the infrastructure to develop.

"So, two things are happening: We have to move the platforms forward but also make sure that the infrastructure is put in place.

The exciting picture I see, certainly within the next ten years, is some pretty high-speed roads and some pretty neat cars."

The Authors' Insights

Throughout ThinkPad history, the IBM executive team had the insight to change general managers as business needs dictated. As cited by Professor Kosnik, profound leadership is critical to building an enduring brand, and ThinkPad was fortunate enough to experience this throughout its history. Despite the team's disappointment in the perceived early departure of Claflin and the sporadic focus of Formichelli during his tenure, Steve Ward's arrival was accepted as a necessary change. His operational expertise was well known before his arrival and instilled confidence throughout the group. He leveraged the skills of his organization while perfecting long-neglected processes. His direct style drove long days and nights, but the team was committed to achieving operational efficiencies. As a result, operational efficiency was the hallmark of 1996 and, it is hoped, beyond.

1996 Product Line Additions

System	560	760E/ED/FL	365X/XD
Form	Ultra	Notebook	Notebook
Processor	Pentium 133/120/ 100MHz	Pentium 100/120/ 133/150MHz	Pentium 120/133MHz
Memory	8/72MB	8-16-32/104	8/40
Storage	810MB 1.08/2.1GB I/II/III PCMCIA	810MB 1.35/2.1GB II/III PCMCIA	810MB 1.08/1.35/2.1GB II/III PCMCIA
Display	12.1" TFT SVGA 11.3" Dual Scan	12.1" XGA TFT 12.1" SVGA TFT 11.3" SVGA DSTN	10.4" TFT 11.3" DSTN 11.3" TFT
Operating system	Windows 95 PC DOS 7.0 OS/2 WARP	Windows 95 PC DOS 7.0	Windows 95 PC DOS 7.0 Preloaded SW
Weight (lb.)	4.1	6.4/7.4	5.9/6.4
Other	Infrared PCI bus Ext FDD TrackPoint III	Video subsystem ISA or PCI Mwave DSP TrackPoint III Infrared	Integrated CD-ROM Audio chip Security TrackPoint III Infrared
Announced	5/21/96	10/15/96	10/15/96

Awards

ThinkPad 560	*Byte*	Best of Comdex - Portable
	PC World	Top 20 Notebooks
ThinkPad 760	*Mobile Office*	First Class Award
	PC Magazine	Best of the Year
ThinkPad 365	*Computer Life*	First Place

CHAPTER 28

ThinkPad After ThinkPad

The history of design at IBM is the history of innovation and hard work. Innovation distinguishes the leader from the follower, never satisfied with what has been, but with what will be. It is the driving force of the creative spirit, sensitive to change and the changeless. It focuses not only on what is right, but also on what is exceptional. Surprise, not predictability, is its hallmark.

—Paul Rand, 1990

A highlight of Ward's first year was the ThinkPad 560, which, like the original ThinkPad, won all major portable industry awards. Analysts renamed this class of products *ultraportable*—those lightweight portables with all bays removed and focused on the essentials. Statistics indicated approximately fifteen percent of portable users sacrificed the built-in accessories in order to gain the advantage of lower weight, forcing the ultraportable to be recognized as a niche product category. To achieve a profitable participation, IBM needed to increase the appeal of these portables to a larger group of users. With this goal and the pursuit of award-winning products in mind, the IBM ThinkPad team thoroughly researched each new product concept.

Erica DesRoches, a member of the IBM Personal Systems Group's Worldwide Market Intelligence organization, managed ThinkPad market research in the late 1990s. According to DesRoches, "I defined the research requirements and translated them into research questions and research designs. I then reported the findings of these primary market research projects, along with specific recommendations on the product(s) under evaluation. So, although we were not part of the line ThinkPad team, we were part of the matrixed structure. Our group was as strongly committed to the success of the product line as if we reported to Ward."

This market research helped to create the ThinkPad 380 for the small and medium business segments. Each of these models sold more than one million units, the result of strong product management efforts. In 1995, David Nichols, an executive recruit, was hired as the product manager for this ThinkPad. In his role as product manager, Nichols worked with the market research organization, as well as the Yamato development team. But, his efforts were not slowed by his adaptation to the IBM environment. He experienced less culture shock than Jim Bartlett three years earlier because professional hires had become more commonplace. Nichols spent less time fighting the bureaucratic culture and, thus, could be more effective faster. IBM had established programs to assimilate the professional hires into the organization with a little less pain.

Nichols reflected on his move to IBM: "In July 1995, I was working for a wireless data communication company. I decided that it was time for a career move and called Gerry Purdy, who had numerous contacts in the mobile industry. I asked him what kind of career move he thought a young mobile computing marketing guy like me might want to consider. I remember, that was on a Wednesday, and by Friday I was talking to Jim Bartlett, the executive director of Brand Marketing for the IBM ThinkPad Group. I was attracted to IBM because of its great ThinkPad brand. Although it had great products, it needed to expand beyond the large enterprise market and move into other segments, like retail and small-to-medium businesses. It fit perfectly with my prior experience at Sony and this wireless data communications company.

"My first interview with Bartlett was over the phone. It was an in-depth and probing interview, one of the most challenging I ever had. Bartlett asked me not only how I looked at markets but also what type of opportunities allow expansion within a given market. He asked me how you take an established brand like ThinkPad and link it to a different type of product designed for a new market. Following the call, I was invited to Raleigh to meet the rest of the team.

"I interviewed with Tim Peters (now at Dell Computer Corporation), Bob Sachsenmeier, Jay Johnson, John Madigan, and Kevin Clark. The ThinkPad organization was now using the team approach to adding outside personnel; no longer did just the receiving manager interview a candidate. Because I was to be part of the team, the team got to vote on me as well. Based on the interviews, I knew right away that exceptional people surrounded me. I encountered people who thought hard about what they were doing. They asked hard questions and challenged those responses they didn't understand or didn't accept.

"I have to admit that the bureaucracy I encountered during this process turned me off a little bit. I wasn't sure that I was prepared to deal with it, coming from a small company. I actually turned down the first offer I got from Bartlett. I declined his offer because I was convinced that the culture would affect my ability to succeed at IBM. To his credit, Bartlett didn't just pass on this. By the next day, I had a phone call from Joe Formichelli, then the general manager of the

ThinkPad brand. I then received a phone call from Per Larsen, vice president of Marketing. I was very impressed that both long-time IBMers told me that their jobs were to ensure that the traditional IBM culture didn't get in the way of the Mobile Computing team.

"My wife accompanied me on the second trip to Raleigh because accepting the job would require a move from California to North Carolina. This was an opportunity to work with a brand moving from number three and aggressively pursuing number one. IBM wanted to dominate the portable computer market and to bring out new and exciting new products. With such a challenging environment, I accepted IBM's revised offer.

"I joined IBM on October 2, 1995. The first year was quite enlightening. I was immediately thrown into what I would consider some very old IBM ways of doing things, which set off my warning signals. I had come here to do product marketing, but at the time, there was no product marketing position open. I was put in charge of service and support and the customer satisfaction programs.

"This assignment provided some great understanding of how IBM looked at things. I saw how IBM took care of its largest customers. I got to measure their satisfaction and then put plans in place to improve it. It gave me a chance to learn the ThinkPad product line while getting acclimated to the IBM culture. It certainly proved to be different from any other culture I had experienced. I counted on Bartlett's and Larsen's commitments to move me into Product Marketing after I got some initial experience under my belt.

"In January 1997, I became a product manager. As the segment manager for the small and medium business market, I was in charge of focusing ThinkPad on the needs of this segment. I was not put in charge, per se, of a ThinkPad product and told to find out who would buy it. Rather, I was in charge of a customer set and told to develop a ThinkPad product to meet the customer needs.

"Working with the Market Research organization, I began to analyze the users in my segment and to determine the product attributes they valued most highly. I then drove those attributes into requirements for the ThinkPad products to be offered to the small and medium business market segment. I decided on the final product definitions and the launch campaign for the 380.

"Our research showed that small and medium business owners didn't have an MIS department to configure their machines. Instead, they themselves had to manage their portable computer resources, or they would use a part-time consultant. This told us that an integrated portable with all the features built in would be attractive to this segment. Therefore, we built in the hard disk, CD-ROM, and floppy drive with the distinctive look and feel of a ThinkPad.

"Our research also demonstrated that this class of buyer was very price sensitive. Therefore, we worked hard to minimize cost in the unit. As a result, we brought out a fully configured ThinkPad 380 portable well under three thousand dollars. This just had not been done before. In fact, it was a challenge because many people believed that IBM built only high-end expensive portables. The 380 was different. We provided great value instead of the very highest performance. So, our go-to-market strategy was to broadly communicate that the 380 was an affordable portable.

"We launched the ThinkPad 380 in May 1997. It was an instant hit. Our orders were backlogged for months. We had thought that if we could sell a couple hundred thousand in a year, we'd be doing well. Order rates came in well above that so we had to make some production adjustments. In just eighteen months, IBM reported that the ThinkPad 380 had sold more than one million units, making it the most successful single model of a portable computer produced in the market to date."

At the time of the announcement, Ward commented that "the ThinkPad 380 series all-in-one design represents the next step in mobile computing because the power and features now available in notebook computers match those of a desktop. Mobile computers are no longer desktop alternatives, but truly desktop replacements."

Press and market analysts were also gung-ho about this offering. Mike McGuire, senior industry analyst at Dataquest, said, "Notebook computers offering leading-edge technology at affordable prices have been the sweet spot of the overall mobile PC market for the past two years. The ThinkPad 380 represents a solid contender in this market segment."

USA Today echoed the forecasted success in an article "IBM Record Punctuates Its Rebound," published just before the ThinkPad 380 announced. Two days after IBM's Big Blue computer and software beat the world's human chess champion, IBM's stock surpassed the decade-old record high of $175 7/8 (August 21, 1987), hitting $177 1/8. According to the article, by Lorrie Grant, "Analysts say another reason for optimism was IBM's launch of an all-in-one ThinkPad notebook that integrates a hard drive, floppy drive, and CD-ROM."

The ThinkPad team also tried some innovative introduction strategies. To encourage customers to experience the ThinkPad 380 and to find out where to buy ThinkPads, IBM created the ThinkPad 380 series World Wide Web site on the Internet. At the Web site, customers also found out how to participate in the ThinkPad 380 "A Better Place to Think" sweepstakes. Beginning May 13, 1997, for six weeks, a ThinkPad 380, as well as related prizes, was awarded according to the terms of the sweepstakes.

But, the team did not stop there. One month later, the brand announced enhancements to the ThinkPad 760 and 560 series. The enhancements included 13.3-inch active matrix displays and faster Pentium processors. The systems were also available through the IBM System Care program. This program enabled customers to experience the total benefits of ownership by refocusing assets on their core businesses rather than on managing their PCs. According to Ward, "Backed by the IBM System Care Program, combining technology, financing, and service and support in a single, comprehensive program, these ThinkPads not only led the cutting-edge technology but were also the easiest to manage mobile PCs in the market. Our customers could now focus on their business and let us manage their mobile infrastructure."

"A Better Place to Think."

Ward's team was on a roll. Not only had they improved their operational performance, but they also announced innovative, award-winning products. They went for their third homerun: the ThinkPad 770. The ThinkPad 770 announced on September 8, 1997, with a 14.1-inch screen. It was billed as the first in a new series of "extreme performance" mobile computing solutions that integrated powerful processors and multimedia capabilities with maximum-size displays, advanced communications, Windows NT, and massive data storage. The ThinkPad 770 also featured several enhancements to the TrackPoint pointing stick device, an integral part of the brand's recognized personality. New Press-to-Select or Release-to-Select features allowed tapping of the TrackPoint itself to speed application launches and reduce keystrokes. A new programmable button located under the mouse buttons enabled fast scrolling of Web sites and large documents. When coupled together, these features enabled Ward to assert that "With the ThinkPad 770, IBM is once again asserting its leadership role in notebook computing."

Ward was leading a championship team on its journey to becoming the most recognized brand in mobile computing history. During 1997, the ThinkPad team made significant progress toward its vision of "providing the most powerful and convenient way to work anywhere in an interconnected world." It delivered product choices that fit customer requirements and budgets. It expanded and demonstrated its commitment to service and support after the sale. Quality processes that ensured continual improvement of ThinkPad's reliability and serviceability were established. Stocking spare parts to service older machines took precedence over revenue targets driving the ultimate goal of Total Customer Satisfaction.

Ward knew that these successes should be documented. He made one more decision before the end of 1997 that eventually became tied to the legacy of the brand. On Tuesday, November 12, 1997, during the annual Comdex trade show, IBM celebrated its fifth anniversary of the first ThinkPad announcement at Piero's restaurant in Las Vegas.

Gerry Purdy had arranged to meet Debi Dell at this celebration. Dell arrived early in hopes of spending time with her old friends from the ThinkPad team. As she entered, she noticed an attractive, silver-haired gentleman and wondered who he was. Finding two members of the former Boca Raton ThinkPad team, they gathered around one of the many tables laden with food. Halfway into her first glass of wine, she noticed the distinguished-looking gentleman walking toward her; she also felt some nervousness on the part of her tablemates. The gentleman walked over and introduced himself as Steve Ward. Recognizing the name of the current general manager for IBM Mobile Computing, Dell extended her hand in greeting. Ward immediately recognized her name (the irony of her working at IBM with the surname *Dell* was seldom lost on IBMers or customers) and said, "So, let's talk about why you want to write a book about ThinkPad."

Dell related her role on the original ThinkPad team and how the experience had been the source of several papers during her recently completed masters of technology at the University of Miami. She described the benefits of telling this successful story about the creation of the ThinkPad brand and its award-winning portable PC products. She was enthusiastic about the interest of professors and industry headhunters in how this brand's journey began.

Ward then asked a probing question, the type so typical of someone who is very precise: "What will make people read this story? How do you make this story interesting and not just a case study?" Dell responded that it would be a personal story, a story told by the real players and not from just a technology perspective. They discussed Ward's view on the critical elements of the story and his pride in his team.

After wishing her luck with the project, Ward was then called away to host the anniversary event, where he gave a spirited talk to his guests. He acknowledged IBM's success with ThinkPad during its first five years in existence. He related that IBM had stayed true to many of the things that made ThinkPad unique and successful: TrackPoint, innovative industrial design, and the black color.

He highlighted the move from twelfth in the industry to second in volume and first in revenue in only five years. He thanked the team for making it happen and then thanked the analysts and press for their support.

The anniversary was not the last thing to be celebrated in ThinkPad's history, at least from Nichols' perspective. Nichols was very fortunate to have come from the outside, survived the culture shock, and then produced a ThinkPad that became an instant hit. He joined the team during a very productive and rewarding period, culminating in the anniversary celebration. And his luck continued. After his experience with the 380, he became the segment manager for the performance segment. Whereas the "extreme performance" segment was focused on the high-end, latest technologies, the performance segment was a new market for the mobile team. Research showed that performance users wanted to have a thin and light portable with the attributes of high-end machines. They also wanted a portable that included a bay that could hold a CD-ROM or other accessories, such as a second battery or floppy drive.

Different form factors were tested with customers through worldwide focus groups. Over and over, one form factor stood out. It was thin like the ThinkPad 560 but included a bay that was only twelve millimeters thick, instead of the typical seventeen-millimeter bay common to most portables. The responses indicated that such a machine would be a real winner. Nichols reflected that "Based on the research of Tim Peters and Erica DesRoches, we went to work and developed such a portable. The unit weighed only slightly less than five pounds. We followed up the concept focus groups by showing prototypes to major accounts and medium businesses. They loved it. The only exposure was that this product might draw users away from the ThinkPad 380 and 560 because it was much thinner and lighter. Also, this machine provided the capability to have a CD-ROM anytime, anywhere that software might have to be loaded."

DesRoches augmented Nichols's thought: "In the case of the ultraportable, we didn't stop with the ThinkPad 560's design. Comprehensive research, both U.S. and international, honed the product's definition and the design of its performance-based follow-on, the ThinkPad 600. Our efforts predicted its market acceptance. We clearly demonstrated its superior performance relative to other concepts under evaluation. This product was reviewed from several perspectives: from early qualitative discussions of its pros and cons, to quantitative estimates of how it would do in the target marketplace, given the other competitive options, to in-depth discussions of its industrial design."

In June 1998, IBM introduced the ThinkPad 600, one of the fastest selling portable computers in IBM's history. Performance users in both large and medium accounts desired it. It won industry awards for its sleek design, high performance, and low weight. The minor design challenges, such as the audio placement, did not slow down this rocket in the market. In fact, according to IAC member Jerry Michalski, "The 600 was just awesome, the only machine I use. Hard to believe, but the difference between the 560 and 600 was definitely noticeable. One just has to wonder how much longer these innovative designs can continue."

If David Hill, manager of the Personal Systems Group design center, has his way, these creative designs will continue indefinitely. Hill commented on this dimension of the brand: "The original design idea for the ThinkPad came from Richard Sapper. He was [is] a noted industrial designer with a long list of accomplishments, one of the most important designers of the twentieth century in product design. He has been IBM's corporate design consultant since 1980, and his ideas affected many aspects of the ThinkPad.

David Hill, manager of the PSG design center.

"I felt that the design of the original ThinkPad was special because it was dramatic. It had a mysterious quality. Yet, the fact that the design was very simple added a timeless quality to it. Take the pyramids in Egypt, which are an incredibly simple, yet powerful and timeless shape. Or take the Washington Monument with its very simple shape. Take the Vietnam War Memorials, an incredibly simple shape but a powerful design because of that simplicity."

In addition to Richard Sapper and the ThinkPad team, Hill also worked with the industrial design team in Yamato, Japan, headed by Kazuhiko Yamazaki. An extended team, it was important that they all operate under the same perception of what ThinkPad needed to be. Hill continued, "The ThinkPad design was an evolution, not a revolution. Consider the Porsche 911. If you looked at a Porsche 911 today, and you looked at a Porsche 911 from fifteen years ago, you would clearly see how different the car is, but you would still know it was a Porsche 911. The car evolved without destroying the basic underlying design elements. In fact, the door handles and the overall contour of the two Porsche 911s remained almost identical. All the 911 changes occurred out of purposeful evolution to make it better and, yet, hold on to the design heritage.

"When you have a wonderful design, you have to be careful how you advance it. Just as the Porsche design team slowly advanced its product, we did the same with ThinkPad. When you don't have an industrial design that is special, you can change it every year without impact. But, when you have a special design, you treat it very carefully. We knew that the initial ThinkPad design was something special.

"Lots of companies tried to create some sort of a design theme for their notebooks. We saw some things that were interesting and some things that, frankly, looked a little bit more like a cheap boom box. The ThinkPad design was so simple, so strong, and so transferable. By *transferable*, I mean that we could make big ones, small ones, thick ones, and little ones, and they all looked alike because their simplicity allowed migration across size lines. Thus, we carefully experimented with the ThinkPad design during this phase in IBM's portable history. Consider the ThinkPad 600. The first time you see it, you know it's a ThinkPad. But, you get this feeling that somehow it's a little bit different. It has just a bit of a surprise when you open it up. The ThinkPad 600 design screams at you artistically. That was very intentional.

"We discovered in testing the ThinkPad 600 against the competition that thinness seemed to trip people's emotions. The ThinkPad 600 design was reworked to emphasize and create the illusion of added thinness because it's such a strong communicator of advanced technology. We chamfered the bottom of the chassis, so the computer appears to float above the table.[1] When you see a ThinkPad 600, it appears to be almost as thin as a ThinkPad 560. It has that element of magic or mystery, like 'How did they make a box the size of a 560 that has a CD-ROM in it?'

"Interestingly, although it proved to be an award-winning design, the ThinkPad 600 does have some glaring mistakes. The most noticeable is that the audio speakers sit right underneath the hands. Typing on the 600 can interfere with the sound coming out of the speakers. Because good design is the melding of both form and function, the ThinkPad design fell a little short. Form and function are inseparable. So, we will have to modify the ThinkPad 600 to provide better sound and yet retain its sleek and special appearance."

While the market research and planning communities were working on the features and functions of their soon-to-be-announced products, Adalio Sanchez worked the product line from another perspective. Sanchez recalled, "In 1996, I got a call from Joe Formichelli asking me to help out with the ThinkPad line. After ending my assignment with Mii-san in 1994, I became the director of manufacturing for the PC business. Formichelli felt that I had the expertise necessary to help with the new ultra-portable 560, the high-end 760E, and the 365 series. For a time, I worked on the ThinkPad problems while still doing my nine-to-five job as director of PC Manufacturing. Eventually, the mobile assignment required my attention full-time. What started as a three-month special assignment turned into a promotion to vice president of ThinkPad development in the fall of 1996. I stayed with the team through the 380 and 600."

1. Nathaniel Wice, "Thin," *Time Digital* (November 2, 1998): 25.

Ward continued as general manager during the ThinkPad 770 and ThinkPad 380 development cycles. But, Bartlett's earlier words proved prophetic. As was the case with Claflin and Formichelli, when his mission was accomplished, Ward moved on. He was promoted on March 5, 1998, and Adalio Sanchez assumed ThinkPad's key management role and saw the ThinkPad 600 to announcement.

Before his departure, Ward's final comment emphasized his love for the mobile effort: "I looked at this job as the gem in IBM. I was honored to have this job. Whenever I got a chance to speak in front of large audiences, I always stopped and said, 'My name is Steve Ward, and I am privileged to represent the IBM ThinkPad brand.' It was a great deal. You got a ton of support from everyone in IBM. Everyone really wanted to help, to be part of a winning team."

Ward was not the only one to move on. Two successes in a row, the ThinkPad 380 and the ThinkPad 600, led to the IBM Group promoting Nichols to manager of Mobile and Consumer Options in Options by IBM (OBI). He was encouraged by Per Larsen to expand his experience beyond portables. Nichols summarized his ThinkPad experience and joining the ranks of IBM, "IBM people are smart, intelligent, bright, and aggressive. It was refreshing not being the smartest person in the company. I don't mean that I was the smartest person in the other companies, but it was refreshing to say something and know that it was going to be challenged. It improved my thinking, and it improved my critical skills. It helped me become a better person, helped me to grow. Somehow, I survived the bureaucracy of IBM and made a contribution to the mobile business."

Adalio Sanchez.

The Authors' Insights

Sometimes, when a product comes to market, it is a "one-hit wonder" with no follow-on success. Seldom does such a one-hit wonder result in an enduring brand. In fact, the test of an enduring product brand is to develop and bring to market successive products that are as good as or better than the original. Thus, the brand increases its reach and continues to hold its preferential position in the market. In 1992, no one knew whether the ThinkPad 700C was a one-hit wonder or whether IBM could build a truly enduring portable brand. Throughout its abbreviated history, IBM demonstrated an ability to create lasting equity in the ThinkPad brand. The team developed successive ThinkPad products that reached new markets and added value to the overall brand.

Like Claflin and Formichelli, Ward's era was brief; only time will tell whether it was too short. Despite feelings of the team to the contrary, history has shown that the departures of Claflin and Formichelli were well timed and that the ThinkPad journey was not negatively affected. Perhaps it was inevitable that IBM rotate mobile general managers every two years; after all, the market changes significantly in the same brief time frame. But, then again, hindsight is 20/20 vision, and anything can be justified when it is associated with success.

We will never know what ThinkPad might have achieved if the same general manager stayed in place long enough to live with the successes, failures, and constantly changing competitive landscape. But, we do know that Ward achieved what Professor Kosnik calls the importance of running a successful business. After all, a company has one primary objective: to make a profit. Ward helped ThinkPad grow from a start-up enterprise into a major business for IBM.

The Brand Expands

System	380	560E	770	600
Form	Notebook	Ultra	Notebook	Ultra
Processor	Pentium w/MMX 150MHz	Pentium w/MMX 166/150MHz	Pentium w/MMX Mobile Module 200/233MHz	Pentium 266/233MHz
Memory	16/80MB	16/80MB	32/256MB	32/256MB
Storage	1.08/ 2.1GB I/II/III PCMCIA	2.1GB II/III PCMCIA	5.1/ 10.2GB	3.2/ 4.0GB
Display	12.1" Dual scan or TFT	12.1" TFT SVGA 11.3" Dual Scan	14.1" Active matrix 13.3" Active matrix	13.3" Active matrix
Operating system	Windows 95 Windows 3.11 Windows NT DOS 7.0 OS/2 Warp V4	Windows 95 Win 3.11 Windows NT DOS 7.0 OS/2 Warp	Windows 95 Windows 3.11 Windows NT DOS 7.0 OS/2 Warp V4	Windows 95 Windows 3.11 Windows NT DOS 7.0
Weight (lb.)	4.6	4.1	7.0	4.6
Other	Integrated CD ZV port enabled Enh Port replicator Preloaded NetFinity	Infrared PCI bus Ext FDD System Care	Second hard drive Opt internal Iomega Zip drive Opt 20/8 CDROM 3D sound Enhanced TrackPoint	Swappable CD-ROM and diskette drive Enhanced TrackPoint UltraBay Built-in modem
Announced	5/13/97	6/10/97	9/8/97	4/29/98

Awards

TP 380	*PC Computing*	A-List
	Computer Shopper	Top 100
TP 560	*Home PC*	Reviewer's Choice
	Fall Comdex	1997 MVP Award
	Home Office Computing	1997 Editor's Pick Award
TP 770	*PC Magazine*	Editor's Choice
	Fall Comdex	Technical Excellence Award
	Fall Comdex	1997 MVP Award–State of the Art Notebooks
TP 600	*PC Today*	Top Pick
	PC Magazine	Editor's Choice Award

CHAPTER 29

The IBM ThinkPad iSeries

Only a fool thinks that price and value are the same thing.

—Antonio Machado

The winning ThinkPad team responsible for the most valuable brand in mobile computing knew that they had to have a game plan to stay ahead of the competition and to address the changing market demographics. ThinkPads were selling well in the enterprise segment, but now individuals wanted the systems as well. It was time to get back to basics and design a line of portables deserving of the *ThinkPad* name and satisfying the needs of individual buyers.

Individuals are much more in tune with style than corporate buyers. For example, they buy Sony Sports Discmans not only for the sound but also for the look. Similarly, individuals who purchase portables with their own money want them to reflect their own image and personality. Individuals want to make a statement to the people around them. As multimedia and sound permeate the portable market, individuals want systems that sound as good as they look. The sound needs to be accompanied by bright displays to handle the action graphics of today's game software. Most importantly, individuals want to use this latest and greatest technology right out of the box, connecting to the Internet in a straightforward manner. No hassle, no bother.

Five groups of buyers are interested in portables designed for individuals. First is the college student, who is always on the move. Although dorm rooms are filled with desktop computers, there is a rapid switch to portables. Analysts predict that almost all college students will have portables instead of desktops within a few years. Portables can be used in the dorm, in the classroom (where appropriate), or the library and then easily taken home for breaks.

Second on the list is the family that is buying a second or third computer. Portables provide more flexibility because they can be moved from room to room, family member to family member. The third group is recent college graduates buying personal computers for the first time. They know the benefits of a portable, whether used in their first apartment or small cubicle. Fourth are small business owners who also need the flexibility of taking computers to client sites. Finally, the group expected to grow fastest over the next twenty years—retirees. As knowledge workers retire, they are expected to travel more and, yet, want to stay in touch with their children and grandkids, probably via the Internet. Whether in a small condo, camper, or recreational vehicle or just visiting new locales, this group will not want to be burdened with cumbersome desktops. Thus, portable manufacturers are pursuing products that appeal to the interests of the individual instead of the enterprise. It should prove to be a smart move as this market grows to millions of units a year.

The 5th Wave   By Rich Tennant

"THE LCD DISPLAY WAS GOOD, PLASMA DISPLAYS WERE A LITTLE BETTER, BUT WE THINK THE LIQUID LAVA DISPLAY THAT JERRY'S DEVELOPED IS GONNA ROCK THE WEST COAST."

Early in 1997, IBM decided to pursue this market and to develop a ThinkPad portable product line designed for individuals and small business owners. Jim Bartlett brought forward the initial concept because he felt that IBM needed to offer a ThinkPad tailored to the individual buyer. Under Bartlett's direction, John Biebelhausen conducted some early market research on what a portable for individual buyers should be. Brian Dalgetty from the Aptiva PC group was then asked to lead the effort; in essence, he was to head up this new IBM business with direction from both the Consumer and the ThinkPad groups.

Dalgetty studied robotics at M.I.T. and graduated with a master's degree in 1984. He lived all over the world, from Hong Kong to Australia to Belgium. This experience led him to seek a position at an international high tech company, and he joined IBM. He first developed serial dot matrix printers, with responsibility for the electromagnetic heads that did the actual printing. He was a charter member of IBM's PS/1 consumer team in Lexington, Kentucky.

In 1993, he was promoted to head product development for Ambra North America. Ambra was IBM's attempt to set up a direct organization like Dell Computer Corporation. Although Ambra worked from product and logistics perspectives, it just did not fit IBM's enterprise computing model. Following Ambra's demise, Dalgetty was asked to head the Product Marketing team on the Aptiva S Series. Shortly after, Jim Firestone asked him to manage IBM's development effort for a portable designed specifically for individuals.

Said Dalgetty, "At the time they asked me to do a consumer portable, I had several mentors inside IBM: Jim Firestone [now at Xerox] and Steve Ward [now IBM CIO]. They convinced me that I should take this job and create a new portable line different from the enterprise portables developed during the past five years. They told me, 'Don't just use an existing ThinkPad and put a fancy marketing program around it.' Rather, they told me that I should focus on meeting the needs of the individual and small business buyer."

Erica DesRoches described this approach, which included her market research: "Because my group was responsible for the entire PC product line, we did significant research in seven countries across the world on this new product line. We found that individual buyers wanted the advanced technology desired by business purchasers, but they also needed the products to be easily accessible and quite affordable. We knew that the product had to look sharp and include only active matrix TFT displays, competitive differences for IBM. These individual buyers, part of the fast-growing segment of the portables market, purchased these products with their own money and definitely wanted value for their dollars."

Dalgetty added, "We went off and did a lot of research. It told us some very interesting things. First, users hated the existing low-cost portables with the passive matrix DSTN displays. If they were going to use a portable for personal productivity applications and the Internet, users wanted a bright display with great response to motion graphics. That insight told us that all our portables needed active matrix TFT panels. These users also turned out to be experienced users of technology. If they bought a portable, they wanted it to be a true desktop replacement.

"They wanted an IBM-quality keyboard. So, our portables had to have the same look and feel as the keyboard on our business portables. They also wanted a great sound system, with the speakers positioned on the front of the portable. They did not want their hands to cover the speakers while typing and playing a CD.

"Speaking of CDs, a standard CD player was desired in the front of the portable, with industry standard buttons and an LCD display. Users wanted to be able to play a music CD without turning on the computer. With these objectives in mind, the iSeries team got together with Altec Lansing and designed a totally new speaker system. It was thin and vertical, so it could be embedded in the left and right sides of the display."

Dalgetty continued, "Users wanted their personal portable to be more stylish than a business ThinkPad. We refreshed the design and included red, green, blue, and yellow bars just above the keyboard to identify customizable 'shortcut' keys. These corresponded to four function keys that could be easily programmed to launch any Web site or application. We included easy-to-use sound adjustment wheel and drop-down legs so that the keyboard would be positioned for easy typing.

"One ease-of-use innovation was the Access ThinkPad software that resided on the desktop. It allowed users to do the most common tasks right from a drill-down menu. They did not have to go inside the machine. It was right there whenever needed. Our research and our usability lab told us that users wanted to do their typical tasks easily. Other areas of IBM will probably use this approach in their products."

The team investigated adding a touch pad just below the left and right mouse button. But, in typical fashion, Yamato Labs came up with something even better. They provided an Internet Scroll Bar button that allowed the user to scroll a Web page without moving the cursor all the way over to the right side of the display to scroll down the page via the slider bar. Pressing the scroll bar and moving the TrackPoint caused the whole page to move without the user having to move back and forth to the slider bar.

A lot of time was spent on developing the product positioning, customer value proposition, and associated branding. The team wanted to position future IBM "consumer mobile" products for personal productivity and business use. They desired to leverage and extend the ThinkPad brand to the individual segment, while providing enough separation from existing ThinkPad offerings to preserve the current equity with corporate customers. They contracted with Communications Development Corporation (CDC) to conduct naming research in the U.S., Europe, and Japan. The product needed a name that was more personal and conveyed the attributes of affordability, convenience, freedom, fulfillment, and achievement.

"More than three hundred names were evaluated, covering a wide range from *X Pad* and *X Series* for the generation Xers, to *TrekPad* and *Aptiva Note Personal Series*," recalled Dalgetty. "Many of these options appealed to a younger audience but left retirees out in the cold. When the iSeries popped up in a team meeting one day, I remember saying, 'Hey, that's it. Let's leverage the *i* in *ThinkPad* to represent individuals.' Everyone got excited about it. The research confirmed this as the best choice and indicated that the letter *i* had also become a contemporary descriptor for the Internet. Many of the marketing messages were built around a personal enablement theme using 'i can' and in-store materials featuring the tag line 'i can do anything!'"

Dalgetty managed the development of the iSeries with a very small staff but also with help from the entire ThinkPad team in Raleigh, the Personal Systems design team, and development via Yamato Labs in Japan. The worldwide resources of ThinkPad were leveraged to develop a new focus on individual buyers. One of the resources that not only was leveraged but was also a critical aspect of this effort was the industrial design organization.

David Hill, head of design for the IBM Personal Systems Group, was in charge of the design for the iSeries notebooks. He talked about this project in detail: "When we worked on the industrial design for the new ThinkPad iSeries, the challenge was to come up with a more attractive and personal design than the ThinkPad 380. The 380 was an *all-in-one* design—meaning that it included a hard drive, CD-ROM, and floppy all in the same unit—but it was kind of clunky. It was on the wrong end of the spectrum of the ThinkPad design language, where being thin was the focus of the appearance.

"The ThinkPad 380 did not have the advanced design signals of the 600. Our concept was to take the idea of the chamfer and exploit it even more in the iSeries so that when you see the iSeries for the first time, it looks really thin. It's easier to pick it up, and it feels better when you carry it. It has a completely different elegance to it.

"It still had to be a ThinkPad, but with a more personal design. When you open a ThinkPad iSeries for the first time, you see the little red, green, blue, and yellow bars above the keyboard. That use of color was a way of communicating more personal affiliation with the user than the more corporate feel associated with the

ThinkPad 600. It was very intentional and did an excellent job delivering a feeling of a more personal product.

"Remember that the original idea of ThinkPad was simplicity that, when opened, revealed a surprise. What we did with the ThinkPad iSeries was to make the surprise bigger. Instead of the same old thing, we made it so that when people opened it, their eyebrows raised. We sculptured the palm rest more. We gave the appearance a fun character—a little bit more personal style in terms of how the palm rest and the buttons were treated for the scrolling feature and the TrackPoint buttons.

"We wanted to create a different sensation for how sound would come from this product. We made it more like a TV, so the speakers were adjacent to the screen rather than sitting on the palm rest. We liked the idea of rapid access keys, similar to what we had introduced on the Aptiva desktop PC. We couldn't create dedicated keys because of space limitations, but we had this concept of using the function keys to create a sense of personality so that you could launch applications from them. Users could assign them to be whatever they liked, for example, making the blue one launch AOL. So, we came up with the idea of four colored bars that would act as memory joggers. Then we had to decide what color to make them.

"We decided to make the color bars associated with the colors used in the ThinkPad logo today: red, green, and blue. We put them as stripes just above the function keys. We used yellow as our fourth color. It is the color of the connector for the AC adapter in ThinkPad notebooks. Thus, we picked up the four primary colors we were already using in ThinkPad and put them in sequence inside to provide a personalized touch in a comfortable and friendly way. The use of color created this element of fun. You can remember which keys are which, based on their color.

"We also took the design one step further into the screen itself. We helped the usability engineering folks develop a new feature called *Access ThinkPad*. We were responsible for the interface design. We incorporated simplification of the technology in a compelling, interesting, engaging way. We used animation that runs with the letters that tell you the different categories. We developed a top ten list that describes those how-to-do things for ThinkPad that everybody wanted to do. We thought this was another good use of design—to help create an enjoyable experience for the user."

IBM introduced the ThinkPad iSeries on Tuesday, October 13, 1998. Reviews were very favorable. The iSeries group was challenged immediately with making enough of them for people who clearly wanted a stylish, affordable ThinkPad. With the iSeries, IBM was the first to introduce a TFT color portable for less than fifteen thousand dollars. More and more individuals could now buy a portable that provides the flexibility and functionality of a desktop system.

Erica DesRoches summarized the efforts of the mobile computing team, first under Ward and currently under Sanchez: "The aesthetic and ergonomic appeal of notebook industrial designs was elevated to a primary focus of our research. The extended Mobile Computing design team worked on the natural evolution of the ThinkPad while retaining its unique character and design signatures. This evolution was well executed from the start, with substantial resource investment helping the brand stand on its own. IBM's continued commitment to high-quality standards made purchasers seek out new models of ThinkPad. The ThinkPad team's commitment to keeping in touch with customer wants and needs and preferences was pivotal to the design of each new ThinkPad, whether it was the 560, 600, or iSeries. Like so many before us, we are proud to be a part of this continuing saga."

The Authors' Insights

The iSeries ThinkPads shook up the competitive landscape for portables designed for individual buyers, a space previously owned by Compaq and its Presario line of integrated portables. But, just as the requirements of individual buyers differ, so will the reactions of the portable manufacturers who decide to pursue this space.

Throughout the past decade, IBM has continued to perfect its branding strategies. With the iSeries, it focused on the individual, not the "consumer." The distinction is important. A Sony Walkman or Discman is a consumer product, a product designed for the masses. IBM is not known as a consumer electronics company. Thus, they had to correctly position the iSeries in a more amenable value space around the individual, not the consumer. It had to focus on personal productivity, not entertainment. According to Jim Forbes of *Windows Magazine*, "the iSeries showed a new side of IBM or side of IBM that was not generally acknowledged. It showed their awareness of first-time computer buyers or individual buyers. It showed their willingness to address one of their weaknesses during the last few years—paying attention to price."

The team also knew that the iSeries had to be a complete package appealing to the targeted market. Just branding and positioning would not be enough; industrial design would play as important a role as the technology and product attributes. IBM demonstrated that it had learned how to deliver a new product to a new market segment. The group built a system that was attractive to the target group while retaining the equity of being a ThinkPad. They incorporated all the ThinkPad attributes into the iSeries. They used innovative technology to create an integrated portable, made sure that it was a world-class product, put top talent in charge of the effort, and built a successful business. And the naming scheme—leveraging the ThinkPad brand and then migrating it further with iSeries—was masterful. Its mastery linked two of Professor Kosnik's key qualities: a world class product and a trustworthy brand.

CHAPTER 30

The Journey Continues

If everything seems under control, you're not going fast enough.

—Mario Andretti

As with most legends in history, the story usually continues in some way or another. Sometimes the legend languishes, and few enhancements are made to the story. Oftentimes, the players take a wrong turn and things go awry. Preferably, the players remain true to their plan, and the legend remains intact and maybe even grows. Such was the case of the ThinkPad brand in the last year of the 1990s.

The ThinkPad team wanted to remain true to the brand's original personality. However, things were rapidly changing in the mobile market, and they realized that something truly innovative was needed to stymie the competition. Faster processors, larger displays, and enhanced TrackPoints would not be enough to capture the interest of the ever-expanding number of portable users. The team looked outside itself for inspiration, and the inspiration was found in the most unlikely place.

Ask any purchaser of portable computers about the latest machines on the market, and he or she could probably give you the speeds and feeds. Ask any kid about a transformer, and he or she knows that it's an amazing toy. Although it's an ordinary-looking action figure, when you twist and turn its parts, it transforms into something completely different—something that's unexpected and amazing. On April 20, 1999, IBM announced its amazing new portable and, like its toy counterpart, it, too, could be called a *transformer*. The ThinkPad 570 looks just like any other desktop replacement portable with its built-in CD-ROM (or DVD), diskette drive, and modem . But, with the push of a button on the front of the notebook, the top piece detaches, and the unit transforms into a svelte, four-pound ultraportable phenomenon.

How did IBM conceive this amazing marvel? You might think that IBM's innovation had run its course after creating one of the industry's most successful notebooks with the ThinkPad 600 and creating a consumer line of award-winning notebooks with the ThinkPad iSeries. However, by applying proven creative talent to this challenge, a better solution was designed than anyone believed possible.

The concept of this ultraportable grew out of the ThinkPad's experience with the subnotebook. The subnotebook journey began with the ThinkPad 500 and 510. The ThinkPad 510C was limited in its acceptance, to some degree, because of its small keyboard and display. Users, especially outside Japan, still preferred a full-size keyboard (that is, a 19mm pitch or distance from the center of one key to the center of a key to the right or left) while desiring full-function, lighter machines. In 1995, the team announced the ThinkPad 701, known as *Butterfly* throughout the industry because of its innovative keyboard, which fanned out when the system opened. Although the 701 addressed the full-size keyboard requirement, its limited processor and display prevented its being a long-term alternative for individuals who need power while on the road. Users not only wanted the fastest processor but also preferred a display that is easy on the eyes and makes text comfortable to read. Subnotebooks had forced users to compromise on these attributes, causing a general resistance to portables described as *subnotebooks*.

So, the subnotebook portable category was found lacking by the mobile industry. Yet, users knew that they wanted a "smaller" notebook, one that was thinner and lighter but with a standard keyboard and large display. As these requirements gained widespread popularity, the industry coined a new category, a new term for this class of machine: *ultraportable*. The term, sometimes attributed to Gerry Purdy, described a full-function notebook that incorporated an ultra amount of portability.

Building on its subnotebook experiences, IBM's first attempt to deliver an ultraportable was the ThinkPad 560. Introduced in April 1996, the ThinkPad 560 became an instant hit with its 12.1-inch SVGA (800×600 pixel resolution) display. A standard keyboard similar to the one used on the ThinkPad 700 series was incorporated. To keep the 560 as thin as possible, the vertical travel of the keys was reduced slightly, a change that was almost imperceptible to the user. This portable remained a competitive portable offering for almost three years because of, in part, its solid keyboard and display, something that most other ultraportables failed to provide.

This is not to say that competition within the ultraportable category did not exist. In 1997 and 1998, Fujitsu Personal Computer Corporation announced and enhanced its LifeBook 600 series. An ultraportable similar to the 560, the LifeBook 600 mated with a "slice" that sat underneath the portable component. Unfortunately, getting the portable on and off the slice was complex. Often, the pieces did not fit together properly. But, it provided something that the ThinkPad 560 did not: It enabled all the additional media components to be collected in one place. The slice contained the floppy drive, the CD-ROM drive, and all the ports in one thin accessory. The ThinkPad 560, on the other hand, provided external floppy disk and CD-ROM drives as accessories that were connected via cables.

As the market indicated its acceptance of the concept of a slice, the ThinkPad team was designing the ThinkPad 560 follow-on. Gerry Purdy was asked to work with Ron Sperano, then the ultra-portable segment manager, on this project. In 1997, Sperano invited Purdy to a meeting in Building 205 at the IBM facility in Raleigh, North Carolina.

"Ron, have you seen the Fujitsu LifeBook 600?" inquired Purdy.

"Yes," responded Sperano. "We've evaluated the unit as part of our competitive positioning and PFV [Price Function Value] ranking. The keyboard and display are nothing like what we have in the ThinkPad 560. And we don't think that it has nearly the ease of use of the 560. The portable does not connect very well to the slice, making access to the media devices and ports difficult. Even more of a concern, what do users take with them on the road? What is the office alternative? There must be a docking solution as well."

Purdy mused, "The idea of a slice similar to what Fujitsu has done makes sense; users would take it on the road. But, I agree that you have to provide docking as well. What if the slice were connected to a port replicator that would always stay in the office? Think of it as the 'three-piece suit' scenario for the ultraportable. By incorporating three pieces into the system, the customer has a portable that connects to the media slice, which, in turn, connects to the port replicator." As they talked, Purdy proceeded to draw a portable, a slice, and a port replicator on the white marker board in Sperano's office.

Ron Sperano.

"It's a great concept," said Sperano. "If we could take the follow-on to the 560 in this direction, we could have a real winner.
We knew that we wanted to take the best of the 560 and yet
address its deficiencies. This concept is different from what others
have been thinking, but I think it's a direction to consider."

Both Sperano and Purdy knew that it would take some careful industrial design engineering to make the design work properly. The portable had to mate easily with the slice and include *hot docking* (the capability to detach the portable from the slice without having to reboot the system). The portable and slice then needed to easily mate with the port replicator. They also felt that the entire system should resemble the ThinkPad 380's follow-on, an integrated all-in-one portable (later named the *ThinkPad 390*). This desire helped to solidify using the mating design of the 380 with its bus connector on the bottom versus connectors on the back, like the ThinkPad 600. It could drive a common port replicator across the IBM ThinkPad line.

Maintaining a family look and feel had been a hallmark of the ThinkPad brand. As their discussion continued, Sperano and Purdy also agreed that the ThinkPad 560 follow-on should use the keyboard and display used in the ThinkPad 600. The design would include the latest processor and largest storage available in the market while keeping the TrackPoint and other industrial design favorites.

Sperano did not get the chance to see the design through to its completion. He soon accepted a less demanding staff position, which allowed him to pursue his Ph.D. in technology in education. Bill Tsang became the worldwide segment manager for Ultraportable and Companion Products, with responsibility for taking the product from concept stage through announcement. To accomplish this, he worked with the engineers in Yamato, Japan, and tested it with target users in the U.S. and Europe.

Tsang and the IBM market research team did extensive, sophisticated market research on two continents to determine the feature set that ultimately went into the 570. This research showed different skews in the feature preference for small and light notebooks between North American and Japanese users. The challenge of the 570 was balancing and coming up with models that could appeal to both geographies.

"We enjoyed testing mock-ups of what is now the ThinkPad 570 with focus groups worldwide," said Tsang. "We showed them the portable sitting on the table. When participants looked at it, it appeared to be a full-sized desktop replacement portable—and a very attractive one at that. We did not tell them anything about how it worked. We told them that what they saw was a portable computer that weighed 6.5 pounds and included a CD-ROM, floppy, keyboard, 13.3-inch display, standard ports, and built-in modem. And it was an IBM ThinkPad. They commented that it sounded like a great portable but that it seemed big in comparison to other portables in the market.

"At that point, we lifted off the Ultraportable with one simple motion. Reactions varied in degrees of amazement. We then showed them how it easily snapped back into place, and we demonstrated how the pieces worked together. By pushing the little release button on the right side, the Ultraportable popped off in one easy motion. Reactions by the focus groups were consistent worldwide—smiles and acceptance."

The ThinkPad 570 was, indeed, designed in three pieces as originally conceived. In addition to the Ultraportable, the UltraBase slice has two bays. It supports all the typical media: CD-ROM, DVD, and so on, in one and floppy drive or other smaller device in the other. A second battery can also be charged in the UltraBase as well.

Completing the three pieces in the overall design, a Mini-Dock accepts either the Ultraportable alone or the underlying slice. The bus connection is on the bottom, so the unit simply attaches with a drop-down and then pops off when disengaged. The Mini-Dock has all the standard ports replicated on the back of a standard portable, a PC Card slot, and, optionally, ethernet. The Mini-Dock is integral to the entire solution. Users can attach all cables to the Mini-Dock and then detach either the Ultraportable or the slice, depending on their needs. According to Sam Dusi, a key member of the ThinkPad marketing team, "Managing the secondary devices so critical to the mobile user was a major consideration in our design efforts. We knew that users wanted flexibility on the road and when they returned to the office. We were concerned, however, that such an alternative form factor might not get the executive support and funding necessary to survive. We needed to view this product differently and offer proof of its potential.

"We discussed this potential in terms of usage scenarios and the size of the opportunity associated with the users. If the user just needs the Ultraportable at a meeting, at home for the evening, or on a short trip where multimedia isn't needed, the Ultraportable can be taken off the UltraBase. In this configuration, the user has a lightweight (3.9 pounds for 12.1" display, four pounds for 13.3" display) portable that's easy to carry around and yet provides the same keyboard and display as the ThinkPad 600. However, if the user needs multimedia, such as a CD-ROM to play music, a DVD to play a movie, a floppy drive, or other media, the Ultraportable and UltraBase can be taken off the Mini-Dock. The user then has a full-function desktop replacement that weighs 6.9 pounds when configured with a CD-ROM and floppy."

Sam Dusi.

the new thinkpad 570.(dramatization)

The IBM ThinkPad 570.

Knowing that the ThinkPad 570 was to be used by road warriors, the mechanical housing and design were deemed very important by the product team. They decided to use an UltraCarbon housing based on a carbon fiber–reinforced plastic developed by IBM Researchers. UltraCarbon is the lightest and most durable composite material available in the marketplace today. A derivative of carbon fiber composites used in sporting goods equipment, the UltraCarbon housing results in a thinner-walled, higher-strength unit that enables efficient heat dissipation and room for high-performance internal components such as the latest Intel processors, large IBM hard drives, and long-life batteries. Beneath its rugged exterior, the IBM ThinkPad 570 has a full-size, full-stroke keyboard; an ergonomically designed palm rest; and IBM's TrackPoint pointing device, with the Internet Scroll Bar button and magnifying functions to help users breeze through spreadsheets and Web pages. Ease of use and durability were definitely key components of this product.

"We knew that we had a winner with the ThinkPad 570, although its gestation period was a little longer than we anticipated," said Leo Suarez, director of Product Management for the Mobile Computing group and Dusi's manager. "We wanted to maintain market leadership in this space, so we knew that it was better to take longer and get it right. Users quickly saw a distinct improvement over the 560, which was, until the introduction of the 570, the most successful ultraportable on the market. The 570 extended the ultraportable franchise, potentially eating into some sales of our integrated all-in-one ThinkPad 390 and the ThinkPad 600. The ThinkPad 570 will also bring new customers to IBM, those who were thinking of buying a sexy looking ultraportable but wanted one that delivered a total solution."

Adalio Sanchez, general manager, IBM Mobile Computing, expounded on Suarez's thought: "As notebooks become the sole computers for business, users are torn between full-function models and ultraportables. Now they can enjoy the best of both worlds without sacrificing performance or functionality. To make this happen, ThinkPad must operate on all cylinders right now. We have to focus on producing ThinkPads worldwide so that they are ready when and where customers want to buy them. And we have to make sure that our product line covers the requirements of the varied segments of portable users."

To round out its family of mobile offerings, the ThinkPad team introduced the Ultralite ThinkPad 240 in June 1999. This portable was designed for people who have a desktop computer but want a small, lightweight portable to use when out of the office. It filled the niche for users for whom system weight was the most important feature, users usually found in Japan, where mininotebook form factors have met with great success.

The Ultralite ThinkPad 240 has a 10.4-inch display and a keyboard that, although slightly smaller than the 570 (with an 18mm pitch), is large enough that even most Western users can touchtype without difficulty. Like the ThinkPad 570, the usability and ergonomics of this smaller, nonstandard-size keyboard were extensively studied and tested with users, resulting in one of the best machines in its class. Steve Wildstrom, in his June 28, 1999, "Technology and You" column in *Business Week* described the entry of the ThinkPad 240: "I have been searching for a long time for a really small laptop for the road. But, everything I looked at, from Windows CE to mini-notebooks like the Toshiba Libretto to ultralites like the Sony VAIO 505, demands too many compromises. Compromise is a fact of life in a laptop this small, but in the ThinkPad 240, IBM has made choices I can live with."

IBM ThinkPad® 240 — Draft version. For information only and subject to errors.
Final version at http://w3.pc.ibm.com/pcinstitute/psref/ after announce

IBM® ThinkPad®	
Processor	Intel® Mobile Celeron™ 300MHz[1] / 66MHz system bus
Processor features	No upgrade / processor on Ball Grid Array (H-PBGA)
L2 cache	**128KB / onboard (full speed)** / synchronous pipelined burst / ECC / write-back
Diskette drive	External 3.5" 1.44MB / connects to left side with FDD port / includes case and cable
CD-ROM	*Option:* External CD-ROM / 20X-8X[8] speed / connect via PC Card slot
DVD-ROM	*Option:* External ThinkPad Proven DVD drive / connect via PC Card slot
Type-model	**2609-21U**
Processor	**Celeron 300MHz**
Disk - size / ms	**6.4GB** / 13ms read / 14ms write / Ultra DMA/33 or PIO Mode 4 / S.M.A.R.T.[29]
Preload (see side)	**Windows 98**
Available date	June 1999
Display - size and type	**10.4" TFT color** (264.16mm) / **Active Matrix**
Display - techology	**SVGA** / 800x600 / 15ms refresh (typical) / 50 to 110 nits
	16.7 million simultaneous colors / 250 to 1 contrast (typical)
Graphics - controller	**NeoMagic® MagicMedia128XD™** (NM2160C) / 128-bit accelerator / DDC2B
	2MB / SGRAM (embedded) / color space conversion
Graphics - features	Simultaneous LCD and CRT / 180 degree tilt / multiple-monitor support [26] / ext SVGA to 1024x768 with 65,536 colors
Memory - std / max	**64MB** / 192MB[33]
Memory - features	SDRAM / non-parity / 66MHz / 3.3 volt / 64-bit
	2 sockets for JEDEC 144-pin SO DIMMs / one socket used by std memory /
	socket accessed by removing three screws and keyboard
Disk controller / disk	EIDE / PCI 2.1 / supports one internal disk / customer can not remove
	disk (IBM or dealer service required)
Keyboard	Keyboard palm rest / 95% full-size main typing keys / 18mm key pitch
Pointing	TrackPoint® / Press-to-Select / Release-to-Select / dragging / click pace /
	sensitivity / spare caps
Dimensions	10.2 x 8.0 x 1.05" (86 cubic inches)
Weight[2] (w/ batt/disk)	2.9 lbs (1.31 kg)
Case material	PC/ABS plastic
Battery - type	Li-Ion (3 cell) / intelligent / left side
Battery - life[10]	1.9 hrs
Charge time[10]	3.5 hrs on / 3.0 hrs off
Architecture	**Intel 440DX AGPset / Intel 82371EB PIIX4E** (EIDE, PCI to ISA bridge, USB) /
	Texas Instruments® **TI1211** PCMCIA controller / NS PC97338 (FDC, IR, I/O)
	PCI 2.1 / 32-bit / 33MHz (EIDE, graphics, PCMCIA, USB, audio, modem)
	ISA (diskette, serial, parallel, infrared)
Docking station	None
Port replicator	None
PC Card Std slots	1 Type I or 1 Type II / CardBus 32-bit / PCMCIA 2.1 / no Zoomed Video support
USB / serial / parallel	One USB / one 9 pin; 16550A / one (IEEE P1284-A, EPP, ECP, bidirectional)
Other features	APM-aware BIOS / Ultraslim AC adapter, barrel, 3-prong, 56 watts
Video (TV) out	None
MPEG decoder	None (software support for MPEG-1 in Windows 98)
Data/fax modem	**56K**[37] / V.90 / integrated in system / mini-PCI Type IIIb / Lucent 1646 /
	not voice-capable
Audio	16-bit SoundBlaster Pro™ compatible / ESS 1946 / PCI / full duplex
Speaker	One internal speaker (.5 watt???)
Audio features	Internal microphone / Fn+PgUp and PgDn volume control with mute
Audio in/out jacks	Microphone jack (stereo) / headphone jack (stereo) / line-in jack
Infrared ports	Infrared port on left side / IrDA 1.1 compatible / up to 4Mbps
Security	Power-on password / setup password / disk password / security keyhole
Supp oper systems	Windows 95, Windows 98, Windows NT 4.0
Limited warranty[11]	**1 year** - carry-in or ThinkPad EasyServ™[13] (door-to-door depot repair service)
Service options[16]	On-site[32], M-F, 8-5, next bus day (72 cities) / serv up to 5 yrs from purchase date

WINDOWS 98 PRELOAD[18]
- Microsoft® Windows® 98
- Online User's Guide
- ThinkPad Configuration Program
- ThinkPad Utilities
- ThinkPad on the Net
- Access ThinkPad
- IBM Update Connector
- RingCentral Fax
- Ergonomics
- IBM Registration
- Puma IntelliSync 97 (infrared)
- IBM Global Network Dialer
- Netscape Communicator
- Lotus® SmartSuite Millennium™[20]
- PC Doctor
- ConfigSafe
- Norton AntiVirus (OEM Version)
- Universal Management Agent
✧ Software Selections CD
✧ Lotus SmartSuite Millennium CD-ROM
✧ Recovery CD-ROM (Windows 98)
✧ Recovery CD-ROM (Windows 95)[7]

Color depth LCD	External Monitor				OPTIONS		FEATURES
Resolution TFT	60Hz	70Hz	75Hz	85Hz			
640x480 16M	16M	--	16M	16M	- 32MB SO DIMM 3.3v NP SDRAM	76H0294	Wired for Management 1.1a compliant
800x600 16M	16M	--	16M	16M	- 64MB SO DIMM 3.3v NP SDRAM	20L0241	DMI 2.0 compliant
1024x768* 64K	64K	64K	64K	64K	- 128MB SO DIMM 3.3v NP SDRAM	01K1150	PC 98 compliant
1280x1024 --	--			--	- High-capacity 6-cell Li-Ion Battery	02K6580	ACPI ready (APM enabled)???
* Virtual screen mode					- Ultraslim 56 watt AC Adapter (3-prong)	02K6545	Wake on LAN™ support[28]???
					- 20X-8X Portable Stereo CD-ROM Drive	1969011	Setup Guide, User's Reference, Windows
					- 20X-8X Portable CD-ROM Drive	1969010	OS manual, and Quick Reference Card
All models:					- V.90 PC Card Modem with XJACK[24]	10L7393	System Status Indicators
- C: drive is FAT16 of 2GB					- 10/100 Ethernet CardBus PC Card	08L3147	Reset switch on bottom
- D: drive is FAT32 of remaining space					- 10/100 EtherJet plus 56K modem	28L3261	Plug and Play 1.0a
					- Turbo 16/4 Token-Ring PC Card	28L3670	Standby, suspend, redifsafe, and
					- DC Auto Adapter	02K3381	hibernation modes
Pressing F1 during startup brings up IBM					- Smart Card Security Kit		ENERGY STAR compliant
BIOS Setup Utility					- ThinkPad Proven™ solutions[12] (visit	10L7333	International Warranty Service[14]
					www.ibm.com/pc/us/thinkpad/proven)		IBM SystemXtra™[35]
							24 hour / 7 day telephone[30], bulletin
							board, fax, electronic, and Internet
							(www.ibm.com/pc/us) support

All trademarks are the property of their respective owners — No warranties are expressed or implied in this summary
(240) © IBM Corp. June 1999

The IBM ThinkPad 240.

The Authors' Insights

As the 1990s draw to a close, the mainstays of the ThinkPad brand
are intact. With new additions to its family of products, the team

did not compromise the design and ease of use fundamental to the brand's personality. They remained as concerned with attention to detail and quality as they had since the brand's inception in 1992. Despite how few of the original team members were still part of the ThinkPad organization and how matrixed the organization was within the chameleon-like IBM, the brand personality survived. Members of the original team had consistently conveyed the vision and brand blueprint throughout time, driving innovation as a fundamental element of the plan.

This innovation was captured in the ThinkPad 570 and ThinkPad 240. Yet, the team realized that their challenge, in addition to remaining true to the brand, was to address more markets and segments than development funds might allow. The team needed to allocate money not only for its traditional product family but also for emerging categories of adjunct tools. The ThinkPad brand had to be extended beyond the category of notebooks and ultraportables.

The *ThinkPad* name was expanded with the addition of the CrossPad to IBM's product line. This joint venture between IBM and A.T. Cross allows users to record notes using a standard pad and an active pen, broadening input capabilities beyond the TrackPoint so integral to the ThinkPad brand. But, the pen was not the only tool required for the mobile line.

In 1998, ThinkPad licensed the Palm Pilot from Palm Computing and named it the *IBM WorkPad*. The WorkPad, part of a category of electronic tools, enabled pervasive computing. Pervasive computing, an initiative from the office of IBM Chairman Lou Gerstner, combines the benefits of personal computing with data communications. It allows IBM to pursue a business model that is beyond just selling a device—it extends the value chain. To extend this value chain, all parts of IBM must work together.

According to Tom Grimes, a ThinkPad brand manager and recent addition to the ThinkPad team, "The value of having something as recognizable as the ThinkPad brand is the value it creates by allowing one-to-one relationships with our customers and with other parts of IBM. ThinkPad enables us to take the best IBM has to offer and extend its capabilities through a network of partners who recognize the value inherent to the brand. We can address the changing needs of our customers while delivering on the promise of IBM and ThinkPad. It was this ability that made me choose IBM as a place to work. It is this ability that ensures ThinkPad's desirability in the minds of our customers. It is this ability that will continue ThinkPad's status as the most recognizable brand in mobile computing history."

System	570	240	WorkPad z50
Form	Ultraportable	Ultralite	Companion
Processor	300/333/ 366MHz Mobile Pentium II	300MHz Mobile Celeon	NEC VR 4121 131MHz
Memory	64/192MB	64/192MB	16/48MB 20MB ROM
Storage	4.0/6.4GB	6.4GB	I/II/III PCMCIA
Display	12.1/13.3" TFT	10.4" TFT SVGA	8.2" VGA DSTN
Operating system	Windows 98 Windows NT	Windows 98	Windows CE— H/PC Professional Edition V 3.0
Weight (lb.)	4.0/6.9	2.9	2.6
Other	UltraBase Infrared	56K modem	Infrared
	Enh TrackPoint	Card Bus	33.6 Kps modem PC Card
Announced	4/20/99	6/99	5/99

These products demonstrate IBM's commitment to address the ever changing needs of its customers.

PC Magazine, April 20, 1999:

IBM goes the thin-and-slice route with the 4-pound ThinkPad 570— and the result is a success.

"Latest ThinkPad: Nice, Any Way You Slice It," *PC Week*, May 3, 1999:

The near-flawless execution that IBM brought to previous-generation ThinkPad notebooks can be found in the ThinkPad 570.

The Authors' Final Insights

Success has a thousand fathers, while defeat is an orphan. Ultimately, we will be judged not by our rhetoric or our rationales, but by our results.

—President John F. Kennedy, after the Bay of Pigs

Well, you have completed our book, *ThinkPad: A Different Shade of Blue*, about a high tech success that has changed the landscape of the portable market. We hope that reading it was as enjoyable for you as writing it was for Gerry and me. We had more source material and more individuals who wanted to be interviewed than we ever thought possible. We also found that President Kennedy was right—the more successful a certain aspect of the ThinkPad story, the more individuals claimed that they were responsible.

Early on, some individuals who had built careers on their contributions to the ThinkPad story and were afraid that some aspect of this book might affect their credibility threatened us with lawsuits. Despite such intimidation, we continued to work hard and to present the real story behind the ThinkPad brand. We attempted to introduce you to the main characters, those with whom either Gerry or I had personal contact. Regretfully, it was not possible to introduce you to each and every person who has ever touched the ThinkPad product line. Many wonderful and talented people contributed to this narrative, either during the writing process or as part of the actual ThinkPad development and marketing. We could never do all of them justice. But, hopefully, you now feel as though you know a few of our favorite characters.

This book represents the best of what we personally experienced, we remembered, we learned, or we discovered. As with any story, other versions probably exist, but we diligently scrubbed the fifty-plus interviews to find those dates and meetings that could be verified or validated. We encouraged our contributors to tell us both sides of every incident. As you would expect, we did not find as many individuals who came forward and admitted their mistakes. For those who did, such as Bruce Claflin, our admiration only increased.

Gerry and I also learned a lot from writing this book and from discussing it with such knowledgeable individuals as Dr. Dave Bradley and Professor Tom Kosnik. While Dr. Dave kept us straight on the technologies, Professor Kosnik's Seven Qualities of Enduring Brands provided a framework in which to highlight ThinkPad's strong points. At the beginning of this journey, the team did not even know that it was developing a brand; it had been asked only to develop a new line of portables. However, in the early 1990s, just as a renewed focus was put on portable computing, IBM underwent tremendous change. A revised approach to branding became part of IBM's transformation and fundamental to ThinkPad's success. The qualities of an enduring brand began to surface within the ThinkPad's infrastructure. To refresh your memory, those seven qualities cited by Professor Kosnik include

- A growing market
- Innovative technologies

- World-class products
- Profound leadership
- A trustworthy brand
- A balanced business
- A global learning network

Allow me to briefly recap how ThinkPad addressed these qualities and how the team members considered each one as they moved forward.

A Growing Market

The personal computer industry has been marked over time by what paleontologist Steven Gould called *punctuated evolution*. What that means is that things go along pretty much as expected until, all of a sudden, a significant occurrence changes the entire landscape. This change might force us to think about things differently. Such was the case for personal computing.

Before the early 1980s, businesses were content to use mainframes and "dumb terminals" for their data processing requirements. Then, on August 12, 1981, IBM changed the business computing paradigm by announcing the IBM Personal Computer. At the time, no one was certain what the "killer app" would be, but almost everyone knew that the way they were doing business was going to change in a big way. The personal computer started exponential market growth, and it is still growing. It started an industry that continues to evolve on an almost daily basis.

But, something happened along the way. Personal computer users started to rely on their systems not only in the office but also at home. They also found that they needed them on the road. PC manufacturers started to address both this portability requirement and the emerging segment of the personal computer market. Compaq Computer Corporation entered the PC scene and showed everyone how to do portability right. IBM stumbled along the way, sometimes getting lost in its own difficulties and not hitting the "sweet spot" of the portable market. But, Big Blue did not give up. It took them almost ten years to find their way in portables, but they did.

IBM became a player in portables because of the vision of executives such as Jim Cannavino and Bob Corrigan. In the early 1990s, a portable team was funded and asked to pursue this exploding market. They were given the latitude to operate as a self-contained unit similar to how Don Estridge had been allowed to run the original PC team. The team analyzed the market, its competitors, and the available technologies. It developed a five-year roadmap for its journey to become number one in this dynamic market space. It learned the importance of having a roadmap and religiously updating it to reflect changing trends and technologies.

An unexpected factor along the way that helped the IBM portable team was the downturn in the economy. Many businesses started to look for ways to be more efficient when it came to office space and personal computing equipment. Even IBM looked inward and found that it could save money by using portable technology to make its employees mobile, to eliminate office space, and to allow employees to work from home. This changing demographic, now known as *telecommuting*, expanded the baseline for the portable market.

Somewhere along this path, the term *portable computing* migrated to *mobile computing*. It took on a new face and included more than just portable PCs. Manufacturers started to look at handheld devices, personal digital assistants, and smart phones. Even IBM could not ignore the different segments of the market now termed *mobile computing*. However, the ThinkPad team stayed focused on its core technology and brand strengths. They limited their foray into these uncharted waters.

ThinkPad has kept pace with this fast-growing market, one that had "legs" and is expected to grow for at least the next decade. According to Jim Cannavino, "This market will continue to grow. In fact, even guys like me who were mainframe bigots use only a notebook PC. A portable computer is the only system I have, and there's a whole segment of the market that operates the same way. Today, the only difference is that we back them up with more sophisticated servers. We can stay linked to the Internet and corporate data while we're on the road."

Cannavino's statement supports the need for IBM and the ThinkPad team to pursue emerging markets. To be successful in the future, as Professor Kosnik cites, the team must address such growing market segments as pen, voice, and data communications. IBM has taken the first steps with its CrossPad, WorkPad, and Pervasive Computing initiatives. But, perhaps the future brings more than just changing form factors and innovative uses. Perhaps, by building on its service heritage, IBM and ThinkPad can establish a reputation as the premier services and technology provider in the mobile computing market.

Innovative Technologies

The ThinkPad product line incorporated significant technological changes in its short history, changes that laid the foundation for an enduring brand. Throughout the story, we highlighted some of those key features and functions that helped to create the ThinkPad brand. By the time you read this book, the team will have incorporated newer, more innovative technologies than those found in the ThinkPad 600, the iSeries, the latest 770, and even the ThinkPad 570.

These technologies will be decided on the basis of the brand's standard requirements processes. The Headlights program has survived from the team's inception and includes both short- and long-term views of the technology landscape. The industry and customer councils continue to be held semi-annually and bring the analysts, consultants, and end user inputs into the requirements equation. The team listens to the Voice of the Customer through forums and user groups and at trade shows. It conducts extensive market research on a worldwide basis to make sure that new products meet customer requirements.

Customer requirements have driven portable computers to be the incubation field for advanced computer technology. In the beginning, portable manufacturers wanted to build machines whose features and functions were equivalent to the desktop. Screens had to be equal to or better than those attached to the desktop, thus, active matrix color TFT displays. PCMCIA slots and cards were developed to handle options and peripheral capabilities. Full-size keyboards were a fundamental requirement, driving mechanical designs and, in the case of Butterfly, some creativity. The technology curve has turned from viewing portables as desktop alternatives to viewing them as desktop replacements. In fact, at one point in ThinkPad's history, executives would not allow the team to refer to its product line as a desktop replacement for fear of affecting its desktop line.

As the portable segment matured, the trend toward greater and greater mobility drove additional technological innovation. Companies such as IBM reduced system weight while increasing hard files and memory. Battery life, basic to the useful portable, necessitated power management to allow for trans-continental flights. Mouse capability had to be usable in confined spaces, resulting in such innovations as TrackPoint, the Trackball, and the TrackPad. The mechanical design and packaging had to be durable and resistant to the ravages of the road warrior environment.

Interestingly, mobile technologies are migrating onto the desktop. Large, flat-panel TFT displays are replacing monitors. Power management is an accepted feature on the desktop. TrackPoints have been added to desktop keyboards. It is possible to conceive of the desktop of the twenty-first century as a portable configured to work primarily in the office.

Adalio Sanchez, ThinkPad's general manager since March 1998, offered this perspective: "We are reaching an interesting inflection point, which Gerstner describes as 'one where information technology becomes much more than a computer on a desktop that forces you to type in order to interact with it. A recent issue of *The Journal of Business and Design* describes this technology as crossing into true ubiquity, finding its way into everything from automobiles to machine tools and household appliances—in effect, disappearing into the fabric of our day-to-day lives. As today's notion of "computers" is replaced by these pervasive "computing devices," there's a new premium on design as an aspect of competitive advantage.'[1] ThinkPad must stay in step with the changing landscape, the innovation that is always on the horizon."

Industry Advisory Council member Leslie Fiering built on Sanchez's thoughts: "ThinkPad must absolutely stay on the cutting edge of technology, always be ahead of the crowd, strive to be number one. To me, innovation will become more and more critical. With the proliferation of devices that people carry around with them, ThinkPad must be leading edge in not only portables but also extensions to the portable, such as WorkPad. They will need to seamlessly link these products together."

The personal computer industry has changed dramatically in its relatively short history; even more so, the portable computer segment propelled forward at rocket speed. During this time, the ThinkPad family embodied a family of technologies that, when

1. *The Journal of Business & Design* (vol. 4, no. 2): 22.

taken together, provided customers with real benefits and value. The brand has a track record of continuous innovation over time, a record that should continue into the twenty-first century.

World-Class Products

The ThinkPad brand has established a high benchmark for excellence. IBM did not just build a slightly better portable; it built a world class, multi-generation portable family. Industry analysts and consultants have consistently rated the ThinkPad brand one of the best, bestowing numerable awards for quality, innovation, and industrial design. Customers have developed a loyalty to the ThinkPad brand equivalent to that of Harley Davidson riders or Starbucks coffee drinkers. ThinkPad has "crossed the chasm" from technological innovation, to useful product, to desired brand.

Profound Leadership

Throughout our story, we described various leadership styles and personalities of ThinkPad's key management team: Watabe, Claflin, Formichelli, Ward, and Sanchez. We illustrated the necessity for management to change as the business changes. The ThinkPad story started with a technologist (Watabe), moved to a marketing genius (Claflin), grew under the decisions of a manufacturing expert (Formichelli), improved the business with an operations master (Ward), and has come full circle to a market-savvy technologist (Sanchez). Each brought his own perspective and experiences to the mission; each succeeded because he listened to his team.

We also explored the vision of Jim Cannavino and Bob Corrigan in funding and supporting the renewed portable effort within IBM. Coupled with the arrival of Lou Gerstner and a sound business strategy, a turnaround was almost inevitable.

We talked about the effect of some of its team members who were not general managers but who still offered profound leadership in their areas of expertise—for example, Bartlett's market management, Larsen's worldwide knowledge, and Higuchi-san and Ikeda-san's technological expertise. We explored the creativity of such leaders as Richard Sapper, Tom Hardy, and David Hill when it came to industrial design. We learned about the planning expertise of such individuals as McHugh, Bower, and Fletcher.

More important than these leaders was the environment they created. The people rallied around the mission and took pride in their contribution to the brand. The team succeeded as a team, and, in those rare instances when there were problems, suffered as a team. Future leaders were groomed throughout the ThinkPad story, including Adalio Sanchez, Leo Suarez, and Rod Adkins. The depth, breadth, and diversity of leadership talent across multiple generations of the product line was remarkable. The trend continues with the addition of individuals such as Kevin Clark, Brian Dalgetty, and Tom Grimes, to name just a few of the current ThinkPad team.

Finally, of the utmost importance, despite their divergent interests or individual career goals, the team respected the capabilities and strengths of each player. They learned to accept the cultural differences and challenges associated with being a worldwide team. Each function was recognized for the part of the journey for which it was responsible.

Jim Cannavino said it best: "The strength of ThinkPad was in the team approach. Centralizing everything under one general manager enabled a clear vision, a clear path toward achieving number one in the mobile space. Should IBM ever decentralize the team, it would be the beginning of the end. It would be a change that ThinkPad's competitors would welcome."

A Trustworthy Brand

An enduring brand must be a trustworthy brand. Customers must trust that what they are buying is what they will get. The brand must endure over time; it cannot be a "flash in the pan." Through a series of good decisions and commitment to a brand personality, IBM built a recognizable brand, one in which customers place their trust.

As Professor Kosnik stated, "building a brand is difficult." It takes more than the five Ps of marketing—product, production, price, placement, and promotion—to create a brand. ThinkPad did the fundamentals extremely well. The team developed innovative products with cache. They eventually produced enough to satisfy the demand, improving their processes along the way. They moved from the perception of high-end pricing to a tiered pricing structure that today even includes the consumer. ThinkPad is now placed not only in dealers but also in retail and direct mail channels. The brand has been promoted from day one, despite IBM's financial challenges of the early 1990s.

But, investment in the five Ps cannot build a brand unless customers trust the brand. Trust is based on product usage, customer service, and technical support experiences. We expect that service and support will continue to grow in importance as ThinkPad goes forward. IBM will have to be more creative in this area to stay in front of competitors such as Dell Computer Corporation. The answer will no longer just be a portable computer with cache but will require a total solution that addresses the entire scope of requirements. By linking the ThinkPad effort with the growing services expertise of IBM Global Services and the Pervasive Computing initiative, IBM can build both its primary brand image, IBM, as well as the sub-brand images of ThinkPad and IBM Global Services. Rob Enderle, of the Giga Information Group and an IAC member, supports this thought: "IBM must focus on what it is they do best—making ThinkPad part of an overall corporate solution or business solution as opposed to a standalone product. As a standalone product, they are at risk by the emerging companies like Dell, Micron, and Gateway. As part of an overall solution, few companies can touch the kind of breadth that IBM can provide."

How will IBM know what services should be offered? Through the continuous two-way communication between product development and the people who use portables, the ThinkPad team will continue to build its successful brand. According to Chris Barr, "Few organizations have mastered the art of customer-company dialogues as well as the ThinkPad team. They continue to dialogue with the most visionary analysts, consultants, and customers year after year, keeping a finger on the pulse of the portable computing user." As a result, IBM created a position in the minds of the user (and the prospective customer) that ThinkPad is a brand people can trust, admire, and enjoy.

What must IBM do to propel its brand forward? According to Scott Bower, the first marketing director for ThinkPad, "ThinkPad must continue to focus on the brand. They must not lose sight of the original personality that customers have come to expect. They must be careful not to allow the systems to look the same. It has to be more than just technology. They have to focus on the value to the customer, not just technology. And they have to stay in touch with their customers."

Sam Dusi, currently a member of the ThinkPad team, continued, "Staying in touch with our customers is absolutely critical. Mobile products are an emotional sale—ThinkPad brings that out in our customers, the team, and our partners. Surely in a world where people identify with the type of pen they use, whether it is a Cross, a Mont Blanc, or a Bic, surely a notebook cannot be viewed as a commodity. The ThinkPad team must continue to differentiate its products—to personalize its products—well into the future."

A Balanced Business

"One of the great things about this industry is that every decade or so, you get a chance to redefine the playing field," Gerstner told *Business Week* in an exclusive interview in 1995. "We're in that phase of redefinition right now, and winners and losers are going to emerge from it."[2] During the redefinition of the portable effort, the management team also realized that it needed a balanced approach to its total business.

The team, through each general manager and each personnel change, worked hard to run ThinkPad as a successful business, even during IBM's most challenging times. Under the watchful eyes of individuals such as Rod Adkins and Steve Ward, the group monitored its financial performance, its customer performance, its internal processes, and organizational learning and product innovation. During its recent history, IBM built a portable business that, by all estimates, is in excess of five billion dollars a year. It is a very profitable unit within IBM, approaching eight percent of IBM's total revenue. In fact, if ThinkPad were a separate company, it would be one of the Fortune 500 companies.

Bruce Claflin recently reflected on ThinkPad's past business performance: "Clearly, ThinkPad has been a real success for IBM. One of the things that used to trouble me was how IBM has never really promoted the brand, despite its success. Just look at the results. In 1992, IBM sold about two hundred fifty million dollars in notebooks and lost two hundred million dollars doing it.

2. "The View from IBM," *Business Week* (October 30, 1995): 142.

So, here it is seven years later, and ThinkPad is likely going to be a very profitable five billion dollars a year. In seven short years, ThinkPad went from essentially nothing to a five billion dollar business for IBM. I'd argue that it might be the most successful computer ever introduced in this industry. Ever. It surpassed the 360 and 370 mainframes. It surpassed anything Compaq did. To be honest, I think that IBM didn't want to promote ThinkPad too much in the beginning because it pointed out just how badly the other businesses were doing. And now that the company is back on track and looking to the future, it isn't necessary. ThinkPad can stand on its own."

According to Jerry Michalski of Sociate and a member of the IAC, "There are still numerous opportunities to push ThinkPad in new directions. IBM could change their revenue model and take advantage of the Net for Web support. It's something I keep bringing up at the councils. Integrating that type of capability would increase leadership beyond the ThinkPad control panel, driving a new way to manage your machine and to change its configuration. IBM has not taken mobility seriously enough; they think that they are in the notebook business, not in the mobility business. Being in the mobility business will cause some fundamental business changes. It will link them with the new corporate ebusiness strategy while propelling ThinkPad to a different level."

Kevin Clark balanced this input with caution: "We have to make sure that we don't change too many things too fast. You have to worry about a step function change and adjust for it. We need to hold on to the iconic value of the ThinkPad brand. We're reaching into a broader segment of the population, even reaching people who buy through retail outlets. We want to offer them relevant, legitimate products without taking the edge off the quality of the ThinkPad brand. We want to extend the brand into new arenas such as pen, voice, and pervasive computing. We want to link ThinkPad with IBM Global Services to seamlessly extend our services heritage to our mobile customers."

Leo Suarez, Director of Product Marketing, provided the last insight on what ThinkPad must do going forward: "First of all, we must realize that we are not in the notebook business. Rather, we're actually in the business of delivering solutions for people who are mobile or need to use a PC away from the office. Railroads thought that they were in the railroad business instead of the transportation business. If they had realized what business they were really in, they might own an airline today. We must never forget that we're not in the computer business. Rather, we're in the business of helping people be productive when not in their personal office. Thus, you will see IBM's mobile computing group develop exciting new products to fit this paradigm. We recently branded the WorkPad for a family of PC companion products that have the mission of helping people be more productive when they are mobile. We will network these products to provide the total solution needed by our mobile customers, to match their life and work styles. ThinkPad will be at the core of IBM's pervasive computing initiative."

A Global Learning Network

Whether it is raising a child or building a brand, no one individual or team can do it alone. ThinkPad's success was due to the hard work of its design, development, planning, and marketing teams. This hard work was reviewed by a network of influencers, both industry and customer. Plans were altered based on this input. A network of option and software providers then supported the products. ThinkPads were sold through a growing network of channels who provided ThinkPads to millions of customers. IBM sales representatives explained the ThinkPad benefits to their customers as an integrated part of their information system. In the future, the IBM Global Services network will support the ThinkPad, offering a total, pervasive solution approach to the mobile segment.

Of course, the network has not stayed stagnant. ThinkPad employees have strengthened other IBM teams. They have also moved to other companies, peppering the portable industry with their expertise. Each of these individuals has kept in touch with his or her former ThinkPad teammates. It certainly made writing this story much easier as this extended network closed around our effort.

The current ThinkPad team has made it easy to communicate with them or to discover information on their products. Simply by "surfing the Web," you can find additional information on ThinkPad at www.pc.ibm.com/us/thinkpad or simply www.thinkpad.com. The Web provides another potential network for this enduring brand. Customers can communicate directly with the team that is designing future ThinkPads, commenting on what they believe has been done right or on what needs to be improved.

How did the ThinkPad team and its network do it? How did it affect a cultural change that resulted in the most recognizable brand in mobile computing history? The ThinkPad journey began with a vision that was executed by a cross-functional team. The team was contained within a flattened, empowered organization. The organization extended its capabilities through its network of industry analysts and consultants, suppliers, and customers, each representing a different stakeholder perspective. These perspectives influenced the technology and innovation of the product line. The product line was well timed and focused on quality. Quality became the hallmark of its global presence.[3] Even the errors along the way were handled with flexibility and provided the basis for lessons learned along the way.

3. Peter L. Brill and Richard Worth, *The Four Levers of Corporate Change* (American Management Association, 1997).

Gerry and I also learned a lot along the way. We learned the power of a can-do attitude. We learned that people love to talk about their successes and even discuss their failures. We also learned that it is possible, through the power of ThinkPad and the Internet, to write a book on separate coasts.

The authors at work on ThinkPad 600 and ThinkPad 560, accompanied by Dell's "laptop" dog, Chrissie.

However, just like the value of face-to-face industry advisory councils, we learned the value of working in the same vicinity. We met in person three times during the writing of this book, with specific objectives for each meeting. We learned that, even in the world of mobile computing, face-to-face encounters enhance communication. This is an important lesson for businesses to consider as they move into the widespread world of telecommuting.

Each element of building an enduring brand and ensuring its continued success has been interlaced throughout the ThinkPad history. We hope that you found it an interesting story. Gerry and I realized during this past year that ThinkPad is truly the legacy of

IBM's founder, not just in its name but in its philosophy. In the prophetic words of Thomas J. Watson Senior in 1915, *"all the problems of the world could be solved easily if men were only willing to think...."* We believe that the IBM ThinkPad brand provides the tools that enable individuals and businesses to do just that.

—*Debi Dell*

Where Are They Now?

Jim Bartlett

In September 1997, Bartlett was promoted to vice president of Marketing—Consumer Division, developing and marketing the Aptiva brand. In 1999, Bartlett left IBM to become corporate vice president and chief marketing officer for StorageTek.

Scott Bower

After twenty-three years at IBM, Bower left to become vice president of Sales and Marketing for Samsung. During his tenure at Samsung, his son graduated from high school, which allowed Bower even more career flexibility. He is currently vice president and general manager of Commercial Sales, Micron Computers.

Dr. Dave Bradley

Dr. Bradley is still working on technology development for the personal computer business within IBM. He is a senior technical staff manager and vice president of the IBM Technology Academy.

Jim Cannavino

Cannavino retired from IBM in the spring of 1995. He was the CEO of Perot Systems from September 1995 through September 1997. He is currently chairman and CEO of CyberSafe, a fast growing enterprise security company in Seattle, Washington. He is also chairman of Softworks, an enterprise software tools company in Washington, D.C.

Bruce Claflin

Claflin left IBM and joined the executive team at DEC Computer Corporation. In 1998, he became the president and chief operating officer for 3Com Corporation. He is still in contact with many of his friends and former employees from IBM.

Kevin Clark

Clark is the brand steward for the IBM ThinkPad. Resident in Raleigh, he maintains the programs that entrench and expand the brand.

Debi Dell

Dell is now the National Principal—Mobile and Wireless Services. She is driving the development and marketing of a consulting and services practice for IBM Global Services. She still resides in southern Florida.

Erica DesRoches

DesRoches continues to conduct market research on behalf of the ThinkPad team. She is the manager of Market Research and Worldwide Intelligence for the IBM Personal Systems Group.

Chris Farrell

Farrell is the brand manager responsible for IBM's eNetwork suite of software products. He still has the Duke basketball poster on his office wall.

Maurice Fletcher

Fletcher is currently chief operating officer of PORT, Inc., based in Norwalk, Connecticut. Fletcher contributed many of the marketing examples found in the ThinkPad history.

Joe Formichelli

Formichelli left IBM to become the CEO and president of Hayes Microcomputer, based in Atlanta. Formichelli is now executive vice president and general manager for Toshiba America in Irvine, California.

Tom Hardy

Hardy left IBM in 1992 after making significant design contributions to the ThinkPad brand. He is now a design strategist and resides in Stamford, Connecticut.

Koichi Higuchi

Higuchi-san is director of Personal Systems National Language and Solution Development. He is based in Yamato, Japan. According to Higuchi-san, the personal computer business in Asia Pacific is growing, and he will need to learn Chinese quickly.

David Hill

Hill is manager of Design for the Personal Systems Group. He still enjoys working on innovative designs for the ThinkPad line of products.

Toshiyuki Ikeda

Ikeda-san is still working on the ThinkPad team, leading innovative product engineering efforts.

Bob Kanode

Kanode left ThinkPad in September 1995 to become president of the U.S. subsidiary of Varta Batteries.

John Karidis

Dr. Karidis is a Distinguished Engineer for the IBM Personal Systems Group. He continues to work on new product concepts and computer form factors.

Sue King

King is presently vice president of Worldwide Methodology Services at Cadence Design Systems, Inc., in San Jose, California.

Per Larsen

Larsen resigned from IBM in 1997 and is currently president for Olicom, Inc., in Dallas, Texas.

Bob Lawten

Lawten is currently vice president of sales for Cognos.

Pete Leichliter

Leichliter is division manager for the American High Technology division for American Recruiters. He still enjoys playing baseball with his son, Timmy.

Bill Lowe

Lowe left IBM for Xerox Corporation and then Hughes Aircraft. He is currently heading his own firm, the Lowe Group, which deals in investments. He is in the process of moving from Chicago to Phoenix, where he hopes to perfect his golf game.

Rick McGee

After getting the ThinkPad process working well, McGee was promoted to vice president. He now has responsibility for developing similar "go to market" processes for other business units (such as servers and desktop personal computers).

Patty McHugh

McHugh left IBM to work for Motorola in Boynton Beach, Florida. In 1998, she returned to IBM as director of planning for voice and pen products. She is still an avid sailor and motorcyclist.

Mark McNeilly

McNeilly is currently program director of Mobile Computing Market Requirements. He was instrumental in providing source materials for this project.

Nobuo Mii

Nobi Mii left IBM in 1995 and is now managing partner of the Ignite Group, a venture capital company in Palo Alto, California. He also serves on the Board of Segasoft, the software division of Sega Electronics.

Paul Mugge

Paul Mugge is still at IBM and is the offering executive for market-based innovation.

Janice Roberts

Roberts, a member of the original ThinkPad pen team, is now director of business development for Citrix Systems, Inc. Citrix is developing application management and delivery for remote and wireless users in the consumer market.

Adalio Sanchez

Sanchez is the current general manager of Mobile Computing. He is responsible for the ThinkPad product line and future extensions to the brand.

Ted Selker

Ted Selker is on leave from IBM, working as a visiting professor in the multimedia lab at Massachusetts Institute of Technology.

Ron Sperano

After an assignment on the PC Company architecture team, Sperano rejoined ThinkPad. He is currently program director for Mobile Market Development.

Leo Suarez

Suarez rejoined the ThinkPad team after a brief stint in IBM Latin America marketing operations. He is currently the director of Worldwide Product Marketing.

Bob Sztybel

After nearly eleven years with IBM, Sztybel joined Port Corporation, Norwalk, Connecticut, where he developed and launched a line of mobile accessories to complement PORT's successful line of carrying cases. In 1998, he became vice president, Group Marketing and Product Brand Development, The TeleAdapt Group.

Rick Thoman

Thoman left IBM to become president of Xerox Corporation.

Kathy Vieth

Vieth worked in a consulting role to Bruce Claflin until the end of 1992. She is now an independent consultant living in Colorado.

Denny Wainright

Wainright retired after a stellar career at IBM and still resides in Boca Raton.

Steve Ward

Ward was promoted after his role as general manager of the ThinkPad team. He is now the chief information officer for IBM.

Jan Winston

Winston retired from IBM and is now an independent consultant. He works with Patty McHugh on IBM's pen and voice products.

Appendix B

ThinkPad Timeline

References

- All awards information was obtained from IBM's PR Firm, Broedeur Porter Novelli. Special thanks to Kim Zuleba and Monica D'Agostino for their help.
- All IBM ThinkPad product release information was obtained from press releases.

Year	Personnel	Products
1981	Estridge heads PC effort. McHugh on original team Dr. Bradley patents BIOS.	IBM Personal Computer
1982		IBM PC XT
1983		
1984	Boca site hits 10,000 employees.	IBM Portable PC IBM PC AT IBM PCjr
1985	Estridge re-assigned. Lowe returns. Boca and Austin become one division (Entry Systems Division).	
1986	ESD Headquarters move to New York. Sapper works on PCs.	IBM PC Convertible
1987	IBM Research initiates "TrackPoint" idea.	Personal Systems/2
1988	Lowe leaves IBM. Donofrio takes over. Boca Mfg. moves to Raleigh.	
1989	Vieth assigned displays. Cannavino arrives. Lawten assigned laptop. Sapper and Hardy develop new "differentiated" strategy.	PS/2 P70
1990	King assigned pen tablet. IBM invests ten million dollars in GO Corp. Decision to centralize portable development in Yamato.	PS/2 P75
1991	Lawten leaves IBM.	
	Pen Project Office	PS/2 L40SX PS/55 Note (Japan)
1992	Brand concept deployed.	N51SX N45SL
	Bartlett joins IBM. Claflin, first Mobile GM. Formichelli takes over displays.	CL57SX ThinkPad 700T ThinkPad 700C ThinkPad 300

Differentiators	Key Competitive Actions
BIOS/Alt+Ctrl+Del	Osborne 1:CP/M System Epson HX-20
Hard disk (10MB)	Grid Compass Morrow Decision Kaypro 1
	Kaypro II TRS-80 Model 100 NEC 8201A Compaq Portable Plus Corona Portable
Infrared keyboard	DG1 (Data General) Commodore SX 64
	Toshiba T-1000, T-1100
Micro Channel OS/2	
	NEC Ultralight Sharp Wizard Toshiba 5100 Compaq SLT
	Compaq LTE, LTE 286 Poqet PC Atari Portfolio
Harvard MBA portable pilot	
	HP95LX
ThinkPad name 10.4" display TrackPoint II Double-speed CD-ROM	Macintosh PowerBook Duo

Year	Personnel	Products
1993	Louis V. Gerstner arrives. Claflin promoted. Formichelli succeeds Claflin. First IAC meets. Larsen appointed division director of Marketing. IBM and Canon jointly produce portable with built-in printer.	PS/Note ThinkPad 710T ThinkPad 720C ThinkPad 750C ThinkPad 750P ThinkPad 500 ThinkPad 350/350C ThinkPad 360/360C ThinkPad 550BJ (Japan)
1994	PC Company announces site consolidation in Raleigh.	ThinkPad 730T ThinkPad 755C/Cs ThinkPad 510Cs
1995	Nobuo Mii leaves IBM. Cannavino retires. Jerome York quits. Raleigh consolidation.Clark joins IBM as brand manager. TP used in "Trial of the Century," the O.J. Simpson double murder trial.	ThinkPad 701C ThinkPad 760CD ThinkPad CD/CV
1996	Ward succeeds Formichelli as ThinkPad GM. ThinkPads used at Summer Olympics.	ThinkPad 560
1997		ThinkPad 380 ThinkPad 560E
1998	Sanchez succeeds Ward. Ward appointed IBM CIO.	ThinkPad 600, iSeries IBM WorkPad
1999	ThinkPad book	ThinkPad 570 ThinkPad 240 WorkPad z50

Differentiators	Key Competitive Actions
IAC ThinkPad Proven Convertible form factor	Apple Newton @ COMDEX
ISA bus	
IACs go worldwide Mwave DSP "Out of Box" with product map. Personalized nameplate	Apple Newton MessagePad 110 Apple PowerBook 500 series Apple PowerBook Duo 260 / 280c
Expandable keyboard 12.1" display	Apple Newton MessagePad 120 Apple Newton MessagePad 130 (backlit) Apple Newton 2.0 O/S Iomega Zip drives
Ultraportable Infrared PCI bus 11.3" Dual Scan display 12.3" TFT display Pentium	PalmPilot DEC HiNote Ultra II OmniBook 800 Apple PowerBook 1400 Apple MessagePad 2000 and eMate 300 Windows CE unveiled NEC MobilePro HPC Compaq PC Companion
Integrated design TrackPoint III	Apple PowerBook (250MHz) REX PC Companion
Low-cost TFT Integrated MMX	Palm III Apple iMAC Sony VAIO
UltraBase	Palm V

PC Timeline

1992

The number of Internet hosts breaks one million.

Creative Labs introduces SoundBlaster 16.

NEC introduces the first double-speed CD-ROM drive.

Apple Computer Chairman John Sculley coins the term *Personal Assistant*, referring to handheld computers that typically operate via a stylus on an LCD display. Sculley announces that Apple Computer will enter the consumer electronics market by the end of the year. He is widely quoted as predicting a three trillion dollar industry.

Intel and Microsoft announce the Advanced Power Management (APM) specification for laptop computers, which allows the system to shut down power to system resources not currently in use.

Intel introduces the i486DX2 microprocessor, with clock speeds of 25/50MHz (external/internal). For the most part, the DX2 is just a 25MHz 486 that internally runs twice as fast. The price is $550 each in quantities of 1,000. Speed is 41MIPS.

Microsoft ships Windows 3.1. More than one million advance orders are placed worldwide.

Apple CEO and Newton champion John Sculley first shows the prototype to the press in Chicago, where he describes not only the device but also the platform strategy.

Apple Computer discontinues the PowerBook 100.

Apple Computer introduces the Macintosh PowerBook Duo

systems, consisting of a 4.2-pound portable computer and a Macintosh Duo Dock desktop docking station.

One year after the introduction of Apple Computer's PowerBook, sales of $1 billion make it the first personal computer to break that threshold. More than 400,000 PowerBooks have been shipped.

Microsoft announces Microsoft Windows for Workgroups 3.1, which integrates networking and workgroup functionality directly into Windows 3.1.

Intel introduces the 486SL processor, designed for notebook computers. Speeds include 20MHz (15.4MIPS), 25MHz (19MIPS), and 33MHz (25MIPS). The processors can address 64MB of physical memory, and 64 terabytes of virtual memory. They use 1.4 million transistors, employing 0.8 micron technology.

Microsoft announces Microsoft Access Database.

1993

Mosaic takes the Internet by storm. The WWW proliferates at a 341,634 percent annual growth rate of service traffic. Gopher's growth is 997 percent.

Apple Computer shows off test versions of its Newton Personal Digital Assistants at the Winter Consumer Electronics Show.

Total sales of Apple Macintosh PowerBook Duo systems reach 100,000.

Intel introduces the Pentium processor. It uses 32-bit registers, with a 64-bit data bus, giving it an address space of 4GB. It incorporates 3.1 million transistors, using 0.8 micron BiCMOS technology. Speeds are 60MHz (100MIPS) and 66MHz (112MIPS). Prices are $878 (60MHz) and $964 (66MHz).

Microsoft introduces the MS-DOS 6.0 Upgrade.

Amstrad begins shipping the Amstrad Pen Pad PDA600 Personal Digital Assistant (PDA) in England. It is the first PDA to be shipped. The Pen Pad weighs less than a pound, is 1 inch thick, and features a 240×320 resolution 3×4 inch screen. It uses a 20MHz Zilog Z8S180 microprocessor and can run for forty hours on three AA batteries. It includes 128KB RAM, with a PCMCIA expansion slot for memory expansion to 2MB.

Microsoft formally launches Windows NT 3.1. Windows NT delivers a powerful, reliable, and open platform for client/server solutions.

Apple Computer introduces the Newton MessagePad 100 personal digital assistant at Macworld Expo in Boston's Symphony Hall. It features 640KB RAM, 3MB of ROM storing applications and the operating system (Newton Intelligence), a low-voltage 20MHz 32-bit ARM 610 microprocessor, 240×336 resolution (85 dpi) 2.8×4-inch LCD screen, one PCMCIA Type II expansion socket, data transfer of 9600 bps and runs on four AAA batteries. Fifty thousand units sell in the first ten weeks, but only eighty thousand are sold during the product's life.

Microsoft Office 4.0.

Microsoft releases MS-DOS 6.2.

Microsoft releases Word 6.0 for Windows.

Microsoft ships Windows for Workgroups 3.11.

Sales of Apple Computer's PowerBook series hit the one million mark.

The MessagePad wins Forbes Product of the Year award.

1994

Java is introduced by Sun.

Intel ships the Pentium processor. The chip uses Intel's new 0.6 micron BiCMOS technology.

U.S. Robotics ships the Courier v.34 28.8K bps modems. List price: $329 internal, $349 external.

Gateway 2000 Inc. sells the first PC powered by Intel's 75MHz Pentium.

Intel confirms that nearly two million Pentium chips have been shipped with a defective floating-point unit.

1995

Intel introduces the 120MHz Pentium processor.

Iomega begins shipping its Zip drives.

Intel releases the mobile version of the 90MHz Pentium processor.

Intel introduces the P6 processor (Pentium Pro).

Intel announces the immediate availability of the 133MHz Pentium processor. It uses 3.2 million transistors, employing 0.35 micron BiCMOS technology. Speed is 218.9MIPS.

Iomega introduces the Jaz drive.

Microsoft releases Windows NT v3.51.

Microsoft introduces Microsoft Office 95.

Microsoft releases Microsoft Internet Explorer 1.0.

A number of Internet-related companies go public, with Netscape leading the pack with the third largest ever NASDAQ IPO share value (August 9).

Windows 95 is launched. It is a fully integrated 32-bit operating system replacing Windows 3.11, Windows for Workgroups 3.11, and MS-DOS as the mainstream desktop operating system. More than one million copies sell at retail stores in the first four days.

Microsoft announces Microsoft Project for Windows 95. This new version, designed exclusively for Windows 95, greatly facilitates project communication throughout an organization and includes improved workgroup functionality, full ODBC support, and integration with Microsoft Office for Windows 95.

Intel releases the mobile version of the 120MHz Pentium processor.

Intel releases the mobile version of the 120MHz Pentium processor.

Cyrix announces the 100MHz CX6×86 microprocessor (formerly code-named *M1*). The chip is manufactured by IBM and priced at $450 each in quantities of 1,000.

U.S. Robotics begins shipping enhanced Sportster v.34 modems capable of transmitting data at up to 33.6K bps.

Intel announces the Pentium Pro microprocessor, at speeds of 150MHz, 180MHz, and 200MHz, available initially for $974 to $1,682. The processor uses 5.5 million transistors.

Advanced Micro Devices begins shipping samples of its 133MHz Am5×86 Pentium-class processor. The price is $93 each in quantities of 1,000.

Microsoft announces the release of the final version of Microsoft Internet Explorer 2.0 for Windows 95. Internet Explorer 2.0 is widely available for downloading at no charge to licensed users of Windows 95 via the Internet. Internet Explorer 2.0 offers full support for Web standards and for current Internet security standards, including secure transaction technology (STT).

Bill Gates outlines Microsoft's wide-ranging commitment to supporting and enhancing the Internet by integrating the PC platform with the public network. Gates notes that businesses will adopt the Internet for internal business use—the *intranet*—for communication with employees, suppliers, and customers and that Intranet applications will likely emerge faster than those for the general consumer market. NBC and Microsoft join forces.

1996

Microsoft ships the thirty millionth copy of Windows 95.

Intel releases the 133MHz Pentium processor for notebook computers. The processor uses 0.35 micron technology and operates on 3.3 volts of power externally; its internal core requires only 2.9 volts. The price is $371 in quantities of 1,000.

Advanced Micro Devices begins shipping the AMD5K86 microprocessor. Prices are $75 each for the 133MHz AMD5K86-P75 and $99 each for the AMD5K86-P90, in quantities of 1,000.

Microsoft releases Microsoft Internet Explorer 2.0.

Microsoft SQL Server, a client/server database management system, version 6.5 is released to manufacturing. Key new features include built-in support for Internet applications, improved support for distributed management tools, and a new locking architecture called *Dynamic Locking*.

Netscape Communications releases Netscape Navigator 2.02.

Intel introduces the 200MHz Pentium processor, shipping it initially in small quantities. The price is $599 in quantities of 1,000.

NEC Electronics begins shipping its R4101 processor for personal digital assistants. The chip includes a 33MHz 4100 processor core, a 2KB instruction cache, a 1KB data cache, a real-time clock, a DMA controller, an audio driver, and interfaces for serial port, keyboard, infrared, and touch-screen interfaces.

Intel begins shipping the 200MHz Pentium Pro with a 512KB cache.

Microsoft releases Windows NT 4.0.

Microsoft releases Microsoft Internet Explorer 3.0.

Intel releases the 150MHz mobile Pentium processor, designed for use in portable computers. The processor uses 0.35 micron technology and operates on 3.3 volts of power externally; its internal core requires only 3.1 volts. The price is $341 in quantities of 1,000.

At the Microprocessor Forum, Advanced Micro Devices announces the K6 processor, optimized for 16- and 32-bit code, supporting MMX, and including 32KB cache memory. The chip will plug into a standard Pentium socket.

Microsoft unveils the Windows CE operating system for handheld PCs. The code name of the project is *Pegasus*. *CE* stands for *Consumer Electronics*.

Microsoft unveils Microsoft Office 97 at Fall Comdex.

Compaq Computer ships the PC Companion, a handheld computer running Windows CE. The weight is less than 1 pound. The unit measures 7 inches wide by 3.5 inches deep. It runs on AA batteries, lasting up to twenty hours. Prices range from $499 (2MB RAM) to $699 (6MB RAM).

NEC Computer Systems ships the MobilePro HPC, a handheld computer running Windows CE.

Hitachi Home Electronics ships the Hitachi Handheld PC, running Windows CE.

Casio Computer ships the Cassiopeia, a handheld computer running Windows CE.

1997

Intel introduces MMX instructions.

Microsoft announces the immediate availability of Office 97, the new version of the world's best-selling productivity suite, which integrates the ease of intelligent applications with the power of the Web.

56K modems appear in market.

The second-generation PalmPilot comes in two versions: the 512K PalmPilot Personal and the 1MB PalmPilot Professional. Both PalmPilots have display backlighting and an Excel-compatible expense-tracking application, and they run under Palm OS 2.0. The PalmPilot Professional model also includes an e-mail client.

Apple Computer announces that it will spin off its Newton Systems Group into a subsidiary company.

Pentium II is introduced at a low entry price.

Steve Jobs and Bill Gates lay out a broad product and technology development agreement between Apple and Microsoft. The agreement includes the production of future versions of Microsoft Office, Internet Explorer and other Microsoft tools for the Macintosh; the bundling of Internet Explorer with the Mac OS; a broad patent cross-licensing agreement for leading-edge Mac technologies; and a $150 million investment in Apple by Microsoft.

Rolodex® Electronics REX™ PC Companion takes portability to the extreme. Ultra-slim, this 1.4-ounce device has Starfish's TrueSync™ data synchronization, so mobile professionals can view their PC organizer data anytime, anywhere.

Microsoft's Internet Explorer 4.0 is released to critical acclaim and enormous customer demand. Internet Explorer 4.0 combines the premier Internet browser, communication, and collaboration tools, innovative Active Channel, "push" content, and true Web integration to offer users an unparalleled Internet client solution.

Apple Computer announces that it will not spin off its Newton Systems Group, as it had announced in May.

The Justice Department files a motion in Federal District Court, alleging that Microsoft has violated a 1994 consent decree dealing with certain aspects of licensing the Windows operating system to computer manufacturers. Specifically, the Justice Department asks the court to stop Microsoft from tying the use of its Windows 95 operating system to the use of its Internet browser, a tool to navigate the Internet.

Palm Computing enters an OEM licensing deal with IBM to produce the WorkPad, which Palm clones. IBM's WorkPad is targeted toward IBM's enterprise customers.

1998

Netscape makes source code for Netscape Communicator 5.0 browser available for free download on the Internet.

Intel releases the 333MHz Pentium II, with a 66MHz bus.

Apple Computer ceases development of its Newton operating system and Newton OS-based products.

The Palm III is the first Palm device to run Palm OS 3.0. This third-generation model comes standard with 2MB of storage, an infrared transceiver for sharing contact information and applications, and a rigid, removable flip cover. The Palm III also has a more rounded design—a portent of future designs.

Intel releases the 350MHz and 400MHz Pentium II processors, with 100MHz memory interface.

Microsoft Corp., 3Com Corp., and Palm Computing Inc. have announced that they have agreed to amicably settle their dispute over the naming of the category of palm-size devices currently referred to by Microsoft as *Palm PCs*.

Microsoft releases Windows 98.

Red Hat Linux 5.2 is released.

America Online buys Netscape Communications for $4.2 billion in stock.

Yahoo! brings Internet content to the PalmPilot.

1999

The Palm IIIx shares many of the design features of the Palm III, but the Palm IIIx, which runs Palm OS 3.1, has 4MB of RAM, a better reflective screen, and reverse backlighting. When the backlight is on, letters light up and the background is darker.

Palm V officially rolls out at Mobile Insights '99. Thinner and lighter than the Palm IIIx, the Palm V also has a glossy metal case. The Palm V comes with 2MB of memory and the same applications as the Palm III and Palm IIIx units. The Palm V shares the Palm IIIx's reverse backlighting.

IBM announces its versions of Palm IIIx (8602-30X) and V (8602-40U) using the *WorkPad* name.

References

Microsoft Museum: Timeline

http://www.microsoft.com/MSCorp/Museum/timelines/microsoft/timeline.asp

Timeline of Computers

http://hyperion.advanced.org/17072/html/normal-html/timeline.html

Hobbes' Internet Timeline

http://info.isoc.org/quest/zakon/Internet/History/HIT.html

PC Magazine—Fifteen Years of PC

http://www.zdnet.com/pcmag/special/anniversary/

Chronology of Events in the History of Microcomputers

http://www.islandnet.com/~kpolsson/comphist/compyear.htm

http://www.macaddict.com/news/9803/newtonretro.html

http://www.islandnet.com/kpolsson/comphist/comp1990.htm

http://www.newtontalk.com/macneil.html

http://hyperion.advanced.org/17072/html/normal-html/timeline.html

http://www5.zdnet.com/zdnn/content/zdnn/0522/zdnn0015.html

http://www.zdnet.com/pcmag

http://www.franklin.com

http://www.tcp.ca/1998/9802/9802smal/palmpilo/palmpilot.html

http://www.palm.com

http://www.infoworld.com/cgi-bin/displayStory.pl?99022.ehpalm2.htm

References

Books

Arnold, David. *The Handbook of Brand Management.* Perseus Press, 1993.

Brandt, M., and G. Johnson. *PowerBranding, Building Technology Brands for Competitive Advantage.* San Francisco: International Data Group, Inc., 1997.

Brill, Peter L., and Richard Worth. *The Four Levers of Corporate Change.* Amacom, 1996.

Carlton, J. *Apple: The Inside Story of Intrigue, Egomania, and Business Blunders.* New York: Times Books, 1997.

Carroll, P. *Big Blues, The Unmaking of IBM.* New York: Crown Publishers, Inc., 1993.

Chposky, James, and Ted Leonsis. *Blue Magic: The People, Power and Politics Behind the IBM Personal Computer.* New York: Facts on File, 1988.

IBM PC Company Sales Advisor. August 1994 and February 1995.

IBM Personal Systems/2 & Printers Sales Advisor. Winter 1991/1992.

IBM Think Magazine. December 1993.

The Journal of Business & Design. Vol. 4, no. 2.

Kaplan, J. *Start Up: A Silicon Valley Adventure.* New York: Houghton Mifflin Company, 1994.

Kaplan, Robert, and David P. Norton. *The Balanced Scorecard.* Boston: Harvard Business School Press, 1996.

mobile LETTER, Insider's Guide to Mobile Computing and Data Communications. 1995–1998.

Mobley, Lou, and Kate McKeown. *Beyond IBM.* New York: McGraw-Hill Publishing Company, 1989.

Moore, Geoffrey A. *Crossing the Chasm.* New York: HarperBusiness, 1991.

The New International Dictionary of Quotations. Selected and annotated by Margaret Miner and Hugh Rawson. Signet Books, 1994.

PC Product Guide. February 1997.

Personal Systems Sales Advisor. Fall 1992.

Porter, Michael E. *Competitive Strategy: Techniques for Analyzing Industries and Competitors.* New York: The Free Press, 1980.

Quinn, James Brian. *Intelligent Enterprise.* New York: The Free Press, 1992.

Reader's Digest Quotable Quotes. The Reader's Digest Association, Inc., 1997.

Rodgers, F. G., and R.L. Shook. *The IBM Way.* New York: Harper & Row, 1986.

Sculley, John. *Odyssey: Pepsi to Apple, A Journey of Adventures, Ideas and the Future.* Harper & Row, 1987.

Seybold, Andy M. *Portable Computing in the 1990s.* Dataquest Incorporated, 1990.

Tapscott, Don, and Art Caston. *Paradigm Shift: The New Promise of Information Technology.* New York: McGraw-Hill, Inc., 1993.

Tennant, Rich. *The 5th Wave.* Kansas City: Andrews and McMeel, 1992.

——*Version 2.0, More BYTE-ing Humor.* Kansas City: Andrews and McMeel, 1995.

Thirty Years of Management Briefings 1958–1988. Armonk, New York: IBM Corporation Communications, 1988.

21ˢᵗ Century Dictionary of Quotations. Edited by The Princeton Language Institute. The Philip Leif Group, Inc., 1993.

Watson, Thomas J., Jr. *A Business and Its Beliefs, The Ideas That Helped Build IBM.* Graduate School of Business, Columbia University, New York: McGraw-Hill Book Company, Inc., 1963.

——*Father, Son & Co., My Life at IBM and Beyond.* New York: Bantam Books, 1990.

Watty, Piper. *The Little Engine That Could.* New York: Platt & Munk, 1930.

Articles

"The Balanced Scoreboard." *Portable Computing* (October 1991): 6.

Bradley, D. J. "The IBM Personal Computer." International Business Machines Corp. (1981).

Brownstein, M. "How We Got Here from There." *PC Portables* (March 1988): 37–45.

Computer Reseller News (February 6, 1995): 50.

Cullum, Cliff. "History: IBM Personal Computer." International Business Machines Corp. (1988).

Essex, David. "Pen Portables Prove Puzzling." *Portable Computing* (October 1991): 27.

Golden, P. "big BLUES'S big adventure." *Electronic Business* (January/February 1998).

Hall, P. "Think Ahead." *I.D. Magazine* (January/February 1999): 81.

Hardy, T. "design saves the brand." *Innovation* (Summer 1998).

Hubbard, Holly. "Global Growth for Mobile Computing." *Computer Reseller News* (January 14, 1994): 44.

Kang, Karen. "The Corporate Positioning Myth." *Technology Marketing Insights* (December 1993).

Larsen, Judith K., and Everett M. Rogers. "Silicon Valley: The Rise and Falling Off of Entrepreneurial Fever." In *Creating the Technolopolis*, edited by Raymond W. Smilor, George Kozmetsky, and David V. Gibson, 99–115.

Martin, E.W. "IBM-Indiana, Case Study I-4." (1992): 179.

"Mobile Computing Guide." *Computerland* (June 28, 1993): 107.

Parade Magazine (March 14, 1993).

Rickert, Joseph. "Field Test of the IBM ThinkPad." *Tell el-Muqdam* (August 1992): 5.

Riley, Kathleen. "The ThinkPad 750 Series: IBM's Comeback Kid." *The Best Practices Report* (February 1994): 5.

"A Road Map for the Revolution." *ThinkTwice* (December 1993): 14.

Sakakibara, Kiyonori, Ph.D. "IBM ThinkPad 700C Notebook Computer." London Business School (September 1994).

Stetson, Christopher, and Jeffrey Frentzen. "IBM's ThinkPad: Cream of the Tablet Crop." *PC Week* (April 27, 1992).

The New York Times (June 1993).

Teitler, Rachel Derby, and Carol Venezia. "Desktop and Laptop PCs." *PC Magazine* (January 10, 1995): 166–167.

"The View from IBM." *Business Week* (October 30, 1995): 142.

Wice, Nathaniel. "Thin." *Time Digital* (November 2, 1998): 25.

Wiley, David. "Star Tech." *Journal of Business Strategy*. London Business School (July/August 1993): 52-54.

INDEX

Symbols

2.5-inch disk drive, 176
700C model, 163-185

A

Access ThinkPad, 429
accessories, PORT and, 253
Acorn code name, 13
active matrix color TFT panels, 167
Advanced Power Management (APM), 481
advertisement, 247
advertising
    coupons, 249
    flyers in shipping content, 250
    initial campaign, 195
    Maurice Fletcher, 248
    media, catering to, 260
    NBA basketball, 248
    slogans, 196
    Thank You from ThinkPad, 248
Aker, John, Steve Ward and, 383-384
Alexis Park hotel, Comdex and, 202
Altec Lansing, speakers, 425
Ambra North America, 424
Amstrad Pen Pad, 483
answering machines, 33
appearance of product, 421
Aquarius, 9
Asia Pacific South, Bruce Claflin and, 146
AT computer, 33
AT&T, Hobbit RISC architecture, 102
Atari, 11
availability, 217, 228-229

B

Bajarin, Tim, 199
barbecue at Debi Dell's, 302
Bartelemeo, Jim, 25

Bartlett, Jim, 49, 129-136, 467
    birthday celebration at Comdex, 208
    Gerry Purdy and, 203
    Joe Formichelli and, 291
basketball, NBA, 248
battery, 245
Bauer, Bob, 25
Beitzel, George, 11
Bertram, Jack (Black Jack), 56
Big Blues: The Unmaking of IBM, 39
BIOS (basic input/output system)
    code, 17
    MS-DOS and, 16
    Zenith Data Systems and, 50
blocks comparison with butterfly keyboard, 314
BMC (Brand Management Council), 220
book writing, 409
boot sequence, MS-DOS and, 16
Bower, Scott, 85, 155, 467
Bradley, Dave, 467
brand development, 189-199, 243-253
brand recognition, 245
brand trust, 458-459
Broward Community College, 32
business balance, 460-462
business plan review, 154
Butterfly, 307, 432

C

CAC (Customer Advisory Council), 216
Canion, Rod, 20
Cannavino, Jim, 56, 96, 467
    Bruce Claflin and, 139
Carberry, Robert, Dr., 41
Caribbean code name, 41
carrying case, PORT and, 253
case, drop test, 111
CD-ROM, 410
    market research and, 425
Charlie Chaplin marketing campaign, 38